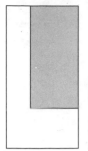

UNDERSTANDING FAMILY COMMUNICATION

SECOND EDITION

webct.pdx.edu:8900/

Janet Yerby
Central Michigan University

Nancy Buerkel-Rothfuss
Central Michigan University

Arthur P. Bochner
University of South Florida

ALLYN AND BACON
BOSTON LONDON TORONTO SYDNEY TOKYO SINGAPORE

This book is dedicated to
our parents and students.

Communication Titles from GSP

Argumentation: Understanding and Shaping Arguments, James A. Herrick

Communicating in Organizations: A Casebook, Gary L. Peterson, Editor

Communication: Apprehension, Avoidance, and Effectiveness, fourth edition, Virginia P. Richmond and James McCroskey

Communication Between the Sexes: Sex Differences and Sex-Role Stereotypes, second edition, Lea P. Stewart et al.

Communication for the Classroom Teacher, fifth edition, Pamela J. Cooper

Conflict: From Theory to Action, Roxane Salyer Lulofs

Interpersonal and Relational Communication, Kittie W. Watson and Larry L. Barker

Interviewing: Skills and Applications, James E. Sayer and Lilburn P. Hoehn

Intrapersonal Communication Processes, Charles V. Roberts et al.

Intrapersonal Communication Processes: Original Essays, SPECTRA

Look What Happened to Frog: Storytelling in Education, Pamela J. Cooper and Rives Collins

Nonpolicy Debate, second edition, Michael D. Bartanen and David A. Frank

Persuasion: Contexts, People, and Messages, Roxane Salyer Lulofs

Seeking Compliance: The Production of Interpersonal Influence Messages, James P. Dillard et al.

Small Group Discussion: A Theoretical Approach, second edition, Charles Pavitt and Ellen Curtis

Teaching and Directing Forensics, Michael D. Bartanen

The Articulate Voice: An Introduction to Voice and Diction, second edition, Lynn K. Wells

Understanding Family Communication, second edition, Janet Yerby et al.

CONTENTS

CHAPTER 5

MARITAL REALITY CONSTRUCTION   110

UNIT THREE

PATTERNS AND PROCESS   145

CHAPTER 6

EXPANDING COMPLEXITY   146

PREFACE

We undertook the second edition of this textbook with the same conviction that motivated us to complete the first edition: we wanted to write a book about communication and the process of meaning-making in the family that would touch our readers as well as instruct them. Our particular concern has been to develop a book that speaks directly to students—one that is written in an engaging manner, integrates theory and research with narrative, conveys a sense of relatedness among the ideas explored, and is organized to provide a clear progression from one area of focus to the next.

Many of the revisions in this edition address what we sense is an increased interest in narrative, cultural, and social construction approaches to family process. At the same time, we have tried to strengthen the text within the general scaffolding provided by the first edition in order to ease the transition for those who have designed courses with this text in mind.

In this edition of the text, as in the first, we have taken a complex view of family communication. Dinner table conversation can include intricate layers of meaning; seemingly minor events may have enormous significance for family members; small gestures can be intensely provocative; dialogue in the present often acquires its meaning from past events and interactions. Because of the complexity of family communication, we take a descriptive rather than a prescriptive approach to communication in intimate systems. We believe that exploring families as meaning-making communication systems is potentially more useful than formulating advice about how families should communicate.

In synthesizing the family communication literature, our goal has been to provide a framework for discussing theoretical ideas about family process that have historical significance for family communication as an area of study. At the same time, we wanted to convey the sense that the study of family systems is an evolving story that, as Paul Rosenblatt (1994) writes, pushes us "toward new constructions." Our intent is that the ideas presented in this book will offer opportunities for "ongoing conversations" about family communication rather than present conclusions about "the way things are." We also encourage our readers to consider qualitative aspects of communication in families and to apply what they learn to their own family experiences.

The book is organized developmentally, introducing students to foundational concepts and examining family communication as the family moves from the creation of the spousal/parental partnership to the more complex nuclear family with connections to the larger culture. Our exploration of family process also includes the possibility for variety in family forms as family members make sense of their lives over time.

The general content and organization of the chapters presented in the first edition are retained. In this edition, however, we have attempted to strengthen the conceptual foundations of the book and reinforce the evolution of ideas and perspectives presented and illustrated here. In an effort to "push toward new constructions," we have added a chapter on family stories and developed ideas and examples that explore narrative approaches to understanding family communication. We also have given increased attention to dialectical processes and reality construction in the family, have synthesized ideas related to current perspectives in the systems view of the family, and have widened our discussion of the influence of the larger culture on communication in the family.

This edition of the text integrates additional examples from diverse family forms (e.g., single-parent families, stepfamilies, gay and lesbian families), includes discussions and examples that reflect a more multicultural view of family communication, and augments discussion of gender issues. Four of the chapters open with new anecdotes—all are well-developed stories from students' lived experience in their families.

Here is a brief overview of chapter content, including significant changes made in this edition:

Chapter 1, "Conceptual Foundations," now introduces social construction theory, systems theory, and dialectical process as the three important conceptual orientations for the book. We explore key terms in our definition of "the family," and we have enhanced our discussion of the uniqueness of the family as a communication context by integrating Burr's presentation of the study of the family as "a unique realm" (Burr, et al., 1987).

Chapter 2, "Communication Processes," contrasts the communication approach to the study of the family with psychological and social approaches and defines what we mean by "family communication." The discussion of the characteristics of communication has been separated into components of communication and communication as a process of meaning-making. Here and in other chapters, we include additional examples related to gender and cultural issues in family communication.

Chapter 3, "The Family as a Meaning-Making System," describes essential features of a systems view of family communication, including system elements and processes. A new section integrates current views of family systems theory into a perspective that emphasizes an individual/system dialectic, a stability/change dialectic, the importance of narrative in understanding family process, social reality as linguistically constructed, the significance of intergenerational influences on family process, and a concern for gender and culture bias.

Chapter 4, "Courtship and Commitment," discusses the patterns of premarital interaction that culminate in the decision to marry, explores the various factors that influence the development of a relationship, and identifies the various escalation phases, turning points, and themes of courtship. In this edition, we have strengthened the organization and visual presentation of the material in the chapter.

Chapter 5, "Marital Reality Construction," focuses on communication in marriage as two partners construct one relationship. This edition of the chapter is enhanced by a new opening story. The chapter also includes an elaborated section on control patterns and refines the terminology used to characterize alternative organizational structures for relationships.

Chapter 6, "Expanding Complexity," describes the family as a system composed of smaller subsystems functioning within a web of larger suprasystems. New examples that reflect cultural diversity and the variety of family forms explore the relationship between the family and the larger environment, and a new section reinforces the importance of the connections between the nuclear family and the culture.

Chapter 7, "Rules," explores the relationship of family rules to communication in the family. The chapter explains and discusses characteristics, functions, types, and origins of family rules and examines the relationship of rules to family change. A new section discusses the relationships between cultural values and family rules.

Chapter 8, "Family Stories," is a new chapter that describes the narrative approach to understanding family process. This chapter focuses on family narrative as comprising the larger communicative activity by which meanings are constructed, coordinated, and solidified in the family. A true story told in the first person introduces the chapter. The remainder of the chapter explores how stories help us make sense of our experience, identifies features of stories, describes the functions of stories, distinguishes among different story genres, explores the influence of popular stories on the construction of personal stories, and discusses how family stories can be deconstructed and reframed. The material presented in this chapter is grounded in social construction theory and connects well with Chapter 9, which discusses family myths, metaphors, and themes.

Chapter 9, "Family Myths, Metaphors, and Themes," is related to the exploration of family stories in Chapter 8. The chapter explores the family's social reality as it is constructed and revealed through myths that are generated in family stories, through metaphors that represent family experience, and through family themes that are reinforced in the conversations of family members. In this edition, we identify four levels of family myths, including cultural, personal, couple, and family myths, that reinforce links among individual, couple, family, and popular stories. A new, well-developed description of the work of Sillars and his colleagues (1987, 1989, 1992, 1993) explores how conversational themes are related to family members' constructions of their relationships.

Chapter 10, "Roles and Family Types," includes a new opening narrative told in the first person. Two new sections discuss the construction of the parental role and explore the issue of gender and family roles, including a description of the distinction made by Walters and her colleagues (1988) between role complementarity and role symmetry.

Chapter 11, "Change and Growth," explores the significance of change in family communication. Specifically, the chapter discusses sources of change in the family life cycle, points of impasse in the family, and qualitative stages in the family and their application to problems in abusive families and summarizes what we have learned about optimal family functioning. A new story, in which two family members share their interpretations of a developmental struggle in the family, opens the chapter. The chapter's expanded section on the characteristics of optimally functioning families is based on an integrative review of the literature and is consistent with ideas presented in the rest of the text.

We have made every effort in this new edition to enhance its readability and accessibility to students. Opening stories and the discussions that follow draw students into the material. Previews of the main sections of the chapter, clear headings and subheadings, well-developed transitions, and links between and among chapters guide readers through the material. Tables and figures present and summarize material visually. Boxed "Applications" allow students to consider and apply the material they have read. Finally, each chapter concludes with a list of key terms; definitions for all terms are included in the book's glossary.

An underlying theme of this book is that the study of family communication can be personally meaningful as well as academically satisfying. As we indicated in the preface to the first edition, we do not maintain that communication can solve all problems or produce a cure for relationship anxieties and difficulties. We do believe, however, that reflecting on one's own family experiences in the process of learning more about communicative activity in the family can create new possibilities for understanding how family experience is constructed.

ACKNOWLEDGMENTS

For this edition of the book, we owe a special debt to our students, who reacted to the first edition and made suggestions for revisions. Our students have also contributed significantly to the content of the book by sharing their family experiences. Some of the narratives included in this edition are from students who gave us permission to use their stories. We are especially grateful to them. Our conversations and discussions with our students have been a source of inspiration and humility for us in both editions of the book.

We would also like to express our appreciation to Carolyn Ellis of the University of South Florida, who has had a strong influence over our approach to the narrative extensions of the book and the way that we have written about this material.

We are grateful to our reviewers, who read the manuscript in various stages of completion and offered suggestions toward its improvement. We appreciate their efforts on our behalf. Special thanks to Dr. Marlene von Friederichs-Fitzwater of California State University–Sacramento and to T. Dean Thomlison of the University of Evansville for their in-depth reviews of the final manuscript. In addition, we want to thank William R. Chartrand, Normandale Community College; Glen H. Stamp, Ball State University; Patrice A. Mettauer, University of New Hampshire Manchester; Thomas J. Socha, Old Dominion University; and Alan Sillars, University of Montana.

We would also like to thank Gay Pauley and Colette Kelly of Gorsuch Scarisbrick, Publishers for their support and editorial assistance at various stages in the writing and production of this book.

This is an exciting time to be writing in the human sciences in general and family communication in particular. Our ideas about family communication are constantly evolving. We encourage our readers to offer their reactions to or suggestions for improving the text by writing to us in care of our publisher.

UNIT ONE

CONCEPTUAL FOUNDATIONS

C H A P T E R 1

PREMISES AND PERSPECTIVES

NANCY VADER-McCORMICK

THE NELSON FAMILY

Ted and Joan Nelson had been married eight years when they decided to start a family. Ted taught economics at an urban university and Joan was a purchasing agent for a large chain of department stores. When the couple decided to have a child, they bought a modest house in a nearby suburb. For the first two years their lives ran smoothly— apart from the usual chaos that a new baby can create. Jamie, their son, stayed with Mrs. Palen, who ran a family day-care operation out of her home. She took care of four children in an environment that was nurturing, creative, and loving. The Nelsons appreciated Mrs. Palen's special affection for Jamie.

Joan's job required her to travel frequently, which was hard on the family. When Joan's employers offered her a management position in one of their large suburban stores, Joan accepted the position primarily because it would reduce the number of her business trips. Ted was pleased. The Nelsons decided to move closer to Joan's workplace and into a house with a little more space. The new location allowed Ted to use public transportation to get to the university and permitted Joan to drive to work in ten minutes.

The move made it inconvenient, however, to continue leaving Jamie with Mrs. Palen during the day. After talking it over, Ted and Joan decided to change their child-care arrangement. They enrolled Jamie in a larger day-care establishment that operated like a nursery school. Jamie was unhappy with the new arrangement and frequently asked about Mrs. Palen. He began having nightmares and crying more frequently. He screamed and cried every time he was dropped off at the new facility. Joan had several reassuring talks with the director of the day-care center, who encouraged Joan to give Jamie the time he needed to adjust. Joan usually felt a little better after these conversations, but the situation did not improve. Jamie became disruptive at home, throwing food at the dinner table and having temper tantrums over small things.

Meanwhile, Ted was working toward a promotion and feeling pressure in his career. He became impatient with Jamie's temper tantrums and disobedience. Night after night, Ted would yell at Jamie, Jamie would begin to cry loudly, and then Ted would drag his son, hollering and screaming, off to his room. After a while, Ted began spanking Jamie as a disciplinary measure, something he had vowed never to do.

Joan disagreed with Ted's methods of handling Jamie, and the couple frequently argued over discipline. Ted hinted to Joan that she might try to take some time off from work, or work half-time temporarily to see if increased attention would reassure Jamie and relieve some of the household tension. Ted's suggestions, always cautiously presented, were upsetting to Joan because she felt Ted was implying that her career was less important than his. The two of them had agreed, even before marriage, that they would give mutual support to one another's careers. Joan knew her hours were less flexible than Ted's and she wanted Ted to leave work early a couple of afternoons a week to spend some time with Jamie.

After a few months, Jamie began adjusting to the day-care situation. He even seemed to enjoy himself and usually had something to share with his mother in the car on the way home. The tension in the couple's relationship, however, continued to grow. To make matters worse, every time they quarreled, Jamie would act up and a family uproar would develop.

Fearful that their marriage was deteriorating, Ted and Joan consulted a marriage counselor recommended to Ted by a colleague. The counselor provided Ted and Joan with the opportunity to talk about the support each needed from the other. They began to feel a little more comfortable sharing their needs with each other. In response to the counselor's suggestion, Joan and Ted started planning some "family time" into their weekly schedules. On Sunday afternoons they routinely tried to take a couple of hours to do something that would be fun for everyone. Ted and Joan also scheduled time to be alone without Jamie. During that time Ted began to disclose his feelings of jealousy about Joan's career. In turn, Joan began to express her anxiety over Ted's impatience with Jamie. Time at home with the family seemed a little more relaxed as a result of the improved communication between Ted and Joan, and Jamie's episodes of screaming and rebellion gradually disappeared.

After about a year, Jamie developed a close friendship with Roger, a boy who lived two houses away. Roger's parents, Jean and Mike, worked, and in the course of short conversations with Ted and Joan about the difficulties of being "working parents," the two couples became close friends. The friendship between their parents pleased Jamie and Roger. When Ted was promoted the two couples celebrated together. By the time Jamie began kindergarten, life in the Nelson household was so stable that Ted and Joan began talking about adopting a second child.

UNDERSTANDING THE NELSONS

The story of the Nelson family illustrates two important points about family communication that are emphasized in this book. First, family life can be seen as a continuous developmental process in which families live out their unique lives.

Second, the experiences and actions that may appear to affect only specific members of the family have an effect on each member of the family and on the functioning of the family as a whole.

The fictitious Nelson family drama has an arbitrary beginning and no conclusion. We could have begun the story at any of several points in time—with Joan's new position, with the move into a new neighborhood, with the change in Jamie's day-care arrangement, with Ted's concern about his promotion, or even with the decision about whether or not to adopt a second child. Our ending is also arbitrary; it does not really finish the Nelson story. While the Nelsons seem to have reached a comfortable point in their lives, the stability (created by weathering a difficult period) has motivated them to consider expanding the family. Adding a new family member will require further change and adjustment. We could continue our story by describing what happens after a second child is adopted. Jamie's growth and adjustment, Ted's promotion, Joan's attachment to her career, and the new support provided from a positive bond with another family are events in an ongoing developmental process.

The influence each member of the family has on the functioning of the family as a whole is as important as the family's history. Several situations in the Nelson family involve specific members: Joan accepts a new position in which she does not have to travel; Jamie is taken out of a comfortable day-care situation and put in a different day-care setting; Ted works toward a promotion. Events that appear to happen to individuals actually affect all members of the family. Sometimes these events change some of the family's habits, routines, agendas, and expectations. At other times, the family develops a strategy for coping that itself creates new problems.

Family members often blame a situation on the personality of an individual instead of trying to understand the interdependence of their responses to each other and to the situation. For example, it would be of little use for us to view Joan's change in her job situation as the cause of the family's problems. The family's response to this change is as critical to understanding family functioning as the change itself.

What would we gain by blaming Ted and Joan for changing day-care arrangements and causing Jamie's difficulties? Is Jamie to be labeled a "bad child" because he throws his food on the floor, breaks something, or misbehaves when his parents quarrel? These behaviors work, don't they? His parents stop quarreling and pay attention to him.

Most of us are used to looking for the causes of family problems in the behavior of specific individuals. We focus on individual family members to explain our own families or the behavior of other families. We say such things as: Joan is too interested in her career to focus attention on her child; Ted is too hard on Jamie and allows his own stress to prevent him from understanding Jamie; Jamie is a spoiled child with bad manners. Such assessments only shift blame from one member of the family to another.

In this book we assume that interpersonal problems should be considered within the context of the whole family and the environment in which the family functions. The behavior of each member of the Nelson family is a product of each individual's perceptions, the specific family context, and the actions and conversations which connect family members to one another. It is difficult to understand family behavior without an adequate description of the historical, physical, emotional, and relational context in which it occurs.

Chapter 1 presents an overview of the ideas developed in the rest of the book. We briefly identify the general theoretical bases for our approach to the study of family communication. Next we define what we mean by "family" and explain essential features of our definition of the family. Finally, we discuss the family as a unique communication context.

THEORETICAL PERSPECTIVES

In our exploration of family communication we make an effort throughout to clarify some of the theoretical perspectives that have influenced our thinking about communication in families. At its most basic level, a theoretical perspective represents a particular point of view toward the subject matter being studied, suggests a framework for organizing our observations and experiences, and specifies the kind of information and knowledge that may be most useful to us.

The literature devoted to the study of the family is extensive and diverse. Families can be studied from any number of perspectives and with various purposes in mind. For example, to understand different achievement levels of adults, it may be useful to explore the influence of family size on personal orientations toward work and careers. Similarly, we could examine the relationships between substance abuse and family violence or compare dual-career with single-career families. In taking a communication approach to the family, however, we focus on conversation, sequences of behavior, and change as primary variables for describing and analyzing families. The question is: How do family members function as they create and negotiate meaning through their communication with one another? In this textbook we view communication as descriptive of how family members function, create and share meaning, sustain identities of family members, and develop particular orientations toward reality. Focusing on a family's communication processes helps us to understand its internal dynamics. In Chapter 2 we elaborate further on this idea in our discussion of the "communication approach" to the study of the family.

For example, studies that attempt to explain the increasing frequency of divorce may utilize information about families to explain the increase. Divorce can be viewed as an outcome of reduced social pressure to remain in unhappy marriages or of changes in the social structure of the family. Our primary goal in this book, however, is to describe everyday family experience, not to explain how individual and social "problems" such as divorce may be affected by the surrounding culture. We want to examine how families operate as social systems. We focus on the question, "What is going on in this family?" Handel (1965) has described this orientation as the "study of the whole family." It is a perspective that treats family functioning as an important phenomenon in its own right, rather than as a cause or product of individual problems or of social patterns.

The analysis of family communication developed in this book is based on conceptions of the family associated with three theoretical perspectives: (1) social construction theory, (2) systems theory, and (3) dialectical process. These three theoretical perspectives emphasize the interdependence of all members of the family and of the forces operating within and upon the family in creating family reality.

Social Construction Theory

A significant number of social theorists believe that symbolic interaction is central to the process of creating a family's social reality (Strykcr, 1972; Berger & Kellner, 1974; Berger & Luckman, 1966; Turner, 1970; McLain & Weigert, 1979; Burr, Leigh, Day, & Constantine, 1979). The concept of **symbolic interaction** suggests that people live in a social world created and sustained through their communication (Stephen, 1984). Communication uses symbols to create messages. Symbols such as words, gestures, signs, objects, or events represent things, ideas, or feelings. Symbols are often used to represent ideas or images that cannot be visualized, such as love, integrity, and faith. Furthermore, symbolic meanings are unique constructions—that is, meanings change from culture to culture and from situation to situation, according to the experience and relationship of the people involved. For example, a hug from a mother to her daughter can mean, "I feel affection for you," or it can mean, "Let's not talk about this anymore." If mother and daughter recently quarreled, it can mean, "I'm sorry." The same mother's hug can mean one thing to the mother ("I'm sorry") and something totally different to the daughter ("Your anger is unjustified because I love you"). The daily life of families is made up of many such communicative acts.

Imagine a nine-year-old girl cooking dinner in the kitchen with her mother. If the child's hand lightly touches the side of a hot skillet, she will pull it away reflexively. Some behaviors are an automatic reflex to events in the environment. Beyond the reflex action, however, the behavior of mother and daughter will depend upon the symbolic content of the event for the two of them. How upset the daughter becomes, for instance, will depend upon the child's relationship with her mother and her experience of her family's responses to minor family mishaps. The mother's reaction will depend upon her assessment of how serious the problem is, her previous experience with family accidents, her previous experience with this child, and what the accident represents for their relationship.

The possible meanings are nearly endless when viewed across families but often predictable when viewed in a specific mother-daughter relationship. In one family, the mother may get excited and run quickly to the medicine cabinet for ointment and a bandage. In another family, she may reach over and pat her daughter on the shoulder, viewing the incident as one requiring gentle reassurance and motherly comfort. In still another family, the mother might merely ask her daughter how serious the burn is; or she might look the other way, perceiving the event as an opportunity for her daughter to solve a problem on her own; or she might scold her daughter for clumsiness and take over the cooking project herself.

The daughter's quick jerk of her hand as she feels the heat is a reflex, but the responses of both the daughter and mother depend upon what the event represents for them in the social world of their family. If the mother and daughter tend to struggle for power in their relationship, the mother may respond by scolding and the daughter may become defensive. If the mother and daughter seek support from each other, a burned finger may be an opportunity for tears, hugs, and a shared ice-cream sundae. The **generation of meaning** is a symbolic and socially constructed activity in the sense that individuals react to events and to each other's behavior on the basis of what the behavior represents in their social world.

The idea that meaning is socially constructed assumes that the interpretations people attach to behavior are central to and a consequence of their social relationships. Furthermore, meaning is not a set of objective facts about the world;

people create meanings in the process of relating to others. Family members negotiate and coordinate these meanings as they interact with one another (Pearce & Cronen, 1980). Meaning is socially constructed through conversations and interactions with others, especially with others who are important to us, such as family members.

The view that reality is not an objective fact but something that individuals create has been developed by theorists associated with the social constructionist movement (Berger & Luckman, 1966; Stanton, 1981a; Gergen, 1985; Von Foerster, 1984; Stier, 1984; Hoffman, 1990; McNamee & Gergen, 1992; Yerby, 1992). **Social construction theory** maintains that the realities family members create (and take for granted) influence their interaction patterns (Stanton, 1981). For example, a family seated around a dinner table takes for granted the meanings attached to a wide variety of behaviors exhibited by family members. A child who begins to eat with her fingers may be told by one of her parents to use her knife and fork. The assumption is that eating with one's fingers is not appropriate behavior at the dinner table. The meaning attached to eating with one's fingers is not an objective fact, even though these parents take it for granted that such behavior constitutes bad table manners. In Pakistan, for instance, food is traditionally eaten with one's fingers. Even in this culture, some "finger-lickin' good" foods are routinely held in sticky fingers, at least in some families. The parents in our example believe that such behavior should be discouraged. The child, in turn, learns to conform to her parents' views about table manners. At the same time, however, the child may repeat the behavior at the next meal as a challenge to her parents. Thus, eating with her fingers has meaning for the family at another level, as a symbol for the enactment of parent–child roles. Dinner time is made up of many events such as this, each validating the meanings the family creates and maintains.

Symbolic interaction and social construction theory emphasize how family reality is formulated through conversation, sequences of action and reaction, and the stories that families tell of their lives together. This theoretical orientation to the study of the family is characterized by an interest in communication as the means for structuring expectations, interpreting and framing events, negotiating meaning, and creating social order.

We have discussed the importance of social construction theory as a framework to understand how meaning and social reality are created in the family through communication. When the daughter in our example burns her hand on the stove, her mother can respond in a variety of ways, and how she responds gives meaning to the event and reflects a particular view of her daughter, their relationship, and the nature of the world. Family systems theory is a theoretical perspective that can help us see the interdependence of family members and describe recurrent patterns that are often revealed in the stories about a family's life.

Systems Theory

Family **systems theory** maintains that, although a family is composed of individuals, the behavior of family members can be understood only in relation to each other and to the functioning of the family as a whole (Beavers, 1977; Bochner & Eisenberg, 1987; Guerin, 1976; Hoffman, 1981; Kerr & Bowen, 1988; Madanes, 1981; Napier & Whitaker, 1978; Sieburg, 1985; Stanton, 1980; Steinglass, 1978;

Watzlawick, Beavin, & Jackson, 1967). For instance, to understand Jamie Nelson's temper tantrums, consider his behavior in relation to Ted and Joan and in relation to the functioning of the family as a whole. Jamie is frequently disruptive when there is tension between Ted and Joan. When Jamie's behavior escalates into a temper tantrum, his parents stop arguing and focus their attention on him. This reinforces Jamie's behavior. Dealing with Jamie's disruptive behavior may be less threatening to the family than dealing with the conflicts in the marriage. Jamie's responsive behavior, then, may itself be seen as evoked by the response of his parents. Ted and Joan may be very concerned about Jamie's behavior; they may spend hours discussing their concerns about Jamie with friends. From a systems theory perspective, however, Jamie's disruptive behavior can also perform a function for the family—it diverts the interaction away from the argument between Ted and Joan and toward Jamie. We gain insights from Jamie's behavior when we understand it in the context of other relationships in the family.

Family systems theory grew from the need of a group of researchers and therapists to explain why recovering schizophrenics often revert to earlier negative behavior patterns following visits from family members (Guerin, 1976; Hoffman, 1981). Their observations led to the hypothesis that the behavior of the schizophrenic can serve a function for the whole family. It made more sense to consider the whole family as "the patient" and to examine the family's patterns of communication rather than to focus attention only on the person with the symptom. A series of premises about family functioning evolved that focused on the tendency of family interaction to be interrelated, repetitious, and patterned. The systems approach to the family provides a language and a tool for studying the family as a unit and for understanding important aspects of relationships in the family. As Napier and Whitaker (1978, p. 48) suggest, systems theory shifts the focus from "studying an individual or an individual species to studying a set of relationships"—a shift that gives us a method for conceptualizing the complexity of the whole family.

Current family systems theory emphasizes the dynamic interplay among the individuals, various relationships in the family, and the family as a whole (Nichols, 1987; Weeks, 1986). There is also a dynamic interplay between the family's tendency to develop predictable patterns of relating and their capacity for spontaneous change, improvisation, and transformation (Doherty, 1986; Hoffman, 1990). Families are continually engaged in negotiating the needs of individual members while attempting to maintain some degree of coherence as a group. They also balance their needs for predictability with their capacity to accommodate to change. The following discussion of dialectical process focuses on this issue of negotiating simultaneous needs in the family.

Dialectical Process

Dialectical process is a term that has been used to describe the relationship between the apparently opposing forces that operate in the family (Baxter, 1982, 1988; Bochner & Eisenberg, 1987; Bopp & Weeks, 1984; Boszormenyi-Nagy & Spark, 1984; Charney, 1986, 1992; Cissna, Cox, & Bochner, 1989; Montgomery, 1992; Rawlins, 1983; Weeks, 1986; Wilmot, 1987; Yerby & Buerkel-Rothfuss, 1982). By opposing forces we mean the polarities, paradoxes, contradictions, and/or competing demands that confront the family as it interacts over time (Bochner & Eisenberg, 1987).

Gestalt family therapists have suggested that families often struggle with the need to integrate polarities (Kempler, 1974, 1981; Zinker, 1977). A Gestalt family therapist might help the Nelsons, who are achievement-oriented, hardworking, and serious, to experiment with humor and set aside more time to play together. Ironically, the Nelson family may find that their work gets accomplished more easily and creatively as they learn to develop more of a sense of play within their family.

Family members can experience opposing forces as dilemmas. Individual family members have needs; a family as a collective unit has needs. Sometimes individual and family needs conflict with each other. A marriage often requires nurturance and support. A couple may find that their obligations and responsibilities as parents, however, make it difficult for them to nurture their marital relationship—and yet, when the couple fails to nurture the marriage relationship, the family seems to suffer. The marriage and the family simultaneously depend on each other and compete with each other. Ted and Joan Nelson, for example, both have jobs that are important to each of them and to the economic security of the family. When they feel good about their work they also bring these good feelings home to the family. At the same time, the commitment that each job requires sometimes produces stress and gives them the feeling of being torn between work and family. Work is necessary to the family's well-being and yet it also seems to drain energy away from the family.

One important feature of dialectical process is what Wilmot (1987, p. 107) has called the "dynamic interplay" between "opposites that appear to be bound together." In the Nelson family, for instance, the work that is so important to Ted and Joan's identity and to the family's security can also be the cause of stress in the family. Another example illustrates further the dynamic characteristic of dialectical process in the family. Joan finds that she is more relaxed with her family if she can get away from them for an afternoon now and then. As a consequence, at least one Saturday afternoon a month she tries to go shopping or go to a movie with her friend Leslie. Ted also finds that an occasional Sunday morning playing golf helps him to feel more comfortable with the demands at home. Because of their busy schedule Ted and Joan often argue over how to fit these activities into their weekend. Yet, when Ted and Joan take care of their individual needs to get away from family obligations, they seem to enjoy more fully the times that they share with each other. The quality of the time that Ted and Joan spend together is in part a function of their ability also to schedule time to be apart.

Bochner and Eisenberg (1987) describe two important dialectical processes operating in the family that are central to the family's functioning: the tensions between integration and differentiation and between stability and change in the family. (See also Bopp & Weeks, 1984; Cissna, Cox, & Bochner, 1989; Rawlins, 1983; Weeks, 1986.)

The first of these dialectical processes operating in the family is the tension between **integration** and **differentiation** (Bochner, 1984; Bochner & Eisenberg, 1987; Minuchin, 1974; Montgomery, 1992; Wynne, 1984; Kerr & Bowen, 1988). Every family is made of individuals differentiated by separate and unique histories of experience, genetic characteristics, and ways of interacting. Kramer (1985, p. 5) has defined individual differentiation in the family as "that capacity of a person to develop his own uniqueness." Likewise, the various relationships in the family have unique characteristics. These unique differences are integrated (with varying degrees of comfort and satisfaction) as the family operates as a unit.

Consider an example that illustrates the integration–differentiation dialectic. Dennis is a twenty-year-old college student who has encountered many changes in the last two years. He suffered through a painful separation from his girlfriend, made some decisions about pursuing a career goal, and became disillusioned with his family's religious beliefs. At home for his older sister's wedding, he tried to discuss with his father some of the things going on in his life. Dennis did not get very far. His father tried to be attentive but found himself distracted by his daughter's wedding. Dennis did get the sense that his father was interested and seemed to understand that the family's energies needed to focus on the wedding. His dad suggested that Dennis come home for a visit in a week or two when things quieted down. The wedding was fun and Dennis felt especially close to his family as he chatted with them at a dinner given for the two families of the wedding couple.

Integration and differentiation are both operating in this example of Dennis and his family. Dennis is a unique individual with particular needs, aspirations, and anxieties. Some of these will be known to his family; others will not be known or will be resisted. Dennis explored his individual identity as he talked hesitantly to his father about what he had been experiencing during the last two years at college. Dennis's father suggested that his son come home for a visit after the wedding, validating his son's need for self-exploration. The acknowledgment of Dennis's need and his uniqueness as a person is related to differentiation in the family. At the same time, Dennis also has a particular place in that family. His father suggested that the wedding weekend may not be the time for him to listen to Dennis's story; without making him feel neglected, Dennis's father indicated that right now everyone in the family needed to focus attention on the family and on the wedding. As he shares in a celebration dinner with his family, Dennis has a sense of being part of—being integrated into—his family. By talking, arguing, and sharing stories at dinner, a climate of family solidarity, union, and integration is created. Each family experiences the processes of differentiation and integration differently. For some families, these processes are difficult, awkward, conflict-laden, and sometimes painful. How families manage the fact that they are made up of separate individuals with distinct identities who also operate as a communal unit is a function of the family's communication.

Another dialectical process operating in the family is that between **stability** and **change** (Bochner & Eisenberg, 1987; Hoffman, 1981, 1990; Weeks, 1986). Family members develop *predictable patterns* of relating to one another. Ted and Joan each expect the other to be home for dinner by 6:30; Jamie typically goes to bed at 8:00; the family usually does errands together on Saturday mornings. In addition to these routines, the Nelson family has patterns of talking with each other. For example, when Ted and Joan arrive home from work, Joan usually shares information about her day, which provides Ted with information about her current mood. Joan makes inferences about the kind of day that Ted had by noticing his posture and tone of voice. He says very little about work until Joan asks questions and probes for a description. If the couple becomes involved in conversation, Jamie will typically show them a toy or ask to sit on Joan's lap until they pay attention to him. The predictability of these patterns imposes a structure on the family and gives the family stability.

The patterns of relating that give the family stability are continually evolving as the family moves through time. Throughout this text, we emphasize both the predictability and stability of communication patterns in the family, and the ongoing, process nature of communication. Inherent in this description is a tension between the forces that induce stability and those that foster change.

Stability provides the comfort that comes from the predictable and the familiar, but families also change. Family members grow older, circumstances are altered, and relationships can develop qualitatively. However, as family members mature, the predictability that gives the family stability may make it difficult for the family to change some of its patterns. Weeks (1986) calls this tension between stability and change the "bipolarity of permanence and change." Others have called it the "union of permanence and change" (Doherty, 1986, p. 255). As Doherty suggests, "Families have elements of identity-forming permanence and elements of transforming changes" (p. 258).

For example, the forty-something heroine of the play and movie, *On Golden Pond*, feels like "a little girl" whenever she visits her aging father; she feels "permanently stuck" in her role with her father. Her father reciprocates by behaving like a paternal tyrant in spite of some of his feelings of childlike helplessness and rage at being old. However, just as family members can participate in stable patterns that resist change, they can also change (sometimes through a spontaneous turn of events or through a slow evolutionary process) in ways that enable them to develop new patterns of relating. At the end of *On Golden Pond*, the daughter and father find a new way of accepting themselves and each other that does not require her to play the role of little girl and him to play the role of paternal tyrant. Some changes that the family experiences or that some members experience can undermine the stability of the family itself (a circumstance that may not always be negative for some family members even if it is painful for others). Two parents in their forties, for example, may find themselves pursuing individual goals that make it difficult for them to remain in a marriage. There is a constant tension between the

APPLICATION 1.1

DIALECTICAL PROCESSES IN THE FAMILY

Answer the following questions.

- Wisdom suggests that parents have performed well in their roles if their children grow into young adults with a sense of confidence in their independence. Have you ever felt as though you were exercising this independence and found yourself in conflict with your parents?

- Describe a situation when you experienced your own goals and needs (differentiation) in opposition to the goals and needs of your family (integration).

- When and why are predictability and stability in daily routines useful for a family? When and why might change in these routines also be useful?

- Why do you think families resist change? What events or circumstances might lead to change?

tendency to resist change in order to maintain familiar and stable patterns in the family and the inclination to change in order to solve problems or adapt to family members as they grow and mature.

The three theoretical perspectives discussed thus far, including social construction theory, systems theory, and dialectical process, have influenced how we have chosen to present our ideas in this book. Taken together, these perspectives represent a view of communication in the family as an interdependent process of generating meaning and of creating the family's social reality, which often includes oppositional and contradictory elements.

DEFINITION OF FAMILY

There is no universally accepted definition of what constitutes a family. Social scientists often make the distinction between the nuclear family (typically identified as a parent or parents and a child or children) and the extended family (which typically includes grandparents and relatives). Yet definitions of the family are not widely agreed upon by families themselves (Jorgenson, 1989). Cultural differences can also influence how the family is defined and who is considered to be included in the family (McGoldrick, Pearce, & Giordano, 1982). For example, boundaries between the generations are much more diffuse in Hispanic, Asian, and African-American families than in some other cultural groups; in these ethnic groups the nuclear family often includes extended family members and/or friends.

It is difficult and ultimately arbitrary even deciding how to define what is meant by the "nuclear family" as differentiated from the "extended family." For example, Tamra and Michael are two children who live with their father and stepmother during the week and travel down the street to live with their mother and stepfather on the weekend and for a month in the summer. These children belong to a stepfamily system. How would one identify the boundaries of their nuclear family? A couple might also think of themselves as a family, as might extraordinarily close friends. A student of one of the authors has adamantly argued that she and her two cats are definitely a family. Given the variety of possibilities, it may be wise to "keep in mind that 'the family' is an abstraction" (Doherty, 1986, p. 259). Offering the reader our definition of the family provides a common reference for our discussions. For our purposes, then, we have defined "family" in the following way:

> A family is a *multigenerational* social *system* consisting of at least two *interdependent* people bound together by a common living *space* (at one time or another) and a common *history*, and who share some degree of emotional *attachment to or involvement with* one another.

In describing the family as **multigenerational** we are emphasizing the importance of relationships between parents and children and the significance of intergenerational influences on the family (Minuchin, 1974; Haley, 1976). Parents have obligations to and influence over their children, at least when the children are young. They have more experience and knowledge than do their children and they have responsibility for nurturing and guiding them. Children learn from their parents how to be independent (or how to remain dependent in some cases) and how to cope (or not cope) with authority. As they grow and mature, children also recognize how they are similar to and different from their parents, though this awareness does not always occur at a conscious level.

Parenting behaviors are often related to how two marital partners feel about their marriage (Napier & Whitaker, 1978). When Ted loses his temper with Jamie, Joan becomes anxious. Joan is uncomfortable with Ted's impatience and anger. Joan's anxiety about Ted's impatience and anger sometimes makes Ted feel unsupported in his frustrations with Jamie. Their feelings influence how they communicate in their marriage and as parents. Likewise, Jamie's awareness that there is tension or conflict between his parents can influence how he behaves.

This situation is made more complex by the fact that some of the negotiating that Ted and Joan must do as they parent Jamie is related to what each of them learned in their family of origin—the family in which they grew up. Joan learned that conflict should be avoided and that "nice people" do not "make scenes." Ted learned that displaying anger is a legitimate way to handle frustration. A family is influenced by the specific nature of the parent–child relationships and also by each parent's experience in his or her family of origin (Napier & Whitaker, 1978; Kramer, 1985; Kerr & Bowen, 1988). Consider the complexity of your own relationship to your parents and the influence of your grandparents on each of your parents. We discuss issues related to the multigenerational nature of families in several subsequent chapters.

The term **system** describes an integrated whole in which the parts or members are interconnected with one another in a complex web of relationships. A system exhibits an organized structure and relatively stable patterns of behavior. However, relationships among the parts of a system are never completely predictable, permanent, or rigidly constraining. Instead, the integration and order that is achieved in a system also permits a significant degree of irregularity, variation, and flexibility in the behavior of its members. As Capra (1982) explains, "It is this flexibility that enables living organisms to adapt to new circumstances" (p. 268).

Interdependence means that each family member's behavior influences and is influenced by every other family member's behavior. Sieburg (1985) has made the point that, "a family is made up of individual people, yet we can never fully understand its behavior by examining its members one at a time" (p. 3). Interdependence implies that no family member is totally in control, inaccessible, or unmoved by the actions of other family members. Although one or more individuals may be accorded more power in the family unit, all individuals are affected by the actions of others. The Milan Group of strategic family therapists describes the concept of interdependence as a way to think about **causality** in the family. Writing of this tendency of family members to influence each other's behavior, Palazzoli and her colleagues (Palazzoli, Cirillo, Selvini, & Sorrentino, 1978) maintain that the

> behavior of any one of the members of the family inevitably influences the behavior of others. At the same time, it is epistemologically incorrect to consider the behavior of one individual the *cause* of the behavior of others. This is because every member influences the others, but is in turn influenced by them. The individual acts upon the system, but is at the same time influenced by the communications he receives from it (p. 5).

Returning to our earlier example of the Nelson family, you will see how one family member influences and is influenced by every other family member in some way. Even a relatively helpless toddler can exert incredible influence over the behavior of parents. Imagine the Nelson family entering a grocery store to pick up some milk and bread. Jamie Nelson asks his parents to buy him a cookie at the

*The family is unique
as a communication context*

NANCY VADER-McCORMICK

delicatessen counter. At first, Jamie's parents resist moderately. Judging that his parents' refusal is not firm, Jamie intensifies his request. As Jamie becomes more insistent, Ted becomes impatient. Joan withdraws as a way of managing her own irritation at both Jamie's demanding behavior and Ted's impatience. Ted interprets Joan's withdrawal as a lack of acknowledgment of Jamie's "bad behavior," which increases Ted's irritation. The interaction escalates until Jamie is carried off crying from the grocery store with both parents as unhappy with each other as they are with Jamie. While it may be tempting to blame Jamie's insistence, Ted's impatience, or Joan's avoidance as the cause of the resulting conflict, all three individuals created the outcome of their interactions. Ted's impatience appears to escalate in response to Jamie's insistence, but it is not directly caused by Jamie's behavior; Ted has many other behavioral options. Ted cannot help being affected by Jamie's and Joan's behaviors (as they are affected by his), but the interaction is based on many situational factors.

Space refers to both the physical and psychological distances that individuals maintain between each other (Kantor & Lehr, 1975; Constantine, 1986). Constantine emphasizes the importance of managing physical space in families and regards space as a metaphor for aspects of the family's emotional closeness and distance, commenting that the "management of space and the use of space as a metaphor is so intrinsic and pervasive in the human experience that it often passes unnoticed" (p. 146). The simple act of a single mother and her teenaged son fixing a meal together might be taken for granted by the pair. But the fact that they share a task, a kitchen, and cooking utensils indicates that the space belongs to both of them—it is not just Mom's kitchen. Sharing the space and work brings them together.

Families share rooms, homes, yards, neighborhoods, and automobiles—physical spaces central to their lives. How family members use their personal space can create conflict and reveal tensions between family members (Crane, et al., 1987). Family members continually negotiate use and ownership of their territories in order to live together. As McLain and Weigert (1979, p. 175) indicate, a central characteristic of being a family is that "within the family's domestic space are special zones legitimately available only to one or another family member, such as father's chair, mother's closet, daughter's drawer, etc."

The Nelson family decided to build a tall fence around their backyard for their two small children and new puppy. They are also going to build a small addition onto the house for Jane to use as a study and a retreat. The boys are told not to enter their parents' room if the door is closed. On Sunday mornings when the door is open, however, they come into their parents' bedroom and climb all over the bed and all over their parents. Families also negotiate how close and how distant family members can be in a psychological sense, that is, how involved they want to be with each other's personal lives. Two sisters, for example, may enjoy sharing experiences and exchanging stories until the late hours of the night, while sisters in another family may value their privacy and keep their feelings more to themselves. A family develops orientations to privacy and ways of being separate as part of the negotiations that define how the family shares its common living space.

Shared history refers to the shared experiences, images, meanings, and values associated with a family unit as it functions and evolves over time. Carter and McGoldrick (1980) emphasize the importance of the family's shared history in understanding how the family operates, arguing that the family's existence "over historical time" influences its behavior "in this time" (pp. 10–11). When two people form a marital dyad, they bring to it the histories of their families of origin: memories of celebrations, conflicts, and affections as expressed in the families in which they grew up. Partners also bring a level of education, social status, and dreams for the future to their marriage. More importantly, they bring a view of themselves and a style of relating to others—of expressing anger, sharing fears, and demonstrating affection. From two unique sets of expectations and experiences, the couple develops the values and principles (or the conflicts over values and principles) that will guide their new family as they develop their own history. The addition of children to the family unit often creates a need for reassessing meanings and values, which creates more history for the family.

Finally, **attachment** and involvement refer to the intimate social bonds that link family members (Wynne, 1984). In most cases, family members paradoxically talk about loving one another, even in the face of conflict, neglect, or abuse. Siblings may fight with each other endlessly and adolescents may rebel against parental authority but underneath the fury lies an attachment, if not commitment, that is difficult to rend. Peggy tells her friends that she and her sister "fight like cats and dogs," but if her sister were hurt or in trouble Peggy would be by her side "in two seconds." It is attachment and bonding in families that enable family members to derive a sense of comfort and security from each other and to feel anxious when confronted with separation (Ainsworth, 1982; Weiss, 1982).

Notice that our definition of the family implies a distinction between marital communication and family communication. As we discuss the evolution of the nuclear family we talk about the married couple as the **architects of the family** (Satir, 1972). The family, in a very real sense, emerges from the foundation that is constructed by the relationship between husband and wife. A marriage is a unique, intimate dyad. Two people with separate histories come together to create and maintain a relationship, participating in a series of choices as they invent their relationship. As the partners progress through stages of attraction and commitment, the patterns that they develop influence the structure of the larger family.

TABLE 1.1   Key concepts that define the family.

KEY CONCEPTS	THE NELSON FAMILY
A family is multigenerational.	Ted and Joan are parents as well as spouses. How Ted and Joan function as spouses and as parents is influenced, in part, by the families in which they grew up. There are differences in authority and responsibility between Jamie and his parents.
A family is a social system.	Ted, Joan, and Jamie have predictable patterns of relating to each other and to their environment. These patterns, which structure their relationships in the family, may change as family members go through stages in their life together.
Family members are interdependent.	Ted, Joan, and Jamie influence each other and are influenced by each other as they interact.
Family members are bound by a common living space.	Ted, Joan, and Jamie negotiate the spaces that they share and the emotional closeness that they experience with one another.
Family members are bound by a common history.	Ted and Joan have a history that began in their courtship and that continues in their marriage. The history that Ted, Joan, and Jamie create began when Jamie was born. Ted, Joan, and Jamie accumulate shared experiences and images of their life together that will evolve as they grow older and their relationships develop.
Family members are attached and involved with one another.	Ted and Joan care for one another and for Jamie. Ted, Joan, and Jamie all see each of the others as central figures in their lives.

The complexity of patterns increases when the first child enters a family, and the number of relationships leaps from one to four. Consider the number of relationships in a family of three: mother–child dyad, father–child dyad, husband–wife dyad, and father–mother–child triad. Possibilities exist for any two family members to unite to gain more influence over a third (Haley, 1976; Kerr & Bowen, 1988). We discuss such relationships in more detail in later chapters of this text. Haley (1976) describes the complex relationships that can develop when two family members team up against a third family member. A mother and daughter, for example, might join together against a father, whose notion of how late his sixteen-year-old daughter should be allowed to stay out with her friends is perceived to be too rigid by mother and daughter.

In addition to the possibility of two members uniting against a third, a structure of responsibility and authority normally emerges (Minuchin, 1974; Haley, 1976), dividing the authority and responsibility of family members by age and gender. Sometimes the relationships between one of the parents and a child can confuse or contradict the structure of responsibility and authority among parents and children. In our example, one parent teams up with a child in order to mitigate the authority of the other parent. Contrast the complexity of relationships in a family to the one relationship of the marriage. It is not only the presence of a child but also differences in the complexity of structure that causes us to distinguish marital from family communication.

THE UNIQUENESS OF THE FAMILY

Many scholars in recent decades have turned to marital and family communication as their primary area of teaching and research (Fitzpatrick & Badzinski, 1985; Fitzpatrick, 1988; Bochner & Eisenberg, 1987; Gottman, 1982; Raush, et al., 1974, 1979). Other researchers have asked: "Why *family* communication? Why not relational communication? Or dyadic communication?" They legitimately ask: "What is specifically unique about the family as a communication context that justifies examination of this field as a separate entity?"

Those who resist the claim that it is useful to study family communication as a unique area of communication frequently maintain that a family is really little more than a set of dyads (parent–child, spouse–spouse, sibling–sibling) and, consequently, can be studied adequately by using tools developed in other areas of interpersonal communication (Miller & Knapp, 1985). Similar processes are involved whether we examine communication in an organization, a social group, or a family.

From our perspective, however, it is the emotional complexity and compulsory nature of relationships in a family that make the family context unique. Families involve genes and heredity, in-laws and cousins, family secrets, patterns transmitted through generations, traditions and heritage—in short, a complex system of interrelationships into which we were born. Carter and McGoldrick (1980) have argued persuasively that the family is a unique social system:

> As a system moving along through time, the family has basically different properties from all other systems. Unlike all other organizations, families incorporate new members only by birth, adoption, or marriage, and members can leave only by death, if then (see Terkelsen, chapter 2). No other system is subject to these constraints. A business organization can fire members it views as dysfunctional, or conversely, individual members can resign if the structure and values of the organization are not to their liking. The pressures of membership with no exit available can, in the extreme situation, lead the family down the road to psychosis (Cecchin, 1979). In nonfamily systems, roles are filled by different individuals at different times. In the main, though, the functions of the system are carried out in a stable fashion (or else the system self-destructs) by the replacement of those who leave for any reason. While there are roles and functions in family systems, the main value is in the relationships, which are irreplaceable. For example, a stepmother may take over the role and functions of a mother, but will never completely replace her (p. 12).

Burr and his colleagues (1987) have eloquently described "the unique nature of the family realm" and the significance of its uniqueness for the study of families. Our explanation of the uniqueness of the family as a communication context is compatible with and incorporates many of the ideas and terminology developed in their work. We identify six characteristics that, when examined together, distinguish the context of family communication from other interpersonal contexts:

1. Families include relationships that, except for the members of the marital dyad, are nonvoluntary and permanent.
2. Families develop and maintain the self-concept of members as total persons.
3. Families exert an influence over members which endures for a lifetime and extends beyond one generation.

4. Families have the potential to produce high levels of commitment and intimacy among members.

5. Families are motivated by qualitative purposes, altruism, and nurturing much more than are other social institutions.

6. Families are complex interactional systems with the capacity for simultaneous orientation toward multiple relationships, goals, and tasks.

Nonvolition and Permanence

As Carter and McGoldrick (1980), Burr, et al., (1987), and others indicate, families are a unique form of relationship because they involve **nonvolition**. You choose your friends from the social contacts available to you and you can choose your field of study or line of work, but you do not choose to be born into a specific family. You do not select your position on a family tree or choose your relatives. Even if you want to disown them, you can't; they are yours for life. Even children who are able to legally divorce their parents remain connected to them biologically. When you are born into a family, you are provided with a history and a set of relationships with a network of "relatives."

Nonvolition can work to strengthen the relationships within the family system because it encourages the development of an attitude that calls for all family members to work together as a "family." However, nonvolition may also work against the family because it may cause family members to feel trapped in a situation over which they have little control. Family members may become alienated from or be in conflict with one another, but their bonds as a family cannot be easily broken. Heidi can decide that Bonnie is no longer her friend, but even if he is not speaking to her, Peter is still her brother.

Self-Concept of the Total Person

We learn much of what we know about ourselves—physically, psychologically, and conceptually—through interaction with others. However, most of the people with whom we interact relate to aspects of ourselves that we have selected to reveal or that others encounter because of our particular role relationships with them. As Burr, et al., (1987) have pointed out, family members relate to each other differently; they "tend to deal with each other as whole persons" (p. 4). The family is where, as infants and children, our identity is first developed and it is also the place where the multiple dimensions of who we are get expressed—where, as Burr and his colleagues suggest, we can "be ourselves" or "let our hair down." As a consequence, family members, for good or ill, often experience a wider range of each other's identities than they do in other contexts.

During the critical years of infancy, childhood, and adolescence, a person obtains information from family members that contributes to his or her overall self-concept. One's **self-concept** is composed of those positive and negative feelings that one has about his or her general self-image. It is in the family context that we first learn how valued, loved, or lovable we are. Although our conceptions of ourselves continue to grow and change throughout our lives, many of the strong impressions we hold of who we are and what we can do were developed at an early age. Concepts of self continue to be reinforced, maintained, and/or modified by information received from family members as we grow older (Winch, 1977; Demo, 1987).

The family context also reshapes and reinforces the self-concept of adult family members. Partners in the parental or marital dyad validate (or invalidate) each other through their primary relationship as spouses. Information about performance, ability, and self-worth may come from people outside the family, of course, but the information an individual receives from his or her spouse usually has a profound and lasting effect on one's general self-worth. Indeed, failure to receive confirmation of one's self-worth within the marital relationship may be a major cause of marriage dissolution (Berger & Kellner, 1974). We may participate in a variety of tasks and roles outside the family, but it is in conversations with spouses and other family members that we typically seek to have our value as a person and our fundamental sense of "who we are" validated and confirmed. Perhaps that is why intimate conflicts are often the most emotional and intense of all conflicts.

Longevity of Influence

Another characteristic of the family that makes it unique as a communication context is the **longevity of family influence**. McLain and Weigert (1979, p. 175) have poetically testified that the "family is unique as that social group to which, most likely, I will always return." Once born into a family unit, you are subject to the influence of family members throughout your lifetime: influence on values, your perception of yourself, your understanding and acceptance of others, how you express your needs or emotions, and how you communicate with and reach out to others in general. Although marriages currently face a fifty percent chance of dissolution, parent–child relationships and sibling–sibling relationships persist throughout the lifetime of each family member, whether or not the people involved remain in close proximity. A mother who lives 2,000 miles away and who infrequently visits her young children may still exert a tremendous influence on them and vice versa. Even a deceased parent or one who was never known to his or her children can influence development in many ways. Moreover, researchers have discovered that family influence often extends from one generation to the next (Kramer, 1985; Framo, 1992). In their efforts to help families, Kerr and Bowen (1988) have shown the power of families to transmit behaviors from one generation to the next, maintaining that a "family does not change from very good functioning to very poor functioning in one generation" (p. 13). The family context differs fundamentally from every other interpersonal context because family membership involves an enormous, largely inescapable influence over the entire course of an individual's lifetime—and through several generations. Furthermore, the activities, events, conflicts, conversations, and stories that family members share have a lasting effect on each person's life, which does not end with one generation.

Commitment and Intimacy

The second fundamental characteristic of the family context is the high level of commitment and **intimacy** typically associated with family members. Much of the interaction that occurs in the family is not visible or accessible to bystanders (Burr, et al., 1987). Neighbors and grandparents do not see Ted Nelson slap his son, nor do they hear Joan scream at her husband. A family shares experiences and secrets that are hidden from the "outside" world. They see each other under all kinds of circumstances, good and bad, and in many different moods. McLain and Weigert (1979, p. 175) describe the family as "essentially different from other social institutions" primarily because it can be "characterized by a unique intimacy and intensity as well as a unique mutual knowing." It is difficult, if not impossible, to maintain a "false face" over an extended period of time with family members.

Being vulnerable in the presence of others—which we call intimacy— is closely related to maintaining commitment among family members. Family members reveal their vulnerabilities to one another, often with a sense of trust and usually with the hope that their vulnerabilities will not be used against them. For a family to live in the presence of each others' vulnerabilities and to stay intact, all members make an agreement (implicit or explicit) to maintain the family unit, at least at some minimum level. This commitment is essential to developing bonds that help family members trust one another in spite of their potential vulnerabilities.

Qualitative Purposes

We use the term **qualitative purposes** to refer to the prominence of emotionality, connectedness, altruism, and nurturing in family life and their significance for communication in the family. Burr, et al., (1987) originally used the term "qualitative purposes" to differentiate the primary concerns and goals of the family from other social organizations. A family coordinates routine activities, such as who will pick up the toddler at the day-care facility, buy a gallon of milk on the way home from work, or decide what to do about a leaky faucet. Families integrate different members' agendas, manage their budgets, negotiate transportation to and from work. These purposes are related to the life skills of a family, which can be measured by their efficiency, problem-solving capacity, and productivity. In most social organizations the ability to control and manage people so that the tasks of the organization get accomplished effectively is central to the organization's survival. But the family is also a place where the qualitative aspects of life are central to its survival.

As Burr and his colleagues write (1987), families "create intimacy, care, concern, nurturing, a place for healing, closeness, a sense of belonging, and tenderness" (p. 6). These experiences are more difficult to measure; they are subjective, ambiguous, transitory, ephemeral, and often governed by different motivations than mere personal gain or satisfaction. Individuals marry, have children, and care for elderly relatives because they are connected emotionally, even though these connections are sometimes the cause of anguish or frustration. It is, in fact, the centrality of emotions in the family that makes the family a unique social system.

Family members are, of course, not always considerate of one another. Economic disadvantage, painful experiences in one's background, conflict, and/or health, work, and social pressures sometimes make it difficult for members to nurture one another. However, the family is a place where caring for others and mitigating one's own interests to those of others is more than just an aspect of living together; it is a *primary obligation*. In a sense, the tragedy of family abuse and violence is the violation of this contract. Family members have the right to expect physical and psychological protection, love, comfort, and validation, even if they do not always receive it.

Feminist theorists and feminist family therapists (Gilligan, 1982; Goodrich, Rampage, Ellman, & Halstead, 1988; Gouldner, 1985; Lerner, 1986; Leslie & Glossick, 1992; Walters, Carter, Papp, & Silverstein, 1988; and others) have explored the importance of understanding the need for cultural values that acknowledge the importance of individual well-being. They also examine the qualitative purposes of family life and the need to encourage and support men's participation in nurturing its members. Such participation may require changes in how men relate to the family and in the gender-based division of labor in the family.

The problems in the Nelson family are not about how Ted and Joan will manage their careers, manipulate their schedules, or control their child. Their struggle is about how they can nurture and support each other a little better. The Nelsons seem able to work out their problems because both Ted and Joan are willing to risk sharing their feelings and commit themselves to improving the climate in the family. Meeting the emotional needs of family members is difficult in any family. It may be especially challenging for families who are under economic pressures or in families where one parent has the sole responsibility for the family's qualitative life.

Simultaneous Orientation

We use the term **simultaneous orientation** in the same way that Burr and his colleagues do. Simultaneous orientation describes the tendency for family members to engage in several activities that typically involve more than one family member and to pursue several goals at the same time. As Burr, et al., (1987) write, "Living in the family realm is typified by interruption, discontinuity, lack of completion, and constant juggling of attention among individuals and their different schedules, activities, preferences, and needs" (p. 5).

Work organizations usually separate the spaces where employees work from spaces where they "play." A company may have lunch rooms, lounges, or outdoor picnic tables where workers may relax and enjoy themselves. Families, however, are places where members often get their work done *through* play. A father, for example, may be "doing the important work" of connecting with his son and nurturing the boy's self-confidence *as* he plays a game of Scrabble with him. Father and son might also take advantage of the opportunity to enjoy each other's company while they fold laundry together, watch television, and play with the dog. At the same time, they might be interrupted by a sibling who scolds them not to get dog hair on the clothes, by a phone call from a grandparent, or by another adult in the family who wants to talk about the dinner menu. An hour later someone else in the family might finish the half-folded laundry, while father and son go to the grocery store for a loaf of bread and some toilet paper. As Burr and his colleagues suggest, "We support, reinforce, work, encourage, reprove, teach, embrace, kiss, hold close, listen, and sympathize in a jumble of multi-dimensional, polychronically organized patterns" (p. 5). As a consequence, interactional goals are in a constant state of flux as conversations between two family members include other family members or are subject to interruptions or spontaneous encounters from people inside and outside the family.

In the dialectical sense, this potential for discontinuous, irregular, and disorderly interaction becomes just as important for our understanding of families as is the regularity of patterns of interaction that one can observe and predict within a family. The family's capacity for simultaneous orientation reflects the tension between order and disorder, continuity and interruption, and between patterned regularity and improvisation in family life. Sillars and Weisberg (1987) have explored the tendency for relational conflict to be disjointed and disorderly—characteristics of family life in general. While much of the research in communication has tended to focus on the patterned and predictable nature of interaction, we may see more research in the future that focuses on phenomena such as the effects of interruption on family interaction. For example, an artist who works at

APPLICATION 1.2

THE UNIQUENESS OF THE FAMILY AS A COMMUNICATION CONTEXT

Think about the following questions as you read this section.

- How do you think the circumstance of nonvolition might create positive and negative feelings in the family?

- Do you think that the commitment and intimacy that family members feel for each other is similar to that experienced in friendships? Do some friendships feel like "family relationships"? How? Why?

- What are some of the ways that the family can influence a person's self-concept? Can you give an example?

- Do you agree that families can be differentiated from other social organizations by the prominence of emotionality and connectedness and by the importance of altruism and nurturing in the family? Why or why not?

- Describe an episode in your family that illustrates the family's capacity for simultaneous orientation.

- Suppose that a young adult has moved far away from her parents because of the pain or conflict that the parent–child relationship produces. How might the influence of the parent–child relationship continue even though the parents and child are separated?

- In your own words, explain what is meant by opposing forces operating in a family. Give an example.

- Can you describe a "small behavior" (such as having breakfast together) that might significantly influence the communication of several family members? How does the situation illustrate interactional complexity?

home and has small children may have to cope with interruption as a primary issue related to her vocational situation (Jorgenson, 1993). In the case of the Nelsons, one could also ask if Jamie's behavior and his parents' responses would have improved spontaneously, without counseling, when Jamie made friends with Roger, a child from down the street. We will talk later in this book about the importance of enhancing our awareness of patterns of interaction as well as acknowledging the interactional complexity and discontinuity in the family.

SUMMARY

Family members operate as a collection of individuals, as partners in a marital dyad, as participants in parent–child dyads, as members of sibling relationships, and as a whole family with goals and values. Families are nourished by the variety of their relationships and at the same time experience competition among them. Joan, Ted, and Jamie Nelson are each individuals with particular reactions to the events around them and yet their behavior is also a product of their interactions with each other. Jamie's disruptive behavior, which occurs whenever his parents argue, may provide Joan and Ted with the opportunity to focus attention on Jamie and avoid a marital confrontation that makes the couple as anxious as it does Jamie. Joan has a particular set of needs related to her career and her sense of self; these may be in conflict with the relationships she has developed with Ted and Jamie. The same is true for Ted. The potential for pain and nourishment, joy and conflict, validation and disconfirmation that simultaneously permeate all family life are our concern in this book.

"It is the family that provides the framework through which human beings pass from nonbeing to create the meanings and values that shape their lives" (Bochner, 1976). Every family is unique in the specific way it manages its system; some families deal with their dilemmas and contradictions more constructively than others. Being able to talk about what goes on in a family from a communication perspective may help you to appreciate the complexity of family life and to gain increased insight into the operation of your own family.

We characterized family life as an evolving process in which day-to-day events are important and occur within a historical framework. Relationships are interdependent: members evoke behaviors in one another as they create and maintain their relationships; behaviors that appear to affect only specific members of the family have an effect on the functioning of the whole family. A process-oriented approach toward the study of the family seeks to describe family life as the product of a continual sequence of events that acquire meaning and take place through the medium of the family members' communication with one another.

In this chapter we describe a communication approach to understanding the family that emphasizes pattern, process, and change. We briefly describe social construction theory, systems theory, and dialectical process, which provide the foundation for our discussion of many of the ideas and concepts that are to follow. Several important terms are introduced in our definition of the family: multigenerational, social system, interdependence, common living space, shared history, and attachment and involvement. We indicate why we believe that the distinction between marital and family communication is useful and how the partners in the marriage relationship can be seen as the "architects of the family."

We argue that nonvolition and permanence, the importance of the family in the development and maintenance of a person's whole self-concept, the longevity of the family's influence, the potential for commitment and intimacy, the prominence of qualitative purposes in the family, and the family's capacity for simultaneous orientation make the family unique as a communication context. As you develop your understanding of family communication, we invite you to become an "observer" of your own family experiences and processes instead of proposing solutions to problems or arguing your own biases about how families "should" function.

KEY TERMS

architects of the family

attachment

causality

change

dialectical process

differentiation

generation of meaning

integration

interdependence

intimacy

longevity of family influence

multigenerational

nonvolition

qualitative purposes

self-concept

shared history

simultaneous orientation

social construction theory

space

stability

symbolic interaction

system

systems theory

CHAPTER 2

COMMUNICATION PROCESSES

NANCY VADER-McCORMICK

THE JACKSON FAMILY

The Jackson family gathers in the kitchen to prepare breakfast together as they typically do. The family engages in their usual early morning conversation. Family members talk about the rainy weather and make comments about each other's clothes. The primary function of their conversation, however, is to make plans for the day. Frank Jackson is leaving for a business trip today and will be gone for four days. Conversation focuses on the need to make certain that his domestic tasks get taken care of while he is away. A decision also needs to be made about how he will get to the airport and how he will get home when he returns.

Meredith, who is thirteen, has an appointment at the orthodontist this afternoon. Her father has fairly flexible working hours and he usually takes his daughter to her appointment and picks her up. Since he will not be able to do this today, Meredith is concerned about how she will get to and from the orthodontist's office.

Regina, who is eleven, has an important test at school and is worried about it. She also feels neglected because no one was available last night to help her with some difficult math problems. Mom was at a school board meeting and Dad was busy packing. Regina is a little irritable this morning. Her shoulders are slumped over her chest and she has a scowl on her face as she sits down at the table.

Bobby, the seven-year-old son, is the youngest member of the family. He does not like the idea that his father will be gone for a few days. Frank helps Bobby pack his lunch for school before they sit down to breakfast, at the same time rehearsing in his head the things that he would like to mention to his family before leaving for four days. Bobby insists on sitting near his dad at breakfast. As Frank glances over at Regina, Bobby asks his dad to eat the same cereal that he is eating. Frank reaches for the cereal, begins pouring milk into a pitcher, and notices that Bobby's voice is high-pitched and that he is talking faster than usual.

Mary Jackson tries to coordinate plans for the evening before she leaves the house to take her husband to the airport. She is also waiting for a phone call to find out whether or not a friend of the Jacksons can meet Frank at the airport when he returns. Mary cannot leave work in time to meet her husband's plane. She would like to be able to tell Frank whether someone can meet him or whether he will have to arrange to take a limousine home from the airport. Mary also needs to remind Meredith to take the bus home from her orthodontic appointment. In addition, she wants the girls to start something simple for dinner because she will be a little late this evening and Frank will not be home. Mary notices that Regina has a sour look on her face. Mary asks Regina how she feels about her test. While she listens to Regina's response, she runs her hands affectionately across her son's shoulders, aware that Bobby would rather his dad not leave today.

Reaching for more toast, Frank tells Mary that the plumber is coming Saturday morning to replace the laundry faucet in the basement and he wants to make sure that Mary will be home. Frank thinks to himself that he needs to remind Meredith to take the bus home from the orthodontist; he knows that she hates to ride the local shuttle. The last time he left town no one took the garbage out to the curb to be picked up and he tells everyone to notice the note that he wrote on the refrigerator. He is also a little concerned about how Regina feels about her test. Frank isn't sure whether or not to say anything. He feels that Mary is too easy on Regina but he wonders if bringing up the problem of Regina's performance in school will incite an argument with Mary. He really wants to leave with everyone in a good mood. Noticing the attention that he is receiving from Bobby, Frank makes a mental note to play with his son when he gets back. He observes that Mary looks especially attractive today and thinks to himself that he will miss her.

Mary reminds Meredith to take the bus home from the orthodontist. Meredith is about to protest, but she notices the nod from her father reinforcing Mary's instructions and says nothing. As Frank starts to say something about the plumber, he admonishes Regina to eat her breakfast and quit playing with her food. Regina glances at Mary. Mary responds to Regina by saying "she is just worried about her test." The parents are silent for a moment and then Frank gets back to talking about the plumber. Bobby asks his dad if he wants to hear a funny joke he heard at school. Everyone takes a moment to listen to Bobby's joke. The parents laugh. Meredith groans and Regina mumbles that she has heard the joke a thousand times. By the time the family has finished breakfast and it is time to leave, the Jacksons' friend has called and confirmed that he can pick up Frank. Plans for the day have been made and the parents hug their children good-bye as they prepare to leave for the airport and for work.

UNDERSTANDING THE JACKSONS

Except for the fact that Frank Jackson is leaving town, this morning is not very different from other mornings in the Jackson household. Through their conversation and interaction with each other, the Jackson family has managed some important family activities simultaneously. They have made decisions about the day and coordinated their activities; they have validated each other's roles and acknowledged one another's concerns; they have negotiated agendas and exchanged affection; and they have reinforced routines and patterns— all during breakfast. The Jacksons also reveal feelings and anxieties. Notice how they communicate with their actions as much as through their conversation. Regina's shoulders are slumped over her chest and the pitch of Bobby's voice is higher than usual, behaviors that do not go unnoticed by the children's parents. As they interact, family members seem aware of one another's behavior. Meredith is about to protest the fact that she has to take the bus home when she notices a nod from her father reinforcing the decision. Several things seem to happen simultaneously. Frank and Mary reinforce their roles as parents and as husband and wife. The children compete for their parents' attention. Family members may be making plans for the day, but there is much more going on here also.

Communication is the process through which families manage their lives together. In this chapter we attempt to show how the communication approach to the study of the family differs from psychological and sociological approaches. In so doing, we develop our definition of family communication. We then use that definition to highlight important characteristics of the communication process and introduce terminology and concepts associated with the communication approach to the study of the family.

THREE APPROACHES TO THE STUDY OF THE FAMILY

One of the best ways to describe the communication approach to the family is to compare it to psychological and sociological approaches. Although the three approaches overlap to some degree, each provides a unique perspective on the study of the family. To distinguish among these approaches it is useful to relate our discussion of the communication approach to the theoretical perspectives discussed in Chapter 1. Social construction theory, family systems theory, and the concept of dialectical process provide us with a framework for understanding the internal functioning of the family as a social system. The study of family communication involves an exploration of the internal dynamics of family life, including the family's construction of meaning and reality; how the family functions as a system; and how the family copes with the contradictions, dilemmas, and paradoxes of family life. The following sections compare these aspects of the study of the family.

The Psychological Approach

A **psychological approach** to the study of the family focuses on the individuals in the family. Scholars who study families from this perspective generally examine the effect of the family on the development of the individual; they often focus on personality as an outcome of family interaction. Variables of interest to psychologists include values, beliefs, attitudes, developmental levels, abilities, self-esteem, cognitive development, and behaviors of family members. A psychologist might examine topics such as the extent to which divorce influences the social adjustment of school-age children (Kline, Johnston, & Tschann, 1991); the extent to which child-rearing practices affect the self-esteem of children (Barber, Chadwick, 1991 & Oerter, 1992); or the extent to which a daughter's relationship with her father influences her psychological well-being (Barnett, Kibria, Baruch, & Pleck, 1991). In the Jackson family, for example, it is evident that Frank takes an active role in the domestic life of his family. He is aware of the emotional state of his three children; he helps Bobby pack his lunch; he frequently takes his daughter to the orthodontist; and he coordinates domestic chores with his wife's work schedule. A psychologist studying the Jackson family might study how the father's active involvement in domestic activities affects the sex-role attitudes of his children. The psychological orientation toward the family usually focuses on the family as a source of influence on the development of characteristics and predispositions of individuals—particularly children.

The Sociological Approach

A **sociological approach** toward the study of the family focuses attention on the relationship between characteristics of the family and social forces in society. Sociologists see a dynamic relationship between the norms and roles of a society and the common forms of family life found in that society. Families embody many of the norms, roles, and values of the society in which they function. Families are assigned the crucial function of preparing children for responsible participation in society, what sociologists call socialization.

Consider the fact that the United States is a pluralistic society made up of people who settled this country from many other countries. Those who immigrated to the United States brought with them common practices of family organization and other cultural traditions. These practices and traditions influenced their assimilation into the larger culture as well as the development of the many subcultures that make up our society. The United States is also pluralistic in its diversity of family forms and role relationships. The dual-career family, for instance, in which both husband and wife pursue careers outside the home, has become common (Hanson & Ooms, 1991; MacEwen & Barling, 1991; Sears & Galambos, 1992). This form of marriage can affect many aspects of the work environment, as well as standards of living and child-rearing practices. Economic conditions may make it difficult, if not impossible, for a family to make ends meet on only one income. One outcome of this social force may be that men, who are no longer the sole breadwinners, must now negotiate on even terms with their spouses. A sociologist studying changes in husband–wife roles might examine the relationship between a dual-career lifestyle and the inherent stresses of and adaptations to work.

Family sociologists are interested in what family patterns reveal about the fabric of society and how the societal context affects the structure and functions of the family. Sociological variables include socioeconomic and educational levels of the family, ethnic and cultural backgrounds, changing roles, varieties of family forms (such as single-parent and remarried families, gay and lesbian families, and multigenerational families), unemployment and welfare, health-care availability, religious and political orientations in the family, and the resources available to families with special problems. A sociologist studying family violence might examine the relationships among income level, family structure, and reported incidents of family violence. Suppose that Frank and Mary Jackson are college-educated and each makes a high salary. A sociologist might view the Jacksons as representative of families in which there is a relationship between the educational and socioeconomic achievement and the tendency to trade off roles in the family. In other words, the sociologist might study the relationship between family social status and family role orientations. Family characteristics are examined for what they reveal about cultural change and social issues.

The Communication Approach

The communication approach focuses on the process of creating and sharing meaning as family members interact with each other. The assumption underlying the **communication approach** is that family processes are important in their own right rather than as a way of understanding individuals or society. The processes of change and stability within a given family or type of family are of central concern. The focus of study is on how individuals organize their relationships with other family members and how those relationships affect family functioning.

The communication approach focuses on topics such as how rules change as family members grow older; how coalitions in families are maintained through the family's communication sequences; and how family stories give meaning to experience in the family. Communication researchers have also shown interest in issues such as the themes that emerge from conversation in a newly formed stepfamily, what communication reveals about the role structure and decision-making patterns of single-parent families, and the ways in which family culture is developed and maintained through family talk.

Someone studying communication in the Jackson family might be interested in how nonverbal messages are used to communicate feelings. Recall that Bobby's pitch and rate of speech increased as the time grew nearer for his dad to leave, and Mary rubbed Bobby's shoulders comfortingly as she talked to other family members. Nonverbal indicators may say much about family dynamics in the Jackson family. Taking a communication perspective of the Jackson family would also call your attention to sequences of behavior that may be indicative of relationship patterns in the family. When Frank admonishes Regina, Regina glances at her mother, who then speaks for Regina in a protective way. The "protective" coalition between Regina and her mother is reinforced by Frank's hesitancy to speak directly to Regina. If this pattern recurs over time, the coalition between Regina and her mother may prove to be an important element in the Jacksons' communication patterns. Similarly, you might ask a variety of questions about the Jacksons: How are interpersonal relationships in the Jackson family maintained as they help each other set the table and discuss the day's agenda? What attachments and alliances are apparent among the Jacksons? What does the content of the family's talk reveal about the issues and cultural values that are important to them? What conversational patterns are repeated in the family and what do these repeated patterns reveal about how the family views themselves and the world around them? These are the kinds of questions asked when we examine the family from a communication perspective.

Distinctions among sociological, psychological, and communication orientations toward the study of the family provide a point of departure for focusing on the objectives of this book. The internal dynamics of process and change in families is our primary concern, rather than the impact of the family on individual personalities or the relationship between family characteristics and the larger society. Nevertheless, it is impossible to focus on family relationships without occasionally referring to psychological or sociological variables; these variables help to provide the context in which communication occurs. The differences among the psychological, sociological, and communication approaches to study of the family are highlighted in Figures 2.1 and 2.2.

FIGURE 2.1   Three approaches to the study of the family.

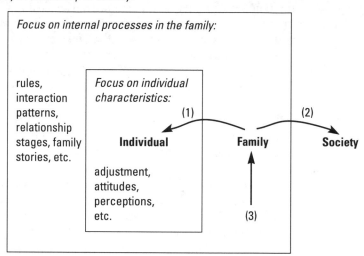

Focus on the family's relationship to society:

child-rearing trends, divorce rates, demographic characteristics of different family forms, family culture, etc.

Focus on internal processes in the family:

rules, interaction patterns, relationship stages, family stories, etc.

Focus on individual characteristics:

(1)   (2)

Individual   **Family**   **Society**

adjustment, attitudes, perceptions, etc.

(3)

(1) = Psychological Approach
(2) = Sociological Approach
(3) = Communication Approach

FIGURE 2.2   Examples of three approaches to the study of the family.

The Psychological Approach: Family variables are studied for what they might reveal about individual characteristics and behavior.

Brad's father suffered from severe depression during Brad's teenage years. Brad is now trying to understand the effect his father's depression had on his own feelings and attitudes. He has been reading studies conducted by psychologists on depression and self-esteem.

The Sociological Approach: Family variables are studied for what they might reveal about the family as a social institution and about social forces in the culture.

Larry Holt has been studying the correlations among marriage at an early age, divorce rates, and levels of marital satisfaction. He has found that early marriages are more likely to end in divorce. However, early marriages that do not end in divorce tend to produce as much satisfaction as later marriages.

The Communication Approach: The focus is on understanding the dynamics of process and change in the family and how these relate to family functioning.

Monica Fitzgerald recently read a study on the conversations of couples with children at three different stages in the family's life cycle. The study identified distinctly different conversational themes for each stage of family development.

CHARACTERISTICS OF THE FAMILY COMMUNICATION PROCESS

Communication is a word frequently used in our everyday life, yet the language used to describe it often fails to capture the complexity and richness of its meanings and functions. When people discuss communication, they usually refer to a person's typical way of speaking or how effectively messages are exchanged between two people; however, there is much more to the communication process.

Communication has been defined in a variety of ways. Littlejohn (1992) has summarized several alternative definitions of communication. Some writers have defined communication in terms of its elements, including a source who sends a message through a channel to a receiver who, in turn, responds and provides feedback (Berlo, 1960). Others argue that definitions that focus on elements in the communication exchange fail to capture the tendency for the communicators simultaneously to influence each other. Proponents of this view describe communication as transactional and emphasize the tendency of communicators to "adapt and change their own communication—even as it is occurring—based on how they perceive the other person is communicating to them" (Cooper, 1988, p. 4). Other definitions emphasize the importance of attaching meaning to the cues that the communicators exchange (Wilmot, 1987). Still other definitions focus on the emergent and ongoing nature of communication. Such definitions view attempts to assign a beginning and an end to an exchange of verbal and nonverbal cues as

---

APPLICATION 2.1

COMMUNICATION AS A PROCESS

A process orientation views communication as complex and continually changing. How does the following example illustrate a process description of communication?

> As her father raises his eyebrows and stiffens his spine, Jill gets up and moves to the television set to turn it off. Jill's dad begins to chastise her for leaving toys and clothes scattered about the living room. Jill doesn't wait for her father to get more than five words into his speech before she starts to pick up her things. Her dad continues to talk, asking Jill if she has finished her homework. Jill's face flushes as her dad speaks. She tells him, "Mom said I could watch TV." He responds, "Well, I say you can't watch TV until you finish your homework." Jill stomps upstairs and her dad heads for the kitchen, angry at his wife. In the last two months, Jill and her dad have had this conversation about three times a week.

Create your own example of a communication situation and indicate how the interaction illustrates a process view of communication.

arbitrary (Watzlawick, Beavin, & Jackson, 1967). These latter definitions tend to take a **process orientation** toward communication as complex, ever-changing, and influenced by past interaction while simultaneously influencing future interactions.

In this book we take a process view in defining and conceptualizing family communication. Simply stated, **family communication** is the symbolic, transactional process of generating meaning in the family. More specifically, family communication is an evolving and complex process of mutual influence. This process includes verbal and nonverbal messages; family members' perceptions, feelings, and cognitions; and a cultural, environmental, and historical context for interaction. Family communication results in the creation and sharing of meaning that is both stable and constantly changing and that is generated and interpreted at several levels simultaneously. Family communication characteristics fall into two categories: (1) components of family communication and (2) the process of creating and sharing meaning. The components of communication include the what, who, and where of family interaction: (1) verbal and nonverbal messages; (2) individual perceptions, feelings, and cognitions; and (3) the contexts for family interaction. The meaning-making process (1) is a process of mutual influence; (2) involves the generation of meaning; (3) includes meanings at multiple levels; (4) is a functional process; (5) can be unintentional as well as intentional; and (6) is patterned and predictable over time. The remainder of this chapter discusses these characteristics in more detail.

Components of Family Communication

Family communication involves three basic components, each of which contributes to the type and quality of family interaction. Verbal and nonverbal messages provide the content of family interaction. The individual perceptions, feelings, and cognitions of family members explain the influence of individual family members on the family communication process. The contexts in which family interaction occurs (including culture, place, and historical frame of reference) provide the setting (and expectations) for meaning-making in families.

Verbal and Nonverbal Messages

Communication contains both verbal and nonverbal components. Basically, communication is the process of manipulating verbal and nonverbal symbols to create and share meaning. When people think of communication as symbolic activity, they generally think of words and language. How families use **verbal symbols** to create meaning is an important part of family communication, which we will discuss throughout this book. A mother, unhappy with her son for spilling a glass of milk, can tell him that he is clumsy and better "shape up." Or she can say that she feels bad for him that he spilled the milk, ask him to clean up the mess, and suggest that he pour himself another glass. She might even chastise herself for letting him use a too-large glass or for filling it too full for him to handle. Each of these verbal constructions creates a different reality and attributes a different meaning to the act of the child spilling his milk. How families use labels, make requests, gain compliance with demands, talk about feelings, coordinate goals, and manage other family activities depends to a significant degree on how family members verbally construct their messages.

However, in any interaction communication is achieved not only through words but also through nonverbal actions that accompany what is said (Burgoon, 1985). **Nonverbal communication** refers to nonlinguistic forms of communication. A wide range of behaviors is involved in nonverbal communication, including facial expressions, vocal cues (such as tone of voice), eye contact, gestures, posture, touch, odor, physical appearance, dress, silence, and the use of space, time, and objects.

As Regina tells her mother about her day at school, Regina's eyes, tone of voice, and posture also tell a story. By the pace and pitch of her voice, the way she moves her body, and what she does with her eyes and face, Regina can describe the "B" she made on her math test with pleasure and enthusiasm or with disappointment and concern.

For our approach to communication in the family, two important aspects of communication are: (1) the potential for contradiction between the nonverbal and the verbal components of messages, and (2) the dominance of the nonverbal over the verbal component of the message in many situations. These aspects are discussed in the following sections.

Potential for contradiction between verbal and nonverbal communication. Every message contains the potential for contradiction, as well as reinforcement, between the words and the nonverbal behaviors that accompany them. Verbal compliance with a request for help, for instance, can be accompanied by a tone of voice, facial expressions, and body behaviors that can confuse, color, or subvert the verbal offer of help. Frank Jackson can comply verbally with Regina's request for help with her homework but at the same time sabotage that offer to help by indicating nonverbally impatience, irritation, and petulance. Similarly, a mother may verbally indicate interest in hearing about her child's day but continue to read an article in the newspaper as the child speaks. While these kinds of contradictions can create problems, it is important to understand that they are also unavoidable (because humans are not perfect) and are part of living in the close proximity of others who love each other and/or who make demands upon one another.

Significance of nonverbal messages over verbal messages. Research in nonverbal communication indicates that people are likely to attend to nonverbal cues over verbal cues when the two appear to contradict each other (Burgoon, 1985). When Frank asks Regina if she has finished her math homework, Regina replies in a tentative, hesitant tone of voice, avoiding Frank's eyes as she responds. Because of Regina's nonverbal cues, Frank may have doubts about whether or not the homework is completed or how confident Regina feels about the work that she did. In many family interactions, the nonverbal messages convey the significant information—tone of voice, facial expression, or posture can often communicate as much or more about how that person is thinking or feeling than can the words being spoken.

Meredith tells Mary that her weekend with the grandparents was "okay." Because Meredith accompanies what she says with a sigh and a shrug of the shoulders, Mary immediately wants to know if anything went wrong. Imagine Mary talking with Frank about a frustrating experience at work. Frank hears the frustration and irritation in his wife's voice. In responding, it is not so much her husband's choice of words that makes Mary feel understood and supported, but the way that he attends without distraction, nods his head in agreement, and makes eye contact with his wife as she speaks.

Individual Perceptions, Feelings, and Cognitions

The influence of **individual perceptions, feelings, and cognitions** on communication involves the process by which family members take in information from the senses, make interpretations of the data based on their unique characteristics and background of cultural and social experiences, react emotionally to those interpretations, and identify behavioral options based on the interpretations and reactions. For example, a parent who tends to feel a strong need to complete tasks quickly may experience frustration with a child's tendency to waste time and see that behavior as a deliberate attempt to create conflict. A person with a more leisurely approach to getting things done may view this child's behavior as entertaining or may not notice it at all. The perceptions, feelings, and cognitions of individuals in the family can significantly influence how they interact with other family members (Sillars & Scott, 1983).

In our opening example Regina was feeling neglected because no one was available to help her with her math homework. It may be that she interprets receiving help with math as a demonstration of love and caring from her parents; she may also feel insecure about her math performance this year. Maybe she has a modest learning disability that makes mathematical and spatial problems difficult for her. Or perhaps she believes that Bobby and Meredith have been getting more attention from their parents than she has lately. Whatever the underlying cause, she displayed her negative feelings through slumped shoulders and a scowling face. Mary acknowledged Regina's negative feelings by asking her about the math test and by defending Regina when Frank made a disapproving comment about her table manners. Regina's glance at her mother following her father's comment may indicate that Mary has defended Regina before. In fact, Regina's display of negative feelings as she walked into the kitchen may have occurred with the unconscious awareness that her behavior would produce support and sympathy from her mother because it has in the past.

Other plausible explanations for Regina's perceptual processes are possible, of course. We could speculate also about the ways that the perceptual processes of Mary and Frank influenced their responses. Mary's defense of Regina may signify differences between Mary and Frank in their beliefs about effective parenting styles. Perhaps Mary believes parents should reinforce good behavior whereas Frank tends to focus on disciplining undesirable behavior. We do not have any information about the marital history of Mary and Frank, but perhaps the couple chooses to focus on differences in their parenting styles rather than on other issues in their marriage. This could be one area in their relationship in which disagreement between them feels safe. On the other hand, it may be that Mary and Frank simply have different concerns about Regina. Perhaps Mary wants Regina to feel happy and good about herself, while Frank is primarily concerned about Regina's success in school. Each family member's perceptions have validity in that they reflect his or her own unique experience of reality. Whatever the underlying differences, the point is that individual perceptions, feelings, and cognitions can have an impact on communication.

Contexts

Meanings emerge from the context in which they occur. Any interaction between two people takes place within a setting which sets constraints on and expectations for the communication process. The **context of communication** is the background and frame of reference in which the interaction occurs. The social situation or context can be a **place** in which the present interaction is occurring (e.g., breakfast table, library, church, picnic), a **culture** that affects the rules and expectations for interaction (e.g., some cultures value open challenges of authority and sharing of concerns while others do not), or it can be an event or series of events that provide a **historical frame of reference** for the current interaction (e.g., this conversation follows a heated argument at breakfast, pertains to a subject both people have found difficult to discuss in the past, etc.). In any communication transaction, the ways in which the participants perceive the communication process depends on the context to a significant degree.

For example, what is considered appropriate talk by a spouse in one environment may not be considered appropriate in another setting. The communication context, then, is related to the *place* in which the communication occurs. A newly married man may not mind his wife teasing him about his housekeeping habits when they are alone. He may even perceive her teasing as an expression of tolerance and acceptance for his lack of concern about domestic tidiness. On the other hand, if his wife teases and complains about his lack of neatness in front of his parents, he may interpret his wife's behavior as a hostile action intended to embarrass him or manipulate him into changing. What is appropriate for the couple to talk about in private, and how they talk about it, may not be appropriate at his parents' home. The man's negative reaction to his wife's teasing may be further exacerbated based on the *culture* in which he was raised. If his parents embrace cultural values that place the male in a dominant power role in the family, the man may feel humiliated and disgraced in his parents' home by his wife's disregard for those cultural expectations.

Previous episodes in a family are important to understand the historical *context* for an interaction. An **episode** can be defined as a communication event that includes a sequence of actions or messages in which some internal structure or routines can be determined (Wilmot, 1987; Harre & Secord, 1973; Pearce, 1976). Sometimes we attach labels, names, or definitions to communication events, such as "conversation at breakfast," "discussing plans for Saturday night," or "having an argument" (Pearce, 1976). Usually an episode can be perceived by the participants as capable of being named even if there is disagreement about how to name it. Regina, for example, may perceive an interaction with her father as "a fight" while Frank defines it as "a discussion." In any case, the sequence of events has enough structure so that family members can identify it as a specific communication event. Previous communication episodes often provide the historical frame of reference that determines future episodes.

A description of an episode involving a couple that has undertaken a home improvement project illustrates what we mean by the significance of historical context in communication. Keith and Vanessa have been married for about five years. Keith is a successful dentist; he is outgoing, organized, and meticulous in his personal habits and in completing tasks. His friends tease him about his neatness and perfectionism. He plans everything he does, attends to details carefully, and always does a good job on any project.

Although she admires these qualities in Keith, Vanessa, an insurance agent, sees herself as ambitious and energetic. They both have successful careers, an attractive house, and interesting lives. Keith's perfectionism, however, drives Vanessa crazy. Sometimes she wishes they could get more things done; she feels that having to do everything perfectly is limiting in some ways, and her feelings are hurt when she senses that Keith is critical of her lack of attention to details. Keith has a good sense of humor, however, and is aware that he tends to be a little demanding. Vanessa is also aware that she tends to cut corners sometimes and the two of them probably balance each other in the relationship.

One particular weekend they agree to wallpaper a room together. Each time they wallpaper (they have done two other rooms), Keith takes over as leader and criticizes the way Vanessa works; Vanessa approaches the job hesitantly and tentatively. Several times they have fought over the job. They both joke to their friends that if their marriage can survive the wallpapering work it can survive anything.

Today, Vanessa has promised herself that she will not be overly sensitive to Keith's comments. Keith has told himself that he will not be critical of Vanessa's work. They get up early on Saturday morning, have breakfast at Ryder's Cafe a few blocks away, come home and get ready to wallpaper. Keith has already assembled most of the supplies. Vanessa takes out the wallpaper and walks over to the southwest wall to begin. Keith says, "You're not going to start in that corner are you?" With that one comment, Vanessa turns around, red-faced and angry, and stomps out of the room.

An observer might wonder why Vanessa bolts after only one critical comment. This particular interaction, however, is embedded within the context of the previous episodes. It is the history of their working together on similar tasks which influences the interpretation of communication in this situation. In this sense, the history of previous episodes becomes the context for attaching meaning to communication in the present. In families who share a history of experience with each other, as virtually all families do, the context of the interaction influences the meaning attached to messages.

Understanding the characteristics of family communication includes learning about symbols, perceptions, and contexts. In addition, it is important to understand the ways family members create and share meaning through their interactions.

The Process of Creating and Sharing Meaning

The process of meaning-making in the family is an evolving process of mutual influence which involves the generation of meaning at multiple levels. Meaning-making in the family may be unintentional as well as intentional and tends to be both patterned and predictable. These characteristics of the family communication process are discussed in the sections that follow.

Mutual Influence

Communication is an interactive process in which participants mutually influence one another. **Mutual influence** means that each person in an interactional situation simultaneously influences the behavior of the other. As Mary speaks to Frank, she is influenced by the cues he gives her. If she notices that what she is saying about a friend who is very ill brings tears to his eyes, she may try to sound optimistic or pause to let him recover. Conversely, the cues that Frank sends are influenced by Mary's behavior. As Mary modifies her message, Frank may make an effort to stop the tears as a way to show that he can handle the emotionality of the situation. In this sense, *communication is a jointly constructed activity in which participants mutually evoke verbal and nonverbal messages from each other and modify their own messages in response to the feedback they receive.*

Consider Linda, a single mother with a young child. Every weekday morning, Linda must get herself off to work and her daughter, Holly, to a sitter who looks after the child until it is time for Holly to walk to school. Linda has to drive a considerable distance to get to work. She believes that, out of necessity, their mornings have to be routinized and planned. The general strategy is to sleep as late as possible and then to move quickly through dressing, conversing, and eating breakfast as each prepares to leave for the day. There is an unspoken tension between the two of them as they move about in the morning. Linda strives to get going quickly, but the more she tries the more Holly resists being hurried. Holly's resistance, in turn, makes Linda attempt to push the child along even faster. Parent and child are involved in a process of mutual influence in which each person's actions are reciprocated and structured by the other person's actions.

The reciprocal nature of the communication process has led researchers to describe transactions between family members as a "dance" (Rogers, 1984; Miller, Wackman, Nunnally, & Miller, 1988; Pillari, 1986). Family members synchronize their steps with one another, move to specific rhythms, establish distances between themselves and sometimes tug and pull at one another. The concept of mutual influence helps us to understand the tendency of family members to evoke behavior from one another. Communication is not something that one family member does to another. Understanding the reciprocal nature of family communication may help you to avoid blaming any one person in the family or attributing causality to only one person's behaviors, and to pay more attention to the "dance" that the participants have created together.

The dance metaphor helps us track the development of family communication over time. Communication can be described as **reflexive and evolving** rather than linear. By reflexive and evolving we mean that communication does not move forward in a linear fashion from cause to effect. The "dance" is likely to move forward, to the side, and even double back upon itself. Communication emerges from, is influenced by, and is dependent upon the previous messages or experiences of the participants. Current communication simultaneously influences or directs the course of future communication, acting like a coil as it moves forward.

The description of communication as reflexive and evolving emphasizes causality in communication situations. **Linear causality** generally describes a condition in which A causes B. We are accustomed to thinking about causality in this way. Touching her hand on the hot stove will cause Regina to jerk her arm away.

In communication transactions, however, one person's response to another becomes the stimulus for the other's action. Communication is reflexive in that self's actions can be seen as emerging from the response of other to self's actions. In families even the initial act in a particular interaction sequence is based on previous experiences that individuals have had with one another. In a sequence, every communication influences what follows it and is a response to what precedes it. When Frank tries to talk with Regina about how she is doing in her math class, he does so as a consequence of recent or immediate cues that he has received from Regina. His communication is also influenced by the context of previous events that have structured their relationship. Regina's reaction to her father both as he is speaking and when he finishes speaking is a response to her father and a direct message about what he can say or do next. As action moves forward it is continually being directed back upon the previous acts of the participants. That is, interactions in the present moment take their meaning and form from events just past and, at the same time, influence immediate actions to come. One person's behavior evokes a pattern of past experiences to which the receiver may respond. The concept of linear causality is not necessarily "wrong"; it merely oversimplifies the process. Reflexivity implies mutual, cyclical causality.

Linda's behavior in the previous example is both a stimulus for and a response to Holly; and Holly's behavior is both a stimulus for and response to her mother's messages. Linda's behavior is simultaneously a "cause" and an "effect" of Linda's striving to get her daughter moving a little faster. The interaction of mother and daughter moves forward in this way until they leave the house. This is what we mean when we say that communication is reflexive and evolving. The drawing in Figure 2.3 represents this image of communication as moving forward like a coil. Causality in family communication is illustrated as reflexive and evolving rather than linear.

Although communication can be described as reflexive and evolving, individuals typically interpret situations from their own particular point of view. Usually this means that a specific actor sees his or her behaviors primarily as a response to the other person and not as a product of mutual influence. The process of attributing causality on the basis of one's "point of view," as though one were only reacting to the behavior of the other person rather than influencing it, is called **punctuation** (Watzlawick, Beavin, & Jackson, 1967). Punctuation is an important concept in describing how family members and others who interact perceive and attach meaning to their own communication experiences. Watzlawick, Beavin, and Jackson (1967, p. 56) have made the point that "disagreement about how to punctuate the sequence of events is at the root of countless relationship struggles."

Ivan and Thea are in their twenties and have been married for several years. Thea enjoys going to dinner, a party with friends, or a concert on Saturday evenings. Social evenings that require her to get dressed up make Thea feel playful and romantic. When Ivan is feeling romantic he prefers to spend a quiet evening at home alone with Thea. Ivan and Thea frequently struggle over this issue and it has recently intruded on their sexual behavior toward one another. On Saturday evenings Thea often finds herself resisting Ivan's suggestion that they stay home for the evening. She complains the two of them stay home too frequently because Ivan "never wants to go anywhere fun or romantic." Ivan resists Thea's suggestions, insisting that Thea "never wants to just spend a quiet evening

FIGURE 2.3   Communication is reflexive and evolving.

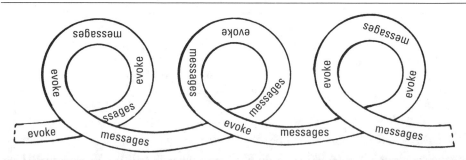

at home" alone with him. Ivan and Thea have different images of the meaning of an "intimate evening" and both of them attribute the cause of their quarreling to the other person. Each person punctuates the flow of communication by interrupting the sequence (in the reflexive coil) at the point where one's own behavior is experienced as a response to the other person ("you never want to go out" or "you never want to stay home") rather than as a product of mutual influence. Punctuation influences the tendency to blame the other. A person may see his or her

APPLICATION 2.2

PUNCTUATION

She:

"If it were not for me, there would be no bond or contact between you and the children."

"I defend your actions to the children and listen to their complaints."

"I try to help them understand why you do the things you do and why you are so demanding of them."

He:

"If it were not for your interference and monitoring, I could have a more cordial relationship with the children."

"You undermine my authority and inspire the children's rebelliousness so that I have to be firmer than I would like to be."

Ordering sequences in one way or another creates what, without undue exaggeration, may be called different realities. This is particularly evident in certain kinds of human conflict. A mother may see herself as the bridge between her husband and her children: if it were not for her, there would be no bond or contact between him and them. Far from sharing this view, the husband sees her as an obstacle between him and his children: if it were not for her constant interference and monitoring, he could have a much closer and more cordial relationship with them. If we do not bear in mind that this is a problem of punctuation—and not of one way of behaving *rather than another—we may become victims of the same fallacy as the two parents and consider one of them mad or bad, the typical charges made when communication breaks down as a result of discrepant punctuation of jointly experienced sequences of behavior.*

from *How Real Is Real?* (p. 62)
by Paul Watzlawick

Question

From your own family experience, can you generate an example of two family members who attach different meanings to each other's actions because they punctuate a common series of events differently?

behavior as a response to the other person—and therefore perceive that the other person is "to blame" or is the "cause" of one's actions. In reality, both participants are part of an episode or sequence of interaction in which each person's response contributes to the other person's actions. The punctuation of an event is related to how each person interprets the cause of a situation from his or her personal perspective. While communication is a reflexive and evolving process of mutual influence, participants' responses to each other are often influenced by how each person punctuates the interaction.

Generation of Meaning

Communication is the vehicle for "meaning-making" in all social systems. When Frank asks Regina if he may look over her homework, Regina becomes defensive. She interprets his inquiry as "nagging" and blurts out, "You don't trust me!" Frank views her response as rebellious and he, in turn, responds by saying, "I have the right to check over your homework, young lady!" Both Frank and Regina are attaching meaning to each other's behavior. **Meanings** are the values, interpretations, and constructions of reality which individuals attach to people, events, and behaviors. Regina and her father have some choice about the meanings that they attach to each other's behaviors. Regina could interpret Frank's inquiry as a supportive offer of help. Frank could interpret Regina's defensiveness as a lack of self-confidence. Meaning is not an objective fact; it emerges from the personal experiences and the history of the relationship of the communicators. **Meaning-making** is the way that meanings are coordinated in the family through the family's communication. Coordination of meaning—meaning-making—refers to how family members interpret and respond to each other's actions and conversation in the context of their relationship—how individuals "intermesh their own actions with those of someone else" (Pearce, 1976).

The meanings attached to interactions make up one's **social reality**—our experience of ourselves, other people, and our relationships. As we indicated in Chapter 1, social reality is not an objective fact, even though most of us take our social reality for granted and behave as though it were an objective fact. Social reality is created through communication as people comprehend, explain, and evaluate events and behavior, that is, as they attach meaning to what goes on around them. In families, relationship meanings are especially significant. It is important to ask: "What do the transactions of family members indicate to each other, as well as to observers, about their relationships?" Consider a simple request from a spouse who is seated comfortably in a chair. As his or her mate leaves the room, the spouse asks for a drink of water. There is a wide range of potential responses to this question, each response signifying something different about the relationship. Here are some alternative responses to the question, "Would you get me a drink of water?"

1. "Sure." (the mate leaves for the kitchen)
2. "Get it yourself."
3. "Ummmm okay." (hesitantly)
4. (pretending not to hear) "Did you catch the weather report on the news?"
5. "If you'll say please."
6. "Whatsa matter, your legs broken?" (goes to get the water)
7. "You look tired, honey—anything the matter?"

8. "Oh, what would you do without me!" (sigh)
9. "A drink of water? I thought you only drank beer."
10. "Okay—while I do that, how about getting the newspaper off the porch?"
11. "Huh? What am I, your slave or something? You must be nuts!"
12. "I'm too tired—why don't you get us both a drink?"
13. "Why don't I make us some lemonade instead?"
14. "You want any ice in your glass?" (leaves and returns with water) "That reminds me—when are you going to call the landlord about that leaky faucet?"
15. The partner goes to get the water but looks mad and slams the cupboard door where the glasses are kept.

Each of these responses attaches a different meaning to the nature of the request and to the relationship between the participants in the interaction. The first response indicates a willingness to wait on the other person in this situation. Perhaps the couple frequently does such favors for one another, or perhaps one person in the relationship is more demanding and the other usually complies. A response that asks, "Whatsa matter, your legs broken?" may communicate hostility in which the request is construed as a legitimate context for potential conflict. Responding with a question such as "Why don't I make us some lemonade instead?" allows the spouse to comply with the request while, at the same time, taking control over how it is implemented. In this situation the equality of the participants is maintained while the spirit of the request is met. You may want to go through each of the responses and describe something about the nature of the relationship that is revealed in each request/response sequence.

Family members also create and sustain meanings that are related to their experience as a group or a collective unit. Imagine, for example, that Meredith Jackson asks her parents for permission to go to a friend's house for dinner. Mary tells her daughter that she needs her help with dinner and Sunday evening chores. Frank joins in and says to Meredith, "You know we like you to reserve Sunday evenings for the family. We're firm about that." Meredith reluctantly telephones her friend and declines the invitation. A particular image of what it means to be a member of the Jackson family is sustained by the interaction of Meredith, Frank, and Mary.

Levels of meanings. As we indicated, communication cues carry information about how participants are to interpret each other's messages and about the nature of their relationships. Regina says that she has finished her homework, but her nonverbal cues give additional information about how to interpret her message. By verbal indications that he and Mary are firm in their decision, Frank asserts parental authority over Meredith in the demand to reserve Sunday evenings for the family. Two concepts that help us to understand how communication carries information about the ways participants are to interpret each other's messages and define their relationship are metacommunication and content and relationship levels of messages.

Metacommunication. Communicators often give each other information about their communication. **Metacommunication** is a term used to describe communication *about* communication (Watzlawick, Beavin, & Jackson, 1967). Communication about communication provides information about how messages are to be interpreted.

JANET YERBY

Communication in the family functions at various levels simultaneously.

Sometimes communicators provide others with verbal instructions about how to interpret their messages. Suppose a husband says to his wife, in response to a request for a drink of water, "Whatsa matter, your legs broken?" And then he follows up his remark with the comment, "Don't worry, I was only joking." The statement, "Don't worry, I was only joking," verbally indicates how the previous message is to be interpreted.

Sometimes nonverbal cues are used as metacommunication. In response to her parents' inquiry, Meredith says that she would like to go out for dinner with her parents, but she does so with a total lack of enthusiasm in her voice. Her nonverbal behavior, in this case, contradicts her verbal message. Meredith's words indicate that she wants to go out to dinner with her family, but her nonverbal message indicates that she does not. Metacommunication can qualify or disclaim ownership of a message ("I was only joking"), contradict a message ("Yes, I want to go, even though my tone of voice says that I do not"), or define the relationship between communicators ("I am asserting my responsibility as a parent in expressing the firmness of this decision").

Content and relationship levels of meaning. The distinction between content and relationship levels of meaning explains how messages define the relationship between communicators (Watzlawick, Beavin, & Jackson, 1967; Sieburg, 1985). The **content level of a message** communicates information about the literal meaning of a message. Suppose that in the middle of doing her math homework Regina says to her father, "I have a headache." At the content level Regina's statement gives her father information about her physiological condition (her head aches). This is the literal meaning of her message. The **relationship level of a message** is an implied command about how the other person should interpret and respond to the message. The command aspect of the message is especially important in the negotiation of a relationship between communicators. Regina's statement that she "has a headache" may be a call (or a demand) for sympathy from her father. She may be implying that her father should help her with her math problems, feel sorry for her, or let her quit doing her homework.

Nonverbal cues are important in providing information about the relationship between two family members. Linda, for example, may wish to ask her daughter, Holly, to pick up after herself. How she makes her request is important. She can do so with a tone of voice, facial expression, and posture that asserts her right as a parent to make demands of her daughter. Or, she can make her request hesitantly, with eyes averted, as though she expected her right to make such demands to be denied. Holly can respond by complying and, therefore, validating Linda's right to make a demand on her. She can also resist or protest and thereby challenge the definition of the role relationship between mother and daughter suggested by Linda's request. The statement, "Please pick up your clothes," conveys information at the content level about a request from one family member to another. In this case, one family member is asking another family member to handle a household chore. The relationship component of a message can indicate how the speaker is feeling, suggest what the speaker expects from the other person, and indicate who has the right to define and control the relationship. The fact that Linda feels free to ask for Holly's compliance implies an authority relationship in which mothers can ask their daughters to do such things. Thus, the verbal message conveys information about the relationship. The nonverbal message is especially important, however. Linda can say to Holly, "Please pick up your clothes," in a way that suggests that she does not really expect compliance or she can make her request assertively. The nonverbal cues that accompany Linda's request will help to structure her daughter's response.

Literal meanings are only a part of the meaning in any communication episode. The emotions and feelings, the sense of support or the apparent tug-of-war that is going on between participants is also part of the communication. In the Nelson family we can imagine Ted saying to Joan, in response to her inquiry over whether he is unhappy about her promotion, "I said I was pleased, didn't I?" Literally, Ted is stating his support for Joan's promotion. At the same time, primarily through nonverbal cues, he communicates information about his perceptions of their relationship. There is tension, impatience, and apprehension in his voice. The two of them may not understand what the promotion means for their relationship and, as a consequence, they are engaged in a struggle to define the situation in terms that are comfortable for each of them. Ted is not sure that Joan will be able to devote as much time as she has in the past to their domestic life. Ted may be asking himself what sacrifices he will have to make for the sake of Joan's promotion. These concerns emerge as nonverbal cues in Ted's response and they reflect a struggle to define the situation in terms that are comfortable for each partner. Communication at the relationship level often takes place beyond the family's conscious awareness. Nevertheless, relationship messages reveal a great deal about a family's life together, much more than do literal meanings.

Specific acts and periods of silence can function as highly significant relationship messages. A spouse who is usually home at a specific time each evening may communicate anger by showing up late without calling. The partner acknowledges and validates the message by balancing the scales and engaging in the "silent treatment" for the rest of the evening (Zuk, 1965). In this situation, being late conveys anger over some earlier grievance; silence distances and punishes the partner for being late. The couple may never exchange a word about the tardiness or the silence, but each knows that the other is angry and dissatisfied.

Another couple has a school-age daughter. As a new year starts, both parents feel as though their daughter has grown significantly during the past summer. One indication that their assessment is correct is that their daughter has taken charge of planning and packing her own school lunches this year. Her father used to do this job for her. The simple act of their daughter making her own school lunch is a communication behavior that asserts her view of herself as more independent. By letting her pack her own lunch—and not interfering when she makes what they consider to be a mistake—her parents confirm her view of herself as more mature and less dependent on them. Mother and father, in turn, may express affection for their daughter and appreciation for her new assertiveness by repairing and painting her old desk. By responding to their efforts with enthusiasm, their daughter can indicate nonverbally her feelings of affection and appreciation for them. It is important to recognize that relationship messages are frequently embedded in such commonplace actions as being late for dinner, being distant or silent for an evening, making a lunch for school, and repairing and painting a desk.

Functional Nature of Communication

Communication can perform a variety of functions for the participants involved. The **functional nature of communication** refers to the tendency for communication to achieve goals and produce consequences for the individuals, the relationship, or the family as a whole. During the conversation at the Jackson breakfast table, Mary and Frank demonstrate cohesiveness in their relationship through their ability to work together as they plan their agendas. By having the girls help with dinner, Mary is supporting a family belief, maintained by her parents, that everyone should share in the family's work. Each of these interactions reflects a variety of goals and consequences for individuals, for specific relationships, and for the whole family.

FIGURE 2.4   Levels of communication meaning in families.

Metacommunication: Communication About Communication

"I didn't really mean it when I said that I hated you."

She said that she thought the new car was fine, but there was disapproval in her voice indicating that she really did not mean what she said.

He said that he didn't object to going to her parents' house for Friday night suppers, but he always managed to make them late, and was usually too tired to talk during dinner. When she suggested that they not go every Friday, he indicated his approval but he did not say much. She knew how much he meant what he said because his energy level seemed to improve dramatically on those evenings when they went out with friends instead of to her parents' house.

Content Dimensions of Meaning: The Literal Meanings of a Message

"Yes, I think that I can do the grocery shopping on Saturday."

On one dimension, this message provides a response to a question and indicates an intent to act.

Relationship Dimensions of Meaning: The Command Aspect of Messages

This dimension provides information about how the respondent is to interpret what is said, suggests a definition of the relationship, and often makes an implied demand of the other person.

Margaret usually takes the children to the dentist. Today she asks if Carl can call the dentist's office to verify their daughter's appointment. As he is leaving, Carl says, "Can't you take care of it, honey? My day is pretty overloaded as it is." Margaret gets very angry and stares coldly at Carl. She has heard Carl say this before and perceives his response to be a lack of involvement in the children's affairs and a tendency to take her role for granted. Carl backs down and says that he will ask his secretary to call.

Jeremy, who is nine years old, is upset because his parents will not allow him to go to summer camp with his older brother. He pouts for three days to demonstrate his anger and frustration and to challenge his parents' right to make this decision.

Messages do many things: they can protect identities, validate self-images, express feelings, confirm values, and gain or redirect attention. Messages can also punish, control, instruct, socialize, reassure, protect, avoid, and confuse. Several goals can be achieved simultaneously for the participants in an interaction episode. Mary Jackson can use communication to instruct as she helps seven-year-old Bobby learn to play baseball. At the same time, the attention and interest that she focuses on the child also expresses affection and caring. In this case, communication performs a socializing and an expressive function.

Dialectical processes in the family's interaction become evident as family members cope with the often opposing functions of communication messages (Bochner, 1984; Bochner & Eisenberg, 1987; Rawlins, 1983; Wilmot, 1987). Family members frequently have to manage contradictory demands in their relationships and interactions with one another. Mary and Frank Jackson believe that it is important for family members to be honest with one another. Mary and Frank also try to encourage their children to be sensitive to each other's feelings, and to validate each other's self-image. When Meredith asks her sister what she "really" thinks of Meredith's new haircut, Regina indicates that "in all honesty" she thinks it is "weird." Meredith's feelings are hurt, and Regina replies, "Well, you asked

APPLICATION 2.3

CONTRADICTORY GOALS IN COMMUNICATION MESSAGES

Mary and Meredith Jackson

Meredith is thirteen. She talks frequently and openly with her mother about her friends. Her mother, Mary, does not like Nicole, one of her friends. One evening while they are cooking dinner together, Meredith asks Mary what she thinks of her friend Nicole. Mary and Meredith have always tried to be honest with each other. If Mary is honest with Meredith, Mary may hurt Meredith's feelings, undermine her confidence, or even provoke Meredith into hanging on to her relationship with Nicole as a way of asserting her independence. Mary is also concerned that Meredith might stop seeing Nicole just to please her. Mary wants her daughter to make her own decisions. But if Mary does not tell Meredith how she feels, Mary is afraid that she would be violating the openness and honesty that characterizes their relationship.

Question

How would you describe the dilemma that confronts Mary? What are some of the potential consequences of responses that Mary might make to her daughter's inquiry? Try not to suggest what Mary should do, but describe what choices she has and what consequences these choices might have for her relationship with Meredith.

for my opinion." One function that Regina's message performs is to reinforce the value of honesty in the family. However, Regina's honesty threatened Meredith's self-image. Each of these communication functions—reinforcing the value of honesty in the family and supporting family members' self-images—makes particular demands upon the communicators and sometimes these demands can be experienced as contradictory. In this case, Meredith indicates that she wants her sister to be honest and, at the same time, to confirm her self-image.

Understanding the multiple functions of communication episodes enables us to better understand family relationships. A young adult in her late teens who begins telling her parents more about her sex life than her parents want to hear may be using the conversation to reveal something important about herself to her parents. Knowing that they are uncomfortable with her behavior, she may also be using self-disclosure to challenge her parents' values. In another family, frequent bickering may be a way that the family makes sure that no one member has more authority than another, as well as a way to express differences in the family. Self-disclosure can be used to confront as well as reveal, and bickering can help maintain stability as well as disrupt. Understanding more about the multiple functions of communication helps us to understand more about how these families manage struggles over authority issues. In order to make generalizations about communication in a given family, it may be important to recognize the function that the communication episode performs for the family. Often this recognition requires taking both the context of the interaction and the relationship dimension of the communication into account.

Unintentionality

Unintentionality refers to the idea that communication can take place in spite of family members' intent not to communicate, or lack of awareness that certain of their actions have communication value for other family members. Watzlawick, Beavin, and Jackson (1967) coined the phrase "one cannot not communicate" to describe the concept that all behaviors, including attempts not to communicate, have communication potential. If Meredith, one of the Jackson children in our opening example, is angry about something that Regina did and decides not to speak to her sister for a week, she will certainly be sending a message to Regina. Avoiding or refusing to talk about an issue can communicate specific attitudes and feelings depending upon the context of the situation and the history of the relationship.

Naturally, avoiding a topic may result in a variety of interpretations. Imagine that Mary had not asked Regina how she felt about her math test. What impact might that have had on Regina? Would it have communicated to Regina that her mother was not interested in her and validated Regina's feelings of neglect? On the other hand, suppose that Mary's failure to acknowledge Regina's test anxiety was perceived by Regina as confidence that Regina would probably do well on the math test. In this case, Mary's failure to mention the math test might have made Regina less preoccupied with the test and more inclined to accept responsibility for her performance. We would need more information about Regina and the Jackson family to decide how Regina might have construed her mother's failure to mention the math test. Each explanation, however, illustrates the important point that not talking about something can have communication value.

Actions that are not intended or advertised as communicative messages can also have influence. The classic patriarchal example is represented by the distant and detached father who quietly reads the newspaper in the living room as mother and daughter yell at each other in the kitchen; he spends weekday evenings at his office and retreats to his basement workshop on weekends. The physical distance clearly communicates this man's refusal to become involved in the emotional life of his family, whether or not the message is sent intentionally.

Other acts that may not be viewed as communication by family members can have communication value in the family. Imagine Frank Jackson peeling apples for a fruit salad. He likes the red color and the crunch of the apple skin, but he peels the apples because Meredith enjoys the salad only if the apples are peeled. She notices and smiles after looking into the salad bowl. Or consider a woman who has been trying to get her teenaged son to clean up his room. He usually leaves the door to his room open; one morning after her son has left for school and before she leaves for work, she goes up to his room and closes the door. That afternoon the son makes an effort to pick up a few things off the floor and opens his bedroom door again. Or imagine a woman who is angry with her husband because he made plans for them to spend Thanksgiving with his parents without consulting her. She spends the evening watching a television program she knows he hates while working in silence on a piece of needlework. The next day he suggests that they think about spending Christmas with her folks. Family members are continually communicating with each other through such actions and routine daily episodes, though they may not always be aware that they are doing so.

Patterns and Predictability of Interaction

Communication among those who are familiar with each other develops into patterns of interaction based on past experience. A **communication pattern** is an organized sequence of interactions.

Ted Nelson is an instant starter in the morning and enjoys a hearty breakfast during which time he typically plans his day. His wife, Joan, on the other hand, has difficulty getting going in the morning. It became a ritual for Ted to fix breakfast for both of them. Joan enjoyed having Ted prepare the coffee, cereal, fruit, and toast that they usually ate. In exchange, she worked hard to wake up and spend time with Ted discussing their daily agendas. The sequence of the tasks, their nonverbal behaviors, and the conversation between them became a morning ritual. Their morning activity developed into a pattern of interaction. As their relationship grows over time and their family grows in size, new patterns emerge.

After their son was born Ted and Joan continued the early morning ritual in which Ted prepared the breakfast and they planned the day. Joan would get Jamie ready to go to the sitter in the morning while Ted fixed breakfast. They continued to talk about their agendas at breakfast, but their ritual expanded to include Jamie. When Jamie was a toddler, one particular interaction pattern was repeated two or three times a week. The parents talked about work and their agendas; they attended to each other rather than to Jamie. After several minutes Jamie usually made a mess, banged his spoon on the table, and started to eat with his hands. The parents directed their attention toward Jamie, fussed at him a little, and began to include him in their conversation. A couple of days later, Ted and Joan would again get distracted discussing their agendas; Jamie would interrupt the conversation, forcing his parents to direct their attention toward him in order to discipline him and then include him in their talk. Neither of the adults seemed to be perturbed by the sequence of events. The morning ritual established when Ted and Joan were newlyweds was merely expanded to include Jamie. Every family's life is filled with many similar patterns of interaction.

The characteristics of family communication and the components of the meaning-making process present both a set of concepts and a language for taking a process orientation toward family communication. Considered together, these features of a process view of communication show how rich and complex family life can be.

SUMMARY

In this chapter, we distinguish between psychological, sociological, and communication approaches to the family. We explore alternative definitions of communication and describe a process orientation toward communication. A process orientation views communication as complex, ever-changing, and influenced by past interaction while simultaneously influencing future interactions. We also define family communication and describe both the characteristics of family communication and the process of creating meaning.

In any family, what is avoided can be as important as that which is stated; what one family member does, as well as what he or she says, can evoke responses from others; and what appears to be an innocent remark can have significant consequences for individuals and relationships in the family. We indicate in this chapter that communication is influenced by the unique characteristics and behavioral choices of family members. However, we wish to emphasize the point that the communication process is much more than the sum of individual messages and responses. Understanding communication in families requires that we appreciate and attend to the complexity of the process.

We stress that communication is a joint construction of all participants. Family members do not merely send messages to one another; they evoke behaviors from and mutually influence one another. Communication is not something that one family member does to another but is instead a reflection and consequence of the family's interconnectedness. This tendency for communication to reflect the interdependence among family members is an important link between the communication approach and the systems view of the family.

KEY TERMS

communication approach

communication pattern

content level of messages

context of communication

culture

episode

family communication

functional nature of communication

historical frame of reference

individual perceptions, feelings,
  and cognitions

linear causality

meaning-making

meanings

metacommunication

mutual influence

nonverbal communication

place as context

process orientation

psychological approach

punctuation

reflexive and evolving

relationship level of messages

social reality

sociological approach

unintentionality

verbal symbols

CHAPTER 3

THE FAMILY AS A MEANING-MAKING SYSTEM

NANCY VADER-McCORMICK

THE MARTIN FAMILY

The Martins live in a suburban neighborhood near Chicago, where Paul Martin works as a city planner. Jane Martin teaches reading readiness part-time at a nearby elementary school and spends much of her free time as a volunteer for a local hospice. The Martins have two children: eleven-year-old Julie and fourteen-year-old Anne. Both girls attend junior high school.

A neighbor and close friend of Julie's recently moved away, which was a tremendous disappointment for her. To compensate, Julie began to hang around and probe into the affairs of her older sister. Anne had been developing an increasing need for privacy as part of her emergence into adolescence and resisted Julie's new interest in her.

In an attempt to free herself of her sister's constant company, Anne tended to be curt with Julie and to say things that hurt her feelings. Julie usually retaliated in some way and their interactions frequently ended in conflict. Both parents tried to be understanding, but sometimes they would get angry and frustrated with the girls.

The girls' mother, Jane, began to make an effort to spend time with Julie in activities that were intended to keep her away from Anne. Jane taught Julie how to knit, for instance, and took her to the indoor pool at a local community center one or two times each week. Jane was not always comfortable, however, with the demands that this made upon her time and energy. She had been thinking about going to graduate school. She now worried that such a change in family routine would be too disruptive at this time.

Jane wished that Paul would take more of an interest in the girls. She would get irritated whenever he suggested that the girls were simply "going through a stage" and would probably return to being friends in a few months. Jane accused Paul of being a workaholic and tried to pressure him into spending more time with the family. From his point of view, Paul felt unappreciated for the hard work and long hours that he put in at his job, something that his own father had never done for his family. Conversations that began as discussions about the girls often turned into arguments about the larger issue of how much time each parent should spend with the family.

To ease some of the demands made upon her, Jane began to rely more on Julie and Anne to help her with the tasks around the house. Initially, Jane asked the girls to help with the dusting, vacuuming, yardwork, and some of the cooking. The girls complained at first, but Jane developed the habit of treating them to dinner at a restaurant, a movie, or some other reward when they did an exceptional job. These rewards seemed to motivate them. Eventually, Julie assumed more of the housekeeping chores as a matter of routine. Anne took charge of much of the meal planning and even suggested that she, Julie, and their father do the cooking together on weekends.

The girls began to work together more cooperatively, to feel good about their increased responsibilities, and to enjoy their father more. Paul realized that he enjoyed cooking with his daughters on weekends and noticed that the household seemed more tranquil with the girls getting along better. He shared his perceptions with his wife, thus opening the lines of communication between them. Jane began to realize that she and Paul quarreled less than they had a few months earlier and she began to think again about going back to school. With less energy focused on internal family problems, at least temporarily, family members began to attend more to other relationships outside of the family: work, school, friends, and others.

UNDERSTANDING THE MARTINS

Families function within a certain range of day-to-day predictability. As illustrated by the Martin example, family members continually negotiate their relationships with each other as the family strives to reach its goals. Families also evolve and constantly change as members interact with each other, with their extended family, and with the environment.

What are the causes of the Martin family's problems? Is Julie to blame for the conflict that occurs between Anne and her? Should Paul feel guilty because he believes that his work prevents him from helping more around the house and spending more time with his family? Can we say that Jane is selfish because so much of her behavior seems to be guided by a desire to attend graduate school? How you answer those questions depends, at least in part, on the theoretical perspective you use for understanding family communication.

In the previous two chapters, we indicated that our preferred view of the family includes a systems theory orientation. This chapter will discuss systems theory and will apply the tenets of systems approaches to family communication. The first section of the chapter will examine the notion of causality and its relationship to a systems perspective. The second section will describe the elements and processes that underlie all family systems. The third and final section will examine current perspectives in the systems view of the family.

CAUSALITY AND FAMILY SYSTEMS

Every theoretical perspective brings with it some assumptions about the world and the events that occur within it. A major assumption underlying systems theory is that all components of a system are interrelated and interdependent. They work together to perform various system functions. Consequently, when we consider family communication, a systems perspective requires that we focus primarily on the relationships between family members and the ways in which family members work together to attain family goals. We think of communication messages as interwoven patterns of interaction that stretch through a family's history together rather than as singular events. Each message is simultaneously a response to someone else's message (real or anticipated) and a stimulus for future responses.

These interactions become patterns that tend to be repeated in family relationships. Thus, communication between family members can be studied as an interactive phenomenon in which all family members participate. When we examine the family from a systems point of view, no one person or one thing in the family can realistically be identified as the "cause" of a problem. Instead, we try to understand situations, problems, and "ways of being" in families. We examine the influences impinging upon the family, behaviors that are evoked between and among members, the sequencing of events over time, and how family members fit together.

As is evident from the opening example, individuals frequently talk about their families only in terms of what specific family members did and how they felt. Julie turned to her sister when her friend moved away. Jane was resentful because she believed she would have to postpone graduate school. Paul found that he enjoyed cooking with his daughters. People describe their own families this way: "My younger brother doesn't like competition." "Mother gives Dad 'the silent treatment' when her feelings are hurt." "My sister has been much easier to get along with lately."

To understand events in the Martin family, however, it is important to think about their behavior from the perspective of the family as a whole rather than just from the perspective of the individual. Consider what happens when behavior is viewed as emerging from what Hoffman (1981) calls "the social field" in which it occurs. Rather than acting independently, family members invite responses from each other through their actions, conversations, and place in the social unit. Jane became more content about Paul's involvement in the family when she saw how much he enjoyed cooking with his daughters on weekends. When Julie started to become dependent upon her sister, Anne pushed her away, hurting Julie's feelings and producing a retaliatory response. Although these episodes must necessarily be phrased to sound as if there was a cause (Paul became more involved with the family) and an effect (Jane became more content), these statements merely describe arbitrary starting and ending points for the episode. We could just as easily observe that Paul's desire to help his wife drew him into a closer relationship with his daughters or that Anne and Julie encouraged their father to work with them out of their needs to both help their mother and feel closer to him. The connections between and among family members and the need to maintain the family system produced the communication episodes just described.

People, however, typically perceive their own behavior only as a response to other members in the family. Imagine Anne Martin saying, "You've got to do something about Julie; she is driving me crazy!" From Anne's point of view, it is Julie's persistent attempts to pry into Anne's affairs that are the source of the problem between the two girls. From Julie's point of view, however, Anne's secrecy and lack of interest are the major problems.

While the responses of each sister reflect authentic feelings and experiences, the girls also tend to justify each of their behaviors by blaming the other. Behavior of all family members is evoked by other family members in significant ways. When behavior in the family is seen primarily as interactive, then it is possible to conceive of episodes as occurring within a sequence of events. How members and subgroups in the family are connected and how the family makes adaptations in their relationships over time also become more apparent. Notice, for example, how Anne and Julie were drawn closer together when they became involved in managing the cooking. When they included their father in the task, some of the distance between Paul and his family was also reduced. Because Paul was more involved in the family, Jane may have felt a little more comfortable putting more distance between herself and her family so that she could go back to school. You can begin to see that the influences affecting the family are complex—influences impinge upon the family from outside the nuclear family, from responses to each other's behavior within the family, and from the individual predispositions of family members.

As we discussed in an earlier chapter, concepts related to *causality in the family* are viewed differently in thinking about how family members, through their communication, are related to each other over time. From a communication perspective, there is little value in blaming Julie, or the neighbor who moved away, for the problems that developed in the Martin family. Why not begin with the fact that Julie had only one close friend in her neighborhood instead of two? Nor do we decide that Anne is the cause for the stress in the family because she needed privacy and pushed her sister away. Why not, instead, blame Paul's investment in his work or Jane's resentment over the increased demands on her time for the tension in the family? Blaming individuals does not help much to understand the family and the processes that influence family behavior.

A focus on the social unit allows you to think of family interaction as ongoing, choice-governed, and somewhat circular. Communication episodes isolate bits of the family's interaction but all episodes are tied together by an ongoing family history. Each episode builds on some prior event rather than beginning anew. In addition, it should be clear that choices about behavior are made in concert with responses received from other family members. Anne chose to be short with Julie partly because her curt responses achieved the desired reaction from Julie: distancing in their relationship. Had Julie's response been different, Anne may have selected another strategy. These episodes reflect overall family functioning and communication rather than individual messages and responses. Family members can predict outcomes in a given situation based on outcomes from prior episodes, which provides a sense of circularity. Thus, family communication can be seen as somewhat patterned and predictable.

Focusing primarily on the social unit rather than on the individual will lead you to think less in terms of causes or of blaming individuals for problems that develop and will change the interpretations of what you observe. Different kinds of concerns are, instead, addressed: what influences do family members exert over each other through their actions and their conversations? How do family members display their connectedness to one another? How does this family manage conflict? What patterns of interaction are repeated and what function do those patterns serve for the family system? What needs do family members satisfy for each other; how are these needs identified; how do they change? How does the family's communication influence and reflect the degree of integration and individuation of family members? What influences outside the family exert pressure on family members and how does the family system cope with those influences? Questions such as these help to identify the interrelatedness of family members. As we will discuss in the next section, the systems view involves a focus on a set of systems elements and the processes that make the systems work.

FAMILY SYSTEMS THEORY: ELEMENTS AND PROCESSES

An early theory of systems called general systems theory (GST) was developed largely by Bertalanffy (1968) and expanded by other social and physical scientists (Buckley, 1967; Laszlo, 1972; Mesarovic, 1970; Pepper, 1972). According to Bertalanffy, the development of systems theory met a need of biologists to describe biological systems and organic phenomena. In particular, the need arose to describe systems that, unlike mechanical or physical systems, are changed by input from the surrounding environment and, in turn, exert an influence on that environment. These biological systems—phenomena like tide pools, insect colonies, various animal habitats, and families—exhibit a number of traits not easily studied using cause-and-effect models. Capra (1982) has called general systems theory a "turning point" in how we think about living organisms and about life in general on our planet.

GST was extended by Miller (1978) in his benchmark work on general living systems theory. Miller argued for the construction of a general theory that would allow researchers to examine hierarchical relationships between the smallest possible unit of analysis (the individual cell system) and the largest (the supranational system).

Because human families are living phenomena that both influence and are influenced by changes from within and without the family unit, they can be studied effectively using a systems approach. In their article in *Contemporary Theories About the Family,* Broderick and Smith (1979) argued that the "systems perspective seems to have no peer among the theoretical perspectives available to family scholars" (p. 126) for examining family communication.

The shift in focus from interest in individual entities to studying relationships as they exist in systems was not lost on therapists and researchers working with troubled families. Although trained from a psychoanalytic perspective, which calls for diagnosis of mental illness within a single identified patient, early therapists began to consider the influence of other family members on their patient's behavior. (For a detailed description of this evolutionary process, see Guerin, 1976.)

This application of a family-centered approach to family therapy emerged simultaneously in several areas of the country. In California, Gregory Bateson and colleagues Jay Haley, John Weakland, and Don Jackson—known as the "Palo Alto Group," began an investigation into the role of communication in the family system. In Washington, D.C., Murray Bowen undertook his pioneering project to study the families of schizophrenics in an effort to explain the fact that improving patients frequently regressed after returning to their family systems. In Atlanta, Carl Whitaker and colleagues went into a private practice in which they acted as co-therapists to work with troubled families. In their therapy, family members were added one at a time to the therapeutic unit, until whole families and, eventually, members of the suprasystem were included in the sessions. In Chicago, Charles and Jeannette Kramer formed the Chicago Family Institute, now affiliated with the Northwestern University School of Medicine. In Pennsylvania, both the Philadelphia Family Institute and the Philadelphia Child Guidance Clinic provided centers for the study of families, eventually focusing on intergenerational family networks as a place for intervention. Ivan Boszormenyi-Nagy, Geraldine Spark, Salvador Minuchin, James Framo, Ross Speck, and Carolyn Attneave have all been part of the pioneering work in family therapy that was undertaken in Philadelphia. In New York, Nathan Ackerman began to examine the influence of social forces, family roles, and other environmental influences on families, although he retained a psychoanalytic focus in his therapy.

In the sections that follow we describe characteristics of family systems theory that were developed in the formative decades between the 1950s and 1980s. The terminology and concepts we describe reflect what could be identified as traditional family systems theory and provide the theoretical background for much of the current discussion of family systems. Family systems, like all living systems, incorporate two types of characteristics: (1) a set of system elements, and (2) a set of processes that help the system function.

System Elements

System elements are the physical features of the family system. Six types of system elements comprise family systems: (1) interdependent components, (2) inputs and outputs, (3) boundaries and hierarchies, (4) rules for operation, (5) system goals, and (6) feedback mechanisms.

Interdependent Components

The **components** of a human system are simply the parts that work together to create the system as a whole. In the case of the family, the components can be people and the functions or roles that they perform for the family system.

One way to organize your thinking about family systems is to consider the components of a family system to be family members: spouses, parents, children, stepchildren, in-laws, grandparents, and other relatives or nonrelated individuals who function as family members. People can also enter and leave the system at various times as family members are born, marry, divorce, and die.

The size of the family can influence how a family functions. As Broderick and Smith have observed (1979), "Large family systems are structurally so different from small family systems that they should be considered separately in making any generalizations about how family systems operate" (p. 113). Clearly, the four-person Martin family will differ in significant ways from the twelve-person Lueder family. Similarly, there will be many differences among single-parent families, blended families, ethnic families, two-generation families, and gay families that will not be reflected in just their sizes.

Roles are sets of functions that individual members are expected to perform in the system, such as caregiver, breadwinner, or scapegoat, based on the rules established for specific relationships. We discuss family roles in Chapter 10.

By *interdependent* we mean that the actions of each component affect in some noticeable way other components in the system. The behavior of one family member has an influence on other members. When Jane returns home from a frustrating day at school, her frustration will invite responses (or nonresponses) from Anne, Julie, and Paul. The ways in which they respond (or fail to respond) to her

FIGURE 3.1   System elements.

1. **Interdependent components:** people and/or sets of role functions.
   Examples of people components: parents, grandparents, newborns.
   Examples of roles: wage earner, nurturer, problem child, initiator, scapegoat.
2. **Inputs and outputs:** information that flows into the system and the products or energy of that information returned to the suprasystem.
   Examples of inputs: newspapers, radio broadcasts, phone calls.
   Examples of outputs: work, volunteering, money to charity, attendance at church services, support for friends and family.
3. **Boundaries and hierarchies:** a series of ever-wider arbitrary dividing lines separating subsystems, systems, and suprasystems.
   Examples: marital dyad subsystem, sibling subsystem, nuclear system, extended family suprasystem, community suprasystem, world suprasystem.
4. **Rules for operation:** guidelines that prescribe what is expected, allowed, and prohibited in a given set of circumstances.
   Examples: parents make the rules, when a parent has been drinking the rest of the family compensates, children may solve conflicts using physical force with each other but never with parents or people outside the system.
5. **System goals:** desired outcomes of family functioning at a particular time.
   Examples: prosperity for family members, happiness, social recognition, promotion of self-worth among family members, maintenance of an unhappy marriage, support for a parent's alcohol dependency.
6. **Feedback mechanisms:** devices that indicate the degree to which family systems are headed toward (or away from) satisfaction of their goals.
   Examples: conflict between spouses may indicate movement away from self-worth goals, chores left undone may indicate movement away from family harmony, cheerful participation in family events may indicate movement toward a goal of happiness.

---

feelings of frustration will, in turn, affect her responses to them. Similarly, when one family member is ill, absent from the family, or otherwise unable to perform the behaviors usually expected from and associated with that person, the entire family system is altered. Because roles help to structure family interaction and stabilize the family system, family members will compensate for each other when roles are not performed.

To fully grasp the concept of interdependence, imagine large, stretchable rubber bands linking family members to each other. For example, imagine strong bands connecting Jane and Paul Martin. As a married couple, they feel strongly tied to one another. As one partner moves, the movement tugs on the other partner, resulting in some movement on his or her part. For example, Paul's long hours at work pull on Jane's rubber band, resulting in tension and frustration in their relationship. Now imagine rubber bands stretching from each parent to each of their children and bands connecting Julie and Anne to each other. As one family member experiences a change—for example, the loss of a close friend who moves away—the bands that connect that family member to all others may stretch. This increased tension in the system will affect each of the other three system components. If the influence is temporary, the tension in the rubber bands might be released, requiring no systemic change; if the change is major, the tension in the rubber bands will eventually be sufficient to move others in the system in some way. Again, returning to our opening example, Julie's loss of a close friend resulted in tension, or a tightly stretched rubber band, between Anne and her. Anne's attempts literally to pull away from her sister resulted in considerable tugging on the rubber band connecting Anne to Julie and, in turn, on those rubber bands connecting both girls to their parents. To ease some of the tension, Jane and Paul engaged in numerous activities that had the effect of moving them closer to both girls, thus reducing the perceived tension.

In our definition of family, we call the interdependence among family members mutual influence. As a natural consequence of exerting mutual influence over each other, being interdependent means that even the absence of a family member will have a profound effect on the family system. The relationship, for example, between a teenaged son and his parents can change dramatically when the older of two sons leaves for college. The boys' parents might find that they have more time to spend with their younger son. They might also begin to use the departure of one of their sons as an opportunity to begin letting go of their children as they make the transition to adulthood. The brothers, in turn, may find that they are closer, even though they see each other only on holidays, because the competitive edge of the relationship is softened with distance.

Thus, family systems can be thought of as sets of people and roles that are inextricably bound by invisible ties. When one element of the system is affected, all others are influenced in some way.

System Inputs and Outputs

Inputs and outputs are the "matter" that moves in and out of the system. **Inputs** are received and used by the system to perform its designated function or achieve its goals. **Outputs** are the outcomes or by-products of the system's activity that are returned to the environment. Inputs and outputs of family systems can be treated as forms of information or communication or can be thought of as requiring communication (Kantor & Lehr, 1975).

For the typical family system, inputs include information from the media, visits from friends, money from employers, mail, and goods and services. When Anne receives a pleasant phone call from a friend, or Jane brings home a new idea that she struggled with in graduate school, or the family watches a natural disaster on their television screen, the result is an input of feeling, information, or meaning into the family system. Incoming information is dealt with and compared with family images and meanings; some is incorporated and some is discarded. When there is disagreement among family members about the value of the information or how to interpret it, conflict may occur. Similarly, issues concerning money enter the system and decisions are made, usually through negotiation, about how it eventually will be converted to interest or hard goods. In the Martin family, inputs may take the form of values held by grandparents that are communicated to Julie and Anne, television news programs that convince Paul and Jane that Chicago is a safe city in which to raise their children, books that entice them to travel to foreign countries, and unwanted intrusions from the too-friendly next-door neighbors.

Family outputs include work and service in the community, money spent on goods and services, participation in politics (voting), support for friends and relatives, and socialization of children. In families with antisocial members, outputs might include damage to the neighborhood, intense noise, or violence. Outputs from the Martin family system might include Paul's efforts at work, Julie's and

Anne's contributions to their classes and helpfulness to their friends, Jane's volunteer work at the hospice and her financial support for her aging parents, and time that all four of them devote to cleaning up the neighborhood park each spring.

As we discuss in Chapter 6, which explores the family's ecosystem, the amount and kind of influence that a family system receives from its environment can significantly affect its functioning. The quality of outputs a family system provides to its environment affects its place in that environment. Examining the ways in which inputs and outputs are processed by the system allows you to identify the rules of operation that influence the family system as a whole and to understand better its place in the larger environment.

Boundaries and Hierarchies

A system **boundary** is an arbitrary dividing line that defines the inside and outside of a given system. The boundary differentiates inputs and outputs and identifies the components that will be considered part of the system. The system **hierarchy** defines the relationships among two or more system boundaries.

The boundary may be an arbitrary dividing line that is drawn at the discretion of the person who wishes to describe that system or it may be a shared perception that family members hold regarding elements that belong inside and outside of the family system. In general, it is most useful to think of boundaries as separating system elements that have frequent interaction with one another. In our opening example, we arbitrarily drew a boundary around the four members of the Martin nuclear family system as our unit of analysis because, using our earlier definition of family communication, these are the four individuals of central interest to a family analysis. If our definition of family were broadened to the extended family, we might have included grandparents, aunts, uncles, and cousins within the boundary.

A systems approach to the study of the family often makes distinctions between subsystems and suprasystems in the family. A **subsystem** includes components of a larger system. The nuclear family is composed of several subsystems. Parents and/or spouses, two sisters, four children and their mother, and a father and son are examples of subsystems in the nuclear family. A **suprasystem** is defined as a larger system that is composed of other identifiable systems. The extended family network, the neighborhood where the nuclear family lives, and the larger community within which the nuclear family functions are included in the family's suprasystem.

Systems have commonly been thought of as containing a **hierarchy of subsystems** and as being embedded in a **hierarchy of suprasystems.** As Miller (1978) discusses in his book on general living systems and Haley (1976) describes in *Problem-Solving Therapy,* this notion of hierarchy can help you to understand the structure of the family system in relationship to the structure of its internal organization and outside environment. Just as a family contains a variety of subsystems (individuals, parent–child relationships, the marital dyad, and child–child relationships), each family is one system in the larger suprasystem hierarchy that contains families of origin (grandparents, aunts, uncles), the community system, and the social system. The relationships of interest (child–child, family–neighbors, or family–society) differentiate the "system" of interest from the supra- and subsystems. We discuss the concept of a hierarchy of subsystems and suprasystems further in Chapter 6.

Please note that families create boundaries by the designs of their houses, locks on their doors, fences that surround their yards, and through the dozens of ways that they stake out and defend family "territory." In some family systems, grandparents, aunts, stepchildren, and even nonrelatives are considered part of the system. These individuals nap in the porch swing, borrow the cars, and feel free to drop by whenever they feel like it. They may even live in the same house with the nuclear family. In other family systems, only parents and children qualify as "family"; other family members function as part of the larger suprasystem. These "outsiders" call ahead and schedule time to be with nuclear family members.

The *permeability* of the boundary that surrounds a family indicates the degree to which that system is open or closed to its environment. In "open family systems," many inputs are sought and there is significant interaction with the outside environment. In such families, members expose themselves to many viewpoints and make attachments outside of the system. In "closed family systems," the boundaries are more rigid and are used to screen inputs and outputs more rigorously. Family members keep to themselves and information may be carefully filtered, with only information consistent with family values being allowed to enter the system. Family behavior may be monitored with equal care, with outputs being restricted to a fairly narrow range of acceptable behavior. A relative degree of openness is important for understanding family functioning (Broderick & Pulliam-Krager, 1978; Constantine, 1986; Kantor & Lehr, 1975).

Boundaries also help to identify how individuals and subgroups are differentiated within the family system. They help to distinguish, for instance, what is unique about the relationship of Julie to her sister Anne; they indicate what is shared only by Paul and Jane; and they prescribe ways in which Anne may be considered to be her own person. Anne and Julie may share secrets as a way to differentiate their relationship from other relationships in the family and thereby define their boundary. Anne may keep a diary that her parents are not permitted to read as a way of establishing a boundary between herself and other family members.

Boundaries may be clear in some families and not clear in others. **Rigid boundaries,** or boundaries that are clearly defined and difficult to penetrate, produce different communication interactions than **diffuse boundaries,** or boundaries that fluctuate freely and are easily permeated. For instance, the mother and father in a family may differentiate themselves from the rest of the family by setting aside one evening per week to spend alone together or by making their bedroom off limits to other family members. In their case, the boundary is clear. Another couple may not have defined their boundary as a couple as clearly. As a consequence, they may allow their conversations and conflicts to be interrupted by their children or they may openly disagree about how to handle the children.

Recognizing characteristics of system, subsystem, and suprasystem boundaries can provide considerable information about family functioning. Boundaries differentiate the family from the environment, maintain the uniqueness of subsystems (i.e., dyadic, triadic, relationships, etc. in the family), and preserve the individuality of family members.

Rules for Operation

Rules specify which operations or behaviors are allowed, recommended, expected, and forbidden within the system. The rules for operation provide the framework or structure within which the system components are connected and must operate (Ford, 1983).

The specific rules governing a family are unique to that family and change as that family evolves (Constantine, 1986). Family system rules pertain to such things as roles for family members, subjects that can and cannot be discussed, ways of expressing anger or affection, and authority among family members. In the Martin family, both adults work but Jane divides her time between paid employment and volunteering, suggesting some rule about who is to be the "breadwinner" for the family. We also learn that it is acceptable to talk about one's frustrations in that family, that efforts are made by all family members to maintain some sort of family harmony, and that affection can be expressed by participating in activities with other family members (cooking, going to a movie, etc.). Each of these observations provides insight into the rules that structure the Martin family system. We discuss various types of family rules, their origins, and their influence on family system functioning in more depth in Chapter 7.

Family System Goals

The system **goal** is quite literally what a system attempts to accomplish or achieve at any given point in time. As such, identification of family goals tends to direct family interaction toward attainment of those goals. The goal of a small antique business may be fairly fixed and generally well understood: to sell enough merchandise at prices that will allow the owners to cover their costs and make a modest profit for themselves. Family system goals may not be as clearly articulated: a goal might be to raise the children in a loving environment or it might be to confirm the belief that men cannot be trusted.

A characteristic of family system goals is that they are not absolute. Family goals may change before they are met, a new goal may emerge as an old one is achieved, or two conflicting goals may compete for the family's attention. For example, in the Martin family there appears to be a structure of rules that promotes family harmony, leading to the conclusion that the Martin system has a goal of maintaining harmonious relationships among its members. Achievement of that goal involves family members doing things together, such as cooking, attending sporting events, and going to movies. It also involves intervention by one or more family members when difficulties erupt in one of the subsystems. As you see in the example, however, as relationships improve, family members begin to focus attention on goals that require family members to draw somewhat apart (Jane begins to anticipate graduate school). The goal of family harmony directs family activity inward; the goal of satisfying individual family members' needs draws family members apart. Sometimes family goals are revealed in conversational themes or in the stories they share and the metaphors they use to describe their life together. We discuss family stories, myths, metaphors, and themes in Chapters 8 and 9.

Goals in family systems continually change as the family evolves, and a family system may work toward multiple goals at the same time. A newly married couple with career aspirations for both spouses may be excited about moving to a large urban area where each of them will realize the goal of being employed in a new, challenging job. Once settled and involved in the demands of their careers, they may find themselves needing to spend time working on problems in their relationship. As we will discuss in Chapter 6, the addition of children to the family system necessitates further modification of family system goals, as does every other major life event to follow.

Feedback Mechanisms

Feedback is any response to an operation or behavior that provides information about that operation or behavior. In communication terms, feedback is simply the response to a comment a speaker has made: the answer to a question, a nonverbal confirmation of listening, or any other communicative act that allows for a communication episode to move ahead. In systems terms, feedback provides information to the system about its progress toward or away from system goals.

In family systems the ability to monitor progress toward goals and make changes in structure or behavior with the intention of improving this progress is important. While families are systems, similar to other living systems that are constantly changing, some family members may attempt to stabilize or regulate behavior within the family in ways that keep the family oriented toward specific goals. Other family members may press for faster change, suggest alternative family goals, or resist previous patterns of relating. Communication in the family often provides the family with information that goals have shifted, that taken-for-granted patterns are changing, or that roles are evolving. In traditional systems theory terminology, the regulating mechanisms in a family help indicate member satisfaction, adherence to family rules and norms, and general progress toward family goals. In some families, conversations among family members perform this function on a regular basis. In other families, quarrels and emotional outbursts provide the needed information. As you might expect, not all deviations from family goals are correctable, even when detected by feedback mechanisms.

In the Martin family, conflict between Anne and Julie served as a regulating mechanism to alert family members to a potential problem. Changes in responsibilities and ways of relating to each other helped to put the system back on course.

System Processes

System processes are the characteristics of human systems that describe how the system functions through time. System processes describe the day-to-day conduct and evolution of the family as it maintains itself in some working order and adapts to the course of events and to the environment. In this sense, families, because they are social systems, are constructed, maintain themselves, and adapt to their environment through their communication.

Four types of systems processes are especially relevant to our discussion of family communication: (1) nonsummativity, (2) stability, (3) change, and (4) equifinality. Each is discussed in the sections that follow.

Nonsummativity

The principle of **nonsummativity** refers to the fact that "a system cannot be taken for the sum of its parts" (Watzlawick, Beavin, & Jackson, 1967, p. 125). To understand the family as a system we need to do more than describe the characteristics and behaviors of individual family members. Each member's behavior is influenced by the behavior of other family members. We cannot, therefore, understand how the family operates by merely "summing up characteristics of individual

FIGURE 3.2   System processes.

1. **Nonsummativity:** developing the patterns and relationships in which the whole is greater than the sum of the parts.

   Example: Those who know Eric Morris and his parents perceive them as relaxed individuals who are easy to get along with. Whenever the three of them are alone together for a holiday, however, they all begin immediately to irritate one another.

2. **Stability:** establishing a balanced state that will ensure maintenance of the system.

   Example: The Millars have two young sons who frequently get into physical fights with one another. Their parents typically ignore these combats until one of them gets hurt and begins to cry; then one of the parents will separate the two boys in order to restore peace.

3. **Change:** adapting to the growth and maturation of family members and to novel circumstances for which no roles currently exist.

   Example: When the Robinson twins started kindergarten their mother went back to work full-time as a maternity nurse and their father reduced his hours at work in order to participate more fully in household tasks.

4. **Equifinality:** reaching similar goals from different pathways or achieving different goals from similar origins.

   Example: The Cohen family achieves a feeling of connectedness among family members through frequent hugs and kisses, while the Quinn family achieves the same feelings through frequent arguments, political debates, and heated discussions.

members" (Walsh, 1982, p. 9). It is important to attend to how family members function as a whole, the patterns that they develop in their conversation and interaction, and how they are connected to one another.

For example, the positive changes that occur in the Martin family are not simply the consequence of the separate behaviors of individual family members but of changes in how the Martins relate to one another. Anne and Julie begin to share more of their mother's role and begin to behave more cooperatively toward one another. Paul and the girls develop tasks that they can share. Paul and Jane share positive feelings about the girls and become more comfortable with their parenting relationship. If we wish to understand the Martins, it is important to understand their relationships. It is not enough merely to indicate that Julie gains maturity or Paul opens up more or Jane becomes less stressed.

Nonsummativity is the outcome of interdependence. System components working together can often achieve what individual components working alone cannot. Integrating their parenting styles is something that Paul and Jane can only do together. Regulating the closeness and distance of their relationship involves both Julie and Anne. The patterns of parenting that the couple develop and the rules regulating closeness and distance that Julie and Anne create describe aspects of their family system that "transcend the qualities of individuals" (Watzlawick, Beavin, & Jackson, 1967, p. 135). Because family systems identify boundaries, establish hierarchies, develop rules, and set collective system goals, they are able to accomplish as a system what cannot be accomplished alone. By recognizing the importance of this system principle, we begin to attend more to characteristics that help us understand the family as a group or a set of relationships.

Stability

The tendency for families to seek stability means that they seek enough regularity, order, permanence, and predictability in relationships outside and inside the family to ensure the maintenance of the system (Watzlawick, Beavin, & Jackson, 1967). Families are continually confronted with information and events from outside their system. At the same time, individual family members are growing and maturing. The patterns that create a sense of predictability in the family enable the family to maintain some degree of "relative constancy" in an environment that is constantly changing (Jackson, 1970, p. 1).

Information from outside the family or deviations in behavior from within the family that might threaten its stability are resisted by feedback mechanisms (Walsh, 1982). As we indicated earlier in the chapter, **feedback mechanisms,** sometimes called *homeostatic mechanisms,* are the system-regulating processes that reinforce family rules and patterns. As Walsh (1981, p. 10) explains, "Too great a deviation from the family norm may be counteracted in the negative feedback process in order to regulate tension and to restore the family equilibrium or homeostasis." Parents who "ground" their teenaged daughter for two weeks after she comes home intoxicated one evening are using a feedback mechanism to discourage such behavior in the future. When one component of the family system deviates from expectations or desires, other family members may intervene to ensure the maintenance of the family system. Rather than allow Julie and Anne's subsystem to break apart through their conflict, both Jane and Paul moved in to try to rectify the problem; they assumed roles that allowed the system to establish stability once again. The family's tendency to seek stability or equilibrium is called **morphostasis** (Speer, 1970; Ariel, Carel, & Tyano, 1984). A system that cannot maintain some degree of stability may eventually disintegrate, but stability is different for every family.

For most families, maintaining stability is an ongoing process that is continually challenged. A family that is going through obvious changes may experience the challenge to its stability as more obvious than a family in which changes are more subtle. The tendency to restore order and equilibrium in the family can be seen following any of the many life crises to which families are prone: the birth of the first child, death of grandparents, divorce, unemployment, and so on. Returning to our opening example of the Martin family, it would be apparent that instability began to be a problem for the Martins shortly after Julie's friend moved away. Jane felt overworked, Paul felt harassed, Anne was feeling pestered by her younger sister and unable to attain the degree of privacy and independence she desired. Left unchecked, these feelings could have escalated into a serious explosion among members of this family. Fortunately, the system reorganized to avert a breakdown. Jane, for instance, shifted some responsibilities to Julie and Anne, thus giving Julie something important to do and satisfying Anne's desire to be recognized for her increasing maturity. In system terms, one component (Jane) shifted some of her functions (housework and shopping) to two other system components (Anne and Julie). This shift in responsibility helped the family system to achieve some degree of stability once again. As new roles were incorporated into the rules for operation, a new sense of order was created and the system took on more organized patterns of interaction.

Change

While some level of stability is necessary for the self-maintenance of the family, it is apparent that some flexibility is also necessary as the family evolves over time. Change refers to the tendency of family systems to reorganize themselves and adapt new patterns in response to new "developmental imperatives" within the family (Walsh, 1982, p. 10). A system tends to evolve over time, usually as it encounters novel events for which it has not yet developed standardized ways of responding (Dell, 1982; Speer, 1970; Carter & McGoldrick, 1980). In other words, family members change how they relate to each other as the system encounters surprising inputs from the environment and as it moves through the family life cycle. The family's tendency to change as it evolves through time is called **morphogenesis** (Speer, 1970).

Family systems can generate feedback and can respond to that feedback in ways that may alter goals, functions, and/or rules of operation as well as maintain them. Components of human systems may modify their behavior, appearance, and relationships. They exhibit interdependence and interconnectedness, and their relationships can be modified if necessary. A couple with a new baby may make some dramatic changes in the roles they assume toward one another, the goals they have as a couple, and the patterns that characterize their life together. Such changes are made possible through the couple's ability to communicate and to act on the basis of their conversations and interactions with each other.

It should be clear that a struggle between the need for stability and the inevitability of change across the life cycle involves the family in a dialectical process that highlights the importance of communication. In Chapter 1 we introduced the idea that stability and change may present contradictory demands on the family. Change may be resisted in the family as it attempts to maintain a stable system. Stability evolves from consistency, familiar patterns, and predictable behaviors. However, systems do not stand still in time. Change naturally occurs as the family goes through various life cycle stages. The addition of children, the aging of parents, and myriad other family life cycle crises push the family system into new forms, new patterns, and new pathways. This change, which we discuss in more detail later in this book, makes the struggle for stability more difficult.

Families continually negotiate a balance between stability and change. There is a constant tension between the forces that resist too much novelty in the family and those that cause the family to adapt as it grows, matures, and responds to the environment. Paradoxically, families that cling rigidly to familiar patterns of relating at the expense of adapting to change can be dysfunctional and may precipitate a family crisis that threatens the integrity of the family (Steier, Stanton, & Todd, 1982). Conversely, families that fail to develop adequate levels of constancy and predictability in their patterns of relating may not be able to maintain the stability necessary to keep the family intact.

Clearly, the degree to which families cope with changing circumstances influences family form and functioning. We discuss some of these variations when we describe family patterns in Chapters 10 and 11.

Equifinality

A fourth and final consideration for understanding family system processes pertains to the ways in which families reach goals. **Equifinality**, a term coined by Bertalanffy (1968, p. 40), refers to the fact that the "same final state may be reached from different initial conditions and in different ways." As Walsh (1982, p. 10) illustrates, "Thus one family may be disabled while another family rallies in response to the same crisis; or two well-functioning families may have evolved from quite different circumstances." Similarly, two different systems may attain the same goal by beginning at different starting points and selecting different strategies.

Return for a moment to our opening example. A goal for the Martin family system appears to be to maintain family harmony. When tension was felt following the departure of Julie's friend, harmony was restored through a series of episodes designed to strengthen relationships and bring family members closer together: cooking together, sharing responsibilities, and having honest conversations about feelings. You can probably think of other strategies that might have been used to achieve the same effect: making new friends, getting professional help, taking a family trip, installing a backyard swimming pool, and so on. Family harmony might have been restored in many ways, depending on the characteristics of the Martin family system described in this chapter.

In the Scarzoni family, for example, family harmony is tied to independence. Rather than finding new ways for the family to join together when the tension becomes troublesome, the Scarzonis look for ways to allow family members the freedom to function outside of the family. Family harmony might be achieved by allowing Dad a special fishing trip with his buddies or by saving the money for each of the three children to go to separate summer camps.

Knowing that the same goal can be achieved in a variety of ways allows for creativity in family functioning. The degree to which family members employ the principle of equifinality is tied to the flexibility with which they meet challenges. Similarly, recognizing the potential for two families to achieve the same goal via differing pathways could provide you with more tolerance for different family styles. Rather than labeling the Martins as a "better" family because they solve their problems without shouting and tears, you may want to consider that such outbursts could provide the same outcome for another family—and they might enjoy the outlet that yelling and crying provides!

THREE APPROACHES TO FAMILY SYSTEMS THEORY

In the previous section, we presented the basic terminology of family systems theory in our description of systems elements and processes. It is important to point out, however, that the window through which one may view communication in the family system may differ depending on the particular approach to systems theory one takes. Bochner and Eisenberg (1987) outline three models, originally identified by Carlos Sluzki, which differ in their approach to family systems theory: (1) interactional, (2) structural, and (3) constructivist or constructionist (p. 544; Sluzki, 1983). Each of these approaches to studying family systems adds to our understanding of family communication.

The **interactional view** emphasizes the importance of message transactions in the family system. In particular, this approach analyzes how *patterns of interaction* in the family help to define the nature of relationships in the family system. It is the relationship-defining aspect of messages rather than the content of messages themselves that is important. For example, Colleen almost always initiates suggestions for how to discipline the children in the family, while her husband, Jay, almost always supports her decisions without commenting very much. In this case, the interaction pattern in which the wife's "dominant" moves are typically

NANCY VADER-McCORMICK

The constructionist view of the family focuses on meaning making in the family.

accepted by her "submissive" husband is viewed as more important than the specific content of their talk. The persistent occurrence of reciprocal patterns of interaction among family members within a particular context of episodes that tend to be repetitive is the focus of interest for this approach to family systems. The exploration of family rules as they relate to repetitive patterns of interaction in Chapter 7 is especially relevant to this view of family systems.

The **structural view** focuses on the social organization and role structure of the family system. This view emphasizes how various dyads are organized in the family, examines patterns of triangulation and role conflict, and attends to issues related to how families manage boundaries and negotiate psychological distance and closeness in the family. The structural view also identifies the functions that particular members of the family perform for the family. For example, a family therapist with a structural view of the family would be interested in the extent to which the parents in the family are able to work together so that they can present a "united front" to their children. The therapist would be concerned, for instance, if he or she noticed a coalition between a mother and daughter, who are very close and involved in each other's lives, against a father who tends to be "blamed" for the problems in the family. The therapist might also try to identify the roles that various family members play in an alcoholic family. Fitzpatrick's (1988) work on types of marital role structures is an example of research compatible with this view of systems theory. We address some of the concepts related to the structural view of systems theory in our discussion of the family ecosystem in Chapter 7 and in our discussion of family roles in Chapter 10.

The **constructionist view** of the family tends to focus on meaning-making processes in the family. How does the family construct its particular social reality? What is the family's view of the world and its relationship to it? How do family members' belief structures, their paradigms for living, and their interpretations of events help us to understand their behavior? How is the family's social reality revealed in the narratives or stories that family members construct of their experience together or in the content of their conversations? For example, how do Alice and Ted tell the intensely emotional story of their personal crisis of going through an abortion together (Ellis & Bochner, 1992) or how do a couple's conversational

APPLICATION 3.1

THE BROWN FAMILY

Using systems theory terminology, analyze the communication in the Brown family system:

Sara and William Brown lived in an older neighborhood in downtown Detroit, Michigan. William worked on the assembly line in a steering gear plant that recently began rehiring employees after a series of layoffs. Sara stayed at home, caring for their four children: two-year-old Teddy, four-year-old Robby, and the twins, Lauri and Melissa, both ten.

Sara's parents recently moved back to Detroit after living for eleven years in Arizona. Although she and her mother had always been close, Sara found it difficult to adjust to the daily phone calls and surprise visits that she received from her parents. She disliked that her parents, now retired, seem intent on spoiling their four grandchildren.

To make things worse, William was clearly disturbed by what he perceived to be his in-laws' interference with his family life. He resented the gifts that the maternal grandparents showered upon his four children. He also feared that Sara was too closely tied to her mother and, because Sara's mother had vigorously opposed their marriage, that this would cause marital problems at some point.

Sara felt caught between her parents and her husband. Although she felt loyal to her mother and father, she recognized that she and William had to maintain a life separate from that of her parents. She found herself defending her parents' behavior to William and his attitudes to her parents. She and William frequently engaged in loud arguments that added to Sara's stress. Although she did not agree with her parents' actions, she felt disloyal whenever she perceived herself to be siding with William against them.

Whenever Sara and William began a verbal battle, the younger children became disruptive and somewhat hyperactive. They would frequently run through the house yelling and screaming at each other. Sometimes the older son would throw toys or hit his younger brother. This behavior usually postponed the couple's argument, but it frequently resulted in a redirection of the anger and frustration felt by the parents toward their children which, in turn, made both William and Sara feel guilty.

William's dissatisfaction with the situation continued to grow for some time. He began working overtime to try to keep a little distance between himself and his problems at home and to make extra money for a camping vacation at a nearby lake. Between the long hours he kept and the tension at home, William frequently found himself worn out. The more tired he felt, the more he found himself resenting the fact that Sara could not straighten things out with her parents and make life a little easier for him. At work, instead of concentrating on his job, he found himself wondering what was going on at home and worrying about the long-term effects of living so close to Sara's parents. His blood pressure rose to 180/95 and he frequently complained of headaches.

themes reveal their orientation toward separateness and togetherness in their relationship (Sillars, et al., 1992). The constructionist view is based on social construction theory, which we describe in Chapter 1. Our discussion in later chapters of marital reality construction and of meaning-making in the family as a process of telling stories, as well as our description of family stories, myths, metaphors, and themes in Chapters 8 and 9 are also related to the constructionist view of the family.

According to general systems theory, families can be productively thought of as family systems because they incorporate all of the systems elements and processes we have thus far described. As we have indicated, systems theory terminology provides us with a vocabulary for thinking about communication in the family. For example, you can begin to think about how your own family defines and regulates its boundaries; or try to identify the extent to which particular family systems goals are shared or integrated in the family; or notice how inputs in the family, such as information from the media, are filtered, screened, or processed by the family. Depending upon your approach to family systems theory, you can analyze how the interaction patterns in the family define the nature of relationships in the family, examine the functions that various family members perform for the family, or examine how meaning is generated in the family. In the following section we discuss current perspectives, primarily from the constructionist view, that have made important contributions to the evolution of family systems thinking.

CURRENT PERSPECTIVES IN THE SYSTEMS VIEW OF THE FAMILY

Systems theory began as an innovative way to think about human experience. Instead of perceiving problems in terms of linear causality, that is, as a consequence of the effects of one person's behavior on another, we can pay more attention to the mutual influence that family members have on one another. Systems theory can make us more aware of our interdependence, help us avoid assigning "blame" in the family, show us how to recognize patterns of interaction which often get repeated in the family, teach us about such issues as how families maintain boundaries and monitor and process incoming and outgoing information in the family, and help us to observe how the family regulates the behavior of its members.

However, while the systems view is useful in providing a set of concepts about family process, we do not want to suggest that this view is a way to "decode" daily interactions and communication in the family. Hoffman (1990) has called this the Rosetta Stone fallacy. This fallacy assumes that if we analyze the family's inputs and outputs, rules, feedback mechanisms, roles, repeated patterns, and other dimensions of the system, we will be able to decipher the "real meaning" of communication in the family. Current discussions in the literature of systems theory view this formula approach to the application of systems theory as somewhat simplistic.

Some researchers have expressed the concern that, taken as a whole, the language of family systems theory may give one a sense of the family as a kind of mechanistic organism (Hoffman, 1990). For example, an image of a mobile hanging from the ceiling has been used as a metaphor to describe the family as a system; if one were to bump one part of the mobile, all the parts would jiggle. This image represents the interdependence of family members; there is the danger, however, that it also presents an image of the family as a kind of machine made up of parts that have some kind of permanent relationship to one another.

It is useful to caution the reader against assuming that the categories, types, and generalizations we describe here somehow capture "what a family is *really* doing." The language of family systems theory, in actuality, offers the reader ways to represent family process and metaphors for thinking about family process (Rosenblatt, 1994). That is, family systems theory provides us with a set of ideas and a language for having a conversation about interactions in the family.

Just as with any conversation, discussions of family systems theory concepts are constantly evolving; ideas evolve, just as families do. What we have presented in the previous sections of this chapter are concepts and ideas generally associated with general systems theory. In the following section we discuss some of the more recent ideas and reevaluations of systems theory. These include ideas that have been developed by gender-sensitive family theorists, researchers influenced by social construction theory, family therapists, and those who have a dialectical view of family communication. The critique of systems theory can be thought of as a *shift in emphasis* in several areas of particular importance. There are six characteristics we have associated with some of the newer prevailing views of systems theory: (1) emphasis on an individual–system dialectic, (2) the significance of change over stability, (3) the importance of narrative in the construction of meaning, (4) the focus on language in the construction of social reality, (5) the attention to intergenerational influences and interconnectedness, and (6) the need for awareness of how culture and gender bias relates to our interpretations of family life.

The Dialectic Between the Individual and the System

New systems thinking tends to emphasize the *dynamic interplay between the individual and the family*, which can be related to an individual–system dialectic. Several family systems theorists have made the point that the tendency of traditional systems theory to compare an individual perspective with a systems perspective can create a false dichotomy between the individual and the whole family system (Weeks, 1986; Nichols, 1987).

In focusing on characteristics of the whole family unit, we can see family systems theory as an alternative to social theory that focuses exclusively on the problems and inner experiences of individuals. However, instead of thinking of systems theory as an alternative to an individual perspective toward problems in the family, it may be more appropriate to take a dialectical view of the relationship between the individual and the family system. In contrast to the either/or approach (represented by an individual *versus* a systems perspective) is the dialectical view that suggests that one needs to move back and forth between the individual and relationships in the family to have a full appreciation of how meanings develop in the family. As Weeks (1986) has argued, there is a need to "fully integrate" both individual and whole family perspectives in order to understand problems in human relationships (p. 6). Nichols (1987) has used the phrase "the self in the system" to focus attention on the importance of the individual in the family.

Families are made up of individuals whose habits of relating and identities can appear to be enduring and permanent but who also have the potential for spontaneous change and growth. In Chapter 1, we indicated that the family is an "abstraction" (even definitions of the family are somewhat arbitrary). Understanding what occurs in families is a matter of understanding what transpires between and among individuals. For example, one of the author's students indicated how frustrated she was over a rule prescribing that she and her mother were not to talk about the daughter's struggle with alcoholism. The resolution to this problem was not a consequence of confronting and changing the pattern but a consequence of the daughter's own grieving, forgiving, and coming to terms with her mother's inability to discuss the issue. The pattern, which one might call rule-governed, remains the same, but the story that the daughter tells about the pattern is different than it was several years earlier because of how she has explored her own experience. Family systems theory provides us with a language for talking about mutual influence and patterned behavior, but knowledge of individual experience is equally important.

The Dialectic Between Stability and Change

Current systems thinking has also tended to emphasize the idea that *change is just as significant, or more significant, in understanding family process as is the family's tendency to strive for stability*. Stability and change are viewed as inextricably bound together rather than as different dimensions of family life, a view compatible with our discussion of stability and change as a dialectical process. Earlier in the development of family systems theory, stability—the striving for equilibrium or homeostasis—was typically presented as the primary goal of family life (Jackson, 1970). This view sees families as developing typical patterns of interaction which help to maintain predictability and help its members to resist change. Families are seen as using feedback mechanisms, such as sanctions for rule violations, primarily to control members so that stability can be maintained at the expense of change.

Reevaluations of family systems theory, however, have tended to view change as a primary characteristic of family functioning; stability is seen as a secondary function (Anderson & Goolishian, 1988; Hoffman, 1990; Gilligan & Price, 1993). The previous tendency to place stability in the foreground and change in the background has been reassessed in part as an idea compatible with Western cultural values. Some have argued that, in Buddhist terms, "change is the constant and stability is an illusion" (Chang & Phillips, 1993, p. 104). While it is useful to be able to identify patterns in the family's interaction, it is also important for us to remember that families are in a constant state of motion and flux. Our ability to identify stable roles and patterns may solidify our view of the family at a point in time and help us talk about what we see happening in the family, but, in actuality, time and motion, like a river, keep the family in a continuous state of change.

The Importance of Narrative

Recent approaches to understanding family systems have emphasized the importance of *narrative in understanding family process* (Anderson & Goolishian, 1988; Bochner, 1994; Bruner, 1986; Doherty, 1986; Friedman, 1993; Gilligan &

Price, 1993; Hoffman, 1990; McNamee & Gergen, 1992; Parry, 1991; White, 1993; White & Epston, 1990). One way to understand current ideas about the relationship between stability and change is to think of stability as grounded in the stories that family members tell about their lives together. The predictable family patterns that we identify can be considered important pieces of a family's history, which give the family a sense of communal identity. In this sense, a family's stability is the set of shared memories that help to make behavior in the family predictable.

A **shared memory** represents how family members recall their previous interactions; memories are related to the stories that they create about their experiences together.

The following example helps to illustrate the relationship between experience, memory, and family stories. Jack is a senior in college and is about to graduate; he is concerned about finding a job after graduation. Jack's father is worried about Jack's future also, so he frequently offers Jack advice. Jack's car is ready for the junkyard and Jack is planning to ask his father to loan him money for a new car. Jack's last discussion with his father about money helps him to predict what the upcoming discussion might be like. In the past, when Jack has asked his father for money or a loan, his father usually "comes through," but not without asking Jack a lot of questions about how he manages his money and how Jack is going to use the money he is asking his dad to loan him. This usually makes Jack defensive and angry, which he tries to hide. The rule seems to be, "Whenever Jack asks for a loan, Dad gives Jack a lecture." As a consequence of this rule, which describes a pattern that has occurred in the past, Jack is anxious and nervous about asking his father for a car loan, even though he knows he will. The rule seems to reflect a stable pattern in their communication.

Jack remembers previous episodes and constructs a scenario, a story, that represents how the interaction in the present is likely to go. He assumes that his father will quiz him about whether he actually needs the car, criticize the type of car Jack would like to buy, and indicate to Jack that buying a new car at this time is a big responsibility, especially now, when Jack has not yet found a job. When he talks to his father, Jack is tense and hesitant. In response to Jack's request, his father is quiet for a long time and then tells Jack that he would like to buy his son a new car for graduation. Furthermore, he thinks that Jack should make his own decision about what car to buy, within a reasonable price range. Father and son agree on a price range, a figure that turns out to be very close to what Jack wanted, and end their transaction agreeably. Jack is elated—and very surprised. The story of Jack's interaction with his father has taken a new twist, and Jack knows that, in the process, their relationship has changed.

In their conversations with one another, family members shape the present moment from the memories of past interactions. These memories become family stories. **Family stories** are the narratives that family members construct about their life together, just as Jack's memory of a discussion with his father is a story that he remembers, or a conversation between two family members that reflects a family theme. But there is a tension between memory and the flow of life as time moves forward. Jack has a memory of the pattern, but the story keeps evolving. One can grasp the simplicity of this concept by noting that every day they are together, family members are getting older, their biology is changing, and the concerns related to their particular stage of life are changing. All of these changes make interaction in the present a little different from conversation in the past. As a consequence, the stories that family members create from the memories of their experience are constantly evolving.

An infinite variety of factors can affect the evolution of family stories. Even your own exposure to the ideas in this book will influence the story that you tell about your family. As you think about the ideas discussed here, you may begin to look for rules in your family or think about other aspects of how your family functions as a system. By paying attention to your family's communication, you may put a different construct on what you observe in your family and on your own family experience. When you finish reading this book, you may view your family a little differently; that is, you may tell a story about your family that is a little different from the one you might have told six months ago. Consequently, as your understanding of your family changes, the rules and patterns in your family will have the potential to change, too.

White (1993) has summed up this narrative approach to understanding family process:

> The idea that it is the meaning which persons attribute to their experience that is constitutive of those persons' lives has encouraged social scientists to explore the nature of the frames that facilitate the interpretation of experience. Many of these social scientists have proposed that it is narrative or story that provides the primary frame for this interpretation, for the activity of meaning-making: that it is through the narratives or the stories that persons have about their own lives and the lives of others that they make sense of their experience. Not only do these stories determine the meaning that persons give to experience, it is argued, but these stories also largely determine which aspects of experience persons select out for expression. In addition, inasmuch as action is prefigured on meaning-making, these stories determine real effects in terms of the shaping of persons' lives.
>
> This perspective should not be confused with that which proposes that stories function as a reflection of life or as a mirror for life. Instead, the narrative metaphor proposes that persons live their lives by stories—that these stories are shaping of life, and that they have real, not imagined, effects—and that these stories provide the structure of life (p. 36).

Social Reality as Linguistically Constructed

Recent approaches to systems theory have tended to emphasize the importance of *families as meaning-making systems whose reality is linguistically constructed through conversation* (Anderson & Goolishian, 1988; Hoffman, 1990). While this concept may seem overly technical, it describes the relatively simple idea that the interpretations or meanings that family members assign to actions and events are directly related to the language or discourse they use. For example, imagine a scenario in which a sixteen-year-old daughter who has just gotten her driver's license asks her mother if she can drive alone to visit a girlfriend who lives eighty miles away. The mother deems the daughter's request "utterly ridiculous." This mother's response attaches a different meaning to the request and to the relationship between mother and daughter than a response that would present a series of questions to the daughter: "Do you think you are an experienced enough driver to travel that far alone? Isn't it dangerous for a teenaged girl to be going that far by herself? Shouldn't you find someone else to go with you and try to stay overnight at Sharon's house?" Each mother in this illustration is resistant to the daughter's suggestion. In the first case, the mother holds an implicit judgment that the daughter's request is not legitimate or reasonable. Imagine that the daughter walks away, feeling foolish. Imagine also an alternative scenario in which the daughter gets angry at her mother and accuses her mother of being "overprotective"; mother then argues that her daughter is being immature and self-centered and the argument escalates until the daughter stomps off to her room and slams the door. Different experiences have emerged from these two different scenarios of conversations between mother and daughter.

Current family systems analysis sometimes refers to this process of attaching meaning to events (including requests like the one in our example) as a description of how families **frame** such encounters through their conversations with one another. Similar encounters between mother and daughter may be framed as "fights," "unreasonable suggestions," "rebelliousness," or "overprotectiveness," depending upon the conversation between mother and daughter. Family systems therapists and researchers often try to understand how family members talk about their experience. How do family members frame their experience or tell stories of their encounters with one another in ways that may be painful or adversarial and how can they be helped to generate different meanings through their conversations?

In her work analyzing conversations between family therapists and the families they are trying to help, McNamee (1989) has described the way that a family therapist can help a family reframe the interpretations that they make of their experience by questioning and expressing curiosity about the taken-for-granted meanings that have been generated in the family. One example McNamee gives shows how a son's "bad behavior" is reframed by a therapist as "lively." The therapist expresses curiosity about the adversarial nature of the son's relationship to his father and frames it as an "interesting" way for father and son to connect. In conversations with the family, the therapist explores different possibilities for how the *family* might describe what is happening in their relationship. The therapist helps the family to reframe their experience through conversations that use language in a different way. How the mother and daughter in our example interpret or frame their experience depends upon how they label, describe, and talk about the daughter's request. Thus, the patterns, rules, and other aspects of the system can be seen as linguistically constructed through their discourse. The emphasis on meaning and reality as linguistically constructed suggests that systems characteristics, such as rules and patterns, stem from how family members communicate with one another. The conversation produces the pattern as much as the pattern produces the conversation.

The Significance of Intergenerational Influences

Current perspectives on family systems theory have also tended to focus *more attention on intergenerational influences* on the family (Boszormenyi-Nagy & Spark, 1984; Kramer, 1985; Framo, 1992). As Boszormenyi-Nagy and Spark have argued, "If one accepts the premise that it is essential to study the interconnectedness between an individual and his family system, then the boundaries of the family must be extended to include the interlocking between a nuclear family and families of origin (including the in-laws)" (p. 216). Families are not viewed as closed systems but as intimate communities with histories that extend beyond one generation. It may be helpful to analyze how a family functions within the framework of concepts that we have described in this chapter, but it may be equally helpful to include an examination of the influence of previous generations on the family.

The family's history includes the experiences that the parents, or the spousal dyad, have had in their family of origin. The conversations among family members in the present may be influenced by relationships and experiences in previous generations. Framo (1992) has made the point that "individuals incorporate aspects of their parents' marital relationship as well as characteristics of their individual parents" (p. 125). Attention to intergenerational influences on the family includes recognizing that rules and styles of communicating as well as gender orientations often get passed down from one generation to the next (Fink, 1993).

In addition, the struggles of one generation of parents often have an impact on the problems that children, as adults, have in relating to their own mates and children. As Framo (1992) suggests, "The invisible bonds of loyalty to the family of origin exercise their irresistible influence throughout one's lifetime" (p. 123). In order to understand and appreciate fully what has happened in the current generation, it is often useful to understand intergenerational patterns and influences. In a later chapter, we discuss the "baggage" that couples inevitably bring with them as they create their own families. Framo (1992) describes the influence of his family of origin on his own first marriage and offers testimony that most of us can relate to:

> I think that in some ways, in my marriage to Mary, I felt similar to my father in his marriage to my mother. On a deeper level, I suspect that our hostility to each of our opposite sex parents got displaced onto each other. . . . It took me years to rework the image of being a man that I got from my father, and this change may have something to do with why, in my second marriage, I am more free to give and get love (p. 227).

In the passage above, Framo poignantly describes the influence that his family of origin had on his first marriage. Kramer (1985) provides an example of the way that the different patterns that each spouse learned in his or her family of origin can influence communication in the nuclear family:

Dan: My mother came over the other day. She was repeating things three or four times—I mean, she *repeated* them. I can look at it more objectively now.

Helen: I could see how it was affecting me. I can accept her doing it more than I can accept Dan's needing it. When I tell him something and then he comes back and says, "Now, what did you say?" or "Tell me that again," I just think: "You baby! I told you! Damn it!" But, interestingly enough, and this is really fascinating, the school wants to test our oldest son, Jeff, for learning disabilities. They think he has an auditory difficulty—that he cannot process what he hears the first time.

Dan: Is it connected to my family? My family did not write notes and Helen's did. And there was the need to repeat and reinforce things from my side, versus Helen's side. It happens with my brother or sisters or mother.

Marian will call me up and tell the story, then Ann will call, and then if I talk to my mother, she'll tell the same story—it's repeated and I can't say, even at this time, "I heard it."

Helen: She'll ask if you heard it and you'll say, "Yes," and she'll tell it anyway . . .

Dan: . . . and it goes on and on to the point where I need less and less of that, but those patterns are still there.

Helen: Your mother was always there as the source of information. That wasn't true in my family—we were always coming and going so if you wanted to tell someone something, you wrote it down. And his dad did it, too, and his uncle did it.

Dan: Also, since the family did not read a lot, vocabulary was limited. We used words as simply as possible and as repetitively as possible to get the message across.

Helen: Did they repeat because they knew they needed to repeat, because they all needed it? Because they had trouble processing auditory things? Or did they lose the ability to process things because they didn't use it? Which came first?

Jan: Then it becomes a pattern in which children are taught that it is so difficult to process things auditorily, even if it isn't difficult for you, that it really *is* difficult, like it is now for Jeff.

Dan: You are taught that the first time around you don't have to catch it.

Jan: It will come around again—as a matter of fact, if you catch it the first time, you're going to be bored!

Dan: That's it! Isn't that Judy!

Helen: Yes, our daughters—none of them are like that, but our son *is* like that.

Jan: It looks like it's coming down the male line.

Helen: Oh, yes. They couldn't be more different in terms of what their abilities are. Judy gets real annoyed when you tell her something twice. She says, "I heard you!"

Jan: (to Helen) But that's like you.

Dan: Oh, ho! The parallel's there!

Helen: I know she's a mirror. It's funny and scary at the same time (pp. 14–15).

In discussing this dialogue, Kramer comments, "As Dan and Helen were able to step back and see the patterns in their families, there bubbled up an escalating enjoyment in discovering the parallels and the process" (p. 15). When we include a description of patterns in previous generations in our search to understand behavior in the present we often "discover the parallels." In subsequent chapters, we explore further some of these issues in our discussion of marital reality construction and the family's ecosystem.

Given the importance of intergenerational issues in the family, you might wish to find out more about the relationship of your parents to your grandparents. Shawn, one of our students, tells the story of her father, Quinn. Quinn used to get irritated every time his mother, Shawn's grandmother, would look disapproving and leave the room when his father told a joke or shared a story about his youth on the farm. Quinn appreciated his father's jokes and stories, as most people who knew him did. His mother's disapproval of his father bothered Quinn so much that if his wife was not totally enthralled when Quinn, on rare occasions, told a joke or story of his own, he would get irritated with her. His perceptions changed, however, when he heard a cousin of his mother's share a story of her own.

Apparently, Quinn's mother at one time was quite pretty, loved to dance and sing, and before she was married she acted in community theatre groups. Quinn's father's family, however, never approved of Quinn's mother's theatrical interests; after they were married, all of her in-laws, who lived nearby, put pressure on Quinn's mother to end her amateur acting career. And Quinn's father refused to go dancing with her because dancing was against his religion. However, he captured the attention and admiration of friends and family through his teasing, humor, and skill in telling jokes and stories. Quinn's father got the kind of attention and admiration that Quinn's mother had experienced in her theatrical adventures. Quinn began to understand that his mother's "disapproval" had much more to do with her own disappointment and sense of being denied attention than it did with her "sour disposition." When Quinn heard his mother's story, he developed compassion for what must have been difficult years early in her marriage. As a consequence of the compassion he developed for his mother, his wife's response to his own occasional bid for attention seemed much less important to him. Shawn also felt more connected to her grandmother, who had been somewhat stern with her, and she understood something about the tension between her parents that she sometimes observed at social gatherings. Sometimes one's own behavior can change as a consequence of curiosity about the previous generation.

Concern for Gender and Culture Bias

Family systems theorists have, in recent years, emphasized the *need to examine family systems terminology for potential gender and cultural bias*. Feminist family theorists and researchers argue the importance of examining the extent to which a systems theory view of the family may reflect male cultural values or minimize the power differences between women and men and between adults and children (Ault-Riche, 1986; Goodrich, Rampage, Ellman, & Halstead, 1988; Gouldner, 1985; Hare-Mustin, 1978; Leslie & Glossick, 1992; Luepnitz, 1988; Libow, Raskin, & Caust, 1982; MacKinnon & Miller, 1987; Morgaine, 1992; Taggert, 1985; Walters, Carter, Papp, & Silverstein, 1988).

Walters, Carter, Papp, & Silverstein (1990) suggest that a common understanding of what is meant by "feminism" is important in discussing this issue. They offer the following definition:

> Feminism, we agreed, is a humanistic framework or world view concerned with the roles, rules, and functions that organize male–female interactions. Feminism seeks to include the experience of women in all formulations of human experience, and to eliminate the dominance of male assumptions. Feminism does not blame individual men for the patriarchal social system that exists, but seeks to understand and change the socialization process that keeps men and women thinking and acting within a sexist, male-dominated framework (p. 17).

Using this definition as a starting point, Walters and her colleagues (and others as well) have explored the ways that systems theory may have been used to "disadvantage women" (p. 17). One example of this problem relates to the issue of family violence. We must take care that in discussing the tendency for family members mutually to influence one another, we do not make the mistake of "blaming the victim" or believing that the victim of abuse is just as "responsible" for the problem as is the perpetrator of violent acts. This caution does not mean that one cannot feel compassion for abusers, who were often abuse victims themselves, or that violent couples do not sometimes participate in mutually destructive communication patterns. However, it does mean that individuals who behave violently should be held accountable for their actions and that cultural values and mores, which may reinforce violent patterns in the family, should be examined.

Furthermore, feminist family theorists and therapists caution us to question taken-for-granted assumptions that may emphasize certain systems processes at the expense of others. Gilligan (1982), for example, has argued that there are differences in values between men and women that suggest they inhabit two different cultural worlds. If gender differences in values exist, it is important to attach equal worth to each set of values. Women often tend to value connectedness, relatedness, expressiveness, nurturing, caretaking, and interdependence more than men. In taking a systems perspective of the family, it may be equally important for us to be consciously aware of the need for interdependence and connectedness as it is to understand how well a family establishes clear boundaries among family members. We may also need to take care that our acceptance of a father who is somewhat aloof and distant is not *greater* than our acceptance of a mother who may be perceived as overinvolved in her family members' lives. Researchers may also need to emphasize the qualities of male expressiveness and emotion in their exploration of the effects of a crisis on intimate relationships (Ellis & Bochner, 1992).

In addition to acknowledging the potential for gender bias in our study of family process, it is also useful to be aware of how our view of the family might

TABLE 3.1   Current perspectives in the systems view of the family.

1. *The Individual–System Dialectic*
    Emphasizes the need to view individual and relationship dynamics as interrelated, rather than take an either/or view of individual and whole family perspectives.

2. *The Stability–Change Dialectic*
    Emphasizes a view of the family in which families are thought of as in a constant state of motion and flux rather than striving primarily for equilibrium.

3. *The Importance of Narrative*
    Emphasizes the idea that the lives of families are shaped by the constantly evolving stories that family members construct of their life together.

4. *Social Reality as Linguistically Constructed*
    Emphasizes the idea that the meanings that are generated in the family emerge from the discourse and conversations that they share.

5. *Intergenerational Influences*
    Emphasizes the influence and interconnectedness between the patterns of one generation and another as the family's story unfolds.

6. *Gender and Culture*
    Emphasizes the need for an awareness of how one's taken-for-granted assumptions about the family or what one chooses to notice or value can be a reflection of gender and/or culture bias.

reflect cultural bias (McGoldrick, Pearce, & Giordano, 1982; Sue & Sue, 1990). This issue becomes increasingly important as cultural diversity increases in the United States and as the planet becomes more of a "global village."

Shon and Ja (1982) provide an example of the importance of understanding the influence of culture on communication in the family in their discussion of Asian families. In Western culture, we tend to value individuality, argumentative skills, and admire someone's ability to express their ideas and feelings. Most Asian cultures, however, do not attach the same values toward openness and free expression of one's thoughts and feelings. Instead, communication that contributes to the harmony and peace of the family are valued. The idea that there is a dialectical tension between differentiation and integration in the family (as we describe in Chapter 1) is a concept that one should view differently in Western culture than in Asian cultures. In Asian cultures, family members are not expected to differentiate themselves from the family but to behave in a way that will promote the family's integration. Direct confrontations are avoided, face-saving behaviors are important, and talking around a point is often more highly regarded than directness because people in Asian cultures believe that directness might lead to disagreement and confrontation. Shon and Ja (1982) tell the following story to illustrate the importance of indirectness in Asian culture:

> For example, consider this story of two Malaysian families. A daughter from a higher-class family fell in love with the son of a lower-class family. The son approached his parents and told them that he wanted to marry the girl from the higher-class family. His mother said she would approach the girl's family to see if it were acceptable to them. She made an appointment with the girl's mother and went to the home on the proper day. She was greeted by the mother and was shown into the sitting room. Refreshments were brought in consisting of tea and bananas. The two mothers talked about the weather and other things, but they never mentioned their children. After a period of time the boy's mother thanked her hostess politely and left. Upon returning home she told her son that the marriage was unacceptable and, therefore, not possible. The boy's mother knew this because in Malaysia tea and bananas are not generally served together. The girl's mother had given the message that her daughter and the other mother's son did not belong together. By doing it in this way she avoided direct discussion, which may have led to hurt feelings and a loss of face, not only for the boy's mother, whose son was rejected, but also for the girl's mother, who would have caused the other mother embarrassment and shame (pp. 216–217).

Family interaction may be influenced by the cultural background of the family, by differences between various subcultures that often exist side by side, and by differences in values between the generations. Differences in family forms and the impact of economic disadvantage are just as important as an awareness of cultural differences in understanding the family (Chilman, Nunnally, & Cox, 1988). Gay and lesbian families must cope with a culture that can be homophobic and that may stereotype family members. A new stepparent may have difficulty relating to her stepchildren because she feels that she has to live up to the cultural expectations of a natural parent. How does one apply systems concepts to the rules and communication patterns of a homeless family? Without

APPLICATION 3.2

CURRENT PERSPECTIVES IN THE SYSTEMS VIEW OF THE FAMILY

Describe a significant event, circumstance, issue, or conflict in your family. Indicate how the episode or situation illustrates one of the six characteristics that summarize current perspectives of family systems theory. For example:

> Tory is a 24-year-old divorced Caucasian woman with a toddler. She is going to school while she is living on welfare; her plans are to complete a nursing degree. Her parents who live nearby help her out by babysitting their granddaughter, occasionally buying groceries, and helping with car repairs. Tory has met an African-American student in one of her math classes and has begun dating him. Edward is considerate and funny and gets along well with Tory's baby. Within a matter of just a few months the relationship has become serious. However, Tory's parents do not approve of interracial relationships and argue continuously with Tory about her relationship with Edward. They like Edward well enough, but they do not believe that interracial marriages can be successful and they do not want to see Tory fail in a second marriage. Some of Edward's friends—especially his female friends—do not hang out with him anymore because of his relationship with Tory, but Edward's closest friends and family are generally supportive. Despite her feelings of guilt and obligation toward her parents, Tory is considering breaking off relations with her family if they cannot accept her growing love for Edward.

1. How does the situation illustrate the dynamic relationship between the individual and the whole family?
2. How does the situation illustrate the family as a system that is continually changing?
3. How does the situation illustrate how families are shaped by the stories that they construct?
4. How does the situation illustrate the way that meanings emerge from the conversations that family members share?
5. How does the situation illustrate the influence and interconnectedness of the generations as the family's story unfolds?
6. How does the situation illustrate the influence of cultural and/or gender bias in the family's interaction?

an acknowledgment of the influence of culture and economic disadvantage into a systems approach to understanding the family, the identification of the family's rules, role functions, and communication patterns may seem abstract and inconsequential.

One additional point needs to made: Sometimes the need to avoid gender bias and respect cultural differences may be contradictory, especially if one is attempting to appreciate a family whose parents grew up in a culture with a more rigid patriarchal structure than our own. We would like to suggest, however, that sometimes contradictions such as this cannot be resolved. Ultimately, each family must be understood in terms of its own complexity and uniqueness. What we can do, however, is become more sensitive to our own biases and assumptions and to appreciate that those theories that are most useful in understanding any phenomenon are probably those that are still evolving.

In conclusion, this discussion of current perspectives of family systems theory should indicate that conceptual approaches to understanding family process are constantly unfolding. As Hoffman (1990) suggests, recent views of family systems make it clear that "the development of concepts is a fluid process" (p. 3). The sense that ideas about family systems are fluid and constantly unfolding helps to keep them vital and alive by inviting you to think about your own family experience and consider what fits for you. In this way, we hope that you come to see these ideas as opportunities for further dialogue and conversation rather than as rigid prescriptions about family process.

SUMMARY

The purpose of this chapter is to describe the systems perspective for understanding the family, because this perspective underlies the chapters that follow. The systems perspective, based on general systems theory, stresses the interdependence of family members and the importance of communication in the family system.

Six types of system elements compose family systems: (1) interdependent components, (2) inputs and outputs, (3) boundaries and hierarchies, (4) rules for operation, (5) system goals, and (6) feedback mechanisms. Communication is linked to all six in specific ways. Communication skills differentiate system components (family members) and allow them to develop relationships with each other, manage their designated family roles, and interact with the various suprasystems. Communication messages and other types of information form the inputs and outputs that flow through the family system. Nonverbal markers such as fences and door locks help to designate physical boundaries around family systems, just as messages differentiate one subsystem from another within the nuclear system. Family rules emerge from family interaction and govern future interaction. Similarly, communication makes it possible for families to establish goals and seek information about their progress toward or away from these goals.

Four types of systems processes are especially relevant to our discussion of family communication: (1) nonsummativity, (2) stability, (3) change, and (4) equifinality. Again, the messages that permeate a system provide the vehicle through which individual system components are able to combine their abilities into a collective whole that allows the system to accomplish more than the components could accomplish independently. Furthermore, family systems tend to strive for stability even though they are constantly changing.

In this chapter, we also discuss the influence of current perspectives related to the systems view of the family. Recent discussions of family systems reflect the influence of social construction theory and the dialectical view of family process, as well as influences from feminist family theorists and therapists and those concerned with the variety and diversity of family life. Six issues were identified in our discussion of current perspectives in the systems view of the family: (1) the individual–systems dialectic, (2) the stability–change dialectic, (3) the importance of narrative in understanding the family, (4) social reality in the family as linguistically constructed, (5) the significance of intergenerational relationships in the family, and (6) the importance of an awareness of gender and culture bias in one's thinking about the family.

Overall, the notion of a system provides the theoretical groundwork for the material to follow. Treating family interaction as an ongoing set of episodes with no beginning and no ending point avoids many of the pitfalls common to an analysis of family functioning such as blaming one family member for problems in the system. From a systems perspective, it is generally possible to identify functions that problematic behavior serves for the larger structure. A systems perspective allows you to appreciate the incredible complexity of family communication. Messages perform many functions on many levels; focusing on just one message or one episode in a family's collective history is futile. Finally, a systems perspective unifies a number of seemingly diverse topics such as rules, roles, themes and narratives, family types, and the family life cycle, which allows us to achieve a degree of relatedness and continuity in our approach to family communication.

KEY TERMS

boundary	interactional view
components	morphogenesis
constructionist view	morphostasis
diffuse boundaries	nonsummativity
equifinality	outputs
family stories	rigid boundaries
feedback	role
feedback mechanisms	rules
frame	shared memory
goal	structural view
hierarchy	subsystems
hierarchy of subsystems	suprasystem
hierarchy of suprasystems	system elements
inputs	system processes

COMING TOGETHER & WIDENING THE CIRCLE

C H A P T E R 4

COURTSHIP AND COMMITMENT

JANET YERBY

ANITA AND CARL

Anita Morales was dating someone else when she started going out with Carl Tyrrell. She and Carl were introduced by a mutual friend; Anita was a freshman in college and Carl was a sophomore. At the time they had started to date each other, neither of them was involved in a relationship that they really cared about. From their first date, their relationship was very intense. They were very physically attracted to each other; they also liked to do the same things together and they liked the security of being together. Anita was outgoing, funny, and intelligent. She had never before experienced the kind of feelings for anyone that she felt for Carl. She felt excited and alive when she was around Carl. Carl was attractive and serious. He made excuses to see her whenever he could and spent every free moment with her.

Their relationship progressed very quickly—it was exciting but a little scary, too. Carl planned to transfer to another university to study engineering the following year and Anita was wondering how they would take the separation. That summer they each had jobs near their families and within traveling distance of each other. They saw each other when they could on weekdays and on every weekend. Toward the end of the summer, Carl and Anita began to quarrel with one another over inconsequential issues; their conflicts seemed to emerge suddenly and without warning.

When she went back to college in the fall, Anita decided to join the staff of the college newspaper. She threw herself into the responsibilities that she was given. Carl came to see her on weekends, but it seemed to him that all Anita talked about was her work and the new friends she had made on the newspaper. He accused her of not being interested in anything he was doing. Anita felt betrayed by his accusations since it was Carl who had transferred to another school and encouraged her to get involved in other activities in order to meet new people. She accused him of being possessive and jealous. Carl began to call long distance more frequently during weekdays. If Anita was not home when he called, the next time that he called Carl would ask where she had been. These conversations always had an edge to them.

Anita began to date a friend on the newspaper staff without saying anything to Carl. One weekend when Carl came to visit, Anita announced that she was dating someone else. Carl exploded and they spent most of the evening arguing. Anita told Carl that she thought they should quit seeing each other for a while. Carl left at the end of the weekend feeling angry and despondent. He called her every night the following week. Their conversations were stormy. Carl would plead for Anita to try to work things out and Anita would try to hold her ground. She said that she really cared for Carl, but that she needed some distance between them right now. Carl accepted Anita's wishes and started writing occasional letters instead of calling. After a few months, the intensity of Carl's letters began to diminish and he began to share more factual information about what was going on in his life. Carl also began to date other women occasionally. Anita wrote to Carl from time to time, sharing what was going on in her life and inquiring about his.

One weekend when Anita was home to celebrate her mother's birthday, Carl stopped by to see her. The school to which he had transferred was not far from the town where Anita's family lived. They spent an evening together. At first, they were a little more formal with each other than they had been in the past and they did not get physically involved with each other. They had a wonderful evening, however, and parted without saying much about what would happen next. Anita went back to school expecting Carl to call her that week. When he didn't call, she finally called him. She said that she thought they ought to start seeing each other again to see if they still had strong feelings for each other. Carl said that he would come up that weekend. They spent the entire weekend together. Three weeks later Carl proposed marriage and Anita accepted.

UNDERSTANDING ANITA AND CARL

Do Anita and Carl have a solid foundation on which to build a successful marriage? How confident can they be about their decision to marry? Out of all the millions of people in the world, how did they happen to find each other, fall in love, and decide to get married? What factors will determine whether their decision will prove to be right? Did they choose each other rationally or were some irrational factors involved in their selection of each other as mates? These questions draw attention to the functions of communication in the process of courtship and commitment to marriage.

Why do some marriages succeed and others fail? This vexing question has frustrated students of the family for a long time. Scholars have searched and probed, queried and pried, examined and reexamined, trying to unlock the mysteries of a happy marriage. Yet little ground has been gained in the battle to triumph over the interpersonal perils of marriage. The divorce rate remains extremely high and each year thousands of adults and children experience the pain and suffering that go along with breaking up a family.

Ironically, there is no shortage of advice about what constitutes a good marriage, how to form one, and what to do to make it last. The problem is that the experts have many different versions of the ideal marriage. The range of conflicting advice found in trade books and primers on marriage is bewildering. It is also depressing. There is so much contradictory evidence, so many different sociological and psychological factors correlated moderately, but not substantially, with successful marriage, that it is easy to be left not knowing who to believe or what advice to follow. The information is so confusing that you may be left wondering whether there is anything more to say than, "It takes a lot of luck to have a happy marriage!" This remark may sound like something a cynic would say. But before dismissing the possibility that the "good luck" proposition contains a grain of truth, let us consider what is involved in the decision to get married.

This chapter examines patterns of premarital interaction associated with the decision to marry. The first section reviews theories of mate selection and interpersonal attraction. A distinction is drawn between why people are attracted to each other and what people say and do to facilitate attraction. The development of a relationship is problematic because its course largely depends upon what each person says and does. The second section builds on the idea that the development of a relationship is a problem that hinges on what people say and do to each other as they move toward commitment. The problem of resolving issues of ambiguity as the couple negotiates how to characterize their relationship in its early stages and the importance of momentum in carrying the relationship forward will be discussed. Five forms of escalation are presented, which advance the view that courtship involves persuasion. We also explore the ways in which a relationship becomes objectified, idealized and, occasionally, functions as a resolution of an identity crisis for both partners. The third section discusses decisive episodes called turning points, which can make or break a relationship. These decisive moments center attention on whether the relationship is sufficiently loving, the partners are sufficiently virtuous, and the bond between partners is sufficiently resilient to make the relationship "marriageable." The fourth section describes four uniquely different patterns of courtship that revolve around different relational themes. These quite different patterns may lead to the same result: the decision to marry. Overall, this chapter attempts to dispel some of the myths that exist about what brings people together. As we look at what people say and do to each other during courtship, it will become clear that if logic and rationality were insisted upon, all communication would have to cease (Freedle, 1975), and far fewer people would be willing to commit to marriage.

SELECTING A MARRIAGE PARTNER

Courtship as Decision Making

On what basis does one person decide that another person is "marriageable"? *The decision to marry is a prediction about how one person's life with another person will evolve in the future based largely on how it has evolved in the past.* In this sense, we can conceive of **courtship as decision making**. Each person assumes that he or she can rely on the past to predict the future. It is taken for granted that the attitudes, feelings, and experiences that bring two people together are the same ones that will keep them together. If you ask a couple why they want to get married, they are likely to give you one or more of the following reasons: (1) we have a lot in common; (2) we get along really well; (3) we are very attracted to each other. But how do they know that they still will have a lot in common five or ten years from now? How do they know that they will be able to talk as freely and as effectively then as they do now? What makes them think that they will stay attracted to each other as they grow older together?

The cynical view is that most people contemplating marriage for the first time have no real idea of what is in store for them. Dating couples sometimes face issues related to religion, racism, abortion, class, and gender. Too frequently, however, the toughest decisions a couple will face include what to do when close friends fail to support the relationship or whether or not to engage in sex before marriage (not including the decision to marry itself). Are these experiences a sufficient foundation for anticipating how they will cope with the many unforeseen events that can alter the course of a marriage? How well will they function if she loses her job; he becomes critically ill; they have a child born with a severe handicap; or they are forced to move to an unfamiliar place where they have no friends. Considering these possibilities, it is difficult to anticipate the course a marriage will take. In Bergman's famous film, *Scenes from a Marriage*, Marianne and Johan look upon the marital selection process as something akin to "luck of the draw."

Perhaps the secret to predicting whether a marriage will turn out to be happy is that there is no secret. Marriage is a calculated risk. Even though the decision to marry may place your emotional health in jeopardy, marriage is nonetheless a ubiquitous experience. More than ninety percent of all people will get married. Not only will most people get married, but those who marry unsuccessfully probably will marry again. This odd pattern of "repeating the error" makes it apparent that the selection of a marriage partner is not an altogether rational process.

Mate Selection

You might like to think of courtship and commitment as moderately rational; however, the events that move two people toward marriage sometimes seem to have a life of their own. Consider the following testimony from a study conducted by Rubin (1976):

> We met at this place and I kind of liked her. She was cool and kind of fun to be with. Before I knew it we were going steady. I had this class ring from high school and she kept wanting me to give it to her. So finally one night I took it off and did. And the next thing I knew, she took it down and had it made smaller. She made a big thing out of it, and so did her family. Don't get me wrong; I liked her good enough. But I just didn't think about getting married—not then anyhow. But then, after we were going together for almost a year, it just seemed like the thing to do. So we did. (p. 164).

In Chapter 5, we will describe how a relationship develops after two individuals decide to marry. Our discussion of the marital relationship will explore the expectations that each individual brings to a marriage. But as important as expectations may be to the future of a marriage, this factor alone cannot explain how two people become committed to marriage. If marriage is viewed as the development of a relationship, then the entire history of the relationship needs to be examined. Taking a relationship perspective on marriage draws attention to the importance of considering what happens *before* two individuals commit themselves to each other.

For many years the selection of a mate was viewed as a psychological act in which certain measurable traits could account for why one person chooses to marry another. Two theories were advanced, one which hypothesized that mate selection could be explained by **homogamy** (similarity), the other which emphasized **heterogamy** (complementarity of differences) (Altman and Taylor, 1973; Knapp, 1978). Do birds of a feather flock together or do opposites attract?

Both of these theories have been shown to have some merit, but neither theory provides a forceful explanation of why one person selects another. The research on mate selection suggests that the most crucial factor is **differential contact**—typically, the "field of eligibles" is a confined social network. This may explain why demographic factors such as race, religion, education, and social class usually are more predictive of mate selection than social-psychological variables such as attitudes or personality profiles. For most individuals, the field of eligibles is narrowed considerably by socialization experiences that limit the range of other persons with whom one will interact. Since individuals with more similar demographic profiles are more likely to hold similar attitudes and values, demographic similarities tend to cancel out social-psychological factors.

While studies of complementarity have produced some evidence that certain types of individuals will match up with certain other types, the strongest support involves atypical cases in which one of the individuals has a "psychological deficiency," such as a weak ego, which is counterbalanced by a mate with a very strong ego. While this "neurotic" pattern has been found to occur frequently among couples who marry at a young age, it is not characteristic of the broader range of "normal" marriages (Bolton, 1961).

Mate selection has also been viewed as a **filtering process** in which individuals apply different tests of compatibility to each other as they progress toward increased commitment (Kerckhoff & Davis, 1962). The test of whether or not the other is regarded as sufficiently compatible tends to change as time passes and experiences are accumulated. Filtering theories provide a richer conception of complementarity, but they do not adequately explain how individuals will respond to particular combinations of personal attributes.

Even if empirical support for these theories were more convincing, we would not know precisely how similarities or differences affect individuals during premarital interaction because inferences about the selection of a mate must rely on measures taken after the mate has been selected. This standard procedure begs the question of whether or not these traits were important during the process of selection. Did Anita choose Carl because his political, religious, and moral values were similar to hers, or did their attitudes merge after they were attracted to each other?

There is another line of research that has examined the question of whether or not similarities between attitudes leads to interpersonal interaction (Byrne, 1969, 1971). These studies have tested the hypothesis that "the more similar another person's opinions, interests, or personality characteristics [are] to those of a perceiver, the more will the perceiver come to be attracted to the person" (Fishbein & Ajzen, 1975, p. 255). The studies that have been conducted to test this hypothesis have followed a standardized procedure. First, each subject in the study is asked to complete a questionnaire dealing with attitudes and opinions on a variety of issues. A few weeks later, subjects are given a copy of the same form and told that it has been completed by some other person. This person is sometimes referred to as a "bogus stranger," since no such person really exists. But subjects are not told that they have received fictitious forms.

The questionnaires are systematically distributed in such a way that some subjects receive forms with responses that are nearly identical with those they

NANCY VADER-McCORMICK

Theories of mate selection often overlook the importance of communication and the progression of a relationship toward the commitment to marry.

gave earlier, while others receive questionnaires containing responses that are highly dissimilar to their own. After the subjects are given an ample opportunity to look over the "stranger's" responses, they are asked to report the degree to which they would tend to like this person and how willing they would be to work with this person in an experiment. The results of these studies repeatedly and conclusively show that the more similar the bogus stranger's attitude profile is to the perceiver's, the more "attractive" the bogus stranger is likely to be to the perceiver. Under these restrictive circumstances, then, attitude similarity leads to attraction.

Unfortunately, studies of interpersonal attraction underestimate the *significance of conversation* (Bochner, 1984). The fact that people talk to each other should not be taken for granted; it must become a part of the attraction equation. The problem is that research on interpersonal attraction is not interpersonal at all. As Levinger stated, "research on interpersonal attraction has tended to confine itself [to] . . . the target of attraction as an object of contemplation rather than a human being who stands in vibrant reciprocity" (1974, p. 100).

The sequence of interactional experiences that typifies the development of a relationship reveals that most of the time individuals become attracted before they know each other's attitudes and opinions, and rarely, if ever, does one person gain access to another person's attitudes through a written mode of communication. Most of what we learn and what we surmise about another person's behavior comes from talking to the person or observing his or her behavior. When research procedures have been modified to include conversation, the association between attitudinal similarity and attraction has been shown to be considerably more complicated. For example, Sunnafrank (1984) found that attitudinal similarity predicted interpersonal attraction only under circumstances in which conversations were highly atypical of what people say to each other when they are getting acquainted. Following more typical encounters, individuals tend to become more attracted to dissimilar people once they have the opportunity to interact with them (Sunnafrank, 1984). As Stephen (1985) has suggested, there is increasing evidence to support the view that it "may be as much the communication exchange between partners that determines the progress of their relationship as the background factors themselves" (p. 956).

To sum up, neither the research on mate selection nor the research on interpersonal attraction can tell us very much about *how* Anita and Carl's relationship evolved to the point where they were prepared to commit themselves to marriage. This is because mate selection and interpersonal attraction have not been considered as processes that evolve over time. Bolton (1961) was one of the first writers to point this out:

> Perhaps mate selection must be studied not only in terms of variables brought into the interaction situation but also as a process in which a relationship is built up, a process in which the *transactions between individuals* in certain societal contexts are determinants of turning points and commitments out of which marriage emerges. Seen from this viewpoint, the development of a mate selection relation is a problematic process. By problematic is meant the outcome of the contacts of the two individuals is not mechanically predetermined either by the relation of their personality characteristics or the institutional patterns providing the context for the development of the marriage— though these are both certainly to be taken into account—but that the outcome is an end-product of a sequence of interactions characterized by advances and retreats along the paths of available alternatives, by definitions of the situation which crystallize tentative commitments and bar withdrawals from certain positions, by the sometimes tolerance of and sometimes resolution of ambiguity, and by the tension between open-endedness and closure that characterizes all relationships that have not been reduced to ritual. In short, the development of love relations is problematic because the product bears the stamp of what goes on between the couple as well as of what they are as individuals (pp. 235–236).

Viewing the development of a relationship as problematic brings into focus the importance of examining what goes on between the two individuals; that is, what they say and do to each other. Once a relationship begins, its members are faced with the problem of making it work. The metaphor of "work," in fact, has become part of the ordinary language of relationships. When Jane says to her boyfriend Bill, "We need to spend some time working on our relationship," she is expressing a need to talk with him about what's happening between them. She may also be implying that the relationship has become a problem. If they let the relationship run its natural course, Jane thinks the problem will become worse. She assumes that by talking about their relationship, they can "work things out" (fix the problem).

In one episode of the former television series "Moonlighting," Maddie says to her lover (and colleague), David, that she doesn't know where the relationship between them is going. She has strong feelings toward David, but she cannot be content with a relationship that is confined to the bedroom. The relationship has to move forward. David is ecstatic about the relationship. He is crazy about Maddie. But he also has a nagging fear that it could end at any moment. David wants to bring some of his things over to Maddie's house, where they've been sleeping together. His response to her concern about where the relationship is going is to say jokingly that he could move some of his things in with her. Then, the relationship could move from the bedroom to the bathroom and on to the living room and the kitchen. That's how relationships move for him. David's response is more than good-natured sarcasm about Maddie's anguish. He is concerned about the ambiguity of their relationship. He knows that Maddie's willingness to have him bring some of his things over would signal a more definite commitment on her part.

Each of them is trying to influence the other to extend the boundaries of the relationship, though each defines the problem differently.

MOVING TOWARD COMMITMENT

The communication or relational perspective treats the development of a relationship as a problem in its own right. The problem is that once some initial attraction occurs, individuals must say and do something to facilitate the development of their relationship. This section focuses on how communication can escalate a relationship toward increasing commitment.

Every relationship has a unique history. Some people fall in love at first sight and others move slowly and cautiously toward a commitment to each other. In many relationships affection is asymmetrical. One individual is more attracted to the other, feels more strongly about the other, or is more uncertain about the other's feelings. When one person likes the other more than he or she is liked by the other, this person faces a difficult interactional situation with a lot at stake. Most of us like to think that falling in love is a natural and spontaneous process. But not many of us actually experience our relationships this way. The probability of being discovered by "the one person you were meant to be with" seems rather remote. More often, when you become attracted to a person you think of ways to get that person to notice you. When you like a person, you will probably say and do things to make the person like you.

The point should be obvious: *courtship involves persuasion.* There is a considerable amount of interpersonal influence that takes place as the relationship between two individuals intensifies. The influence is more covert in romantic relationships than in other interpersonal experiences, and frequently, the commitments to which the process is directed are established more implicitly. But the indirect nature of persuasion in close relationships should not be allowed to conceal what is going on. Six factors influence the movement toward commitment: (1) ambiguity, (2) momentum, (3) forms of escalation, (4) objectification of the relationship, (5) defining the other as marriageable, and (6) the relationship as a resolution to an identity crisis.

Ambiguity

Once a relationship moves beyond a state of casual acquaintance, some ambiguity about the definition of the relationship is bound to exist. There are no institutional constraints making the continuation of a relationship compulsory (such as there are in marriage); generally, the individuals proceed voluntarily. The institutional constraints of marriage carry certain premises about the closeness of the spouses and their commitments to each other. This is not the case in a premarital relationship. The meaning and value of the relationship are considerably more ambiguous. This tends to make premarital relationships even more precarious and fragile than marriages. The individuals have to figure out what the relationship means to each of them and then gauge their own perceptions of the relationship against their partner's. Anita may be crazy about Carl, but if she thinks he is not yet wild about her, she may measure her reactions carefully so as not to give the impression that she is rushing him.

Moreover, as our discussion of systems theory in Chapter 3 suggested, a relationship does not exist in a vacuum; it is not sealed off from the rest of the world. The individuals demonstrate how they want their relationship to be interpreted by their friends and families. Is Anita a casual date or a serious one? Is Carl going to continue to go out with other women and Anita with other men or will their relationship become exclusive? What will it mean to outsiders if they decide to live together? They will need to have a way to introduce each other to third parties. Is Carl someone Anita is dating? A steady? A lover? A significant other? Or a fiancé? The language they use to reference their relationship will define not only how they see each other but how they expect others to see them as well (Baxter & Wilmot, 1985).

The process of resolving ambiguity in a relationship is not always an easy one, however. In the following story, Shawna recalls a conversation with her boyfriend that conveys the emotional significance that language can have for one or both partners in defining the meaning of the relationship:

> About three months ago my boyfriend, Cory, and I were watching television in his living room when the telephone rang. He took the call in the kitchen and returned shortly, looking embarrassed and flustered. Cory explained to me that the call was from a woman who was interested in dating him. He said that he had told her "no" a number of times before but that she persisted. I asked him, "Did you tell her that you have a girlfriend?" He responded by saying, "I told her that I'm dating someone, but she doesn't seem to care!" I repeated my question, "But did you tell her that you have a girlfriend?" Then he said, "I already told her that I'm dating someone—isn't that pretty much the same thing?" "No!" I replied emphatically, "It's not! If she's like me, and like most of the women that I know, she probably interprets 'dating' as a pretty minimal commitment. If you tell her that you have a 'girlfriend,' then the implication is that you are not available at present because of your commitment to your 'girlfriend.'" Cory sat quietly for a minute; then I continued, "and if that's the way you see our relationship, as 'dating,' then I need to know, because I view it as much more than that." I paused and waited for his response. "I do too," he said, and added rather sheepishly, "I see your point. I guess I need to be a little more direct."

Momentum

Most individuals do not experience the growth of a close interpersonal relationship as a slow, gradual, and steady development of commitments. Although scholars have tended to describe relational development as an orderly process (Altman & Taylor, 1973; Knapp, 1978), most relationships grow by leaps and bounds rather than step by step. Certain interactional episodes can propel a couple forward suddenly. A **momentum** builds that is "bigger than both of them," providing the impetus to establish firm commitments. One thing leads to another. Each episode conditions the next. The process, however, is fragile and reversible. Unsupportive reactions by significant third parties or sobering experiences with the partner can result in second thoughts that can reverse the direction of the relationship. Once strong commitments have been announced publicly, they become difficult to take back; momentum is a very powerful force.

APPLICATION 4.1 ───────────────────────

ESTABLISHING A RELATIONSHIP

Think of a movie or television program that you have seen in which two people develop a relationship with each other that seems to be leading to some sort of exclusive commitment. Some examples are *When Harry Met Sally,* *Frankie and Johnny*, and *Sleepless in Seattle.*

Trace the development of the relationship in terms of the six factors that move the relationship toward commitment.

Escalation

Our understanding of how commitments evolve has been greatly advanced by Charles Bolton's (1961) study of premarital interaction patterns that move individuals toward the commitment to marriage. **Escalators** are defined by Bolton as sequences of action that have a built-in momentum. Once the first step is taken, the individuals may feel as if they are being swept away as the relationship glides inexorably toward commitment to marriage. The hidden dangers of this process may have been what the famous sociologist Georg Simmel (1950, p. 328) had in mind when he warned individuals not to allow the enchantments of intimacy to lure them into "sending the last reserves of the soul after those of the body."

Five forms of escalators have been described by Bolton (1961): (1) involvement, (2) commitment, (3) addiction, (4) fantasy, and (5) idealization. We identify and provide examples of these five forms of escalators in Table 4.1. Each provides information about the nature of the relationship.

The first form is referred to as **involvement**. The relationship is escalated by interpersonal sequences that have the effect of coordinating one individual's activities and plans with the other's. The more each individual takes the other into account in working out a daily routine, the more involved they become with each other. In the beginning of the relationship, this may mean only that Anita and Carl try to arrange their schedules so that they can walk each other to class or have lunch together. As time passes, they may begin to talk about their career aspirations in relation to each other. Consequently, they may begin to conceive of a future that involves the other person. Some of each individual's personal goals may be revised in light of these conversations, but the important discovery is that the other's goals are complementary to one's own.

The second form of escalation is called **commitment**. Commitment refers to private and public expressions of the special meaning of the relationship and the feelings that define it. These two domains of experience, private and public, are woven closely together. At first, it may be sufficient for Carl to confine his expression of strong feelings for Anita to her alone. But after a time, she probably will want others to know. The promises or pledges that one person makes to another privately carry with them an implicit agreement to define the relationship in

TABLE 4.1   Phases in the escalation of a relationship.

1. *Involvement:* Interpersonal sequences in which two people coordinate their activities, agendas, plans, and schedules in order to spend more time together.
   Tracy and Patrick usually have lunch together on Tuesdays and Thursdays, meet each other after work, and leave their weekends free in order to spend time with each other.

2. *Commitment:* A couple makes private and public declarations of the importance of the relationship for them.
   Gary and Jay make it clear to their parents that they view their relationship as permanent and declare their feelings of love for each other.

3. *Addiction:* Two people become psychologically and physiologically dependent upon each other such that withdrawal can evoke anxiety or feelings of longing to be with the other person.
   When Carl was gone for three days on a job interview, he called Anita every evening on the telephone and would usually talk to her for over an hour. He could hardly wait to see her when he got home.

4. *Fantasy:* Individuals in the relationship daydream or develop mental images of their sexual, romantic, and/or day-to-day life together.
   Shawna thinks about the kind of stepfather that Cory might be for her small son: she pictures Cory taking the boy to baseball games, helping him with his homework when he starts school, and giving him advice about girls when her son is older.

5. *Idealization:* The tendency of individuals to focus on the positive qualities and overlook or minimize the negative qualities of their partners.
   Jake is aware of how much fun he has with his fiancée and how good she makes him feel; he overlooks the fact that she often drinks too much and tends to avoid conflict.

broader terms. She may want him to have dinner with her family. He may invite her to spend a vacation with his parents as an indication that their relationship is exclusive.

Moreover, a time will come when one person says "I love you" to the other. The commitment to love ordinarily precedes the commitment to marry, and in many cases, this message can be perceived as a sign that one is contemplating marriage. It is important, however, to understand how incredibly ambiguous the statement "I love you" can be. Henry (1973) expressed this point vividly in the following passage:

> If a man says "I love you" to a woman, she may wonder whether he means it, whether he loves only her, how much he loves her, whether he will love her next week or next year, or whether his love only means that he wants her to love him. She may even wonder whether his love includes respect and care, or whether his love is merely physical (p. 191).

A third form of escalation consists of what Bolton calls **addiction**. Love is like a potent drug insofar as it can produce a constitutional dependency that the individual eventually becomes terrified to lose. This dependency can have both psychological and physiological manifestations as the term "love-sick" suggests. The individual is afraid of experiencing the withdrawal symptoms that have accompanied the ending of an intimate relationship in the past. The relationship is perpetuated in order to avoid the pain and suffering of withdrawal. Carl remembers how bad he felt and how he suffered when Susan, his first lover, broke up with him. He may do almost anything to avoid feeling like that again.

A fourth form of escalation occurs through **fantasy**. The relationship becomes a symbol for a privately held fantasy to which the individual attaches substantial importance. The relationship is an embodiment of the fantasy. Love and marriage are supposed to go together "like a horse and carriage." Thus, the fulfillment of a romantic or erotic fantasy may lead naturally to the desire or need to broaden the definition of the relationship by institutionalizing it through marriage. Individuals can also daydream about what life would be like with the other person, creating visions of domestic bliss or a life without loneliness.

A fifth form of escalation arises from a process of selective perception referred to as **idealization**. As a relationship evolves, each person tends to inflate the image of the other. Negative qualities of a person are likely to fall outside the other's field of direct perception, while positive qualities are blown out of proportion. A person's self-esteem may become dependent on the degree to which the mate he or she selects is considered to be a person of moral, intellectual, physical, and/or social value. The other side to this is: "if such a terrific person loves me, then I must not be bad after all." Once the relationship becomes so much a part of one's own self-esteem, the continuation of the relationship takes on added importance.

APPLICATION 4.2

ESCALATING THE RELATIONSHIP

Consider the movie or television couple you selected in the last application. Describe the ways in which their relationship escalated, as well as the communication at each step in the escalation process.

Objectification of the Relationship

Escalation pushes a relationship forward by producing certain images about the quality and type of relationship in which the individuals are involved. The first of these is referred to as **objectification** of the relationship. As the relationship escalates it begins to be perceived as something that is as objectively "real" as the individuals who constitute it. The relationship begins to assume an identity of its own, apart from and in addition to the separate identities of the individuals in the relationship. The individuals arrive at the point where they refer to themselves as "we" and this subjective definition of their bond is reinforced by achieving an objective public existence as "a couple." The forms of address used as modes of reference help to legitimize the relationship for the individuals as well as for outsiders. Gary and Jay are a gay couple who provide an example of this process. Gary recalls:

> I think that our relationship took on a real permanence for us when we decided to buy a house together. As soon as we told my parents and took

them to see the house, they seemed more accepting of us as a couple. They talked about how "we" could have them over for dinner now and asked questions about our mortgage and how we were going to finance the house. Making a commitment to "home ownership" made them see our relationship as stable and almost conventional.

Objectification of the relationship removes the fundamental problem of premarital interaction. The ambiguity of the relationship is greatly reduced. Commitments no longer need to be expressed; they can be assumed. The question becomes not *whether* they will marry, but *when*. This level of objectification is achieved in three ways. First, the two individuals differentiate themselves from the field of eligibles composing the general dating complex. They take themselves "off the market." Second, this process of differentiation as a couple must be respected and fortified by the public reactions of others to the relationship. Their network of family and friends now considers them as a couple and treats them as a unit. Violations of exclusivity can threaten the viability of existing friendships. By this time, the other has become "the significant other par excellence" (Berger & Kellner, 1974). This may explain the "Romeo and Juliet effect" in which parental attempts to divide or break up a relationship often have the opposite effect of intensifying and strengthening it. When the couple feels rejected by parents, each partner may gravitate all the more to the other as the primary source of attachment and support. Conversely, parental support can also strengthen the sense that "we are a couple," as is the case with Gary and Jay. Third, objectification of the relationship is formalized by a public announcement that positions it within the larger sociocultural framework of society, either by "going steady," "being pinned," "getting engaged," or becoming monogomous.

Defining the Other as Marriageable

A second outcome produced by escalators is the perception of the relationship as marriageable or permanent. Premarital interaction can be viewed largely as a process of impression formation. Each person presents an image of himself or herself to the other, and each forms impressions based on the other's self-presentation. When the image of the other's character falls within the range of what is considered desirable in a mate, the probability of establishing firmer commitments is enhanced. There is an important distinction to be made between the image of the other and the other's "real" character. Courtship promotes idealized images if for no other reason than the fact that each person tends to put his or her best foot forward. The image each projects is not so much false as incomplete. Newlyweds are often startled to discover how much they did not know about each other before they got married. This discovery should not be surprising; the range of premarital experiences is relatively limited and knowledge of each other is based largely on what the person says or does within the relationship. Rarely does one have an opportunity to form a moral image of the other based on observations of the other's independent actions toward persons outside the relationship.

What does it mean to construe another person as "marriage material"? While some variability undoubtedly exists, there are certain widely shared perceptions of an ideal marriage partner regarding the behavior, character, or personality of the other. These include the following: (1) a person who is a good listener, (2) an "open" person, one who shares feelings freely, (3) a person who would make a good parent, (4) a person with high moral and ethical standards, and (5) a secure and stable person.

There is a second dimension to the process of achieving the perception of marriageability that involves attributions about the relationship. Once the relationship is objectified, it takes on a personality of its own. The individuals then can stand back and consider whether the relationship is sound enough to justify thoughts about marriage. It is common to hear individuals justify the perception of their relationship in one or more of the following ways:

1. We are always comfortable and relaxed around each other.
2. There are certain feelings or thoughts that we can express only to each other; no one else knows me as well as he or she does.
3. We hardly ever quarrel.
4. We are extremely compatible; we hardly ever get on each other's nerves.
5. We've been through a lot together and our love has survived every crisis.
6. We make a good team.

These qualities are not necessarily characteristic of successful marriages. However, many individuals believe that the presence of these traits makes the relationship acceptable for marriage.

The Relationship as a Resolution to an Identity Crisis

A third function of escalators in some relationships is to provide a point of reference for resolving a person's identity crisis. Many persons are particularly concerned about finding a direction in life. For some people, the only structure in their lives is the one exerted through parental control, which they resent. They are troubled by the nagging questions, "Who am I?" and "What is the meaning of my life?" They want to be released from the domination of their parents, but they have not figured out how to escape. Some couples may enter a second marriage to regain lost self-esteem or to restore an image of themselves as loving and loveable. A close relationship offers an expedient solution to identity problems. Premarital interaction may focus on reappraising career goals in light of the opportunity to enter into a firm commitment with another person. The mate becomes a reference point for reconstructing one's identity outside the boundaries of previous experience. In the presence of the other, one feels secure and free. The more dependent these feelings are upon the relationship, the more necessary it becomes to secure a firm commitment from the other person.

TURNING POINTS

Relationships do not always progress logically and sequentially through the phases identified in the previous section. There are often dramatic episodes in the couple's life which either move the relationship forward or cause it to drift backward. When individuals look back on the history of their relationship, they can usually recall several explosive episodes that changed the course of the relationship (Baxter & Bullis, 1986). These decisive episodes in the relationship are called

turning points. Not all turning points lead to dramatic shifts in commitment; some merely cement feelings that existed already. In most cases, however, turning points are experienced either as breakthroughs, after which the relationship soars to higher levels of commitment, or as breakdowns, after which the relationship falls apart. When Anita and Carl weathered the storm of their separation and cooling off period, they reached a breakthrough which propelled them toward increasing commitment and a decision to marry.

We have described the development of a relationship as a communicative achievement that requires partners to work through certain obstacles that stand in the way of commitment to marriage. The major problem of premarital interaction is commitment. Turning points are the decisive moments when perceptions about self, other, and the relationship between self and other materialize or diminish. Although some individuals consider practically every major event to be a turning point (Baxter & Bullis, 1986), there probably are only a few such moments regardless of whether the courtship is brief or prolonged.

Braiker and Kelley's (1979) research on conflict in the development of close relationships reinforces some of our earlier observations about how the **perception of marriageability** is achieved. They identify three sets of perceptions that are associated with increased closeness and greater interdependence. The first set involves *self-perceptions*. Self is perceived as being increasingly connected to the other by virtue of feeling "in love," and being affected by the other's feelings, experiences, and behaviors. The second set concerns *perceptions about the other*. The partner is viewed as a person who is worth spending a lifetime with. The third set of perceptions focuses on *perceptions of the relationship*. The relationship is marriageable because it is special and different in positive respects from less meaningful relationships experienced in the past. Anita and Carl think their relationship has matured because they have worked through their earlier conflicts. This experience gives them confidence that they can survive future difficulties.

As these perceptions mount, so do feelings of dependence on the relationship; the individuals become more attached to and more in need of each other. These feelings of dependence are bolstered by the decision to make the relationship more exclusive. The **norm of exclusivity** is a relationship rule in which each partner agrees to seek sexual and emotional intimacy within their relationship only. Until the norm of exclusivity emerges, there is some ambivalence about the direction in which the relationship is moving. In fact, Braiker and Kelley (1979) found that most of the serious conflicts experienced during premarital interaction occurred early in the relationship, before the individuals agreed to make their relationship exclusive. An agreement to make the relationship exclusive removes a major source of conflict by clarifying the definition of the relationship.

The development of a relationship, then, hinges on three types of turning points. Each turning point has the potential to turn the relationship forward or backward. *First, commitments can turn on experiences that define the feelings of love that exist between self and other.* This is the affective dimension of experiencing feelings of being in love, feeling attached and close, caring about the other, and becoming sexually intimate. Each person must recognize and define the feelings he or she is experiencing toward the other, as well as the extent to which those feelings are shared or reciprocated by the other. One of the most widely shared beliefs in our culture is that people get married because they are in love. But the experience of being "in love" is extremely difficult to define. Erotic feelings and sexual excitement can easily be confused with feeling in love, especially during courtship when, as Lederer and Jackson observe, "individuals lose most of their judgment" (1968, p. 42). Nevertheless, amorous feelings undoubtedly play a large part in the development of commitments.

In their descriptive study of turning points, Baxter and Bullis (1986) reported that "passion" was one of the episodes associated with the largest increases in commitment. Passion episodes ranged from the first kiss to the first sexual encounter and included the first time each said "I love you" to the other. It is not difficult to understand how amorous expression can build momentum in a relationship. The statement "I love you" is not a deniable message. Once these words are expressed, they cannot easily be retracted. Similarly, when a relationship becomes sexually intimate a baseline of affectionate expression is established.

Second, commitments can turn on the basis of experiences that define the other person's character. Each person must determine whether the other is a sufficiently moral and virtuous person to justify a firmer commitment. In our culture, it is presumed that one should take the time to get to know the other person as well as possible. This premise is underscored by Baxter and Bullis's (1986) subjects. They emphasized the importance of episodes that helped them to get to know each other and showed them that they could enjoy doing things together. These subjects also indicated that their commitment increased when the partner made a personal sacrifice in their behalf. In a moment of crisis, the partner was there to help, or one person's reluctant request for a favor received a generous and benevolent response from the other. Apparently, sacrifices contribute positively to the momentum of the relationship by embellishing the image of one's character in the eyes of the other. What emerges is a perception of the partner as a helpful and self-sacrificing person who is worth the commitment of a lifetime.

Third, commitments can turn on the basis of experiences that define the marriageability of the relationship. This dimension of relational experience involves some of the most widely shared assumptions about marriage: (1) Effective communication is essential to a good marriage. The partners should be able to talk about their feelings and work out their problems together. They should function as a good team. (2) Conflicts will arise in the course of a marriage. The ability to resolve conflicts is essential to a good marriage. The individuals must be able to weather a storm. (3) Marriage is a monogamous relationship. The marital bond normally excludes close and/or amorous relationships with others. Baxter and Bullis (1986) found that these assumptions were pervasive in the reports their subjects gave about turning points. They also found that making up after a serious fight or period of disengagement was second only to living together or getting engaged in increasing commitment to the relationship. The ability to make up shows that the couple can weather a storm. The relationship is strong enough to withstand and rebound from painful conflicts. These subjects also reported that exclusivity increased their commitment to the relationship markedly. Exclusivity is a joint decision that publicly certifies the unit, removing all competitors from the scene. It is interesting to note that the partners reportedly engaged in the most talk about their relationship when they were making up and deciding to become exclusive. We can surmise that this relationship talk resulted in the perception that the individuals could communicate effectively, resolve a serious conflict, and establish a monogamous relationship.

Table 4.2 summarizes our discussion of turning points. The escalation of commitments hinges on experiences that provide answers to three fundamental questions: (1) Do I feel in love and is my love shared by my partner? (2) Is the

TABLE 4.2   Turning points as decisive moments of relational development.

DEFINITION IN QUESTION	TURNING POINTS	CONCLUSION
Feelings of love (Do I feel "in love"? and is my love reciprocated?)	Kissing. Making love	We're in love/ we're not in love.
Character of the other (Is my partner a moral and virtuous person?)	Getting to know each other. Doing things together. Making sacrifices. Doing favors.	The partner is worth spending a lifetime with/the partner is not worth spending a lifetime with.
Marriageable relation- ship (Can this relation- ship withstand the pressures of marriage?)	Making up after conflict. Developing exclusivity.	We act and feel married/we do not act and feel married.

character of my partner sufficiently moral and virtuous to justify a lifetime commitment? and (3) Is this relationship stable, strong, and close enough to survive the perils of marriage? The measures that are taken to answer these questions come in the form of amorous interactional episodes, tests of character, and challenges to the wholeness and efficacy of the relationship. The rise and fall of commitments rests largely on the outcomes of these encounters.

PATTERNS OF PREMARITAL COURTSHIP

In addition to the fact that couples can experience dramatic turning points in their relationship which influence the course of the relationship, couples also differ in their particular styles of courtship. We have repeatedly emphasized that there is no one path that leads to marriage. The processes that culminate in the decision to marry are pluralistic—different patterns can lead to the same result.

Short and Long Courtships

The most obvious difference is the length of courtship. Some courtships accelerate very quickly. In this type of courtship, the individuals "fall" for each other quickly,

APPLICATION 4.3

TURNING POINTS IN RELATIONSHIPS

Again, consider your media couple. Identify the turning points in their relationship. Identify the effects that each turning point had on the relationship and the communication that accompanied these turning points.

experience few setbacks, and develop a high probability of marriage within two or three months of their initial encounter (Huston, Surra, Fitzgerald, & Cate, 1981). Marriage is consummated within twelve to eighteen months. At the other extreme are the prolonged courtships that follow a long and winding road to marriage. Prolonged courtships suffer numerous setbacks and changes of heart; commitment to marriage may take as long as three years to achieve and the marriage may take up to five years to be effectuated (Huston, Surra, Fitzgerald, & Cate, 1981). Most courtships probably fall somewhere between these extremes.

Themes of Courtship

The most important dimensions that differentiate types of courtships are the themes of the relationship to which interactional episodes are directed. The **themes of a relationship** are the core issues or ideals that form the basis for prolonged commitment. In this respect, the length of a courtship is a consequence of interaction patterns rather than a cause.

The simplest way to describe different types of courtships is to examine some hypothetical cases. This section describes several uniquely different patterns of premarital interaction that culminate in the decision to marry. These include the following themes of courtship: (1) romantic ideal, (2) identity clarification, (3) relationship viability, and (4) tactical maneuvering.

Case I: We Were Made for Each Other (Romantic Ideal)

Tony and Maria grew up in the same South Philadelphia neighborhood. Although Tony was five years older than Maria and hung out with a different crowd, he had seen her around the neighborhood from time to time as he was growing up. When he was home on leave from the service, a mutual friend introduced him to Maria while they were shopping at the Italian Market. Several months later, when Tony got out of the service, he called Maria and asked her for a date. He was twenty-three years old at the time; she was eighteen. Tony and Maria immediately felt strongly attracted to each other. He was tall, dark, and handsome; she was dark, slender, and beautiful. They were a striking couple. Tony was physically strong and aggressive; Maria was more introverted but she felt comfortable around Tony. They seemed to fit together extremely well. During their brief courtship, they talked a lot about the traditions of the neighborhood and their desire to have a big family. They became sexually intimate quickly. Each viewed the other as a romantic ideal. It did not take them long to express their love for each other openly. Tony's parents became good friends with Maria's parents and the relationship received the blessing of both families. Tony and Maria were married one year after their first date.

This pattern of courtship reflects the meshing of personalities and conforms closely to a romantic ideal. Tony and Maria had very similar backgrounds and shared a rich ethnic heritage. They did not have to spell things out for each other. Indeed, they had an uncanny knack of reading each other's mind. They seemed perfectly matched: physically, temperamentally, and ethnically. Each fit the other's image of the ideal mate. They did not feel a need for a long courtship, because they knew they were right for each other.

Case II: Now I Know Who I Am (Identity Clarification)

Jim met Kathy in an English course at the University of Kentucky. Initially, they talked mainly about the books they were reading for the course. On several occasions, Jim walked Kathy to her car after class, and they stood and talked for long periods of time. Gradually, they started seeing each other more frequently, going out for dinner, studying together, and occasionally going to movies. Their conversations became more and more philosophical. They talked about the purpose and meaning of life, about moral and ethical conduct, and about the future of the world. Initially, they disagreed about many things, but gradually their viewpoints seemed to merge.

During this period, Jim was living at home with his parents. They watched over him closely and were opposed to his relationship with Kathy from the beginning. He resented their interference. The more conflict with his family that Jim experienced, the closer he became to Kathy. Jim and Kathy developed an isolated relationship. They did not mix with others and they even withdrew from their families. Each felt most secure in the presence of the other. They treated each other as equals and felt very compatible. The relationship seemed to rescue them from anonymity and gave meaning and purpose to their lives.

This pattern of courtship serves the function of clarifying the identities of one or both persons. The individuals become comfortable with each other quickly. Although they may have strong differences of opinion at first, their interactions bring increasing agreement on values. Conflict with parents pushes the individuals closer together. Endless intimate conversation is a major ingredient of the relationship. Their bond is very deep and they become very dependent upon each other as they withdraw from outside influences and confine their sphere of activity to each other. As each individual's identity becomes clarified, the relationship progresses slowly toward marriage.

Case III: Nobody Said It Would Be Easy (Relationship Viability)

Linda met Phil at an office party. Their mutual attraction was spontaneous and they fell quickly for each other. The relationship was dominated from the beginning by sexual intimacy. Consumed and absorbed by this overwhelming erotic experience, Linda and Phil were seduced into believing their relationship was viable for marriage. Their initial commitment to each other proved superficial. Linda began having serious questions about what she really meant to Phil and whether the relationship had any depth to it. Phil was uncomfortable about Linda's constant pressure to talk about the relationship. The relationship became a roller coaster. They would fight, break up, and then reunite. When they were apart, they would experience a lot of jealousy. Every time they got back together, they would feel closer than ever. But the feelings would not last. Phil and Linda were strongly connected to friends and colleagues at work. They experienced considerable outside pressure to maintain their relationship.

The central theme of this pattern of courtship is the viability of the relationship. This is the stormiest type of courtship. Commitments are superficial and tentative. Numerous breakups and makeups occur. The relationship is not grounded on shared understandings and agreements. Yet, there is a strong amorous identification cementing the relationship, and the pressure from outside forces makes it difficult for them to give up on each other. There is more talk about the relationship and more conflict than in any other pattern of courtship.

Case IV: We'd Be Happier If We Were Married (Tactical Maneuvering)

Fred and Amy were raised in traditional families. The members of Fred's family got along well with each other. There was never much conflict among them. Amy's mother and father did not get along well. They frequently yelled and screamed at each other. Occasionally, Amy's father would become violent. Amy was afraid of violence, and she was easily intimidated by loud and aggressive individuals. When Fred and Amy met, the main thing they shared was a dislike of conflict. They were gentle and kind to each other, but they did not express their feelings openly. Most of Amy's friends were married already and she had become increasingly concerned about whether she would ever find someone to marry. Amy fell in love with Fred quickly and was eager to secure a firm commitment from him. She raised the question of marriage on numerous occasions, but would back down when Fred expressed resistance. Fred had not had much experience in close relationships and had very little confidence in his attractiveness to women. Amy bolstered his confidence and fed his ego. As time passed her subtle attempts to secure firmer commitments paid off. He did not want to lose her.

This is a tactical courtship. Backgrounds may be similar but personalities do not mesh. One of the individuals feels a greater attraction than the other and cautiously presses for commitment. The individuals are not as dependent upon each other as they are upon the relationship. One needs the relationship to fulfill a fantasy, the other to resolve an identity problem. The lack of similarity in their definitions of the relationship makes it necessary to employ tactical maneuvers and friendly persuasion. Their preference for avoiding conflict heightens the probability of a marital commitment.

CONCLUSIONS ABOUT COURTSHIP

Theories of relationship development often leave the mistaken impression that all relationships follow the same general trajectory. From our examples we can see that different relationships take different paths. Courtship patterns might also differ depending upon the cultural conventions or age of one or both partners or whether either partner has been married before. Our purpose in presenting these fictitious cases is to indicate that the themes of courtship can be diverse. These cases may seem like stereotypes and to a certain extent they are. However, each case represents one of the types of courtship patterns described by Bolton (1961) on the basis of extensive interviews with recently married couples.

From Bolton's research and our own analysis, we draw the following four conclusions about courtship:

1. Love does not always precede the desire to marry. Some individuals find marriage to be expedient and desirable in comparison to other available alternatives.

2. Relationships with family and friendship networks can have a significant effect on attachment to the relationship. Rejection from outsiders can

increase attachment to the relationship; when the attractiveness of the relationship is lessening, support for the relationship from outsiders can strengthen it.

3. Subtle forms of persuasion and manipulation are often used to induce greater commitment, particularly when attractions are not equal.

4. The knowledge on which individuals base their decision to marry is necessarily incomplete and imperfect. It is as if they are looking at each other through a crack in the wall that distorts the image. The image of the person is "real," but the picture is not placed in the proper perspective. An idealized image is not so much false as it is incomplete.

It is very difficult to predict the course a marriage will take. Individuals are forced to make a decision about an uncertain future (marriage) on the basis of a rather superficial past (courtship). There is no way to avoid this problem. Even cohabitation (living together) prior to marriage does not improve one's chances for success (Macklin, 1983). The decision to marry is a calculated risk. There is no way to simulate the experience, no way to guarantee a positive outcome. Does this mean that we are opposed to marriage? Not at all. Marriage offers the potential for expanding the meaning of our lives and heightening our sense of significance. Our purpose is not to question the validity of marriage but to increase your understanding of how individuals develop a relationship they perceive as marriageable.

Commonly it is assumed that people get married because they are in love. Lederer and Jackson (1968) point out that this is a false assumption. They suggest that many people mistake romance for love and are swept away by a tidal wave of passion and lust. Nevertheless, people do think that they get married because they are in love; it is easy to forget about other factors that may affect decisions to marry. Our observation of the ways that individuals develop and strengthen their commitments to each other indicates that people decide to get married for many reasons, including: (1) that individuals in our society are expected to marry; (2) that as we grow up, many of the books, television shows, and movies to which we are exposed romanticize marriage; (3) that parents can unintentionally increase a son's or daughter's commitment to a relationship by opposing it; (4) that loneliness and insecurity can make a person feel desperate for companionship; and (5) that low self-esteem can make marriage seem like the best way to improve one's lot in life.

SUMMARY

This chapter has argued that the process of selecting a marriage partner involves a significant amount of decision making and persuasion. Mate selection is not so much a matter of whether we choose partners who are similar to us or who complement our personalities and needs, but it is more likely an outcome of interpersonal processes. Once two people express an interest in each other, their relationship tends to progress through various developmental stages. We describe six factors that influence the development of a relationship: (1) ambiguity, (2) momentum, (3) escalation, (4) objectification of the relationship, (5) defining the other as marriageable, and (6) the relationship as a resolution to an identity crisis. Several phases were identified in the escalation of a relationship: (1) involvement, (2) commitment, (3) addiction, (4) fantasy, and (5) idealization.

We have discussed the importance of turning points as decisive events that either move the relationship forward or cause it to move backward. Three types of experiences seem to characterize turning points: those that (1) define feelings of love that exist between self and other, (2) define the other's character, and (3) define the marriageability of the relationship. In describing patterns of premarital courtship, we identify differences between short and long courtships and discuss several themes of courtship. Themes in four different patterns of courtship include: (1) romantic ideal, (2) identity clarification, (3) relationship viability, and (4) tactical maneuvering. Finally, we caution the reader against assuming that people get married simply (or only) because they love each other. It is somewhat sobering to recognize that a complex set of circumstances influences the decision to marry. Certainly, when it comes to "affairs of the heart," our emotional and intuitive responses are enormously significant. That is as it should be. But the rates of success for marriage in this country also suggest that one needs to be as informed as possible about the choice that he or she is making.

KEY TERMS

addiction	idealization
commitment	involvement
courtship as decision making	momentum
differential contact	norm of exclusivity
escalators	objectification
fantasy	perception of marriageability
filtering process	themes of a relationship
heterogamy	turning points
homogamy	

C HAPTER 5

MARITAL
REALITY
CONSTRUCTION

LISSA ADDINGTON

NINA'S STORY

Gail: Tell me about your family.

Nina: The family that I grew up in?

Gail: Start there. Then you might talk about the family you helped to create.

Nina: Okay. What do you want to hear?

Gail: Well, just tell me your story.

Nina: Okay. My parents are older. They are about seventy years old. They were married during World War II. Right after the war was over they moved to Texas. We have four children in our family. We lived there until I was about fifteen years old. I never really thought of my father as an alcoholic, but in looking at old pictures of my family, I see there was always alcohol in the pictures. And yet, I never realized as a child that that was going on. I wasn't aware of it. Anyway, at fifteen we moved back to Milwaukee (where we were originally from), and it was sort of like our family exploded at that point. Maybe that was just the last straw . . . I don't know. Maybe that would've happened anyway. I don't know.

Gail: The difficulties—the stress—of the move added to your problems.

Nina: Right. The stress added to everything else. My parents are still married. They've been married almost fifty years, but they really don't have any kind of relationship. I can see that I've had a lot of problems in my life, and my brothers have both led very unusual—what I would call unusual—lifestyles as a result of our upbringing.

Gail: Tell me something about each of your brothers—the different paths that your brothers have taken or that you've taken.

Nina: Okay. My oldest brother was very, very well liked

and popular. A lot of people thought of him as the "golden boy" in our family. He was very smart and very successful. He got a lot of praise. I have a brother who was just three years younger than him, who quit high school. He couldn't wait until he turned sixteen so he could quit. He's led a very bad life. He's been in prison. He's done drugs. He's dealt in drugs. He still lives that wow-wow lifestyle . . . "don't bring me down." It's that kind of stuff. And then there's me who I think has always tried to be the "peacemaker" of the family.

Gail: The good girl.

Nina: I try to keep everybody happy. Then I have a younger brother who is two years younger than me. He moved back to Texas when he was twenty-four. He's very determined to become financially successful. He's driven to prove that he's okay. There's a lot of extreme bitterness that I can see. He's doing a lot of things just to prove that he's okay.

Gail: How is your relationship with him?

Nina: My brothers and I sort of banded together against our mom, which probably wasn't terrifically healthy. But we took refuge in each other because my mother was very aggressive. She would slap . . . she slapped easily. She flew off the handle very easily. She is a very frustrated person, I would say.

Gail: She has a lot of anger?

Nina: She had a lot of anger, and she took it out on us. Not too long ago I tried to confront her about it. She is in complete denial over the whole thing. She just absolutely goes into this whole thing about how I must think she's just a terrible person, and the way I make her sound she must have been the worst mother in the world.

Gail: How did your father and mother get together?

Nina: How did they meet?

Gail: Yes. What are some of the details of their marriage? Do you know much about that?

Nina: Not to be bragging or anything, but both of my parents are very, very nice-looking people. Or they were. My father is an extremely handsome man—just gorgeous, really. People say, "Oh, wow," when they see my parents' pictures. My mother was just a beautiful, beautiful woman. I think that they strictly got together because they were both so good-looking. I really do.

Gail: There was a mutual attraction or admiration between them.

Nina: Yeah. My father was Italian and very unacceptable socially. I could tell you stories that you . . . that he felt unaccepted socially at the time. My mother was Algerian, so she was blond with blue eyes. He was very dark with brown eyes. They were kind of opposites. They were striking together. We have pictures of them. They look just like they could be from Hollywood. They were just . . . my mother . . . my grandmother, my mother's mother, didn't talk to my mother for six months after they were married because she knew he was Italian. She accorded him with the lower class.

Gail: Your grandmother didn't speak to your parents after they were married?

Nina: Yes. Yes. The rest of their relationship has been sad. . . . I know that my father has had affairs. Not lots and lots of them, which I think would be easier for my mother to accept, but he has had two long-running affairs that I know of. I mean that have lasted for more than ten years. My father's affairs made my mother very bitter. I see it as the old Italian thing where the husband can have his women on the side and have home and children, too. I think that he thought that that was okay. And yet, we were just neglected emotionally.

Gail: And your mother became very angry?

Nina: Yes. And in the meantime, my mother is frustrated and mad and angry and taking it out on us when he's not there. And who knows . . . I started thinking about this not too long ago. I was thinking that I've always just been mad at my mother. I funneled that energy toward her behavior. What I really see as an older person, I see why she felt all that. It's because of what he was doing. She just didn't do anything to stop it. She didn't have enough courage to leave or stand up or whatever it was going to take to stop it.

Gail: You think she should have left or stood up to your father even though you don't like what she did?

Nina: Right. Right.

Gail: How do you see your place in your family? You said you were the "peacemaker"? Do you still have that role?

Nina: Yes. Although I began to resent it.

Gail: That's understandable.

Nina: Yes, I basically, still . . . the thing is all three of my brothers moved. We all came back to Milwaukee and then they moved back to Texas. My oldest brother tried for years to get me to come out to Texas. He promised me . . . he even came out to get me one time in his truck to move me. I couldn't go. I just couldn't leave my parents. I know it's pathetic, but I felt that I was abandoning them. I worried about leaving them. They needed me to keep their relationship intact because without the kids between them it was terrible. That's all they do is fight. After all these years, it's still that way, I think. Although they are peaceful around us. So one of the children needed to stay. I couldn't just leave them.

Gail: So you felt that if you left and went to Texas they would really destroy each other?

Nina: Right. Right. Right. I guess in the long run I'm glad that I didn't go. Ten years ago I moved about 200 miles from where they live, which was just far enough to be able to go back for birthdays and holidays and any time of the year. That has helped me a lot.

Gail: When you talk about your parents and siblings, I have some sense that you've done some reading, or that you seem to understand what's going on—understand the problems in your family. Have you done some reading in the literature about alcoholism? Or done some things for yourself that have helped to heal some things that have been painful for you?

Nina: I've done a number of things. I've done some reading, but I've also been involved in some twelve-step programs, which I don't participate in. I did for a while, and I found the information in the literature helpful, but I did not feel that attending the meetings was particularly helpful. Something that really changed was that I began to take my religion seriously. I have a different perspective on things now. I am trying—it's like a process—to forgive things that have happened in the past and to see them as they happened—not hide from them—and why they happened. I can change, because I don't want to repeat. I don't want to repeat with my daughter what happened to me.

Gail: What about your present situation? Do you have a family at home?

Nina: Uh-huh. I was married very young and divorced. I married someone who I thought, because he came from the same culture—he came from a half-Italian, half-something-else family—I thought we had many, many things in common. Yet, I couldn't be married to him. It just didn't work. I was miserable. But, anyway . . . so then I was single for, like, seven years, and I remarried ten years ago to a person who is the complete opposite personality of my first husband. So I went from one extreme to the other trying to make up. The man I'm married to now is much more reserved, less aggressive. It's only been really—we've been married about ten years, and it's only been in, like, the last five years that we've really started to function well. So, we're on the road.

Gail: What is his family like?

Nina: His mother is widowed. His father died when he was six. He comes from not a good situation either. His mother is very German. She is very staunch, unemotional, and task-oriented. He did not have a good relationship with her.

Gail: Was she stern?

Nina: Yes, yes. Very stern.

Gail: How do they get along now?

Nina: They don't. Derek has no relationship with her at all. I've tried to encourage him to spend some time with her and make comments and stuff, but he says he doesn't have the energy. He says it is just not worth the effort. I can understand, kinda. He has tried before and it just doesn't work.

Gail: It's just too much for him.

Nina: Yeah. So he keeps his distance. They don't have much contact.

Gail: Do you have any children, the two of you?

Nina: No, we don't have any children together. I think that if we were where we are now, if we were younger—I'm almost forty and my husband is forty-four, and if we were younger we would have a lot of children, but I don't think that we will now, although over the last year or so we have been doing very well, and my husband has started to talk about it. Before that he was completely and totally against it. The door is not closed on the matter yet. Like, I said, we're becoming a family and who knows?

Gail:　Well, do you have a child?

Nina:　I have a child.

Gail:　You have a child from your first marriage.

Nina:　Seventeen-year-old daughter. We do great together, I'm happy to say. We're very close.

Gail:　How does your daughter get along with your second husband? Are they close?

Nina:　Very close.

Gail:　What do you think is the key to the success of that relationship?

Nina:　Um [pause] well, when we were first married, I felt that I had to be the mediator in that relationship, and it didn't really go very well. And like I said, about five years ago I realized what I was doing, so I just took, like, a major step backwards and when one would come to me or another one would come to me to side with them in the usual conflict, I'd say inside that I really think that that could be worked out directly, and suddenly they started working things out themselves, and just everything changed.

Gail:　Everything got much better.

Nina:　Yes. Because when either one of them tried to work through me, it seemed like they were irrational. They were almost calmer with each other.

Gail:　How do you see that your husband's family influenced him?

Nina:　How? Well, his mother . . . I used to always say to him that (this was mean), but I used to sort of make fun of him and say that business came before pleasure because he couldn't do anything until—when he would come into the house he would put things away and start a load of laundry and do all this work around the house. He had to put away his good clothes and get into his other clothes and look at the mail and put things in order before he could even say hello. It was like—to me it was like a joke because I was not like that at all.

Gail:　Attending to chores that need to get done before affection?

Nina:　Yes. But that is exactly how his mother trained him. The minute he would come home from school—and she prided herself on this—but when he came home she had a list of things for him to do, and he had to do every-thing on the list first. When he got that done then she could talk to him or spend time with him or whatever. It has taken him a long time to break that terrible training.

Gail:　To feel like the chores don't come first?

Nina:　Uh-huh. [Pause] Another thing too is that when I met him, we moved here, and it was 200 miles. I had all my friends and family long distance. Well, they never made long-distance phone calls. His mom called him once a year on his birthday and that was it. He never, never, never made long-distance phone calls. It was just something they didn't do. After I moved here our phone bills were like well over a hundred dollars for a long, long time. He just hated it—we fought like cats and dogs over it. I tried to explain to him repeatedly that I couldn't completely sever all ties with everybody. I could write some letters, but I was not going to sever all my ties with everyone immediately just because he thought I shouldn't make long-distance phone calls. So we had a lot of serious fights about it, and then again all this sort of changed five years ago. He said, "Okay, I've come up with a budget. We are allowed to spend seventy-five dollars on the phone—on long-distance calls." This was quite reasonable.

Gail: Sort of a compromise that you worked out?

Nina: Right. Halfway in between over a hundred and nothing.

Gail: This sounds like the long-distance phone calls represented a struggle over the fact that he has this kind of distance in relating to his family and you are more emotionally expressive.

Nina: Oh, yes. Definitely. But, we are getting there. We're getting there.

Gail: Slowly, but surely, you're making progress.

Nina: That's right; we *are* making progress.

UNDERSTANDING NINA

In the conversation we have used to introduce this chapter, Nina briefly describes the family that she grew up in, her role in the family, her first and second marriage, and something about the differences that she and her second husband have struggled with in their relationship. She discusses the difficulty that she has with her husband's task-oriented behavior when they arrive home after work and describes a dispute over long-distance telephone calls. Both of these issues might be thought of as representative examples, or metaphors, for their different relationship orientations. Nina's outgoing, immediate, and emotionally expressive communication style can be contrasted to Derek's more reserved, "business-before-pleasure" orientation. We can see how the family that Nina and her second husband each grew up in has influenced their relationship. Even though Nina expresses more satisfaction with her second marriage than with her first, her story illustrates how challenging and complicated the task of integrating two lives into one relationship can be. As Beck (1969) suggests in his description of what lies ahead for any couple:

> Once the marriage rites have been celebrated, however, and the glow of the morning fades, the realities of the task ahead become clear in the bright light of noon. Somehow the two must integrate into a satisfying partnership and a conjoint career, plan two designs for family living, two sets of expectations for the relationship, and two dreams for the future (p. 584).

Partners carry "baggage" from their separate histories and families of origin to a marriage. The "baggage" can include such things as habits, preferences, anxieties, skills, and previous experiences. Some of Nina's previous experience, or "baggage," includes being the mediator or peacemaker in an alcoholic family; feelings of frustration with and understanding of her alcoholic father and embittered mother; a determination not to repeat the mistakes of the past; an awareness of and sensitivity to her own feelings, which she developed from her effort to heal the bruises of past family experiences; and a willingness to see compromise as a way to improve the quality of her relationships. Once a commitment to marry has been made, a couple begins the process of coordinating their different backgrounds into a manageable relationship. Through their communication, Nina and her husband reconstruct their lives as they build their relationship. They are confronted with a number of marital tasks in the taken-for-granted everyday activities and conversations of their life together. A good example of this includes Nina's description of interactions with her husband after the two arrive home from work or in her discussion of the conflict over the phone bill. This chapter examines five tasks involved in the process of building the marriage relationship: (1) integrating two sets of expectations into one relationship, (2) co-defining reality in the construction of the marriage relationship, (3) negotiating a communication code, (4) organizing the relationship, and (5) managing differentiation and integration in the marriage relationship.

EXPECTATIONS

Each individual brings to marriage a set of expectations relevant to the relationship. A set of **expectations** is a collection of images, unspoken assumptions, and attitudes about what a partner expects to give in return for what he or she expects to receive (Sager, 1976). Nina, for example, expects that Derek will be supportive and understanding of her emotional needs, something that she did not have when she was growing up. Derek expects Nina to supply the warmth and spontaneity that was missing in his family of origin, without sacrificing his need for order and fiscal responsibility.

Sources of Expectations

Where do expectations for marriage originate? There are three significant sources for expectations about marriage: (1) the families of origin, (2) the immediate culture, and (3) the mass media.

Parents provide a model of marriage for their children by the way they relate to each other as husband and wife: how they reach decisions, show affection, express their hopes and fears, interact with their children, disagree, and cope with stress. Children are taught what it means to be married not so much by what their parents say about marriage but by how they act in their marriage—by their deeds rather than by their words. Of course, some children openly reject their parents' marriage as a model for their own, though they may be unrealistic about how different they are or will be when compared to their parents (Laing, 1972). The formidable influence of parents may be too powerful to overcome merely by wishing to be different (Kramer, 1985; Boszormenyi-Nagy & Spark, 1984). In Nina's case, developing a marriage that was better than the one her parents had meant enduring an unhappy first marriage, participating in a twelve-step program for adult children of alcoholics, and spending a considerable amount of time reading and reflecting.

The myths, values, and assumptions about marriage that a person acquires from the surrounding culture also have a powerful effect on an individual's expectations about marriage (Lederer & Jackson, 1968). In the last century people tended to marry primarily for economic and social reasons. Now, we place much emphasis on companionship and the emotional compatibility of partners. Our culture reinforces the notion that marriage should help us stave off feelings of loneliness, provide friendship and emotional support, enhance personal growth and development, and provide sexual pleasure and gratification for the partners. For a satisfactory marriage in our culture, personal and emotional fulfillment are generally expected. Cultural values may lead to the expectation that one partner should not only like and appreciate how the other thinks and feels about almost everything, but also be capable of filling up the gaps and empty spaces that each partner experiences. As Napier (1988) writes:

> After years of anxiety about being alone, we finally *have* someone: here is a wonderful body to enjoy sexually (and we do a lot of that), to snuggle with hungrily in the night; and here is someone who is always ready to talk, always willing to help. It seems that a lifetime of loneliness is over (p. 250).

The mass media provide another powerful source of influence in the creation of expectations. As we grow up we are influenced by what we read, see, and hear about family relationships (Buerkel-Rothfuss, Greenberg, Atkin, & Neuendorf, 1982). Television often defines the ideal marriage as one in which "love conquers all," physical beauty is primary, conflict can be easily resolved, manipulation is a way to smooth over differences, and energy and money are endless resources.

It is also useful to note that, in general, women and men may bring different expectations to a marriage. Women often value connectedness, interdependence, and emotional expressiveness more than do men, who tend to place more value on autonomy and rational expressiveness (Gilligan, 1982; Walters, Carter, Papp, & Silverstein, 1988). These differences are values that are learned in the culture and may be changing. These differences may also create a disadvantage for women if women's "connectedness is equated with dependency" or if the emotional well-being of the family is left primarily to wives and mothers (Walters, Carter, Papp, & Silverstein, 1988, p. 19). In a culture that values individualism and personal freedom, connectedness may not be valued as much as autonomy. Similarly, the role of maintaining the emotional well-being of the family may be viewed as secondary to providing for the economic survival of the family. A rigid separation of roles in the family can also lead to husbands and fathers underparticipating in the emotional and intimate aspects of family life. Nevertheless, gender differences, reinforced by cultural patterns, can influence expectations.

Content of Expectations

Each spouse brings individual expectations about what life together will be like—the content of expectations for the marriage. Nina may see marriage as a way to heal her wounds, receive the kindness and consideration she deserves, and build an equal partnership with someone who is willing to support her personal growth and development. Carrie, who grew up in a large family in a small rural town, may see marriage as the route to raising a flock of children. In Carrie's case, marriage is seen as the way to have the economic support to create her life as a homemaker and mother. Harry, who always felt close to and cared for by his mother, has the expectation that he will marry someone who will nurture him in the way his mother did. He has the image of a marital partner as someone who will be emotionally and sexually responsive to him without his having to "try overly hard" to

TABLE 5.1   Expectations that Nina and Derek bring to their marriage.

Derek's Expectations	Nina's Expectations
Nina will give him the warmth, acceptance, and open expression of affection that was lacking in his relationship with his mother.	Derek will provide a sense of security, stability, maturity, and loyalty that was missing in previous relationships with her father and her first husband.
Nina will contribute to the family income so that he doesn't need to feel overburdened in the way that his mother did.	Derek will support her in her efforts to return to school and develop a new career for herself.
He and Nina will share responsibility for household maintenance tasks, but Derek will have primary responsibility for managing the family budget.	She and Derek will share responsibility for household maintenance tasks, and he will be open to her opinions and needs regarding their financial matters.
Nina will always be there for him and will not require frequent verbal confirmation in order to know that she is important to him.	Derek will be understanding and supportive of her need to maintain frequent contact with her family and friends.
Nina will be in charge of the couple's social activities and will not require him to initiate contacts with friends and family members.	Derek will accept her suggestions for their social activities.
Nina will provide the cheerfulness, good humor, and positive climate in their relationship so that he does not have to feel overwhelmed by the negative feelings and sober attitude that he sometimes displays.	Derek will validate her view of the world as a place that essentially rewards someone who is kind, cheerful, and a peacemaker. Derek will make an effort to love and nurture her daughter from her first marriage.

please her—a wife should be responsive, as his mother had been, because she loves him.

Couples develop expectations about a wide variety of behaviors and issues. Expectations can include how much time the couple will spend together and how they will manage household tasks and economic decisions, as well as sexuality and the decision to have or not to have children. Couples can also expect that the partner will help them to deal with loneliness, compensate for an unhappy childhood, and make them feel better about themselves.

Often expectations have a *reciprocal quality* to them. Harry may expect that, if he is not overly critical of his wife and works hard to contribute to the family income, his wife, in turn, will provide the kind of emotional and sexual responsiveness that he needs. Jules Henry has pointed out "If the marriage is to succeed, each partner must master the other's unconscious conception of what he wants in return for what he gives. . . . Love-in-our-time is supposed to arise and endure when the man and woman are able to give each other what each wants," (Henry, 1973, p. 196).

Sager (1976, 1981) has developed the concept of the marriage contract to describe the reciprocal quality of expectations. The **marriage contract** identifies what each partner expects to get in return for what he or she is expected to give or do for the partner. Suppose that Nina has the expectation that her husband should be willing to support her return to school and new career aspirations. She expects that she will, in turn, support her husband in his need to achieve financial security.

She may also expect that, in return for her sharing in the economic stability of the partnership, her husband will participate fully in the housekeeping. In forming an idea about what her role is likely to be in a marriage, Nina develops an image of the reciprocal behavior that she expects from Derek. Derek may have the expectation that Nina will be the one in their relationship to initiate social interactions with friends and family. Derek likes the comfort and relaxation of being with family and friends. However, he is also reserved and sometimes has trouble coming up with ideas for social activities or initiating new contacts. Nina's ease with people and willingness to plan the couple's social life gives Derek enjoyment. In return, Derek appreciates Nina's social skills and supports her suggestions in a good-natured way.

Relationship Dimensions of Expectations

Expectations also have relationship dimensions. The relationship dimensions of a couple's expectations about marriage describe how the two sets of expectations fit together. Two important relationship dimensions of expectations are (1) congruence and (2) salience.

The **congruence** of a couple's expectations about marriage has to do with the extent to which individual expectations are similar or compatible (Boss, 1983). Let's go back to the example of Nina and her husband. Nina and Derek each expect a marriage partner to share in housekeeping and home maintenance activities. Nina also expects that Derek will be emotionally faithful and loyal to her, be interested in contributing to the financial well-being of the family, and provide security and stability in their relationship. Derek expects Nina to contribute warmth, good humor, acceptance, and outward displays of affection to their relationship. In both cases, their expectations are congruent and build on qualities that were missing for them in previous relationships.

There are also areas where the expectations of Nina and Derek are not congruent. Nina feels that intimacy is related to being able to talk openly and freely to the person she loves. For her, being comfortable in marriage implies the freedom and willingness of each partner to talk about feelings and negotiate areas of conflict. For Derek, intimacy is related to the feeling that one can trust another person without "having" to tell the partner everything. In this sense, Nina and Derek may have expectations for marriage and for their relationship that are not congruent with one another. The extent to which a couple's expectations are congruent may be related to their satisfaction with the relationship (Craddock, 1984).

In the course of their relationship, a couple's expectations may be modified as they create a life together. **Salience** relates to the *importance* of the congruence or incongruence of a couple's expectations. The need for Nina to "talk about feelings" and for Derek to "keep some of his thoughts and feelings to himself" may become a difference that is relatively unimportant to their happiness together. On the other hand, as time evolves, events and episodes may unfold in their conversations and activities that could heighten the importance of this difference for them.

The conflict between Nina and Derek over long-distance phone calls described in our introductory narrative is an example. Nina wants Derek to understand how important it is for her to talk with family members periodically, to check up on them, to maintain an auditory, emotional connection. Derek is not interested in the "reasons why" Nina uses the phone; he just wants Nina to understand that they "cannot afford the financial burden." Nina gets hurt and angry by

Derek's "unwillingness" to be interested in her feelings; Derek gets irritated and impatient because he believes that Nina's "lengthy discussion" about her feelings only "avoids the reality" of facing up to the issue of their phone bills. In this case, the differences in their expectations may become an important issue for them in their marriage. The extent to which particular expectations are important to a couple is synonymous with the salience of the expectation for their relationship.

Incompatible expectations often manifest themselves as typical patterns in the couple's communication. For example, in the conflict over long-distance telephone calls, Nina expects Derek to understand her behavior in terms of relational and emotional needs; Derek expects Nina to understand what he believes are the factual or rational exigencies of the situation. The difference may be a recurring

APPLICATION 5.1

WHAT ARE YOUR EXPECTATIONS FOR MARRIAGE?

- What are some expectations that you have for your marriage?
- What expectations do you have about having children and the role of children in the marriage?
- What expectations do you have for how economic responsibilities will be managed?
- Will one or both of you pursue careers?
- How will you and your spouse handle housekeeping tasks?
- What will be your relationship with family and friends?
- What role, if any, will religion play in your marriage?
- How will you deal with intimacy, emotions, and the sharing of feelings? How will you expect your spouse to react if you are angry, sad, or have your feelings hurt?
- How will you manage dependence and independence in the relationship? Will you expect to spend as much time as possible with your spouse or will you expect to spend considerable time pursuing different interests or just being alone?
- To what extent are your expectations influenced by your family of origin, the culture in which you live or grew up, the mass media, or your history of experience?
- Are there some expectations that are more important to you than others?
- What do you expect to give your marriage partner in return for what you receive? What do you think marriage should do for the partners in the relationship?

pattern for the couple, a pattern that is reflected in Nina's description of Derek's need to "take care of chores" before he gives his wife an affectionate greeting after work. The issue over a couple's entry behavior after work can become related to how the couple maintains closeness and distance in the relationship (Napier, 1988).

Whether they are congruent or incongruent, expectations are part of the "baggage" that partners bring to the marriage from their family of origin and their history of experience. The "baggage" that each partner brings influences how the couple integrates their lives together and the significant problems that emerge for them in their relationship.

CO-DEFINING REALITY

Because their backgrounds are different, the expectations that partners bring to a marriage may differ. At the same time, even before a couple is married they become more similar in their beliefs, attitudes, and values (Stephen, 1985). As Stephen has written, communication functions "as a persuasive force which shapes an emergent 'couple reality' and bonds the couple in a framework of shared knowledge" (p. 961). As a couple converses and interacts, each partner influences the other partner in a variety of ways. Through their communication, partners reinterpret their separate histories, experiences, and views of the world from within the context of living and conversing with one another. A newly married couple is continually engaged in interpreting specific behaviors, words, events, mannerisms, movements, time, distance, and objects in the formation of their relationship. Marriage requires that each partner match, to some degree, his or her views of reality.

Elizabeth and Daryl are newly married. Elizabeth tells Daryl that she would like to buy a big house. Daryl is reluctant and nervous about the idea. He tells her that a house seems like an overwhelming responsibility to him and he complains about the expense of such a venture. Elizabeth begins to shape a more modest image of a house and explores the issue again with Daryl. Daryl becomes more receptive to the idea. They talk more seriously about what they might consider buying. They pay more attention to houses and talk about what they like and do not like as they drive around town. Every day is filled with events and conversations in which marriage partners shape each other's perceptions in a similar manner. In the process of modifying or clarifying beliefs, suggesting or rejecting ideas, reinforcing or discouraging interests, both partners begin to create a common set of experiences from which to view the world—shared experiences that mold and shape their perceptions over a wide range of issues.

Berger and Kellner (1974) have used the phrase **co-defining reality** to describe how marriage partners reconstruct their perceptions, identities, and beliefs through the management of everyday activities. The impression that one has of other people, the attitudes and feelings about oneself, and the values that provide the philosophical framework for establishing goals and for evaluating oneself and others, are subtly reshaped by marriage. This reshaping is accomplished through communication.

How does a couple do this? In this section we describe how marital communication facilitates a joint reconstruction of reality in four significant ways by (1) narrowing alternatives for the marriage partners, (2) focusing movement and energy in the system, (3) altering perceptions and changing relationships with others outside the marital dyad, and (4) supporting some aspects of each person's identity at the expense of others.

Narrowing Alternatives

Commitment to the marital relationship typically narrows alternatives for both partners. **Narrowing alternatives** describes the ways in which commitment to the marital relationship limits options for the partners. Margo, for instance, might fantasize about living in New Orleans, where she would work as a waitress during the day and write poetry at night or she might have the fantasy of borrowing some money to open up a bookstore in Maine or of going to New York to study dance at a famous dance theatre. After marriage, where she lives and what she does for a living is negotiated with her husband.

When Margo makes the choice to get married, she will begin to redefine alternatives for herself within the context of her relationship with her husband. If Margo is not going to be a Southern poet, or a New York dancer, or a Maine entrepreneur, then what is she going to be? This issue normally is worked through (either satisfactorily or unsatisfactorily) in collaboration with her spouse. As the couple talks, Margo's view of her future and, therefore, of reality is modified.

If Margo and her husband decide to accept jobs teaching at a state university in the Midwest, Margo's (as well as her husband's) alternatives will have been limited. If the couple buys an old farmhouse with the intention of restoring it, her alternatives will have been narrowed further. Every choice that the couple makes narrows alternatives by eliminating options that were not chosen. As alternatives are narrowed, perceptions, identities, and belief systems are affected. The way that Margo views the world will be structured by her commitment to a specific relationship, career, and environment.

Religious affiliation is another example of how alternatives become narrowed through marriage (Berger & Kellner, 1974). Before marriage, one or more partners may experiment with various religious systems. A woman may have grown up in a Catholic family but have an interest in different forms of Eastern religion. She may have roots in Jewish culture but feel detached from any religious commitment. Or, like her parents, she may have only a casual and philosophical interest in religion. He may be from a Protestant family where religion played an important part of the family's life. Through the mutual influence of daily conversations, the two individuals will integrate their orientations to religion. Their conversations may stabilize the degree of commitment which they make to a specific religious organization; they may sever their connections to any formal religious establishment entirely; or they may settle into a pattern of quarreling about religion.

Focusing Movement

Once the available range of alternatives is narrowed, energy and movement in the relationship become more focused (Berger & Kellner, 1974). **Focusing movement in the relationship** means that the couple's interactions and activities become more predictable and goal-oriented. More attention is given to working out the specific details of their lives together, to planning agendas and making decisions that will influence their future. After their marriage, Daryl and Elizabeth spend time negotiating schedules, deciding who will do the shopping, how the cars will be serviced, and planning to spend time with family members. They talk about where they would eventually like to live, whether or not they want to buy a house or have children, and their future dreams. As their alternatives are narrowed through marriage, the couple's interests become more intense and less diffuse. Activity and energy become more focused. The couple's attitudes and orientations toward their careers, for instance, are influenced by conversations that they have with one another. Daryl and Elizabeth spend less time socializing with friends than they did before marriage and more time developing their careers and managing their household. They may save for a summer vacation in New England, a new car, a washing machine and dryer, and, eventually, a down payment on a house. As Elizabeth settles into her home with Daryl, her attitudes toward a woman's family role crystallize as she undertakes tasks in her role as "wife." She will also formulate opinions about her career that will influence how she views herself at work. At the same time, Daryl is undergoing a similar experience.

The context of the relationship alters what is important for each partner. The couple begins to establish a hierarchy of priorities as they talk and engage one another in ordinary activities. The process influences each person's identity and his or her perceptions of marriage and of the world. As energy and movement in their relationship become more focused, the identities of the partners and their views of the world stabilize. Through the couple's daily interactions, each partner begins to develop, adapt, and integrate his or her identity and world view with that of the other partner—that is, they co-define reality as they communicate with one another.

Changing Relationships with Others

Relationships and interactions with other people also change through the couple's process of co-defining reality. Perceptions of others are affected by conversations with the partner. Such conversations alter the social support system (contacts with family, friendship attachments, neighborhood associations, etc.) of the partners and consequently affect the way the couple experiences their lives. In addition, the frequency of interaction with other people changes after a couple marries.

Berger and Kellner (1974) point out that "friendships that precede a marriage rarely survive it (p. 225)." How does this happen? Margo's husband may become jealous of the closeness that she shares with an old friend, Jenny, or he may just have a negative reaction to her. When they talk about Jenny from time to time, Margo's husband may point out negative features about this friend, which Margo never noticed before. Gradually, Margo's image of her friend may change. As Margo's image of her friend changes, she may begin to act less friendly toward her. Thus, the friendship becomes less important to Margo; it may even end. Berger and Kellner have called this the process of **conversational liquidation** since it is the talk of the marriage partners that is responsible for changing the definition of the friendship. The friend outside the marriage has little control over this process. This is another example of how conversation recreates reality (in this case the perceptions of a friendship). This same process works in family, neighborhood, and work relationships as well. As Minuchin (1974) suggests:

> A marriage must replace certain social arrangements that have been given up
> for the formation of the new unit. Creation of the new social system means

the creation or strengthening of a boundary around the couple. The couple is separated from certain former contacts and activities. The investment in the marriage is made at the expense of other relationships (p. 30).

Supporting Identities

As part of the process of co-defining reality, some aspects of each partner's identity are supported at the expense of others. Each partner makes comments about the habits, mannerisms, abilities, and preferences of the other partner. These comments can be met with openness, resistance, humor, or defensiveness. Each partner can also fail to notice or attend to other characteristics of his or her spouse. In subtle day-to-day discourse, aspects of each partner's image of himself or herself are supported, discouraged, and/or altered.

Consider the example of Daryl and Elizabeth. Elizabeth has never been interested in sports. Daryl participates frequently in sports activities, keeps himself in good physical condition, and enjoys being a spectator at sports events. After they were married, Daryl offered to teach Elizabeth how to play tennis. As a way to share some fun with Daryl, Elizabeth accepted her husband's offer. She soon found out that she really enjoyed the sport and began to be more actively involved in sports activities in general. Through her relationship with her husband, Elizabeth began to change an aspect of her image of herself. She became interested in physical fitness and began to see herself as athletic.

While Daryl felt confident when involved in some sports activity, he generally considered himself a little too reserved and awkward with people. He did not find social gatherings and large parties much fun. Elizabeth sometimes wished that she knew more about what Daryl was feeling, but she did see that he was a good listener. He made eye contact with people and looked friendly when other people talked to him. After a party one Friday evening, Elizabeth told Daryl that he was a good listener, that people relaxed in the presence of his easy-going manner, and that she enjoyed being with him in the company of other people. Daryl began to change his view of himself as a loner; he began to enjoy getting together with people and came to see himself as more socially oriented than he had previously.

Through daily interactions and conversations with each other, Elizabeth and Daryl influence each other's self-perceptions in various aspects of their lives. Daryl reinforces Elizabeth's interest in her work, but does not notice how well she cooks, and he tells her that she is incompetent when it comes to mechanical problems. Elizabeth appreciates the fact that Daryl does not seem to bring his work home and is grateful that he is only moderately ambitious. She also thinks of him as steady rather than reserved, ignores the fact that he can play the piano well, and is convinced that he has no real money sense. The perceptions that they have of one another carry over into talk and daily activities. Through their conversations and actions the couple reinforces some aspects of each partner's identity and discourages others.

One significant point needs to be made. The process of supporting identities in the construction of the couple's reality is not something that is done to one spouse by another. Supporting aspects of one another's identities is a process of mutual influence. As Elizabeth finds herself more involved in sports, she is also validating Daryl's interest in sports and his image of himself as someone who can handle himself well in sports activities. Elizabeth may also be validating Daryl's participation at social activities, which also validates Elizabeth's social orientation and need for people. As we have stressed in so many ways in this book, the process is interactive, circular rather than linear.

A couple does not deliberately set out to recreate their world. Yet they do abandon certain behaviors and goals and pursue others. The choices that they make are subsequently pursued with greater conviction and more intensity. Intense commitment to certain activities—work, household maintenance, saving for the future, and so on—influences the couple's view of the world and their reality. Through conversations and shared pursuits, the couple creates a reality that they inhabit together. Their reality includes what is important to them, the evaluations they make of others, and the meanings they attach to events. Their satisfaction in the relationship may depend upon how the couple manages to coordinate their two separate constructions of reality.

NEGOTIATING A COMMUNICATION CODE

Any two individuals entering an intimate relationship bring with them a style of communicating, a set of life experiences, self-perceptions, and needs which make up the identities of the partners. Each partner brings to the relationship a preferred and typical mode of expressing affection, exerting influence, making requests, managing problems, and so on.

As they build a marriage, a couple also goes through the process of negotiating communication in their interactions with one another. The way a couple constructs their relationship depends, in part, on how they develop a mutually understood communication code. Negotiating a communication code, then, is a primary task facing the marital dyad. In this section we discuss the process of creating meaning and coordinating communication codes in marriage.

Creating Meaning

As a couple engages in daily conversations and everyday activities, they develop the meanings that will regulate their lives together (Berger & Kellner, 1974). A couple undertakes the task of **creating meaning** through talk and action. Meaning-making occurs whenever interpretations, significance, and order are attached to actions and words. Interaction provides information to the participants about what is important and unimportant, what behaviors are acceptable and unacceptable, and how they view themselves, each other, their relationship, and reality.

Each partner brings conceptions and behaviors learned in the family of origin to the marriage. These transplanted images and behaviors influence and are modified by the marital relationship. Elizabeth grew up in a large family where there was physical contact among members, flamboyant emotional displays were accepted, and spontaneity was encouraged. When she married Daryl, who grew up in a more reserved family, the couple began to reconcile the differences in meanings attached to a wide range of expressive behaviors. How will she know when he is pleased, hurt, or angry? Will he feel uncomfortable if she demonstrates her affection for him in front of other people?

In another couple, one partner may have been born into a family where a typical response to a child crying over a broken toy was, "How did that happen, sweetheart? Maybe we can find out how to fix it." If the other partner grew up in a family where the typical response to the same behavior was, "Those things happen—big boys learn not to cry," the couple is confronted with the problem of integrating two different meaning systems that each response implies. And this is an example taken from only one event! The meaning-making histories of each of the two persons who make up the marital partnership are composed of a vast array of such episodes.

In negotiating the meanings of their words and gestures, a couple must learn how to interpret a wide range of behaviors. If the family of one partner, for instance, values gift giving and the other partner's family does not, some negotiating of the meaning of the act will very likely take place. A partner who grew up in a family where gift giving was especially important may long for a sentimental gift at Christmas time—a book of poetry or an antique rocker—and feel slightly cheated when he or she receives a power saw or an electric blender. For another couple, it may be necessary to negotiate the importance of verbal expressions of affection. A woman may have a strong need to have her husband state frequently "I love you." He, on the other hand, may feel that "words are cheap" and "actions are what count." Instead of saying "I love you" he may refinish an old desk for her or plan a camping trip for the two of them.

This negotiation of meaning pervades other areas of married life as well. A newly married couple has to negotiate the meanings that they attach to particular habits and sets of behaviors. What, for instance, does a disorderly household mean to each partner? For one partner, a disorderly household may mean that life is not controlled by objects.

Consider, as another example, the meaning of being on time. If Elizabeth is consistently late, Daryl may perceive her behavior as inconsiderate and become irritable. On the other hand, Elizabeth may have difficulty understanding why being on time could possibly be so important to her husband. As a consequence, she may experience Daryl's irritability as a lack of concern for her feelings.

Numerous other examples can be given that illustrate the necessity for a couple to negotiate the meanings of certain acts. A man may interpret his wife's casual grooming habits or her need to be alone during a crisis as a lack of caring for him. In a woman's family of origin the preparation and eating of food may have been associated with feelings of affection and conviviality. If her new mate fails to be enthusiastic about a specific eating occasion she may experience disappointment or resentment. Struggling over or negotiating issues such as these is part of the process of creating a relationship. As Sillars, Burggraf, Yost, and Zietlow (1992) write, "Symbolic interactionists have long pointed out that interpersonal relationships are not so much objective entities as collective fabrications made plausible by the exchange of suitable testimony" (p. 147). In Chapter 8 we will explore more specifically how relational themes are managed through the couple's communication (Sillars, et al., 1992).

Coordinating Communication Codes

A couple's **communication code** includes a set of unspoken principles used to translate words and behavior into meaning. Through the use of a communication code, a person interprets the meanings of gestures, words, and other symbols. A communication code determines the couple's choice of language and those nonverbal behaviors that will be selected to express feelings and ideas.

A newly married couple is confronted with the task of co-defining reality.

A man and a woman may enter marriage with very different codes. Henry may have heard his mother affectionately referred to by his father as "my old lady" and be surprised to learn that his wife is insulted by his use of the term in reference to her. Two people can use the same words and yet mean two different things. A partner who says, "pass the butter, please," may be making a polite request. The spouse might employ the same phrase in order to use formality as a way to indicate displeasure at some previous transgression of his or her partner.

Groups of words may be combined in different ways so that their content is subtly different. Consider the following ways of expressing a desire to leave a social gathering:

1. "I would like to leave now."
2. "I think we should leave now."
3. "We have to get up early in the morning."
4. "Aren't you getting tired?"
5. "Aren't you about ready to go?"
6. "I'm getting tired."
7. "I'm worried about the presentation I have to give tomorrow."
8. "We have a long drive home."
9. "Could we leave pretty soon?"
10. "This party certainly is dull."

Each of these ways of expressing the same desire presents the message a little differently. As the form of the message changes, so does the specific orientation toward the other person. In some of the examples, the request is stated directly, even forcefully ("I think we should leave now"). In others, the choice of words avoids expressing the request directly ("I'm getting tired"), but it is assumed that the message will be understood. The selection of language may present the desire directly but avoid making a demand ("Could we leave pretty soon?"). Another version only hints at the desire to leave—yet the message is clear ("We have to get up early in the morning"). Some requests are even phrased in language that suggests that it is a concern for the other person that underlies the message, whether or not that is the case ("We have a long drive home").

One of the most important tasks of newly married couples is to arrive at an understanding of how to interpret each other's messages. What is worth noting is not that misunderstandings occur, but that so often couples are able to read each other accurately. The spouse who says, "I am worried about the presentation I have to give tomorrow," is confident in assuming that his or her spouse knows that the statement means, "I would like to leave now." Couples often develop an abbreviated style of talking related to their ability to translate a brief communication. They develop a code for exchanging information.

The task of **coordinating a communication code**, then, involves acquiring mutually understood interpretations of the meaning of messages. Rabkin (1967) and Tannen (1986, 1990) have both made the point that marriage partners frequently have problems coordinating communication codes because of differences in their gender, cultural background, or family of origin.

Consider this example: a husband says to his wife, "This party certainly is dull," and his wife responds with, "Yeah, it sure is." Three hours later she then says to him, "I'm tired and would like to go home now." As they leave, the wife notices that her husband is somewhat cool toward her. On the way home he is silent. Finally, she asks him what is wrong. He indicates that he is irritated because they stayed at the party so late and he wanted to go home sooner in order to be alone. His wife's response is, "Well, why didn't you say you wanted to leave?" Angrily, he replies, "I did!" And she retorts with, "You did not!"

The husband's statement, "This party certainly is dull," was intended as a request to leave, but his wife did not interpret or decode the message that way. It may be difficult for the couple to straighten out their confused exchange of messages. It is probable that the quarrel will shift from the topic of "Here's what I meant and understood you to mean," to "You are not sensitive to my needs and my feelings." This example of "uncoordinated communication," as Rabkin calls it, illustrates the problems that develop when one spouse relies on a particular code for expressing preferences and the other spouse has expectations that a different code will be used in making requests.

Another example of uncoordinated communication is the following dialogue reported by Rabkin (1967) in which a husband's failure to respond appropriately to a wife's direct request leads to conflict:

Wife: Would you like to go to the movies? (asked in earnest, information-gathering voice)

Husband: No. (Ten-minute pause)

Wife: You never take me out! Why did you refuse to take me to the movies?

Husband: But you never asked me.

Wife: I never asked! I asked you ten minutes ago. You never listen to me. You don't care about me.

Husband: (to himself) She may be right. I don't remember her asking so I guess I really don't listen to her. Maybe I don't want to hear her (p. 11).

PROBLEMS COORDINATING COMMUNICATION CODES

What problems in coordinating communication codes can you identify in the following dialogue?

Jeff: (At the breakfast table) What are you planning to do this weekend?

Rachael: I thought that I would take Patty (her daughter) out shopping on Saturday.

Jeff: What else do you have planned?

Rachael: I need to do some errands and I'd like to spend some time with Mom. I also need to do some laundry, take the dog to the vet, and I'd like to write a few letters this weekend.

Jeff: Okay, maybe I'll go to a ball game in Detroit with Steve.

Rachael: (She is silent for a moment and then speaks.) You spend more time with Steve than you do with me.

Jeff: What do you mean? You said that you were going to be busy this weekend. Would you like me to stay home?

Rachael: You don't seem very enthusiastic.

Jeff: Look, I'm the one who asked you what you were doing this weekend.

Rachael: But you didn't say that you had something in mind for *us* to do.

Jeff: (Frustrated) That's because I *didn't* have anything in mind. I was just trying to find out what your plans were.

Rachael: Oh, never mind. Go ahead and go to the ball game with Steve. (She leaves the room in disgust.)

In this example, the woman appears to be asking her husband if he would like to go to the movies. In actuality, she is making the statement, "I would like you to take me to the movies." The husband, however, responds literally to the first question because he has failed to identify the intended message. Failing to detect the husband's confusion, the wife makes a judgment about her husband— "You don't care about me."

Why do spouses have coding difficulties like this? One partner in a marriage may come from a family in which members could "read meaning" into each other's words; understanding involved reading each other's minds. Specific requests may have been perceived as aggressive acts or may even have been subtly punished. The other partner may have grown up in a family in which seeking an elaboration of what has been said would be a sign of caring (Bernstein, 1971) and requests or expressions of emotion were made directly. Coordinating a mutually understood code for such a couple would be likely to pose a problem. Yet most newly married couples learn, with surprising frequency, to recognize discrepancies between their own communication code and the codes of their mates. At the same time, they also achieve agreement about what certain messages say about the definition of their relationship.

If Elizabeth's preferred style of communicating is to send explicit, verbal messages in her interactions with Daryl, she may assume that Daryl will be direct in expressing his likes and dislikes. Consequently, she becomes confused or impatient whenever she discovers that he has not been. Daryl's preferred style of communicating is to be less verbally explicit and direct. He, therefore, perceives that he had communicated his enjoyment of a picnic they shared by fixing Elizabeth's broken hair dryer. As they become familiar with their styles of communication, several alternatives become available to them. Elizabeth and Daryl may find that they learn how to read each other more comfortably. They may also find that their differences tend to provoke conflict and turn into routine domestic dramas as each partner tries to change the other. In either case, what occurs in the process of their marriage is some shared understanding of how the behaviors and actions of the other are to be interpreted.

Our point is a simple but critically important one: creating meaning and coordinating a communication code are vital and complex processes for a newly married couple. Patterns of expressing affection, regulating closeness, and making demands or requests become clearly developed, even if the patterns result from an indirect mode of communication. The partners begin with the patterns and interpretations that they learned in their families of origin. Out of these separately developed codes, couples are confronted with the task of coordinating the meanings of the words they use and their nonverbal displays, as well as their interpretations of actions that have significance for one or both of them.

ORGANIZING THE RELATIONSHIP

The partners in any marriage have an almost infinite number of tasks and routines to work out. They must decide, for instance, how they are going to relate to their families of origin, whether or not they are going to have children, how they are going to spend their money, what leisure time activities they will engage in, what occupations they will pursue, and how they will present themselves in front of other people—to name only a few. As they work on these issues, the couple also establishes patterns that will govern how their relationship is organized (Krueger, 1985).

We have divided our discussion of the couple's task of organizing their relationship into three sections: (1) first, we explain what we mean by the concept of organization in a marriage relationship; (2) then, we examine control as a primary aspect of organizing the relationship; and (3) finally we describe competitive, complementary, and parallel relationship structures as alternative ways in which the relationship may be organized.

Organization

In nearly every social situation there are cues, some obvious, others subtle, that influence whether one person relates to another as an equal, as a subordinate, or as a superior. The cues prescribe a certain set of appropriate behaviors. We have no difficulty understanding that birds, insects, or other species behave in an organized and structured manner. Yet, the complexity and diversity of human activity and social arrangements make it difficult for us to see that human behavior is also organized or structured.

In his book, *Problem-Solving Therapy* (1976), Haley writes, "If there is any generalization that applies to men and other animals, it is that all creatures capable of learning are compelled to organize" (pp. 100–101). **Organization** can be defined as a description of the functions or role relationships that exist among interdependent parts. The organization of a system describes the structure of that system. How a couple has organized their relationship is revealed in their communication. In Chapter 10, we discuss the relationship of communication to family roles (Haley, 1976).

The concept of social organization can be easily understood in a nuclear family with children. Parents, who have responsibility for nurturing, teaching, and socializing their children, may be democratic in their orientation toward their children, but they are not peers with their children.

To suggest that families have structures and are, therefore, organized does not mean that parents do not include children in decision making, seek their children's opinions and perceptions, or integrate the children's preferences into the family. It does describe the fact that in social systems there is a structure that indicates how members of that system relate to each other as equals, subordinates, or superiors.

Marriage also involves a process of organization. In part, organization in the marriage relationship is related to the extent to which each partner functions as an equal, subordinate, or superior in various aspects of their relationship. Many couples do not accept a definition of the relationship in which one person, in general, has more status and power than the other (although that may be the case in some marriages). Organizing the marital relationship answers such questions as: How are the priorities and decisions of the couple achieved? What constraints do the couple agree to accept for themselves in their relationship with their partner? How has the couple managed issues related to individuality and dependence (or interdependence)? What are the limitations and boundaries of the relationship? That is, what is each partner allowed or not allowed to say and do as a partner in the marriage?

Control Patterns

The process of organizing the marital relationship describes to a significant degree a couple's maneuvers to control various aspects of their relationship (Haley, 1976). Control of the relationship is related to communication patterns that establish the distribution of authority in the relationship or in various aspects of the relationship (Lederer & Jackson, 1968; Millar & Rogers, 1976; Rogers & Farace, 1975). Simply stated, **control** refers to how each partner functions as an equal, subordinate, or superior in various dimensions of a couple's life together.

A newly married couple develops shared agreements dealing with numerous areas of their relationship (frequently without the agreements being discussed). For example, how does the couple handle who will do the cooking? Does the wife do most of the cooking? Does the husband? Do they cook together, or do they eat out most of the time? How is this decision made? Does one partner make a demand or request of another ("I don't cook") and the other accommodates (happily or resentfully)? How do decisions develop about who is to be the budget planner in the marriage? What social involvements, if any, will the couple establish? Will they go to social events together or will one spouse typically participate alone?

How each of these activities is managed reveals something about how the couple has defined authority in their relationship—that is, how the couple has organized their relationship. Organization is accomplished through the couple's communication. Elizabeth, for example, may exert control over the social activities of the couple. Suppose that she is interested in going to a movie that has come to the suburban theatre near where she and Daryl live. She calls up another couple and invites them to go to dinner at a nearby Mexican restaurant and suggests that they all go to the movie afterward. The couple accepts the invitation and Elizabeth tells Daryl when he gets home from a trip to the library that she has made arrangements to go to dinner and a movie with the Sharps on Saturday night. Daryl indicates that he is pleased and asks what time they will be leaving. Elizabeth initiates and Daryl accepts (rather than refuses or suggests that they do something else). Through their conversation, Elizabeth and Daryl have coordinated their agendas. They have also established that Elizabeth is "in charge" of planning the social activities of the couple—that is, she has control of this aspect of their relationship.

One spouse may have primary influence over certain aspects of the relationship and the other spouse may have primary influence over other aspects of the relationship. A couple can also compete for control in areas of their relationship. Elizabeth has primary control over the couple's social activities. Daryl has primary control over the research that goes into the purchase of a new appliance. He might, for instance, return home from the library on a Saturday afternoon and indicate to Elizabeth that he has read an article in a consumer magazine and decided which vacuum cleaner they should purchase. Elizabeth says, "Great!" She tells Daryl to go ahead and purchase the one that he thinks is best—and then she tells him about her plans for Saturday night. Another couple might negotiate almost every issue, including which vacuum cleaner to buy and what to do on Saturday night. Still another couple might argue repeatedly over whose influence will prevail in almost every situation. In any case, couples will develop patterns of communication for managing these issues that reveal the nature of the control in various aspects of their relationship.

Organizing the relationship is achieved through the establishment of generally unspoken rules that indicate who has control over various aspects of the relationship. The couple develops patterns for who is to control what is to take place in what areas of the relationship and thereby control the definition of their relationship in those areas (Haley, 1963). In Chapter 7 we will discuss at length the concept of rules as governing mechanisms in marital and family communication.

In addition to establishing rules, a couple also reaches agreements regarding who is to define the rules in each area of their marriage. In Chapter 2 we discussed the concept of metacommunication as a description of a couple's communication about their communication. Similarly, conscious or unconscious agreements that identify who has the right to establish certain rules are called **metarules**.

Suppose that Elizabeth has become concerned about how busy she and Daryl are pursuing their careers. She is interested in creating more time for them to be together. She might announce to Daryl, "I want us to agree to take Sunday afternoon off to be together." Daryl agrees. Not only is Daryl agreeing to make it a "rule" to take Sunday afternoon off to be together, but he is supporting a rule that suggests that it is acceptable for Elizabeth to propose a rule that they structure their time in a specific way. The rule suggesting that it is okay for Elizabeth to propose a rule concerning the couple's time allocation is a metarule. Daryl might have argued with Elizabeth; he might even have resisted her suggestion and indicated that it was impossible for him at this time to take Sunday afternoon off. He would not only be disagreeing with her suggestion, he would be challenging Elizabeth's "right" to make such a rule for the couple.

Negotiations over rules are accomplished through the couple's communication. In their conversations and interactions with each other, marital partners define the nature of control in their relationship. As Krueger (1985, p. 128) writes, "It is within the stream of communication that one discerns the obvious maneuvers and subtle nuances of control." Imagine a wife at a dinner table neutrally asking her husband to get her a napkin. Each of the following alternative responses reveals a different orientation toward the structure of the relationship:

"Honey, I'm just too tired to get up."

"Sure, I'll be glad to."

"Okay, that's fair since you made the dinner."

"You are closer to the kitchen than I am—get it yourself."

In Chapter 2 we discussed the difference between the content and relationship dimensions of a message (Watzlawick, Beavin, & Jackson, 1967). The relationship dimension of messages suggests how control in particular situations or in an aspect of the couple's relationship will be managed. Relationship dimensions of messages are usually governed by metarules—rules that indicate who has the right to establish particular rules and patterns for the couple. Metarules often reflect how a couple has managed control in their relationship.

In a program of research developed by Rogers and her colleagues (Millar & Rogers, 1976; Rogers, 1972; Rogers, 1983; Rogers, Courtwright, & Millar, 1980; Rogers & Farace, 1975), **control patterns** are described not as something which one person does to another but as descriptions of the nature of the relationship; that is, control is seen as a reciprocal process reflected in the communication transactions of the couple. How a couple manages control in their relationship is a function of how each partner responds to the other and the extent to which their relational patterns are rigid or flexible.

For example, in our opening story, Nina agrees to Derek's proposal for budgeting their long-distance telephone calls. In accepting his proposal, Nina has accepted Derek's right to control this aspect of their relationship. To the extent that their communication patterns are characterized by assertive moves on Derek's part, which are accepted by Nina, one might describe their relationship as complementary. We know, however, that this complementarity was not achieved without an earlier round of arguments and conflicts, episodes in which Derek's control moves were not accepted. These earlier conflict episodes were characterized by competitive patterns in which Derek's efforts at control were matched by similar moves from Nina. In this sense, one might describe the overall control patterns in their relationship as flexible rather than rigid.

Based on ideas developed by the Palo Alto Group of family therapists, the work of Rogers and her colleagues has provided empirical research that supports descriptions of how couples often organize their relationships (see also Rogers & Bagarozzi, 1983; Watzlawick, Beavin, & Jackson, 1967). Three types of relational organization are competitive, complementary, and parallel (see Figure 5.1).

Competitive, Complementary, and Parallel Relationships

How a couple has managed control over various aspects of their marriage describes its structure or organization. We use the terms *competitive, complementary,* and *parallel* to identify three alternative ways in which a relationship may be organized.

Competitive relationships are ones in which the partners continually struggle or compete for control of the relationship (Lederer & Jackson, 1968; Millar &

FIGURE   5.1   Competitive, complementary, and parallel relationships.

Connie and Stuart Have a Competitive Relationship

They frequently argue over whose views are to prevail in a situation. Connie, for instance, would like to remodel the bathroom and Stuart would like to buy a new car. They often try to "balance the scales" in their relationship. If Stuart has to work one weekend, then Connie will tell Stuart that she plans to work the next weekend so that it does not appear that Stuart's work is more important than her work. If Connie insists that they go out to dinner at O'Brien's (which Stuart does not like very much), then Stuart will insist the next time that they go to the Chinese Palace (which Connie does not like very much). Both take care not to let the other person get his or her way more often than the other. Equity is an important issue for them.

Robert and Carrie Have a Complementary Relationship

Carrie enjoys taking care of the children and running the household. Robert, however, makes most of the major decisions for the family. He decides where they will live, what they will do on weekends, and when the children will go to bed. He also makes most of the financial decisions and decides whether or not the family will visit friends and relatives on holidays. Carrie reinforces this arrangement by making it clear to the children that Robert has the final word about almost everything. Most of her decisions take into account Robert's response. If he does not want her to do something, she usually will not do it.

Elizabeth and Daryl Have a Parallel Relationship

Elizabeth balances the checkbook, but Daryl does the income tax. Daryl accepts Elizabeth's suggestions for social activities and Elizabeth accepts Daryl's advice about the purchase of new appliances. Elizabeth does most of the cooking. Daryl maintains the cars. Each partner is somewhat independent, but sometimes lets the other person make decisions for both of them. Elizabeth will visit her family when she wants to do so, knowing that Daryl will not object; Daryl makes an effort to keep in touch with his mother. Elizabeth encourages him to do what he feels he needs to do. They have separate agendas, but they can also do things together without feeling competitive.

Rogers, 1976; Rogers & Farace, 1975). It is possible for a couple to carry on a lengthy dialogue in a struggle over who has the right to define the relationship in particular situations. Imagine a situation in which a husband and wife argue for most of their married life over how to acknowledge each other's birthday. Every year the wife indicates that she would like a nice gift, flowers, and a card for her birthday. Every year the husband forgets his wife's birthday and tells her, when she reminds him that he forgot, to go out and buy something for herself and he will pay for it. She always refuses to buy a gift for herself and does not speak to her husband for several days. For decades the couple repeats this episode. The wife asserts her need to receive a gift acknowledging her birthday. The husband "forgets" his wife's birthday and then offers his own suggestion, thereby asserting his right to refuse to comply with his wife's request and, hence, to control the situation. In response to his refusal to perform the ritual as she prescribes, the wife punishes her husband by giving him the "silent treatment."

This couple is struggling over who is to define the relationship and, by defining it, control an aspect of their relationship. The wife attempts to influence her husband to behave in a specific way. He, in turn, refuses to comply. Neither one is willing to acknowledge the other's needs or to "give in." Each partner interprets the situation differently. After all, the husband did suggest that his wife should go out and buy herself a gift, even after she nagged him about his failure to remember her birthday; he does not deserve her "silent treatment." She, in turn, could say that he was insensitive to her feelings and provoked her behavior. Each partner *punctuates* this situation differently depending upon his or her point of view. The point is that both the act of his suggesting that the wife buy her own gift and the act of her refusing to speak to the husband are competitive acts aimed at winning the struggle over who has the right to set up the rules of the gift-giving ritual. The struggle for control becomes a kind of game that they play together.

In **complementary relationships** one partner does "give in" or relinquish control of the relationship, at least in certain significant areas (Lederer & Jackson, 1968; Millar & Rogers, 1976; Rogers & Farace, 1975). Complementary relationships exist when one partner continually submits to the directives offered by the other partner. By doing this, the one accepts the other's right to control the definition of the relationship. A wife who agrees to help out with the bookkeeping duties associated with her husband's business, in spite of the fact that she isn't happy doing the work, has allowed her husband control over this aspect of their relationship. When one partner, more frequently than not, acquiesces to the other person's plans, decisions, requests, or demands in most areas of their relationship, the relationship can be viewed as complementary. One difficulty with this type of relationship may be that one partner may lose his or her own sense of self by always relinquishing control of the relationship to the other person.

A couple that has agreed to allow one partner control of certain areas of the relationship and to allow the other partner control of other, equally important, areas of the relationship can be described as having a **parallel relationship** (Lederer & Jackson, 1968). For instance, a man may be willing to offer sympathy to his sick spouse provided she agrees to praise his career achievements. Another couple might decide to alternate years when each partner is responsible for paying bills, balancing the checkbook, and monitoring the budget so that both partners share in the control of the family finances. Lederer and Jackson (1968) make the point that, in the parallel relationship, a couple can shift between complementary and competitive patterns, depending upon what is most appropriate or most adaptive to the unique preferences and abilities of each partner.

Keep in mind that the process of organizing a relationship is subtle and complex. The rules that define the nature of control for the partners in the relationship are usually tacit and somewhat covert. They are often out of the conscious awareness of the partners. Neither the husband nor the wife in the gift-giving example may be aware that they are engaged in a struggle over how the relationship will be defined—they each feel "wronged."

Organizing the relationship is achieved, then, through rules and roles that specify both the structure of the relationship and the nature of control in the relationship. Rules that specify what each partner can and cannot do or say or that specify each partner's privileges and obligations also describe patterns of organization in the relationship.

MANAGING DIFFERENTIATION AND INTEGRATION IN THE MARRIAGE

In addition to the tasks of negotiating two sets of expectations, co-defining reality, coordinating a communication code, and organizing the relationship, a couple is also confronted with the need to manage differentiation and integration in their relationship. We introduced the concepts of differentiation and integration in Chapter 1 in our discussion of dialectical processes. Each partner in a marriage is differentiated from the other by unique needs, abilities, and preferences that require attention. The marriage relationship itself also has special needs that require attention. Sometimes meeting the needs of the relationship and meeting the needs of the individual can create competitive or contradictory demands for the couple.

Beth and Rob met when Beth was completing an internship in the University Counseling Center where Rob worked. They became good friends initially because they shared a common philosophy in their work. They appreciated the warmth and sense of playfulness that they each brought to their relationships with other people. In addition, both of them were going through painful divorces and they were drawn closer together as they began to share their feelings with one another.

After a long friendship and an intense romantic involvement, they lived together for a while. The arrangement worked out so well that a year-and-a-half later they decided to get married. Both of them felt that the other person made them happier than they had ever been before. Beth, for instance, felt that Rob brought out the best in her and appreciated aspects of her character and personality that she had suppressed because they had made her first husband uncomfortable. Rob was surprised and inwardly delighted by how sensitive Beth was to his feelings and how she discovered things about him that he thought no one would ever know.

As they began to settle into a life together, Rob began to focus his energies at work on some goals for himself. Now that he had begun to resolve some of his personal problems, other aspects of his life began to take on direction. He found himself committed to a research project that he had been considering for several years. He experienced a new burst of creativity. Beth also began to work on some goals for herself. She was completing her doctorate and instead of just "hanging in there" as she had done for the last two years, she really was making progress toward finishing. As she approached completion of her degree, she applied for a position that she really wanted. When she was offered the position, she was elated.

Their relationship was a motivating force in Beth's and Rob's life. Each partner was able to take pride in the other's achievements as well. As they pursued their goals, however, they began to discover that they had less and less time for each other. This did not happen all at once; the problem seemed to sneak up on them. Beth was also going through changes as she began to experience success. Sometimes she wanted to share this with Rob, but when they had some time together they used it to relax and have fun together. They seldom discussed serious issues. Furthermore, Rob's involvement in his work became so intense that he began working at night and on weekends; his long hours, in turn, gave Beth time alone to study.

The issue of making time for the relationship, however, seemed to get worse, not better. As a consequence, Beth and Rob found themselves barking at each other over little things. A bickering episode sometimes led to a more serious quarrel. Finally, knowing that summer was coming and that they would have some time together on their vacation, they decided to reassess their situation. During the three weeks while they were on their vacation they had a chance to get away from their work, to talk to each other about the changes they were going through, and to work out some plans for establishing priorities in their lives. There were difficult episodes the following year, but, overall, the couple felt that they were managing their lives much more comfortably.

The problem that evolved after Beth and Rob got married reflects one of the tasks that confronts a newly married couple and continues to be an issue in most marriages. The relationship had a positive effect on the identity of each spouse. Each partner's sense of self seemed to be confirmed and validated through the marriage. This new sense of validation gave both of their lives energy, creativity, and direction. Paradoxically, as Rob and Beth began to grow and change because of what the marriage had done for them, they began to pursue their own interests with more intensity. As a consequence, they found themselves wanting to pause and assess the needs of the relationship before they drifted too far from one another. The demand to attend simultaneously to personal needs, to family members, and to the relationship as a unit is an ongoing activity in marriage.

Beth and Rob were involved in the process of managing differentiation and integration in their relationship: differentiation in that each individual is developing a strong sense of identity through the relationship; integration in that the couple is faced with the task of integrating their separate identities into one relationship.

It is important to remember that negotiating differentiation and integration in the marriage relationship is achieved through and reflected in the couple's communication. Sillars and his colleagues (Sillars, Weisberg, Burggraf, & Wilson, 1987; Sillars, Burggraf, Yost, & Zietlow, 1992) have explored how the content of a couple's *conversational themes* can reveal how the couple has managed differentiation and integration in the relationship. For example, the conversation of couples who are more oriented toward integration tends to focus on communal themes, exhibits more "we" terms, and uses language suggestive of "cooperation" and "togetherness." On the other hand, the conversation of couples who are more differentiated tends to reflect themes related to personality differences, to aspects of "separateness" in the couple's relationship, and to individual role performance. In Chapter 9, we explore the topic of family themes in more detail. The point that we wish to make here is that how a couple negotiates differentiation and integration in their relationship can be revealed in conversations about their relationship.

In our opening story, for example, Nina describes her relationship with her husband as one in which her more expressive, affectionate, and affiliative personality can be differentiated from her husband's more reserved and taciturn personality. How Nina talks about her relationship suggests a particular focus in her relationship with her husband. Were Nina to discuss the couple's common religious beliefs or describe their mutual goals, she would focus more on the communal aspects of the differentiation/integration dialectic. Furthermore, Nina suggests that as differences in each spouse's personality needs and preferences achieve some degree of resolution, there is a greater tendency to experience integration in the relationship. Her final comments are "We're getting there . . . we're making progress." While indicating that issues of differentiation are significant in their relationship, Nina's account also illustrates the dynamic relationship between differentiation and integration.

THE IDENTITY–RELATIONSHIP DIALECTIC

In the process of building the marriage relationship, a couple is confronted with the need to simultaneously validate the individual identities of the partners and the integrity of the relationship. Validation of individual identities is related to differentiation in the marriage; validation of the integrity of the relationship is related to integration in the marriage. The **identity–relationship dialectic** refers to the simultaneous need for a couple to maintain personal identities and to maintain the integrity of the relationship. The assumption that couples pursue both a sense of identity and a sense of relationship integrity is a hypothesis explored and supported in the work of Askham (1976, 1984).

Failure to achieve both differentiation and integration in the relationship can lead to disruption or termination of the relationship. There is, however, a dialectical tension between the need for partners to pursue the development of their personal identities and the need to maintain the integrity of the relationship. The pursuit of individual identities and of the integrity of the relationship depend upon each other for their satisfaction; at the same time, fulfillment of one has the potential to undermine the other. Askham's (1976, 1984) term for the dialectical process between differentiation and integration in the marriage relationship is "the identity–stability didactic."

According to Askham (1976, 1984), individuals are attracted to stable relationships because of the opportunity to develop a sense of personal identity through conversations with a significant other. At the same time, the integrity of the relationship may be threatened by activities related to the pursuit of personal identities. Askham illustrates the potential for contradiction and paradox as couples negotiate differentiation and integration in their relationship.

Symbolic interactionists argue that individual identity can be created only as the individual interacts with others. It is through interactions with others that one learns not only the various social roles (wife, mother, husband, father, teacher, doctor) that make up identity but also how one perceives himself or herself as a unique human being. In developing the confidence that a person is who she thinks she is, one needs to interact with intimate others with whom one can discuss such things as fantasies, goals, needs, perceptions, ideas, values, complex feelings, important past experiences, and personal conflicts (Berger & Luckman, 1966). As Elizabeth and Daryl or Beth and Rob share complex feelings with each other, they each discover some things about themselves. Their discoveries, made through interactions with each other, help them to gain a clearer sense of their own identities.

Along with the confirmation acquired in conversations with a significant other, however, contacts outside the relationship are necessary in order to confirm one's perceptions of his or her partner and to give one something to converse about with the significant other. In addition, periods of privacy are required to enable one to reflect on the other's interpretation of reality and to integrate potentially conflicting information about the self. With reflection and privacy also come the potential for change, the impetus to seek new experiences, and the clarification of individual goals.

On the other hand, the conditions necessary for the development of identity are likely to be perceived as undermining the couple's stability. Conversation that highlights the uniqueness of the individual's needs, values, desires, and perceptions of reality may also underscore differences that are perceived as fragmenting the relationship. In the pursuit of stability, contact with others who may offer support for a sense of identity that is incompatible with that of the significant other or who may interfere with the integrity of the relationship are discouraged. As Askham (1976) argues:

> Thus, on the one hand, identity-maintenance requires open and wide-ranging conversation, a certain amount of privacy or independence, the possibility of new experiences and the development for each individual of a minimum of restricting objectification roles, and the chance for intimate interaction with other persons. On the other hand, stability-maintenance requires the inhibition of all these factors (pp. 538–539).

TABLE 5.2   Five tasks in building the marriage relationship.

	EXAMPLE
1. Integrating expectations	How will Nina and Derek integrate their different expectations about the management of the household budget?
2. Co-defining reality	Through conversations with her husband, Evan, Margo gradually changes her perceptions of her friend, Jenny. Likewise, Evan finds that he is more critical of his friend, Bobby, as a consequence of conversations with Margo about Bobby.
3. Negotiating a communication code	Stan gets frustrated with Liz because she does not make requests directly; Liz gets upset because she thinks that Stan is not sensitive to cues that she sends.
4. Organizing the relationship	Elizabeth functions as the leader in some areas and Daryl functions as the leader in other areas of their marriage.
5. Managing differentiation and integration	Now that their relationship is going so well, Stan and Liz are thinking of taking some risks with their careers, knowing that such risks will require them to focus more time and energy on their work.

Strategies for Managing
the Identity–Relationship Dialectic

In her interviews with couples, Askham (1976, 1984) confirmed her hypothesis that both identity and relationship integrity are sought in intimate relationships. In exploring how couples manage the contradictory nature of the two activities, Askham identified some of the alternative strategies that couples develop for coping.

Each of the strategies identified in Askham's work may be viewed as an attempt by the couple to manage paradoxical or contradictory needs. One option is for the couple to attempt a **compromise** in the pursuit of the two activities in which a "certain amount of stability is attained while at the same time each partner is allowed a certain amount of independence, etc., so that their sense of identity is not totally crushed" (1976, p. 545).

APPLICATION 5.3

MANAGING THE IDENTITY–
RELATIONSHIP DIALECTIC

How does the following situation illustrate the identity–relationship dialectic?

Margo and Evan were married while they were in graduate school. Margo completed her degree a year ahead of Evan and accepted a teaching position at a state university in New York. Margo worked hard establishing her career while Evan finished his dissertation. She gained confidence as a teacher and managed to get two research articles published.

After completing his degree, Evan accepted a temporary position in the area. At the end of the second year, however, Evan told Margo that he was depressed about his job. They both decided that Evan should search next year for a new position that was more satisfying for him. Although Margo was very happy where she was, she knew it was important for her marriage that Evan be moderately happy in his career.

Evan found a teaching position at a university in the Midwest. The teaching assignment was not quite what he had hoped for, but he really liked the people in the department and thought he could adjust. The situation was much better than what he had in New York and there were opportunities for Margo. Margo was hired to teach full-time as a temporary faculty member, with the possibility that she could apply for a permanent position should one become available. The couple seemed pleased with the arrangement and they made plans to move.

Would you say that Margo and Evan have managed the identity–relationship dialectic by using compromise, by alternating one need over the other, or by focusing energy at one end of the polarity at the expense of the other?

A second strategy is for the couple to **alternate** in stressing one need over the other. A couple may go through a phase where the integrity of the relationship is stressed and mutual exploration of identity remains relatively repressed. After some time there may be a push to risk the integrity of the relationship in order to achieve a greater sense of personal identity in the system.

Another option may be for both partners to **focus energy** at one end of the polarity at the expense of the other. A couple may subvert their personal identities in pursuit of the maintenance of the relationship or retain their independence and freedom to explore new experiences, risking the permanence of the relationship.

In the process of negotiating a solution to the identity–relationship dialectic, the couple will find themselves caught in a complex set of rules, all of which are compelling and operating at various levels in the system. At the same time that the couple navigates the identity–relationship dialectic, they also negotiate meaning and control in their relationship.

SUMMARY

This chapter discusses five tasks involved in the process of building the marriage relationship: (1) integrating two sets of expectations into one relationship, (2) co-defining reality in the construction of the marriage relationship, (3) negotiating a communication code, (4) organizing the relationship, and (5) managing differentiation and integration in the relationship.

Every individual brings a set of expectations to marriage that gets integrated to some extent (comfortably or uncomfortably) into the relationship through the couple's communication. Interests, goals, friendships, interpretations of behaviors, and other aspects of each partner's life are changed through conversation with one's spouse. In acquiring some understanding of what is meant by each partner's messages, the couple creates meaning in their relationship. Each couple is confronted with having to coordinate their communication codes as they negotiate meaning in the relationship. Through their conversations with each other, partners organize their relationship, assigning duties, rights, and privileges to each partner and developing the patterns that characterize their interaction.

A central concern of this chapter is the communication processes through which the couple manages the issue of differentiation and integration in the system—the fact that there exist two individuals and one relationship to be cared for and that sometimes these components in the system are in competition. It is these processes that establish the foundation for the nuclear family.

KEY TERMS

alternate

co-defining reality

communication code

competitive relationships

complementary relationships

compromise

congruence

control

control patterns

conversational liquidation

coordinating a communications
   code

creating meaning

expectations

focus energy

focusing movement in the
   relationship

identity–relationship dialectic

marriage contract

metarules

narrowing alternatives

organization

parallel relationships

salience

UNIT THREE

PATTERNS AND PROCESS

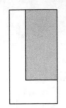

C H A P T E R 6

EXPANDING COMPLEXITY

PEGGY BRISBANE

THE JASINSKI FAMILY

Maggie and Roger Jasinski had been married for nearly eight years. During that time they had managed to fulfill a number of their personal and shared dreams: satisfying careers, a lovely home, an exciting sex life, and visibility as concerned members of their community. Eleven months ago they achieved their final dream: a family of their own. Their daughter, Alissa Marie, was the finishing touch that should have made their lives perfect.

Strangely enough, life in the Jasinski home was not the picture-perfect domestic scene the Jasinskis had anticipated. From everything they had read, they expected parenting to be the ultimate sublime experience, the experience that makes family life complete. For them the picture was very different. Instead of a sweet, smiling, contented baby, Alissa was colicky and difficult to please. Lacking sleep, Roger became short with Maggie, blaming her for her inability to handle the baby. He continued to work long hours in his job, expecting Maggie to take time from her own work schedule to arrange for sitters and to care for Alissa herself. When confronted with the inequity, Roger insisted that the long hours were forced upon him by his employers; he had no choice but to comply. For her part, Maggie resented Roger's implication that parenting was strictly a mother's job and that her career was more easily sidetracked than his. Furthermore, she worried about Roger's apparent lack of involvement with their daughter. The verbal battles were frequent and loud. The exciting sex life diminished to nothing. In a frighteningly short time, Maggie and Roger were discussing divorce.

Maggie sought help from her best friend, Terea, as she had done frequently when the two of them were college roommates. Terea assured Maggie that her demands were not unreasonable and openly sided with her friend. She suggested that Maggie and Roger seek counseling without delay.

Roger confided in his friend and next door neighbor, Fred. He knew that Fred rarely had time for domestic responsibilities, and yet, his marriage seemed to be running smoothly. Fred assured Roger that Maggie merely was suffering from postpartum blues and would soon return to normal. He recommended that Roger buy a dozen roses and try to patch things up.

The roses didn't work. In fact, the problems between Roger and Maggie quickly escalated as the pressures at home collided with the pressures at work. Thinking about Terea's advice, Maggie suggested counseling. Roger agreed, reluctantly. Neither really wanted a divorce, but it began to look as if there were no acceptable alternatives. Neither wanted to face what seemed like never-ending conflicts for the sake of preserving the marriage.

Following their first counseling session, the therapist made a surprising request. He asked both Maggie and Roger to bring their respective parents, and if possible, siblings to an upcoming session! The therapist's explanation was simple: both had learned parenting from the only role models they knew—their own parents. Consequently, discussing their childhood experiences with those role models could provide some insights into their own parenting difficulties. The therapist thought that, at the very least, they might identify choices that they had made strictly on past experience and, in so doing, identify other alternatives that might work better for them.

Maggie had a difficult time convincing her mother, father, and brother to make the long trip from Cleveland, Ohio. Roger had similar difficulty persuading his parents to make the trip from just across town. His sister agreed to visit from St. Louis for a few days, but his brother flatly refused to participate. After considerable negotiation, a time was finally established for the first group meeting, without Roger's brother.

Two additional meetings followed the first; Maggie and Roger learned a great deal about their attitudes toward parenting and the skills that they had acquired. Most importantly, they learned that their past experiences had been very different, a fact that contributed to their inability to select strategies for their own parental roles.

In Maggie's family, the children had always been the center of attention. Both of her parents still thought of themselves as "Mom" and "Dad," even though all of their children had families of their own. Their lover–spouse relationship clearly had taken an inferior role to the parent–child relationships in the family. Maggie's insistence that Roger become much more involved with Alissa and her sudden lack of interest in intimacy with her husband apart from their child was somehow related to the attitude that children should come first.

In Roger's family of origin, children were seen by both parents as a husband's concession to his wife for the fact that he must work long hours outside of the home. Roger's parents had decided to have Roger and both of his siblings so that his mother would have help around the house and someone to be with when her husband was at work. It never occurred to Roger's father that he could take an active role in the parenting process, nor did he want such a role; he assumed that he had become a father in the first place merely to please his wife and his own parents, who felt that having children was a necessary part of being married. There remained a clear understanding that he, the husband, was to be his wife's first priority. The children were there to be companions for her when he was not available.

Having identified the differences in the models they were using, Maggie and Roger gradually realized that they had limited their parenting options. The therapist helped them consider other options and, after nearly a year of hard work, they began working out new patterns of relating to each other and to Alissa that were more acceptable for all of them. Having taken a hard look at their families of origin, they learned ways to avoid the problems that had plagued their relationship with their daughter and with each other.

UNDERSTANDING THE JASINSKIS

Roger and Maggie's experience is not unique. As we discussed in Chapter 5, both partners in the marital relationship bring certain past experiences, expectations, attitudes, and skills learned in their families of origin. This "baggage" influences how the two partners merge to create their unique dyadic relationship.

In Maggie and Roger's case, expectations about the marital relationship apparently had meshed very well with minimal negotiation. In both Maggie's and Roger's families, both parents had worked full-time prior to the birth of their first child. Similarly, both Maggie and Roger pursued careers while taking time off for the things they both enjoy: travel, community service, and time together.

The influences from one's family of origin, however, are not limited to the marital relationship. Lessons learned as a child continue to influence attitudes throughout the life cycle. Parenting, coping with the departure of children, mourning the loss of a spouse, as well as other life events are subject to influence from childhood experience.

Of course, experiences with one's family of origin continue until death. Even when children live many thousands of miles away, telephones and public transit make it relatively easy for them to keep in touch with their extended family networks. In fact, taking a closer look at Maggie and Roger's daily life reveals that Roger calls his mother every Saturday morning, without fail, and that Maggie's parents arrive for short visits at every major holiday. This contact with their parents invariably influences their day-to-day decision making.

It is also important to note the role that Terea and Fred played in this example. People frequently seek opinions and help from their friends, even when they recognize that what works in one family may not work in another. Terea's advice to seek counseling was helpful to Maggie; Fred's suggestion that Roger buy flowers was not.

Other people outside of the Jasinski family also had an impact on communication between Roger and Maggie. Was work just an excuse for Roger, or was his employer badgering him into working those long hours? Were sitters difficult to locate, or was Maggie using the problem of finding a dependable sitter as a way to initiate conversation about the child-care problem?

In Chapter 3, we discussed the notion that every family functions simultaneously as a system in its own right and as a component of a larger suprasystem. For the Jasinskis, this statement means that they function in a three-person nuclear system but that they also function in a neighborhood system (which includes Fred), a social system (which includes Terea), a work system (which includes supervisors and co-workers), and even larger suprasystems. In this chapter, we take a closer look at the influences that people can exert on that system as a whole. We define the term *ecosystem* and explain what it means to examine the family from an ecological perspective. Next, we examine some of the subsystems that can be identified within the nuclear system: the individual subsystems, dyadic subsystems (i.e., the marital dyad, parent–child dyads, and sibling dyads.) We examine the components in the suprasystem: extended family networks, the social support system, and the larger environment. Finally, we discuss the role of communication in the management of system growth and change by focusing on interfaces between the nuclear system and other systems.

INTRODUCTION TO THE ECOSYSTEM APPROACH

In his article on the relationship between family members and family systems, Weeks (1986) introduced a model of family therapy that incorporates a focus on the individual and on the family system. He noted that many family problems may arise from individual or intrapersonal phenomena such as mental illness, chemical imbalance, and chronic illness. On the other hand, as we have argued earlier in this text, an approach that focuses only on the individual misses the degree to which behaviors emerge from and support the functioning of the family as a whole. Weeks's solution calls for a theoretical perspective capable of integrating the individual and systems perspectives, which allows family researchers and therapists to retain the best thinking of both fields. This metatheory should guide us "in transcending the alienating dichotomies of subject and object, individual and system, system and system" (p. 6).

Massey (1986) offered a similar argument in favor of integrating individual, systemic, and contextual variables:

> While various definitions of the family system presuppose that systems are composed of persons, we need to make explicit the social psychological processes that have until now remained largely implicit. A holistic systems theory must integrate both the "inside" and "outside"—the psychological/experiential and the sociological/observational—views of families. In families, personalities interact with social systems reciprocally. An integrative view of family systems neither reduces social structural influences to personal dispositions, nor overlooks social psychological processes in focusing exclusively on context. The what is a who (p. 24).

A family cannot avoid influences from its environment: inputs from work and school, information received from the media, conversations with friends, life cycle changes, fires, floods, and so on. Recognizing how those influences mesh with family communication increases understanding of family functioning. It is especially important to acknowledge the influence of the larger culture on family functioning. Many of the problems faced by homeless families, nontraditional families, and ethnically diverse families are tied to social and political ideologies in the larger cultural system. Furthermore, it would be naive to claim that family patterns always override individual differences. Family communication does not produce individual characteristics such as diabetes, cerebral palsy, epilepsy, high or low intelligence, and other biological and/or genetic variables (although family responses to those conditions certainly influence how they are managed in the family system). Rather than ignore the influence of these circumstances, it is desirable to examine the ways in which different family systems manage them.

A family ecosystem approach examines all influences that affect and are affected by the family system in some way. The term **ecosystem** refers to a depiction of all conceivable interrelated systems, from the small subsystem to the larger macrosystem.

A family ecosystem perspective allows you to view the family holistically, simultaneously considering influences from family members on each other, influences from the family on the suprasystem, and influences from various components of that suprasystem on the family. Just as a systems perspective focuses on the interdependence among family members, an ecosystem perspective highlights the interdependence of individual family systems within their environment. "To the psychologist examining personal experiencing, the elephant looks different than to the sociologist analyzing social-influence processes, but the holistic systems theorist comprehends how these valuable, but different, perspectives conjoin in living social-experience" (Massey, 1986, p. 27).

To use the ecosystem model to examine the Jasinski family, consider the relationships that each parent has with Alissa; the relationship that they have with each other; the nature of the nuclear system; the influences of Terea, Fred, and other friends; the influence of extended family members; the demands and rewards associated with their careers; their position in a work culture that tends to view the male's position as more important than the female's; and so on. The ecosystem perspective also considers individual family members in the systems analysis. Perhaps Alissa is hyperactive, has dyslexia, or suffers from frequent allergic reactions. Functional family interaction alone will not alter the fact that Alissa's body chemistry influences her behavior. Similarly, to focus on the physiology without noting how it supports and is supported by the family system is to miss the interconnections that underlie family functioning. For example, although she hates to see her child in pain, Maggie may see value in Alissa's colicky episodes. When Maggie describes the latest episode to Roger, she may share that story with him as a way to indicate that he needs to spend more time with his daughter. On the other hand, Roger may view Alissa's colic as yet another sign (or metaphor) that Maggie is not performing her role as a mother. For Maggie, Alissa's colic episodes increase her opportunities to engage Roger in conversation about his lack of involvement with his child; thus, the episodes may be viewed positively. For Roger, any increase in the number of episodes would further reinforce his perception that Maggie is not a good mother. Thus, Roger sees Alissa's colic as a negative behavior.

The ecosystem perspective offers many insights into family communication. Just as individual family members exert mutual influence, the family system both influences and is influenced by its surroundings. Influence from the surrounding suprasystem provides inputs to the family system that affect that family's functioning. The inputs influence how family members will interact with each other and the degree to which the system will be able to achieve its goals. Even the most permissive parents may become controlling after they learn that their teenaged son is experimenting with drugs. Even the most resolutely grumpy person may be inclined to smile after winning the lottery. Anxiety over the discovery of asbestos in the city water supply or the installation of a toxic waste dump in one's town may create feelings of rage or helplessness that impair family functioning. Pride in the local football team or a vacation spent building houses for the poor may recharge a family's energy and stimulate positive conversations among family members.

Outputs from the family system to the surrounding environment also influence family communication. Knowing that the Jasinskis contributed funds to plant a rose garden at the local high school, that they never vote in state or local elections, and that they buy their clothing always on sale indicates their preferred means of functioning. Being able to identify a family's place in the broader social and geographic scheme helps in differentiating between two *seemingly* similar families that operate very differently. Income levels, education, proximity to cultural events, social groups, and the government system all contribute to the uniqueness of a family system.

THE ECOSYSTEM MODEL

Figure 6.1 presents our model of a nuclear family ecosystem. Naturally, the model can be adapted for various other family forms: blended families, single-parent families, extended families, gay and lesbian families, and so on. As you can see, we've included the lowest level subsystems of interest, individual family members, and have drawn the outermost boundary around the largest macrosystem, the planet Earth. In sections to follow, we break this model into its component parts to examine the interactions among various systems within the ecosystem.

Our ecosystem model builds on the work of Paolucci, Hall, and Axinn (1977) and their colleagues (Auerswald, 1971; Compton & Hall, 1972; Hook & Paolucci, 1970; Micklin, 1973; Odum, 1971) and is related closely to the systems characteristics presented in Chapter 3. It has also emerged from a focus on family therapy that incorporates individual, family, and contextual variables to understand family functioning. As Pinsof (1984) described in his argument for a broad-based theoretical perspective, the "patient system consists of all the human systems (biological, individual-psychological, familial-interpersonal, social-occupational, etc.) that are or may be involved in the maintenance or resolution of the presenting problem. 'Patient system' encompasses different, hierarchically integrated levels of systemic organization, without locking the therapist onto one level exclusively" (p. 588).

This approach relates to our discussion in an earlier chapter and reflects recent thinking that "integrates social construction theory and dialectical process into a systems view of the family" (Yerby, 1992, p. 17). Social construction theory is concerned with how persons construct reality as they converse and interact with one another (Gergen, 1985). The notion of dialectical process has been discussed earlier in this text as the relationship between "opposites that are bound together" (Wilmot, 1987, p. 107). In particular, two dialectical processes have received considerable attention in the family therapy and communication literature: (1) integration and differentiation and (2) stability and change. Our ecosystem model recognizes that realities are constructed, resulting in somewhat different personal realities for each family member and different collective realities for each family. These realities are coordinated through family communication and through interaction with the environment. Further, the model allows incorporation of the dialectical tensions described earlier in this text and argues that families may strive simultaneously to achieve both ends of the polarities. Finally, our ecosystem model focuses on both individuals and collectives by attempting to identify ways in which the various systems influence one another. "Every family is made up of individuals with different genetic structures, histories of experience, interpretations of reality, preferred ways of interacting, needs for attachment and independence, and so forth. There is a constant tension between those processes that differentiate family members from one another and those that facilitate integration of the family as a communal unit" (Yerby, 1992, p. 15). Similarly, influences from

FIGURE 6.1   The family ecosystem model.

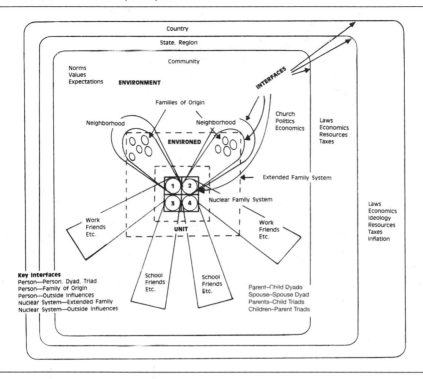

the larger culture play a role in how family members function. Different levels of access to resources, power, and opportunity result in differences in family functioning.

The ecosystem model contains three central elements: the environed unit, the surrounding environment, and the transactions that take place among elements. The **environed unit** is the system of interest, or, in this text, the family. For Maggie and Roger, the environed unit includes both of them plus their daughter, Alissa. Any individual within the family system could also be considered an environed unit. The **environment** refers to the larger systems surrounding the system of interest, such as the neighborhood, the city or town, the state, and the various other systems operating within those boundaries. **Transactions** refer to activity between systems, generally in the form of communication. In our opening example, transactions occurred between Maggie and Terea, Roger and Fred, Roger and his senior partner, Maggie and her family of origin, Roger and his family of origin, and the marital dyad and the therapist. Presumably, the Jasinskis also engage in frequent transactions with co-workers, friends, grocery store clerks, and the other people in their environment.

There are meeting points where the system of interest meets the environment. The meeting points where transactions occur between two systems are called **interfaces**. According to Paolucci, Hall, and Axinn (1977, p. 21), the "interface is that point at which families and environments meet. It is here that information is exchanged and relationships are determined. New opportunities and problems emerge at these points."

For Maggie and Roger, important interfaces include their interactions at their respective places of employment, at church, and with Terea and Fred, their families of origin, their community, and Alissa. They are also influenced by the economy in their geographic region, by the climate and other physical features of their environment, by the laws and ethics of their society, and by the media that provide their news and entertainment. Each contact with another system provides the potential for change or instability in the Jasinski family system.

Focusing primarily on intergenerational interfaces, Kramer argues that "interfaces embody all the interaction and learning that occurs in the psychological spaces among individuals and systems. Each has its own boundaries, with explicit and implicit rules governing transactional patterns of acceptable behavior" (1985, p. 4).

An ecosystem approach analyzes the impact of the extended family system on the nuclear family, the ways in which the community system and family system interact, and so on. The focus of the ecosystem perspective is on the interfaces between components and subsystems in the nuclear family and between the family system and other systems. The ecosystem approach analyzes how outputs from one system affect other systems that use them as inputs. Although our major concern is with communication within the family system, identification of both internal and external influences allows for a clearer understanding of the family.

Family Subsystems

Consider the diagram presented in Figure 6.2, which we call the Bow Model. Again, we have used as our prototype a nuclear family with two children, but the model applies to all family forms. As you see, we have drawn boundary lines around each individual member in the nuclear system. We have also drawn boundaries around other subsystems of interest: the marital dyad, parent–child dyads, parent–child triads, and the sibling dyad. Each subsystem functions separately from others while at the same time retaining interdependence with all other subsystems. Four family subsystems make up the nuclear system: (1) individual subsystems, (2) dyadic subsystems, (3) triadic subsystems, and (4) larger subsystems. The elements of each are discussed in the sections that follow.

Individual Subsystems

Individuals compose the lowest-level subsystem that someone interested in family communication would logically examine. As both Weeks (1986) and Pinsof (1984) argued, the individual is one level in the system and it is important to consider the individual's needs, goals, and personal characteristics as well as the family's needs, goals, and characteristics to understand family functioning. Often, transactions between individual family members and the nuclear system reflect differences between these systems—as when a sixteen-year-old daughter fearfully announces that she is pregnant to her highly religious parents.

Most psychological perspectives on the family examine individual family member components as a way to understand the family. Psychologists may label individual family members as "compulsive" or "depressed" or "violent." We prefer to avoid such labels, focusing instead on needs, past experiences, communication skills, and other abilities and behaviors associated with individual family

FIGURE 6.2 The Bow Model.

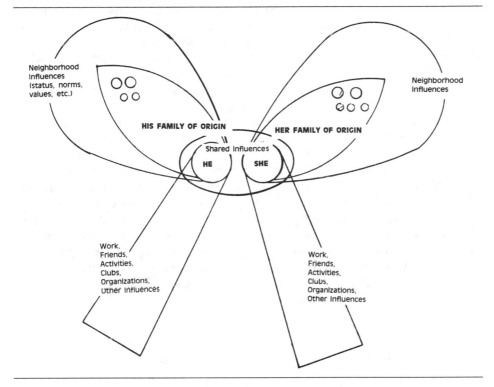

members. Of special concern are the realities constructed by individuals in the family and how those realities support or challenge the collective family reality. From a communication perspective, we are interested in the fact that Maggie keeps a diary, thus separating her identity in a very specific way from other members of her family, and the fact that Roger locks himself in the bathroom to read the newspaper on Sunday mornings, thus allowing himself forty-five minutes of separation from other family members. Rather than label Maggie "secretive" or Roger "aloof," we prefer to speculate on the functions that those distancing strategies perform for the system as a whole and on the interpretations the communicators offer for those behaviors. Perhaps Maggie's diary is a way for her to think through conflicts with Roger before they become too intense; Roger's retreat to the bathroom could be a way for him to differentiate himself from the women in his life. Each individual's construction of reality is unique—and legitimate.

The interface between the individual behaviors and the system as a whole provides information about the communication in that family. Maggie may be encouraged (explicitly or implicitly) by her family to keep a diary because it helps her assert her own identity and to work through her interpersonal problems without involving others, or they may encourage her to keep a diary because it helps her express her needs more clearly after having reflected on them for a while. If asked to describe her diary, Maggie might use metaphors such as "hiding place" or "escape." Such descriptions add to our understanding of the way Maggie views the act of keeping a diary. The diary is a part of her individual subsystem.

The interface between a family member and other systems is identified by the boundaries that separate them. Boundaries around individuals in a family system can often be determined by observing nonverbal artifacts. In the Garber household, each child has a separate bedroom and, although the parents sleep together in the master bedroom, each adult has a separate office/study into which to withdraw when necessary. Possibly more important, each bedroom door has a lock and the room's inhabitant frequently locks the door, thus indicating clearly a need for privacy. In the Huefell household, on the other hand, the focus is on shared spaces. The three boys share one bedroom and their two sisters share another. The family room, dining room, and living room areas dominate the house; all other rooms seem to be an extension of this central space. There are no locks on doors and the only way for a family member to work or play alone is to select an empty room and hope that no one else plans to use that room at the same time. These nonverbal indicators highlight the struggle between integration and differentiation. Individuals continually strive for balance between asserting an individual identity and securing a place in the family. Of course, boundaries may be verbal as well. Maggie may announce that Sunday mornings are her "quiet time," thus indicating her need for differentiation. Or Roger may create a rule that no one may call him at work, thus creating a boundary between him and other family members when he is at his office.

Dyadic Subsystems

Knowing how various dyads within a family relate to each other and to other individuals in the family can tell us a great deal about the family process as a whole. In the opening example, it is clear that there was a change in the marital dyad after the birth of Alissa. Examining the ways in which this new interface within the system affected Maggie and Roger (and Alissa) helps to focus attention on the dynamics of the problem rather than on specific causes. Roger is not a "bad" person because he differentiates himself by spending more time at work. Maggie is not a "bad" person because she differentiates herself from Roger and spends much of her energy interacting with Alissa. However, the degree to which alliances form in the various possible dyads tells us something about family functioning in the Jasinski system. When a child is added to the marital dyad, the number and complexity of relationships increases. When there is more than one child, the number of subsystems increases dramatically.

Imagine that Alissa is now fifteen years old and that she has a brother named Alex. We can then identify a number of subsystems of interest. For one, we might want to look at the relationship between Maggie and Roger when they interact alone, separate from their children. We might want to see how each communicates with Alissa and compare those relationships with the ones between Roger and Alex, or between Maggie and Alex. We might examine the relationship between Alex and Alissa, in the presence of their parents and when they communicate separately. It may be the case that Roger and Alissa have a stormy, conflict-filled relationship, whereas Roger and Alex agree on almost everything. Or, we may find that communication between Maggie and Alissa is open and unrestrained whereas communication in the relationship between Maggie and Alex tends to be superficial and infrequent. It may also be the case that the typical communication patterns in a dyad change in the presence of others. Roger and Alex may express affection for each other through touch when they are away on a fishing trip but connect through verbal arguments when they are observed by Alissa or Maggie.

Remember that researchers are not the only ones who draw boundaries around family members. The family members themselves create boundaries when they wish to interact within one subsystem separate from others. Maggie and Roger may designate Friday evenings as the one time during the week when they can be totally alone. By doing so, they draw a temporary boundary around their dyadic subsystem. Similarly, Alissa and Alex may spend time together listening to music or watching videos. When they voluntarily separate themselves from their parents, they draw an imaginary and temporary boundary around themselves that helps to focus attention on their dyadic relationship and to prevent others from intruding.

Physical features in the family environment may help to reinforce dyadic relationships. For example, the master bedroom may contain its own bathroom, thus facilitating more privacy for the couple. Two sisters who share a room may designate that space as "off limits" to their "baby" brother.

In short, understanding how the two-person subsystems function within the larger system can help to identify potential conflict areas, preferred relating strategies, and many other communication variables. Focusing on the interfaces between dyadic relationships can provide considerable information about the ways in which dyads handle the integration and differentiation dialectic.

Triadic Subsystems

Of course, triadic relationships are also possible in a family of four. Alissa, Maggie, and Alex may find that they often take drives together, leaving Roger at home to amuse himself. As a threesome, they may arrange for activities that they enjoy but that would not be enjoyable to the family as a whole. Similarly, it may be the case that each parent relates very differently with the children. Maggie may interact with the children primarily as a disciplinarian, whereas Roger may spend most of his time with the children engaged in some form of game or sport.

When three members of a family become entangled routinely into a triadic relationship, a potential problem arises called triangulation. **Triangulation** refers to a situation in which a third person serves as a go-between for two other family members, thus sparing those two family members from interacting directly. In most cases, a child serves as a go-between for his or her parents, who are unable to confront each other directly about problems in their marital dyad. For example, imagine that Maggie and Roger are having marital difficulties, but neither one wants to admit that there are problems out of a fear of harming their relationship. Rather than express their feelings openly to each other, especially their anger, Maggie and Roger begin to argue over Alissa's rights as an adolescent. Maggie asserts that Roger is too permissive, that Alissa will experiment with drugs and sex if he allows her the freedom that he feels she should have. Roger responds that Maggie is overly protective and irrational in her dealings with her daughter. By using Alissa as their focal point, Maggie and Roger are able to argue freely, even though the issues behind the arguments have little or nothing to do with their daughter. The real issues may be Maggie's feelings that Roger is losing interest in her sexually or Roger's feelings that Maggie is no longer attentive to his needs. Rather than risk fighting openly about those issues, it becomes much easier to argue over how much freedom to allow their fifteen-year-old daughter.

APPLICATION 6.1

TRIANGULATION

Explain the following situation as an example of triangulation and describe how it has taken place over the years.

> When the oldest McKenzie son, Robert, was fourteen, he had problems adjusting to the family's move to Lincoln, Nebraska. (They had moved to Nebraska to be closer to his mother's parents after his own parents divorced.) He was angry about having to leave his friends and about the attention his younger brother, Mark, was receiving. As a young child, Mark was very ill and demanded considerable attention from Jean, their mother. Mark's health improved as he got older; however, Robert then became a problem. After the move, he had periods of depression and seemed to shut out his mother. He became friends with some particularly adventurous boys at school and was eventually apprehended by police for breaking into a tool shed in a neighbor's backyard.
>
> Robert's remorse over his behavior and the embarrassment he had created for his mother were significant. As a result, Robert vowed to do better in school and to try and turn his life around. He kept his promise. After several months of struggling, Robert discovered a natural gift for math and science and began to pursue special coursework in those areas. Within two years of their move, Robert was excelling in school and seemed destined for a scholarship to study science in college.
>
> Robert's successes had a strange effect on Mark, however. It seemed that the harder Robert worked to please his mother, the more difficult it became for Mark to cope with family life. He began to develop a number of symptoms that caused him to miss school: migraine headaches, stomach pains, and general lethargy. Jean worried that Mark's earlier problems with ill health were returning and frequently took days off from work to be with him.

Some family therapists have suggested that families with an "identified patient" (a member with some sort of diagnosed problem, such as alcoholism, drug abuse, promiscuity, or delinquency) very often suffer from triangulation. Many times a child will take on symptoms such as bed-wetting or temper tantrums or drug use as a way to focus the family away from the marital relationship. Somehow that family member is "elected" by the system as a whole to be the problem. We call the person who temporarily assumes a set of negative symptoms a **scapegoat** (Napier & Whitaker, 1978).

Returning to the Jasinski family, imagine that the relationship between Maggie and Roger has deteriorated to the point where they do not openly fight but they do not speak to one another either. Such a rift in the marital relationship will certainly move the family system farther from equilibrium than the system can allow. Something will have to be done to bring them closer together, and one thing that would do just that would be a problem with Alex or Alissa. Imagine, then, that Alex begins staying out all night, defying his parents' rules, and participating in illegal activities such as joyriding and shoplifting. Taking a systems perspective, it should be clear that Alex has not suddenly turned "bad." Instead, his behavior allows his parents to join forces in their shock and dismay over his behavior so that the focus turns away from his parents' marital problems. Faced with such serious symptoms from their son, Maggie and Roger may pull together to deal with the problem, thus temporarily postponing the battle raging between them. Or, one parent may "side" with the son, drawing closer to Alex and farther from the other parent. Both situations describe classic examples of triangulation.

Closely related to triangulation is the concept that some members of a family system join forces with each other deliberately. Two types of subsystems are possible: alliances and coalitions. **Alliances** refer to subsystems that form for some generally positive purpose. For example, Maggie, Roger, and Alex may decide to plan and maintain a garden together. Their cooperative effort results in an alliance among them. **Coalitions**, on the other hand, are formed as a way to exert *power or influence* over other family members. Just as oil-producing nations join together to maintain the price of crude, or political groups join together to have more clout in an upcoming election, family members may join together to form coalitions within the family system. Maggie, Alex, and Alissa may form a coalition against Roger, thus sabotaging his influence in the family and, perhaps, "punishing" him for some perceived wrongdoing. Two siblings may form a coalition against an older sibling, excluding her from family activities.

It should be clear that the three concepts just discussed—triangles, alliances, and coalitions—have much in common. A major difference is that alliances can be thought of neutrally; triangles and coalitions tend to have more negative connotations because they represent problematic family situations. Remember, however, that taking a systems perspective requires suspending blame. Although it may seem that the parents who allow their teenaged daughter to be scapegoated for their marital difficulties are "to blame" for the problem, the system is far more complex than such a simplistic explanation suggests. The daughter who is scapegoated has been "elected" by the system to perform a role, and she probably gains increased power or other forms of reinforcement as a result. Similarly, while it may seem unfair for family members to form a coalition against others, such behavior may perform a function for a system struggling to find equilibrium. If one family member has become too powerful or too resistant to family rules, a coalition against that member may force that person back into the mainstream of family life.

Larger Subsystems

In families of five or more members, the possibilities for subsystems become unwieldy. In a family of six, it becomes almost impossible to understand the complexities of the two-, three-, four-, and five-person subsystems. Nevertheless, the complexity of the task does not diminish its importance. In a family of six, each individual will influence and be influenced by every other individual in unique ways; similarly, each dyadic relationship will be somewhat different and will interface with every other dyadic relationship in unique ways. In a family of six, we can talk about larger subsystems than triads; in fact, there are over a *dozen* four-person subsystems in a six-member family! The closer family members can come to understanding the uniqueness of those subsystem interfaces, the better they will understand how their family operates.

The Nuclear System: The Family as a Collective

Naturally, the environed unit of special interest to us is the nuclear system. As a collective unit, families develop identities, value structures, ideologies, and a view of the world that all play a role in their interfaces with the outer environment. The Jasinskis see themselves as "survivors," which tends to send them off to work and school with a "can-do" attitude. They also see themselves as self-sufficient as a family unit, which can close them off to influence from their friends, extended families, church, and media.

Most of the concepts that we discuss in this text—rules, roles, images, patterns, and so on—play a role in our understanding of the interactions between the nuclear system and the larger suprasystems with which it interfaces. For example, the extent to which a nuclear family is open or closed determines the flow of information in and out of the family. In general, closed families with impermeable boundaries interface less frequently and with less intensity with their surrounding environment than do more open families (Kantor & Lehr, 1975). In addition, the degree to which rules are known and rigidly enforced may shape family interfaces. Families with rigid rule structures tend to experience less variability in their interfaces than do families with more adaptable rules (Olson, McCubbin, Barnes, Larsen, Muxen, & Wilson, 1983). Family roles also differentiate family types. Families that maintain tight role descriptions tend to follow prescriptions for family members to interface with particular systems (Bernstein, 1971). For example, in families that maintain traditional family roles, the adult male is expected to be the primary wage-earner, male children are expected to participate in "manly"

TABLE 6.1   Levels in the family system.

FAMILY SUBSYSTEMS	POTENTIAL ISSUES
Individual subsystems	management of individual differentiation
Dyadic subsystems	boundary and role definitions
Triadic subsystems	triangulation, scapegoating, coalitions, alliances
Larger subsystems	scapegoating, coalitions, alliances
Nuclear subsystem	influence of family beliefs, ideology, and themes on family interaction; integration of individual, dyadic, triadic, and larger subsystems into the nuclear system

THE ENVIRONMENT	POTENTIAL ISSUES
Extended family network	relationship of nuclear family to the extended family
Social support system	amount and kind of support from friends, work, organizations, and neighbors
Community, culture, and the larger environment	the availability of services and resources; sources of stress that impact on the nuclear system; impact of state and regional resources, laws, values, and characteristics on family interaction; influence of cultural values, economic climate, and politics on family interaction; influence of the physical environment on the stress and coping strategies of the family

activities, such as sporting events and hunting, and the females in the family assume responsibility for domestic and nurturing activities.

If the nuclear subsystems seem complicated, imagine how complex the model becomes when we add the influence of people and events from outside of the nuclear system! We turn now to a discussion of the larger model.

The Environment

Many transactions take place at the interfaces among individual family members as well as between the family as a whole and the surrounding environment. These transactions mutually affect the nuclear system and the surrounding environment. In particular, three systems are especially important: (1) the extended family network; (2) the social support system; and (3) community, culture, and the larger environment. These systems are described in the sections that follow.

The Extended Family Network

The environmental system closest to the nuclear family is the **extended family network**. This system generally is composed of the families of origin—the families and environmental influences—for both spouses. Definitions for what is meant by "extended" will differ, given the fact that some families consider grandparents, aunts/uncles, adult siblings, and in-laws as members of their nuclear system.

Some of the influences of the extended family network are historical: the neighborhood she grew up in, his childhood friends, her school, and so on. Most continue through the present time: calls from his mother, gifts and visits from grandparents, help with the children from his parents, and other similar inputs. Each time the family visits her parents or receives a card or letter from his mother, some influence is felt. When the family (or individual members in it) respond to this influence, an effect is felt in the extended family system. An argument between mother and daughter about how to handle marital stress will affect both mother and daughter; that influence will reverberate through all systems of which they are a part.

It is important to consider influences from the families of origin, given the well-substantiated argument that communication patterns persist across generations (Cohler & Grunebaum, 1981; Fink, 1993; Kramer, 1985). Although much of the research focuses on negative patterns (abused parents were abused themselves as children; alcoholics generally had at least one alcoholic parent; a person caught in a triangle as a child will frequently involve his or her own children in a similar triangle), there is considerable evidence to suggest that an individual's communication ability is shaped in large part during childhood (Fink, 1993; Hopper & Naremore, 1978; Kramer, 1985; Laosa & Sigel, 1982; Satir, 1983). Family rules, patterns of interaction, secrets, taboos, and myths can all influence the ways in which the second-generation family is able to function. Likewise, continued contact with one's family of origin can reinforce those patterns on a day-to-day or week-to-week basis.

Massey (1986) makes a clear argument for a focus on intergenerational interfaces. "Transgenerational perceptions, experiences, and patterns of interactions further reinforce the irreducibility of a systemic context to individual dynamics. Persons exist in the contexts they have inherited and contributed to. These contexts either support the development of competence or inhibit individuation as persons coevolve with ongoing socializing influences" (p. 31).

Naturally, each nuclear family system will interface with the extended family network in unique ways. In Maggie and Roger's family, for example, Maggie's parents are encouraged to exert direct influence over Alissa and Alex, often arriving to care for them while Maggie and Roger leave on trips for business or pleasure. Maggie actively consults with her mother about ways to discipline her children and compares notes on child-care and dual career marriages with her brother and sister-in-law. Roger, on the other hand, rarely engages his parents in conversation about family issues. Clearly, other families develop very different patterns of relating to members of their extended family networks.

The degree to which the second-generation family is able to differentiate itself from the problems of their families of origin while maintaining mutually satisfying ties to those families will directly affect the patterns of communication in that family. A man who was taught to be the "head of the house" can certainly learn to share responsibilities with his mate in spite of his childhood experiences; a man who cannot detach himself from his family of origin and who does not question their construction of reality will, however, more than likely insist upon the same patterns in his own home.

The Social Support System

The second major component of the ecosystem model is called the **social support system**. This system includes the work environment, church, schools, and social relationships. These are the areas outside of the family system in which family members receive emotional support, financial recognition, intellectual stimulation, cultural and aesthetic exposure, and reinforcement (or lack thereof) of their values and beliefs. When Maggie has a productive day at work, she brings good feelings of accomplishment home with her and shares those good feelings with her family. When Alex has a frustrating day at school, his frustrations show in his interactions with his family over dinner. Thus, contacts with the environment both reinforce and change patterns of interaction within the nuclear system. Conversely, outputs from family members shape the work environment, the school system, the neighborhood, and so on.

Naturally, some support sources will be more important to one family than to others. In some family systems, the church may provide a central organizing force for family interaction and shape many family values and rules. In another system, the central force may be inputs from the media or reinforcement from a large and close-knit friendship system. For some families, lack of social support (e.g., an inadequate school system, lack of employment opportunities, and/or an inadequate friendship network) can create many family problems.

Families recharge their energies, gain new ideas, receive instruction, and often suffer pain in interaction with components of the social support system. Participation on a Little League team, active support of the local election, or planning a birthday party for a friend may be sources of energy and pleasure for a family. Losing a job, battling discrimination, or attending the funeral of a close friend can all create stress for the family system. Individual family members will focus on different components in the social support system, with children often receiving considerable influence from television and the school system and parents interfacing with work environments.

Community, Culture, and the Larger Environment

Beyond the social support system are a variety of other opportunities and constraints that influence families. Issues such as social status, class differences, cultural diversity, power, resources, and geographic location play a role in these systems. In particular, this final system includes three categories of influences: (1) the norms, values, expectations, and physical features of the community in which the family resides; (2) the laws, prejudices, ideologies, opportunities, and limitations of the cultural system in which the family functions; and (3) the social, psychological, and physical features of the larger environment surrounding the family.

The Community

The **community system** includes a number of positive and negative influences: threats in the environment, such as crime; quality and affordability of housing; availability of support services, such as libraries, law enforcement, health care, and day-care centers; availability of shopping facilities; and available leisure activities, such as movie theaters, parks, roller skating rinks, and bowling alleys. Again, some interfaces, such as public recognition for alerting a family that their house was on fire or election to the city council, can have an uplifting effect on families. Other interfaces, such as placing a parent in a nursing home or coping with a spouse's arrest for drunken driving, can create conflict and disruption in family patterns. The pressure for both parents to work may affect their roles and their communication. Dad may go to PTA meetings as frequently as Mom. Mom may have to learn about cars and make the decision about buying the car that she will use to drive to work. When the couple talks about such issues, they exchange information and reinforce a sense of egalitarianism in the relationship. In a community in which cultural diversity is the norm, children may grow up with a very different reality from those raised in single-race neighborhoods. The social, political, physical, and ideological climate in a community shape a family's experiences in many ways.

Consider two families: the Stevenses and the Rowandas. Marti and Doc Stevens and their son, Mark, live on the thirty-first floor of a high-rise apartment in downtown Chicago. They live within easy walking distance of a half-dozen theaters, two museums, dozens of stores of all varieties, two libraries, a hospital, a park, and a dozen bars and lounges. Unfortunately, paying for their apartment, utilities, and Mark's sitter takes approximately half of their take-home pay each month, leaving very little for leisure activities. Nevertheless, they spend virtually every evening enjoying features the city has to offer: window shopping, visiting the art and culture museums, taking Mark to the park or a White Sox or Cubs game, and occasionally spending extra money for a play and a nice dinner. Although life is a continual financial struggle, and there are occasional problems with muggings and break-ins in the neighborhood, the Stevens family is enormously satisfied with their lifestyle. They love the excitement of a big city and all that it has to offer the family.

Owen and Claire Rowanda and their three teenaged sons live in a college town of approximately 40,000 residents, half of whom are college students in town for only part of the year. The crime rate is very low, with most police time being spent arresting drunk drivers on Friday and Saturday nights. Most businesses in town cater to the student population: bars, fast-food outlets, discount stores, and party stores. There are three movie theaters, one bowling alley, three golf courses, six drug stores, one department store, five video rental shops, and a dozen bars. The Rowandas prefer a much quieter lifestyle than do the Stevenses. Their typical activities include shopping at the farmer's market on Saturday morning, ice skating on the frozen river in the winter, visiting "Smokey" the bear in the local park zoo, going out for pizza, and watching videos at home. The boys all bowl in a league, play co-ed soccer and softball, and use the swimming and weightlifting facilities at the university. They have time to read, ride bikes, and play video games at the local arcade.

Clearly, the Stevenses and Rowandas interface with their environments in different ways, primarily because of the large differences in their community systems. In truth, the Stevenses might find life very stagnant and boring in a small town, whereas the Rowandas might find the dirt and crime in the city distasteful. Both family systems have adapted to their respective environments, taking the best that those environments have to offer and returning money and energy to maintain and improve those communities. If the Stevenses moved to a small university community, they would, no doubt, make adaptations in their system to allow them to fit into that new community. In all probability, they would work to change the community, as well. We could compare the influence of the community on other types of families, including families with same sex parents, stepfamilies, families with physically or learning disabled members, families whose children are cared for by grandparents, single-parent families, rural families, interracial families, bilingual families, and so on. Each of these families will also interface with the environment in unique ways.

Availability of resources and employment, quality of the educational system, transportation, laws, taxes, political ideology and stability, state services, and other state and regional issues affect the quality of life for individual family systems. Life in highly urbanized areas such as Los Angeles and New York is characterized by lower individual property taxes and easy access to facilities but also more pollution and the threat of environmentally related illness. Various regions develop their own political systems that differentiate them ideologically and pragmatically from other regions. Economic stability and housing availability also affect families. "Drug houses," street violence, and gangs affect family life.

In regions where economic stability is difficult to attain, considerable stress in the family system may originate out of a need to earn and save money. Family decision making may center around finding and keeping jobs, family expenditures, or investments. During long winters in the North, family energy might be devoted to issues related to heat, such as negotiations over how high to set the thermostat overnight. When there are changes in the community system, such as the proposed construction of a chemical dump or the building of a new prison, family energies may rally around responding to those proposed changes.

The Culture

Just as regional politics influence family life in that area, the social and political climate of the country as a whole will have some impact. When inflation is high, increased interest rates influence families directly in their ability to afford consumer goods and services, to purchase houses or make home improvements, and

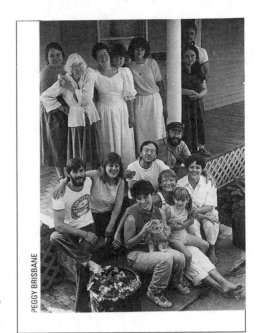

The environmental system closest to the nuclear family is the extended family.

in their ability to save money. Likewise, technological improvements directly affect family mobility, availability of leisure time, and quality of life. The family with its microwave oven, color television, riding lawnmower, personal computer, and compact disk player is likely to function very differently from the family living in its VW camper with no heat, electricity, or running water.

Cultural expectations influence family interaction by imposing a cultural "reality" on family members. In the opening example, Roger's construction of reality included an assumption that Maggie would manage the role of primary caretaker, even if that meant diminishing her role as a working professional. The cultural expectation that the female should handle the major share of child-care responsibilities reinforced Roger's perceptions of how Maggie should behave.

Politically conservative groups argue that American culture should continue to strive for the traditional, patriarchal family form that they believe was standard prior to World War I. In that family type, the father provided for the family financially and made the major decisions; the mother cared for the children and her husband and made decisions pertaining to the household. Of course, this family form does not allow for gay and lesbian families, single-parent households, matriarchal families, and/or blended or extended families. In truth, such a cultural model applies to a diminishing segment of American society. To the extent that employers, educators, politicians, and others in power endorse this family model, families that do not conform to those cultural ideals may suffer. Such family stereotypes may be especially difficult for groups that follow different cultural norms because they face a contradiction between what their own social group expects and what the larger dominant culture prescribes. For example, Dodson (1988) argues that "black American culture and family patterns possess a degree of cultural integrity that is neither related to nor modeled on white American norms" (p. 77). According to Sue and Sue (1990), "the world view of the culturally different is ultimately linked to the historical and current experiences of racism and oppression in the United States" (p. 5).

The Larger Environment

Families also interface with their larger physical and political environments. Size, typography, natural resources, climate, accessibility, political stability, and economic health of the country influence family functioning. For example, in a country of significant geographic distance, such as the United States, geographic mobility may create stress for families. Dad may have a job that requires him to fly from one work site to another on a regular basis or he may live in another town for some portion of the week. Mom may live thousands of miles from her family and/or closest friends and may run up enormous phone bills maintaining those ties. Family communication may focus on managing conflicting schedules, establishing priorities for expenditures, nurturing extended family relationships, finding time for family activities, and any of a dozen other topics related to a mobile lifestyle. Likewise, periods of national recession or high inflation limit employment possibilities and further entrap some families in cycles of poverty (McAdoo, 1988). Moreover, employment opportunities that offer only low-paying wages without health care and other benefits make it difficult to sustain a family.

Finally, families in the 1990s are becoming increasingly aware of their dependence on the nonrenewable resources in their environment. Family activity may now center around tasks such as recycling, and family negotiations may focus on use of resources such as electricity, water, and nonrecyclable materials.

DIALECTICAL PROCESSES IN THE ECOSYSTEM

Adaptation to and interaction with elements in the ecosystem involve management of contradictory polarities. Three dialectical *tensions* are especially relevant to a discussion of family communication: (1) stability and change, (2) individual vs. system dialectics, and (3) family system vs. cultural dialectics.

Stability and Change

How the family system negotiates, through its communication, the interfaces among subsystems, the extended family, and the environment is important in our understanding of the family's ecosystem. The family that retains a focus on family values and patterns away from environmental influences helps to maintain the family's stability. If Mark selects friends whose values and behaviors conflict with those important to the Stevens family, the influence of those friends could challenge family stability. Helping Mark find interesting things to do within the family, thus reducing his time with these friends, can help the Stevenses to reinforce stability. Closing off the family from undesired influences is related to maintaining stability.

On the other hand, being open to the environment is one way for a family to change and grow. Processing new ideas from the environment, thus allowing for change in family thinking, gives family members experience in adapting their point of view. Educational experiences inevitably bring growth and change. Allowing input from extended family, friends, neighbors, and so on opens the family to outside influences and potential sources of support.

TABLE 6.2   Important interfaces in the family ecosystem.

SYSTEM LEVEL	EXAMPLE
Individual dyadic systems	Norma and Jack have different perceptions of how children should be disciplined.
Dyadic family systems	Two teenaged sons find themselves arguing with their parents and younger siblings over how much time the family should spend "doing things together" because they would prefer more time for their own interests.
Nuclear system/ social support system	Maggie's parents take an active role in caring for their grandchildren.
Individual nuclear system/ social support system	Roger's work organization makes no concessions when Roger becomes a new parent, thus reinforcing the values he borrowed from his parents' relationship that parenting should be primarily Maggie's responsibility.
Nuclear system/ community system	Marti, Doc, and their son can take advantage of free leisure and recreation opportunities available to them in a big city.
Nuclear system/extended family community system	Family therapists bring together members of the nuclear family and the extended family in an effort to understand and help to resolve Maggie and Roger's marital stress.
Nuclear system/ larger environment	Marti and Doc worry that urban pollution will make their son's asthma worse and that the cost of urban housing may mean that they will never be able to afford a house.

No family is totally closed nor is any family totally open to the environment. Instead, there is a range on a continuum where families function somewhere between being open and being closed (Kantor & Lehr, 1975). A family that is too closed to the environment will be unable to adapt to natural changes through the life cycle. A family that is too open may be too unpredictable and will endure too much change too fast. Consequently, family systems constantly struggle with the dialectical process of stability versus change in managing interfaces in the family's ecosystem. Recognizing the environmental influences on family experiences and the effects those influences have on family functioning is one way for a family to exert control over its growth.

The Individual and the Nuclear Family

As discussed earlier, individuals struggle with the need to develop and maintain relationships with family members (integration) and the need to retain autonomy and independence (differentiation). Within the nuclear system, family members function as members of family relationships (marital relationships, sibling relationships, parent–child relationships) and as individuals. The woman who is married to a man who tends to be rude to her friends struggles with the contradiction between her desire to be part of the marital dyad while at the same time distancing herself from his negative behaviors when they are with her friends. Although she is his "spouse," she also wants it to be clear to her friends that her communication patterns differ from his in important ways; she is an individual.

APPLICATION 6.2

FAMILY INTERFACES: STABILITY VS. CHANGE

Explain how a family system might adapt effectively to each of the following situations without jeopardizing family stability:

1. The nearby intermediate school will be closed and the youngest child will have to be bused five miles away.
2. A layoff at work of the main wage earner in the family reduces income.
3. The addition of an elderly (grand)parent moves into the nuclear family system as a way to avoid being placed in a nursing home.
4. The oldest child's best friend has revealed that he is gay.
5. A parent or spouse has recently suffered a heart attack.
6. The child-care facility where a single, working mother leaves her two small children announces that it is closing in a month.

Likewise, individuals must manage contradictions between their personal conceptualizations of events and the family's collective perceptions. Imagine, for example, that this woman's family members value "blood" relationships over friendships. In that case, the "rude" behavior may be interpreted by her children as their father's attempt to remind their mother that she is spending too much time with friends and not enough time with family. Her interpretation may still be that her husband's behavior is rude; the collective family interpretation may be that the behavior is necessary. How she deals with the inherent contradiction in perceptions involves her ability to deal with the dialectic between differentiation and integration.

The Nuclear Family and the Culture

Many problems arise when a family's social construction of reality differs from that of the dominant culture in which they live. As we discussed earlier, families who do not fit expected models struggle with two conflicting needs: the need to retain family values and identity and the need to interact positively and profitably with the larger culture. Frequently, a focus on one precludes the other, as in the case of gay families who proclaim their sexual orientation only to be deprived of privileges granted to more "traditional" family forms: the right to legally marry, access to the advantages of marriage (tax breaks, insurance coverages, inheritance rights), the ability to adopt, etc. Other nontraditional family forms, such as families consisting of a female parent with children, also face political, social, and economic difficulties in this culture (McAdoo, 1988). Knowing that being married and, thus, conforming to the cultural ideal, would improve her financial situation, a woman might be tempted to (re)marry. However, such a decision could have profoundly negative effects on her children. In truth, many first marriages might never have occurred had the individuals involved not been pressured by parents, co-workers, bosses, and others in their environment to conform to cultural expectations. Many families might not have been created had the individuals in the marital dyad not bought into their relationship the expectation that the reason to get married is to have children.

SUMMARY

Interfaces are the points at which influence flows to and from the nuclear family system. Key interfaces occur both within and outside of the nuclear family system. Recognizing family subsystems highlights the pattern of alliances, coalitions, and triangles in the family and their function for the family. It also helps to identify ways in which various members of the family relate to other individuals and to other subgroups within the family system.

Other systems of importance include the extended family network; the social support system; and the community, culture, and larger environment. Understanding the degree to which a given family influences and is influenced by these systems helps to identify ways in which families cope with life events through their communication.

A focus on family interfaces provides insight into the ways families cope with the stability-change dilemma. To provide for the continuity and integrity of the family, a family tends to resist influences from the environment as it strives for stability. Conversely, to cope with environmental changes and surprises, a family must demonstrate some degree of flexibility. Other dialectical processes involve the struggle between integration and differentiation and the family's need to preserve its own identity while assimilating into the larger culture.

As we have seen, the family is more than the sum of its members. The family system is a dynamic, goal-directed set of components that adapts and changes in response to influences from its environment while simultaneously effecting changes in that environment. In many ways the family system is dependent upon its environment—for social support, for financial input, for technological support, and so on. In many other ways, effective family functioning involves incorporating only those influences that enhance family life while consciously excluding others. Thus, the family that routinely takes the children to the museum of natural history while prohibiting them access to a television set consciously shapes the interests and experiences that enter the family system. Being able to consciously screen inputs from the environment and compare them with family goals, values, and developmental stages is an important ability for family systems to acquire. Likewise, understanding how the family influences and is influenced by its immediate environment can enhance family functioning.

KEY TERMS

alliances	extended family network
coalitions	interfaces
community system	scapegoat
ecosystem	social support system
environed unit	transactions
environment	triangulation

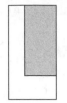

CHAPTER 7

RULES

PEGGY BRISBANE

MARK AND RITA LARSEN

Three couples are sitting around a table at a New Year's Eve party at the home of mutual friends. One woman, Marion Sussex, talks animatedly about a source of conflict between her and her husband, Peter. The couple lives in the same city as the husband's family, and two or three evenings a week his parents visit without giving any advance notice. Marion explains that she experiences these visits as very annoying. She describes the most recent visit, during which the in-laws arrived at dinnertime and casually made room for themselves at the table. According to Marion, her mother-in-law dominated the conversation, talking with Peter and their three sons, David, Andrew, and Justin, pointedly leaving her out of the conversation. Whenever she tried to participate in the discussion, Mrs. Sussex, senior, cut her off as if she didn't exist.

Peter Sussex listens to his wife's description of the scene with a slight smile on his face. After she has completed her version, he asks for equal time and reinterprets the scene from his perspective. His loving but conversation-starved mother came over for dinner to talk to the four fabulous men in her life. With such excellent company available only ten minutes away, how could his mother and father resist dropping by? According to Peter, Marion just can't see how incredible Peter and his three sons really are. Marion groans loudly and both laugh at the exaggerated description of the family scene. It is clear that the couple is able to see the humor in the situation.

A second woman, Rita Larsen, joins the discussion with her own experience, though it is apparent that she wants the conversation to take a more serious tone. She begins to tell the others about her own mother-in-law, who she believes views her as incompetent both as a wife to her husband, Mark, and as a mother to her two children, Toni and Rachel.

The chuckling between Marion and Peter stops, and everyone looks at Rita in surprise, then over to her husband, Mark, to gauge his reaction. Such disclosures from Rita are uncommon in this group. Everyone listens intently to Rita's story, except Mark, who tries to catch her eye and, failing that, looks down at his fingernails.

Rita elaborates on a recent event in their home during the two weeks her mother-in-law spent with the family to celebrate Christmas. On Christmas Eve, the family had gathered in the living room to open gifts. According to Rita, Mrs. Larsen, senior, had been drinking quite heavily all afternoon and was in a foul mood. When it came time for her to open the gift from Rita and Mark, Mrs. Larsen made several caustic remarks about Rita's taste in gift items and her inability to match gift ideas with intended recipients. In fact, Rita's mother-in-law launched into a detailed description of gifts she had received from Rita during the past five years—each of which she described as being more tasteless than the last. Infuriated, Rita stormed out of the room, taking the children with her. Mrs. Larsen followed her out of the room, engaging her in a shouting match and ruining the evening for everyone. During that time, Mark had made no effort to intervene and, according to Rita, gave her every reason to assume that he was taking his mother's side.

Mark Larsen remains silent through much of this description until, red-faced, he finally finds himself drawn into an argument with his wife in front of their friends. Forgetting that there is an audience for their interaction, Mark accuses Rita of exaggerating the circumstances and painting a totally biased picture of his mother. He indicates total outrage at her implication that he sides with his mother against her and demands that she retract that statement. Abruptly remembering the other couples, he becomes embarrassed, insists that they drop the subject, and leaves the room. Ten minutes later, he returns and suggests to Rita that the two of them leave. She is reluctant, but agrees to go.

While driving home, they start to argue again. He asserts that she ruined the evening for him by airing their dirty laundry in public and maintains that she knows better than to draw him into a fight in front of other people. Defending her behavior, she accuses her husband of failing to understand her need to talk to someone about her feelings and explains that she has frequently shared information with these women in the past. She also reminds Mark that their friends have similar problems and asserts that they were not offended over the disagreement. Furious at hearing that Rita routinely shares what he considers to be private information, Mark begins yelling at her. She, in turn, becomes silent, and turns away from him. When they arrive home, Mark takes a pillow and blanket from the bedroom closet and heads for the den; Rita slams the bedroom door.

UNDERSTANDING THE LARSENS

Why is Mark so angry and Rita so defensive? Why wasn't Rita supposed to tell that story about her mother-in-law? Notice that the issue between Mark and Rita at this stage of the conflict is no longer the couple's relationship to Mark's mother. Instead, the argument is about two different issues: whether or not Rita should have publicly disclosed the information about Christmas Eve and whether or not they should have fought with each other at the party. Mark is angry, primarily, because Rita violated two unspoken agreements: one that stipulated that private information should remain private and the other that stipulated that the two of them do not argue in public. Over the years this couple has developed an unspoken contract that "nice people" don't embarrass themselves by criticizing their mates in front of other people or by "airing their dirty laundry in public." Mark is angry at Rita for breaking these rules.

It is not unusual for two people to become involved in a conflict because one of them breaks an agreement that the other believes should not have been violated. This chapter defines "family rules," discusses important characteristics of rules, and identifies three functions that family rules perform for the system. The chapter also examines a taxonomy of rule types, discusses how rules originate and develop in the family, and looks at ways that rules can be adapted to meet changing needs of the family system. By the end of the chapter, you should be able to use the concept of "family rules" as a tool for thinking about the behavior of your family.

CHARACTERISTICS OF FAMILY RULES

As we have discussed in earlier chapters, family systems require a certain amount of predictability to survive. If family members were constantly renegotiating their relationships and their expectations for each other, there would be very little energy left for doing anything else. Families develop sets of rules that guide their behavior. These rules provide the framework for family functioning. Thus, rules provide predictability in the family system and help the system maintain equilibrium. Rules are the benchmarks by which families measure their progress toward family goals.

A wide variety of actions that are frequently difficult to understand can often be analyzed if they are interpreted within the framework of family rules. If a couple does not own a CD player and they have the money to purchase one, how can we explain a conflict that ensues when such a purchase is made? If the Sussexes and the Larsens have similar problems with in-laws, how can we explain the fact that one husband may be amused when his wife shares those problems while another becomes furious? Are there other such contracts in the family that, if violated, produce resistance from certain members? The concept of family rules provides a framework from which to discuss communication and interaction in the family system.

Definition and Description of Family Rules

Possibly the most effective approach for understanding how relationships in the family operate is to identify the rules that govern behavior in the system. Family rules are relationship agreements, established through interaction episodes, that prescribe and limit the behavior of family members over a wide variety of content areas. According to Shimanoff (1980), rules "may function to regulate, interpret, evaluate, justify, correct, predict, and explain behavior" (p. 83).

Family rules can be discovered by identifying the redundancies or repetitive patterns of behavior in the family. Do Janice and Mary Beth spend a portion of their time together discussing problems each of them has at work? Does a wife allow her husband to make most of the important decisions in the family? Does nine-year-old Mary usually hang up her jacket and give her mother a hug when she comes home from school? Is it unusual for Mark and Rita to argue in front of friends of their children? Each of these repetitive behaviors indicates an underlying rule.

We say that family rules are relationship agreements because they are developed through interaction and mutual recognition between individuals in a family system. Suppose that eleven-year-old Jason has a "rule" that he must keep his baseball cards neatly organized. Jason's need to keep the cards neat is a personal but not a family rule. On the other hand, if Jason and his mother have agreed that they will not raise their voices at one another when they argue, that agreement constitutes a family rule. If one or the other violates the relationship agreement, the partner will very likely mention that violation.

Family rules are prescriptions for behavior in that they literally provide guidelines for how family members are expected to behave. If a family member had to get up every morning without any idea of what was expected of him or her or about what to expect from other family members, that person would be exhausted and terribly anxious at the end of the day. Instead, family members typically follow prescriptions for their behavior from the moment they awake in the morning. One family member might be in charge of making breakfast; another might be responsible for getting the paper and setting the table; another might have the responsibility of changing, feeding, and dressing the baby, and so on.

In order for an individual to know or make decisions about how to behave in a social system such as the family, he or she must be able to interpret the actions of others. This is a reciprocal process in which the other person is going through a similar experience of interpretations or meaning assignment.

This coordinated management of meaning (a term coined by Pearce and Cronen, 1980) allows two persons to define the kinds of actions that are permitted, allowed, preferred, or encouraged in their relationship. Rules enable family members to make sense and order out of one another's behavior. They are the prescriptions that govern who can say what to whom, where, and with what effect.

In the previous chapters we indicated that family meanings are negotiated through episodes. Rules are also established through participation in family episodes. *Episodes*, in general, are the units that make up a person's social experience (Harre & Secord, 1973). People don't experience their days as an uninterrupted flow. They tend to recall them as a series of activities such as "getting dressed," "going to work," "paying bills," or "visiting the dentist." Sometimes episodes take the form of small stories and are labeled in order for one to be able to discuss them, to remember them, or to plan an agenda. We speak of "having a fight with," "making up with," or "talking seriously with" another person. Much of our daily lives is constructed in such episodes.

Pearce (1976) distinguishes between different types of episodic situations. Some episodes are accompanied by prescriptions that are shared by almost everyone in the culture or that are established by the institution in which an activity takes place. The protocol that everyone would observe at a presidential banquet is an example of this type of episode. Marriage ceremonies, rites of passage, and greeting rituals are also examples of these kinds of episodes. The rules governing such experiences are widely understood and are usually complied with, within a moderate range of variation.

Once two people initiate an episode that is not as ritualistic, conventional, or routine as a state dinner, however, they negotiate the rules that are to govern their behavior as they communicate with each other. There is no book of family protocol that describes rules universally applicable to every family (though parents sometimes wish there were). Each family must work out its own rules. These are the rules that concern us in this chapter. They influence such things as the conditions under which one member may be allowed to dominate a conversation, how decisions are made and conflicts arbitrated, when family members are expected to be serious and when they may joke, what issues family members are allowed to discuss in front of friends, and other similar expectations. Family rules also dictate the degree to which family members may access information from or provide inputs to the surrounding ecosystem.

One of the main advantages of examining rules in the family system is that it helps us attend to how behavior fits together in the family and enables us to acknowledge relationship agreements that have developed between and among family members. Stafford and Bayer (1993), in their review of research on interaction between parents and children, have made the point that our understanding of communication can best be enhanced by concentrating on "social interaction between persons" rather than focusing primarily on individual behavior that fails to consider adequately "the reciprocal processes of communication" (p. 176). Identifying the rules that govern and organize behavior in the family is one way that we can identify reciprocal patterns of interaction in the family.

Characteristics of Rules

As we discussed earlier, rules are relationship agreements, revealed by repetitive patterns of interaction, which prescribe and limit family behavior. Rules have four defining characteristics (Buerkel-Rothfuss, 1981; Cushman & Whiting, 1972; Shimanoff, 1980):

1. Rules are probabilities, not laws.
2. Rules can be explicit or implicit.
3. Rules exist at different levels in the system.
4. Rules are enforced through overt/direct or covert/indirect sanctions.

Each of these characteristics helps us to understand how rules function in families.

Rules Are Probabilities, Not Laws

We have emphasized that family life is predictable, but it is not absolutely predictable. A basic tenet of theory about rules is that rules only partially predict behavior (Cushman & Craig, 1976). In other words, family rules may be understood as probabilities that specific previous actions are likely to be repeated in any given family.

When we think of laws, we think of the physical properties of science and mathematics that hold true in all instances. However, people are able to make decisions and act unpredictably. There are no "laws" of human behavior, only degrees of regularity with which rules are followed. In identifying a rule, we are making an inference rather than describing a "fact." By noticing regularities in behavior we can infer the existence of a rule. Rules are not "laws" that are static, immutable, or governed by powers beyond the control of the family. Instead, they tend to be demonstrated by *habits of relating* that have developed in a social system at a particular time. A family's habits of relating reflect the value system, ideology, social attitudes, and meanings generated in the family. Rules do not govern behavior directly; rather, they serve as guidelines for how individuals "should" or "ought" to behave in certain circumstances (Gottlieb, 1968). Rules prescribe but they do not guarantee behavior.

For example, the Larsens have a rule against arguing in public. Having a rule does not mean that the rule is always followed nor that tension would result every time the rule was violated. It does mean, however, that the rule would be followed frequently. A rule is not something that operates constantly but is a useful device for guiding behavior in familiar circumstances (Cushman & Craig, 1976).

Rules Can Be Explicit or Implicit

From what has been written so far, it should be apparent that one dimension of rule analysis has to do with identifying the extent to which family members are aware of a specific rule. Rules can either be explicit or implicit. **Explicit rules** are talked about and verbally agreed to. **Implicit rules** remain unspoken and may not be a subject of the family's conversation until they are violated. A family, for instance, may have a rule that any member not intending to be home for the evening meal should call by 5:30 P.M. The rule may never be discussed, negotiated, or verbally agreed to, and yet is understood by everyone. Family members who neither call nor arrive by the appointed time may be in for a lecture, an argument, or punishment of some type. Kramer (1985) explains the force of implicit rules in this way:

> The family member has feelings associated with the breaking of rules—guilt, anxiety, knowing that if other members find out, she will be punished in some way. So she knows rules are there, even though they are not spelled out (p. 14).

Whether a rule is explicitly or implicitly understood depends upon a number of factors: the ways that the rule developed or originated, the extent to which the rule is equally acceptable to each family member involved, the degree of anxiety that surrounds the rule, and the metarules that govern a family's communication behaviors.

If a rule develops without extended discussion and if everyone is comfortable observing it, then there may be little felt need for the family to talk about it. It may simply be one of the assumptions upon which the family's operations are based. Examples of such rules fall under the category of rules frequently called

APPLICATION 7.1

IMPLICIT FAMILY RULES

- Becoming aware of your family's rule system requires a heightened awareness of implicit or unspoken rules as well as those rules that are discussed and made explicitly clear.

- How many implicit rules can you identify in your family system for each of the categories of rules presented in Table 7.2? In Figure 7.2? Would you be able to discuss any or all of these with other family members to check your perceptions? Why? Why not?

"common courtesy": if a family member is watching a program on television, other family members should not feel free to change the channel; if a door is closed, other family members should knock before entering.

If there is tension associated with a rule, it may be more difficult for family members to make the rules explicit. Frequently, families develop *metarules* (rules about rules) to deal with such circumstances.

Laing (1972) has written about those rules that restrict what one may talk about. There are rules that prohibit family members from talking about certain subjects and rules that prohibit talking about the existence of the rule. Metarules frequently tie families into knots. For example, everyone in the Cook family is aware that the oldest daughter had an abortion when she was seventeen. However, there is a rule (established by the parents) prohibiting discussion of the girl's abortion. Other children in the Cook family learn the rule that talking about their sister's abortion is prohibited, and they also learn that one doesn't discuss the fact that such talk is prohibited. It is not likely that questions such as, "Why can't we talk about Sheila's abortion?" would be asked. Consequently, family members are prohibited from seeing all the issues that arise from complying with or breaking those rules. Any problem solving related to a metarule becomes impossible. Nor is it ever possible to change a rule that is "protected" by such a metarule.

Consider an example in which a mother insists on a rule that her three daughters never talk about their brother, who has been in and out of trouble, was finally sent to prison, and has become estranged from the family. When references to the brother surface, mother tells a story that the son "has disappeared," changes the subject, and refuses to talk further about the matter. Not only is there a rule against talking about him, there is a metarule against talking about the rule. Talking about the rule acknowledges the existence of this mother's son and his very existence is so painful for her that awareness of the pain is not even allowed. In this family it is impossible to resolve, confront, or even accept the feelings of anger, guilt, and responsibility associated with the son.

Metarules may also operate out of fear that any change will worsen the existing situation. To admit the existence of a rule is to be open to the possibility of its being changed. The enforcement of a taboo against discussing a rule is further reinforcement that the rule will not be violated. A classic example of this situation for many families revolves around the sexual activity of teenagers in the family. In families where it is difficult to talk about sex, it is often the case that a metarule prohibits talking about the fact that they don't talk about sex. To initiate a discussion of sexuality is to acknowledge that such behavior is a possibility for family members. To prohibit such talk minimizes the probability that rules about sex will be challenged or changed, at least openly.

Reprisals for violating implicitly held rules are just as severe as those for explicit rules, however. If a father assumes that his nineteen-year-old son will be home for supper as usual and he does not come home, the father may become very agitated. Yet there may have been no previous verbal agreement about mealtimes. In this case the rule is discussed only when one party violates it.

One consequence of implicit rules is that a family may be governed by sets of rules that exist outside of its awareness. A family may develop a pattern of behavior in which one parent withdraws in dismay when the children become rowdy, leaving the other parent to act as disciplinarian. If the second parent does not intervene, the household usually becomes the stage for a general uproar. This drama may be enacted frequently, and yet, there may be a lack of conscious awareness by any of the members of the family that this is a regular, rule-governed sequence of events.

Rules Exist at Different Levels in the Family System

Rules can also be examined from an ecosystems perspective. As discussed earlier, rules are relationship agreements that evolve from interaction episodes. Relationships exist at all but the lowest level in family systems.

Jason's rule about organizing his baseball cards is a personal rule. A **personal rule** is one developed by one person that governs only that person's behavior. It becomes a family rule only when it affects another family member in some way, such as when the card collection takes up space in someone else's closet or messes up common living spaces, or when organizing his album takes time away from activities with other family members. Jason's rule is no less a rule—a prescription for behavior—but it is not a family rule. Jason's personal rule becomes important to family communication when it interfaces with other family rules that support or conflict with his rule.

Many family rules develop at the dyadic level. Family members have expectations for how they should behave toward each other (and for how others should behave toward them) and these expectations generally develop into relational or dyadic rules. **Dyadic rules** govern behavior in a two-person relationship. In the opening example, the rule about not arguing in public helped Rita and Mark to identify information that was to remain private between them and information that could be shared outside of their relationship. In this case, their dyadic rule helped to support the boundary around their spousal dyad.

Subsystem rules, or rules governing three-person and larger subsystems within the nuclear family, also develop in triadic and larger family relationships. Children in a system may develop rules about how to relate with one another that differ from how they relate to other children outside of the family. For example, siblings who are generally agreeable toward their playmates may feel free to taunt and even terrorize each other. Parents may relate differently with one child than they do with another; in families where rules follow traditional sex roles, it is common for parents to treat their male children differently from their female children (Stewart, Cooper, & Friedley, 1986). Interaction patterns that result in alliances, coalitions, and triangles are typically governed by subsystem rules (Haley, 1976; Kerr & Bowen, 1988; Napier & Whitaker, 1978).

TABLE 7.1   Rules at different levels in the family system.

Family rules are relationship agreements, established through interaction episodes, that prescribe and limit the behavior of family members over a wide variety of content areas.

LEVELS	RULES
1. Personal rules	Jason organizes his baseball cards.
2. Dyadic rules	Mark and Rita don't argue in public.
3. Subsystem rules	Three teenaged sisters talk with each other, but not with their parents, about boyfriends.
4. Nuclear system family rules	The family has brunch together on Sunday.
5. Extended family system rules	Grandmother can take over the kitchen when she comes to visit.

Family system rules govern the behavior of the family as a whole. These rules are often grounded in family values and power relationships. For example, some families define themselves as "other-oriented" and develop sets of rules that require family members to help others: working as volunteers, donating money to organizations, tithing income to their church, and so on. Other families develop rules about how to treat each other: every family member "sticks up" for every other family member, no matter what, other family members must try to cheer up a family member who is depressed, or children do not yell at their parents.

In conjunction with their extended family systems, families develop extended family rules. **Extended family rules** are rules that govern the interactions at the interfaces between the nuclear family and families of origin. Typical rules at this level of the ecosystem include who will take responsibility for hosting Thanksgiving dinner, which grandparents will be asked to stay with the children when the parents are out of town, whether or not aunts/uncles and grandparents have the authority to discipline the children, the amount of emotional support that can be expected across generations in times of difficulty, the logistics of children's visitations to grandparents in a divorced family, and so on. Ways in which the generations relate to each other are governed by these extended family rules (Cohler & Grunebaum, 1981; Kramer, 1985).

Returning to our discussion of the organization of family systems, it should be clear that rules govern various interfaces in the ecosystem. Multiple levels of rules add to the complexity of the family system; awareness that rules exist at different levels in the system helps us to understand this complexity and recognize the potential for conflict when rules at the interfaces contradict.

Rules Are Enforced by Sanctions

Sanctions are behaviors intended to enforce rules or to punish offenders who violate them, which serve as homeostatic or feedback mechanisms to keep the family system stable. They primarily function in opposition to any change in the system. For instance, imagine a couple with a rule that each partner is to be home for dinner at a specific time every evening and one evening one of the partners is an hour late. There are a number of alternative behaviors open to the partner who is responsible for cooking the dinner. In this case, the partner can simply wait and keep the meal warm, with the expectation that some explanation may be forthcoming. If an explanation is offered, the matter may be closed. If the same circumstance is soon repeated, however, the rule may be changed or altered permanently so that it becomes, "If a partner is late for dinner, supper will be delayed." A partner who makes things unpleasant for the one who is late is engaging in sanctioning behavior to prevent the rule from being changed—for instance, displaying anger, serving a meal that is cold or overdone, or acting especially cool during dinner. If negative sanctions follow a rule violation, as they did in the opening example where Mark yelled at his wife and slept alone in the den, the rule violator is generally inclined to follow the rule at the next opportunity. Any time that punishments or reprisals are not invoked for a rule violation, however, the rule becomes subject to change.

Negative sanctions can be either overt or covert. Overt sanctions are direct sanctions that are expressed verbally and may, in turn, invite a direct response from the recipient. Parents may take away the automobile privileges of their sixteen-year-old daughter for a month when she violates their curfew agreement; a

NANCY VADER-McCORMICK

Rules govern a wide range of behaviors and situations in the family.

wife may verbalize her irritation at her husband for accepting a social invitation without checking with her; a husband may express anger at his wife for staying late at work without calling him.

Socha (1991) has indicated how parents can induce feelings of guilt in their sons and daughters as a particular type of verbal sanction for violating rules. **Guilt inducements** attempt to control the other person's behavior by making him or her responsible for the discomfort or unfair treatment of other family members. For example, a mother might attempt to induce feelings of guilt in her college-aged daughter by telling the daughter that she will be "hurt and lonely" if the daughter does not come home for Thanksgiving vacation as she usually does. A father may indicate that he will be "disappointed" if his son does not work in the family business during the summer. A family can use a wide range of communication behaviors as overt sanctions for violating rules.

Covert sanctions are expressed indirectly, are often nonverbal and may not obviously invite a direct verbal response. Family members can engage in a variety of covert sanctioning behaviors. They can change the subject during conversations, become distant or refuse to speak to another member of the family, retaliate in some indirect way, such as being late for dinner or an appointment, or even become ill. Such behaviors function as tactics to enforce the rule and resist change (Haley, 1963).

Whether a negative sanction is carried out overtly or covertly may depend on a number of factors. First of all, it will depend on the communication skills of the people involved. The injured party must be aware of and feel responsible for his or her feelings about the behavior and be able to communicate them. It may be more difficult for a spouse to communicate hurt than to say, "You made me ruin the meal." Rausch, Barry, Hertel, and Swain (1974) have found, however, that some families can convey messages in indirect ways that are satisfactory for them.

There are other reasons for using covert sanctioning methods, however. If a family is unable to acknowledge or discuss a particular rule, then the sanctions must be covert. In those cases, the metarules actually govern sanctions for rule violations. For example, the Houston family never discusses sex. Furthermore, there is a metarule that prevents anyone from mentioning the fact that the family never discusses sex. Even though their two children are adults, the elder Houstons have never had a conversation with either of them about their sexuality—nor have the children ever asked why such a conversation has never taken place. Whenever one of the children does happen to mention something pertaining to sex in front of the parents, the subject is dealt with quickly—a covert sanction from the parents that indicates that neither the rule (we don't talk about sex) nor the metarule (we don't talk about why we don't talk about sex) can be violated.

Sometimes families may develop covert sanctions because they have a low tolerance for direct confrontation. If a husband is hurt because his spouse violated a rule (and, thus, injured his self-esteem) the husband may give her the "silent treatment" as a response to her behavior and she may endure it rather than confront him. In the opening example, Rita withdrew from the argument in the car and Mark further "punished" her by retreating to the den to spend the night. Although the sanctions were largely covert at that point, both individuals fully understood the message behind the nonverbal behavior.

Family members may also utilize covert sanctions when the status relationship between them is differentiated rigidly. For instance, one partner may perceive himself or herself as "less powerful" than the other. Instead of directly saying, "I am mad as hell at you!" he or she may use a more indirect expression of anger such as pouting or withholding sexual intimacy.

Silencing strategies, or communication behaviors that stifle conversation, are so frequently used by families as sanctioning mechanisms that they deserve special consideration. Zuk (1965) has delineated a number of silencing strategies that he defines as maneuvers designed to avoid dealing with an issue or feeling and/or to punish an individual for some transgression by isolating that person in silence. Silencing strategies are employed to prevent discussion of rules and as reprisals.

An obvious nonverbal silencing strategy is simply to ignore the other person's presence or to give the person "the cold shoulder." This strategy involves the avoidance of eye contact, refusal to interact or make contact with the other person, and maintaining a neutral facial expression when confronted by the other person. Pouting can function as another silencing strategy, as can turning up the volume on the stereo or television. One can engage in silencing another by withdrawal, by not being available to the other person. This can be done by leaving and not returning at an expected time, by sleeping, or by withdrawing into oneself.

Silencing strategies can also involve a complex set of communication behaviors. One can yawn, look impatient, shift body position, break eye contact, grimace, fondle objects absently, appear busy, or look hurt or pained to discourage someone from continuing. Zuk (1965) gives the example of a mother who always looked pained when her daughter began to reveal her feelings about her in front of the therapist. One can silence another by engaging in nonverbal behavior that communicates disapproval, hostility, hurt, or worry and then deny responsibility for it. Consider the following sequence, using the mother and daughter interacting in front of the therapist as the situation:

Daughter criticizes her mother.

Mother looks pained and withdrawn.

Daughter says, "What's wrong?"

Mother responds with, "Oh, nothing."

The daughter halts her criticism, saying that now she couldn't remember what it was she had to say and perhaps it isn't justified anyway.

While silencing strategies can be used effectively as sanctioning devices, they often create problems for the family. They involve communication behaviors that can be confusing and difficult to interpret and tend to reduce the amount of information exchanged. There is evidence to support the assertion that clinical families tend to exchange less information than normal families. According to research conducted by Ferreira and Winter (1968), people in problem families do not seem to talk to each other as they do in nonclinical families. Members of troubled families tend to withhold from each other information about their feelings and wants, often allowing their likes and dislikes to go unverbalized. Hauser and his colleagues (1991) have supported these conclusions in their research with families of adolescents. Families that are able to promote positive self-concepts of their children are characterized as having a higher tolerance for emotional expressiveness and greater exchange of information between parents and children.

FUNCTIONS OF FAMILY RULES

As we have discussed so far, family rules are critical to a family's functioning. Combining some of the system properties of families discussed in Chapter 3 with the notion of family rules, we can identify three central functions of family rules:

1. Family rules enable family members to coordinate interaction in the family.
2. Family rules establish some degree of predictability and stability in the system.
3. Family rules establish and regulate the boundaries and networks in the family system.

Coordinate Interaction

According to philosopher David K. Lewis (1969), rules exist to help individuals choose among alternative behaviors while coordinating their behaviors with that of other individuals. Lewis argued that human relationships require such coordination to maximize goal attainment for all individuals concerned. Imagine, for example, two cars approaching each other on a one-lane bridge. Each driver has several options: (1) back up so that the other can pass, (2) honk the horn, thus indicating an expectation that the other driver should back up, (3) continue forward until the bumpers touch, and (4) drive off the bridge into the water. Obviously, some options are better than others, and some are better for one individual (honk so that the other will back up) while others are better for the other individual (back up so that the other can pass). When individuals encounter similar situations frequently, they develop rules to maximize the outcome for both parties, such as installing a traffic signal at each end of the bridge from the other side, thus speeding up the process of crossing for everyone.

This type of coordination is also characteristic of families. Couples bring sets of expectations to the marital relationship that are not always compatible. The negotiation and evolution of a system of rules allows the couple to maximize goal attainment for each individual in the relationship while allowing completion of system tasks (she chops vegetables; he makes the salad dressing) and allowing for system growth and change (they discuss problems over dinner twice each week). The rules form the structure for successful system operation.

Establish Predictability and Stability

When actions are successfully coordinated in a way that maximizes system stability, those actions become a pattern and, thus, predictable. In the same way, rules become patterned and predictable, thus lending additional stability to the system. As more and more motorists encounter one-lane bridges, more and more traffic signals are installed. Similarly, as family members develop behaviors in the system that help them to coordinate interaction, those behaviors become patterned and predictable. If a husband is almost always praised by his grateful wife whenever he tackles the laundry, the husband may assume laundry chores as part of his role in the system. Knowing that the husband will do the laundry, the other family members can predict that they will have clean clothes to wear, thus maximizing system stability and predictability.

Communication behaviors also become rule-governed and patterned in the family system. Family members can predict the types of responses they will get from each other when they ask for a favor, express anger, criticize, or withdraw from interaction. In general, the more consistent and predictable the responses one gets from family members, the more stable the family system. In fact, research in the area of schizophrenia suggests that mental illness may develop in systems where messages are either not predictable or contradictory (Bateson, Jackson, Haley, & Weakland, 1956). Likewise, research in child-rearing stresses the need for consistency in response to both desired and undesired behavior in children (Smith & Smith, 1976).

Establish and Regulate Boundaries and Communication Networks

As we discussed in Chapter 3, the family system is marked by visible and invisible boundaries that separate it from the outside environment. Boundaries also surround individuals and relationships within the nuclear family. Interfaces connect the individuals to each other within the system and connect the family to other systems in the environment.

The linkages that specify the amount and kind of communication interactions possible between individuals within the system are called networks (see Figure 7.1). Family rules that govern the messages exchanged between family members and the variables associated with those messages (degree of self-disclosure, degree of honesty about feelings, intensity of feelings expressed, volume at which they are expressed, etc.) govern family communication networks.

Thus, *rules are the framework for both boundary definition and network development and regulation in the family system.* Rules describe which inputs are allowed to enter the system and which outputs are allowed to leave. Rules govern who can talk to whom and with what effect—both within and without the family system.

Looking first at dyadic subsystems, family rules help identify relationships within the family system. In the husband–wife dyad, there may be a rule that specifies that they will spend one hour together each evening talking about family events—without interruption. This rule clearly defines the boundary around their dyad during that hour and defines the network that links the two individuals. The couple may also have rules that specify information that should remain private to

FIGURE 7.1   Family communication networks.

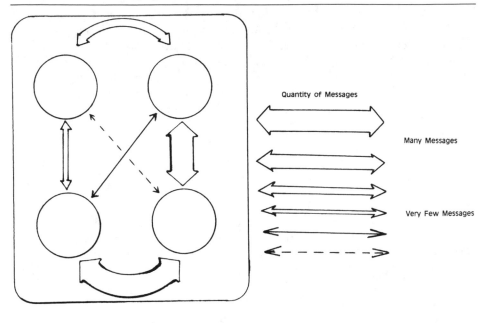

their dyad, how they will deal with conflicts between them, how they will delegate decision-making power, and so on. Relational rules dictate how the couple will respond to each other as relational partners and help to differentiate their relationship with one another from the relationships they share with other family members.

Similarly, rules specify boundaries around triads and larger subsystems in the family system. Three sisters may form a coalition against their older brother. This coalition is go erned by the rules that the sisters negotiate and regulate in their triad. Rules about knocking at their bedroom door, their right to have a private phone line in their room, and their use of a family car may all indicate where the boundary is drawn with regard to their relationships with others outside of the triad. The strength of the communication, and the rules that govern what (and how much) can be said, define the network that links that triad. Rules also establish networks with the suprasystem. Families develop rules for such things as what information is to be kept inside the family, who is to be included in family gatherings, and who speaks to whom if there is a problem to be solved. Taken in combination, family rules identify the connections that the family system will have with the outside environment and the quality and quantity of information that will pass in and out of the family boundary.

A TAXONOMY OF FAMILY RULES

One can identify a specific rule by observing behaviors that repeat themselves. Another way of identifying rules is to specify content areas that the rules could conceivably govern. These two strategies combined can be developed into a classification system for categorizing rules. The classification scheme or taxonomy of rules described in this chapter combines these two rule identification procedures to create categories of rule types.

The content areas were developed from a synthesis of family studies and are certainly not definitive. As a consequence, you may identify a typical behavior pattern in your family that is difficult to assign to a particular rule category. For instance, rules governing the duties and responsibilities of family members may govern family status and authority relationships as well. Nevertheless, such a system does provide a way of identifying alternative types of rules and those behaviors that they govern.

Identifying a rule by identifying behaviors that tend to be repeated can help families to identify patterns in their daily lives. Noting a specific rule-governed behavior such as "dinner is always at 6:00 P.M." or "Rita and Mark do not argue in public" is generally a descriptive, not an evaluative, process. If a family can at least talk about and identify a rule, then they can decide to make the choice to continue, stop, or renegotiate it.

Rules governing the duties and responsibilities of family members are concerned with how the labor or work requirements of the family are divided; which members of the family are responsible for keeping the family accounts; how the child-care duties of the family are allocated; what household tasks are assigned to the children; whether or not there is any hierarchy of tasks established because of the importance value or reward associated with the task; whether or not this hierarchy influences who is assigned to the task.

In some families there may be a rule mandating that one parent is the family breadwinner. In other families that responsibility may be shared either equally or disproportionately between parents. In some families children who live at home past a certain age may be expected to provide a portion of the family income. In

TABLE 7.2   Taxonomy of family rules.

AREAS OF FAMILY LIFE	GOVERNING RULES
1. Duties and responsibilities	It is Jason's job to load the dishwasher.
2. Status and authority relationships for specific contexts	Rita plans their social events; Mark makes decisions about home improvements; they negotiate other financial decisions.
3. Appropriateness of behaviors	Three children may use off-color language when they are alone with each other but not in front of adults.
4. Family members' sexual behavior, physical intimacy, and availability	Rita and Mark do not express affection for each other in public but both of them openly express affection for their children.
5. Personality characteristics of family members	Jason is the "artistic" one in the family; his sister, Rachel, is the one who is "good at problem solving"; their brother, Peter, is the "trouble-maker" of the family.
6. Communication behaviors	Rita may challenge Mark's tendency to criticize her behavior; Mark may give Rita the "silent treatment" when she breaks a relational rule; both Mark and Rita may raise their voices when they argue with each other but not when they discipline the children.

other families, the parents may provide for their children's needs long after the children are married and established in their own family systems. A family may have rules that require that housekeeping chores be assigned according to the gender of the family member. In other families there may be a rule against assigning jobs on such a basis and care is taken, for instance, that son and daughter share or take turns babysitting, doing the dishes, or mowing the lawn. Rules of this nature reveal a family's orientation toward sex roles and parent–child relationships. Notice the nature of those tasks assigned to children. Are they sex-typed, valued by other family members, nonexistent, inconsequential, or are they chores that parents dislike? Are children required to rake leaves in the fall but not allowed to select plants and flowers in the spring?

The rules a family develops in meeting social obligations belong in this category also. If letters are written, what family members tend to write them? How and by whom are social overtures carried out? Some families make complex rituals out of social invitations and events, relying heavily on doctrine from social norms or etiquette texts. In other families, a simple phone call is considered a sufficient invitation to a family gathering.

Families may also develop rules discouraging certain kinds of task activity or competency. A neat uncle who reminds his relatives of Felix Unger from "The Odd Couple" could be discomforting to them when he visits. As he tries to keep the house tidy, thinking he is doing the family a favor, family members may be right behind him deliberately dirtying glasses or scattering newspapers. The tasks that never get done are very often governed by rules that are carefully, albeit unconsciously, adhered to by family members. Disorder and ineptitude can also be rule-governed behaviors. Eddie and his son brag about their messy apartment.

Rules governing the status and authority of family members generally depend on the degree to which such relationships are recognized and enforced. For instance, are the parents strict? Do they emphasize authority and discipline, or are the status differences in the family less rigidly defined and the climate more egalitarian and permissive? Rules that have to do with children's independence and autonomy belong in this category. To what extent do parents establish rules which have to do with where their children can travel or visit, how late they can stay out at night, what activities are forbidden, what competencies should be developed, etc.? How do the child's age and gender influence such regulations? Parents may establish periodic inspections of the children's room but may be outraged to find the children rummaging through the dresser drawers of the master bedroom. As Kramer (1985) indicates, "All family systems have rules forming a covert power structure of operational behavior. Moment by moment, through verbal and nonverbal cues, members are informed of the acceptability of their actions. Even saying or doing nothing carries a message. Every child discovers the rules he must follow in order to survive" (p. 9).

Rules that prescribe how to make major family decisions usually involve status and authority relationships in a family. Does a father whose employer has offered him a position in another city announce to the family his decision to move, do both parents decide for the family, or do parents and children give inputs into the decision? Would the process be the same if the mother's employer requested that she transfer? If a family vacation is planned, do all the members including the children participate in the decision or does one or both of the parents decide and make the announcement to the rest of the family? Who makes decisions about major purchases?

Sometimes a rule may define task behavior and yet its real purpose is to reinforce a status and authority relationship. Marion Sussex is amused at the way her mother-in-law can spend much of Thanksgiving day cooking a sumptuous meal and yet defer the carving of the turkey to her husband, whom she considers the head of the household. Marion's mother-in-law deplores her inability to carve a turkey. In a less traditional family, the task may be carried out by the cook, whether that is mother, father, or one of the children. Carving the turkey has symbolic meaning for the Sussex family, however, and it is seen as a high status task reserved for the father in the family. As we have indicated earlier in this book, family therapists, researchers, and writers are paying increasing attention to how the rules that govern power and status relationships in the family may disadvantage some family members (Goodrich, Rampage, Ellman, & Halstead, 1988; Walters, Carter, Papp, & Silverstein, 1988; Gouldner, 1985). If one partner in a marriage has considerably more status and authority in the family, the person with less authority may not develop a strong sense of self or develop important life skills that could be crucial at another stage in the family's life. If parents do not relinquish control of their children and encourage their children to make decisions on their own as they grow older and mature, children in the family may have difficulties developing a sense of their own personal worth and authority in adulthood (Williamson, 1991).

Rules governing the appropriateness of various behaviors for specific contexts have to do with the time, setting, and spatial regulations governing certain behaviors. Scheduling of meals falls into this category. A rule requiring that the evening meal be consumed between 6:00 and 7:30 P.M., on trays in the living room while everyone watches the evening news, is one example. The rule may be so closely followed that friends generally know not to call during that time period.

Henry (1973) has described "the doctrines of eating"—an elaborate system of rules governing table manners. One category, for instance, includes "the doctrine of quantity." Generally, he writes, "It is hoped that people will eat to their heart's content. Limits are set, however, on the amount of food that may be put on the plate at any one time. The rule is to ask for several helpings of food, not pile it on one's plate, for to do so suggests greediness" (pp. 89–91).

Every family will have its own idiosyncratic eating rules. Such rules may seem trivial and yet a violation of these rules may be perceived as a personal affront to some members of the family. Refusing to eat something, appearing late for a meal, and making obscene noises at mealtime are all behaviors that may be met with strong negative sanctions.

There are also rules that regulate the times when certain behaviors are considered appropriate or that regulate the time schedules of family members. Sunday afternoons may be reserved as a time for the family to be together. A family member who plans to be away from home without significant cause during that time may be negatively sanctioned. It may also be appropriate for young children to run around inside of the house naked but not outside, or to wear pajamas after supper but not at 4:00 in the afternoon. Families usually have rules governing regularly scheduled bedtimes and waking-up times of family members. There may be rules against wasting time or rules governing how much time may be spent at a particular activity. Spending an entire day absorbed in a book may be an acceptable pastime while spending the entire day watching television may not. The book may be a gothic or western novel without literary merit yet not be negatively sanctioned.

While such rules may appear innocent, they often hold much significance. These family rules frequently represent family values. They are also significant for a family's routine and may even be closely associated with rules governing other dimensions of behavior. A mother who requires her children to wipe their shoes off at the door or not to eat with their fingers also reinforces her status and authority relationship to her children.

Rules governing family members' sexual behavior, physical intimacy, and/or availability regulate a wide range of behaviors. Included in this category, of course, are rules that govern the conjugal relationships between the parents. How frequently, when, and where to engage in sexual intercourse, as well as who usually initiates contact, under what circumstances, and the individual behaviors considered pleasurable, distasteful, or irritating may be governed by a series of complex and subtle rules.

Rules that deal with the sexual expression of family members often overlap with rules that govern communication. For example, shame and fear may keep family members from confronting rules of silence that accompany painful or abusive sexual experiences in a family. Rigid rules may be enforced that prohibit discussion of sexually abusive practices in the family. Allen (1980) and Ronai (1994) each describe the pressures that they experienced to keep their father's sexually abusive behavior a secret. The extent to which a family encourages or discourages talk about such issues as pregnancy, birth control, masturbation, menstrual cycles, the initial sexual encounters of teenaged or young-adult children, sexually abusive behavior, and the sexual intimacy of the parents is related to communication and sexuality categories.

In addition to rules governing family members' sexuality and talk about sexuality, families also have rules governing the amount and kind of physical intimacy related to nonsexual contact among family members (Montague, 1971). The extent to which family members cuddle, embrace, fondle, or caress one another is not random but rule-governed. Although these are nonverbal forms of expression, they are differentiated from other communicative acts by their relationship to physical expression, which is a unique category of interaction.

Henry (1973) also discusses the concept of "availability" as it relates to family intimacy. Availability has to do with how a person distributes his or her resources among various persons and activities, including the extent to which one divides time among work, social, and family commitments. A family may function with a rule that makes it acceptable for one parent to be more available to the children than the other. Henry makes the point that when a parent becomes unavailable to his or her family, that parent may be remote from them even when in their presence. Rules that regulate the availability of children to their parents may also develop, especially as children get older. Rules may develop concerning the extent to which children are obligated to be part of family functions, such as family holidays, family vacations, and family reunions. Sometimes children separate themselves from their parents geographically in order to reduce such obligations.

How much time do family members spend with one another? How present are they and how much physical contact do they make with each other? Are some family members more available to the family than others? These phenomena are all governed by intimacy rules.

Rules governing the personality characteristics expected of family members are usually manifested in some labeling behavior. Mother is always calm, Tom is usually cheerful and funny, Mary is the ambitious one in the family, Father is understanding. Aunt Harriet tends to be nervous, Uncle Mac is a good mixer, Cousin Julius is an egghead. Such examples are, of course, oversimplifications. But families may come to depend on specific personality traits of family members as resources or, at least, as a way of predicting the outcome of an interaction. If one family member behaves contrary to other family members' expectations, he or she may generate a negative response or a controlling behavior from other family members who are trying to extract the expected behavior. Predictability increases stability. If serious Kate is clowning around, other members of the family may say she is acting strange or weird. If extroverted Ted is quiet, mother may think that there is something wrong with him. When Rita begins disclosing some feelings she has about her mother-in-law, her friends may listen uncomfortably if such behavior is not typical of Rita's reserved personality.

Rules governing the expectations that family members have for each other may become frozen, reducing the family's ability to be responsive to one another or to adapt to change.

A family may select a few behavior traits of one or several of its members and respond to only those, screening out information that contradicts a favored impression. For example, a father might respond positively to his son's athletic ability, yet be unaware of the child's tenderness with animals. This father may be later surprised to discover that his son would like to abandon a promising career as an athlete in order to become a nurse. The complex and ever-changing personality structures of family members are frequently assumed to be much more simple and stable than they are.

Single-parent families may be especially vulnerable to this problem of developing rules that tend to oversimplify, or even negatively construct, the personality characteristics of family members. Extended family members and society in general often stereotype single mothers as overwhelmed, overextended, and inadequate (Kissman & Allen, 1993). In helping single parents overcome this stereotyping, Kissman and Allen suggest that single mothers often benefit from reframing their perceptions of themselves. They can be given support for acknowledging positive aspects of single-parent family life and for seeing themselves as lacking confidence rather than as incompetent.

Cherie is a single mother who began to talk with her children about the positive aspects of single-parent life. Cherie's children indicated that they thought their family was more democratic than most families and that they were more independent than their peers. New rules governing the personality traits and characteristics of the family evolved around this reframing process. Cherie and her children developed a new rule for her, suggesting that "she was determined and courageous" rather than "overwhelmed." Peggy, her eldest daughter, became "independent" rather than "stubborn and rebellious." The family began to see Dan as the most "honest and direct" person in the family rather than as "rude and disrespectful." As the family began to develop even minor changes in the rules for individual personalities in the family, their interaction began to take on a more positive connotation, which eventually led to a more supportive and accepting family climate for everyone.

Rules governing the communication behaviors of family members are very likely the most significant. Communication is a necessary process in the maintenance of any rule system and, as a consequence, communication rules overlap with those rules in other categories.

Every family develops a set of communication rules. These rules govern what family members are and are not allowed to openly discuss. Whether or not family members can ask questions about certain subjects and the degree to which they can openly challenge or criticize each other, as well as their ability to express approval of and affection for one another are areas governed by communication rules. Who interacts with whom and the frequency of communication among various members of the family are patterned behaviors.

Rules also regulate the clarity and directness with which requests are and can be made in families. Satir (1983) is especially concerned with rules that specify what family members may *not* communicate to each other. Because family members cannot talk about certain subjects, they begin to develop feelings of anxiety about those subjects. The typical example is the child who learns that sex is a taboo subject for family discussion after his mother or father repeatedly changes the subject whenever he asks them a question about his or someone else's body. The child may have difficulty sorting out his or her own sexual feelings if they cannot be openly discussed.

Sensitivity to the rule-governed nature of communication behaviors can be extended by asking certain questions about communication rules. How does a family typically communicate needs to one another? What topics of conversation are avoided? How do family members silence each other or express their anger to each other? To what extent are nonverbal behaviors relied upon to communicate feelings? If you attempt to respond to some of these questions, you will begin to increase your awareness of the rules that regulate your family's interaction and message behaviors.

ORIGINS OF FAMILY RULES

It may be difficult to document when and under what circumstances a particular rule began. Such information may not even be relevant in deciding whether or not the rule has become a problem. However, one generic characteristic of families is that they have histories. A newly married couple may be the exception to this generalization, but it is not uncommon for such couples to have spent most of their time together prior to marriage and, consequently, for them to develop a history before marrying. The rules that govern families, therefore, are often products of evolutionary processes rather than single events. There are advantages to increasing a family's awareness of how a particular rule evolved. If the rule is still in operation after the circumstances that made it functional have changed, then perhaps the family needs to reassess whether the rule should be continued.

Three methods of identifying the origin of a rule involve specifying the history of the behavior governed by the rule. In particular, it is useful to know whether the rule governs (1) a random behavior or initial agreement that evolved into a pattern, (2) a behavior that emerged from the value orientations of the parents, or (3) a behavior that evolved as a bargain between family members.

Lederer and Jackson (1968) suggest that random developments often turn into well-defined patterns. A task, for instance, may be done initially by one person in the family with the result that it becomes his or her job. If one person does something, such as paying the newspaper carrier or setting an alarm clock, that task may become permanently assigned to that individual. No one is likely to take notice of this assignment until the individual asks that some other family member do the chore or until the task fails to get completed. A family that has overslept on a weekday is likely to blame the person who routinely sets the alarm clock in the evening for their collective problem.

FIGURE 7.2 Origins of family rules.

Rules Develop from Initial Patterns or Agreements

Jill and Arnie lived with each other for a year before getting married. When they moved in with each other, they agreed that each person would do his or her own laundry. In addition, Jill would wash the sheets and Arnie would wash the towels. After one daughter and twenty years of marriage, the arrangement is still in operation. Each member of the family, including twelve-year-old Caroline, has a laundry basket and does his/her own laundry.

Rules Develop from Family Values

Whenever Caroline feels unhappy or angry about something she retreats to her bedroom and closes the door. Usually she hangs a sign on the doorknob that reads, "Please do not disturb." Because Jill and Arnie believe that children should be allowed to retreat from the family now and then, the family has a rule that no one will bother Caroline if her door is closed.

Rules Develop as Bargains Between Family Members

Arnie sometimes gets impatient with Caroline because she has a tendency to leave her things scattered about the house. Caroline gets irritated with her dad because he gets impatient with her housekeeping habits. Caroline and Arnie have a *quid pro quo* that specifies that Arnie can nag Caroline about leaving her stuff around the house if Caroline can complain about her dad's nagging. Typically, Arnie releases tension by nagging Caroline, then Caroline picks up her stuff and complains about Arnie's nagging. The two feel better and the episode is repeated in a day or two.

Reciprocated behavior may develop into a pattern of expectations. If she does the dishes, he may take out the garbage. A rule then develops that "it is her job" to do the dishes and "it is his job" to take out the garbage. Sometimes, if a family is not aware of such rules and/or never talks about them, one family member may feel that he or she got unfairly "stuck" with a particular job. As Satir (1983) points out, the rule then needs to be renegotiated. A common protest, "Why is that always my job?" is usually indicative of such a sequence of events. It is not atypical for teenaged children to confess that they never volunteer for a job they dislike for fear of getting permanently assigned to it.

This sort of development is not restricted to rules that govern the duties and responsibilities of family members, however. Some rules may evolve regarding expectations for character or personality. For example, one family member may emerge as especially calm and effective during family crises. Her behavior in one situation may then structure family expectations of her in future episodes. A rule may develop stipulating that "Jane is always the strong one in the family during a crisis." Should she have difficulty coping with a problem, the family may be severely disoriented, insensitive to her signals, or resentful of her apparent weakness.

Rules also develop from the values, attitudes, and beliefs of family members, usually the parents. Some couples possess such similar value orientations that patterns of behavior are assumed without ever being questioned. For example, Glen and Alice believe that household tasks should be shared and that both partners should be responsible for providing the family income. In the Draper family, parents assume that children are not supposed to argue with their parents or openly express feelings of anger and disappointment in the family. In the Rubin family, parents assume that children need to be able to disagree with their parents on occasion in order to develop into independent and self-sufficient adults.

APPLICATION 7.2

TYPES OF RULES

For each of the following rules indicate which of the six areas of family life identified in the Taxonomy of Family Rules (Table 7.2) is affected.

1. No one is allowed to eat in the living room at Grandmother's house.
2. Rob does most of the grocery shopping; Beth supervises the maintenance of the family automobile.
3. Parents kiss, but never passionately, in front of the children.
4. When a child gets hurt, Alicia is the one to handle the emergency.
5. No one talks when we're watching television.
6. The Chens never talk about weird Uncle Harry.
7. Dad makes the rules in this house—period.
8. Knisha takes out the trash; Willie dusts and vacuums.
9. Everyone dresses up for Sunday dinner.
10. Whenever family discussions get tense, Gabriel begins a comedy routine, which makes everyone laugh.

A couple may also assume communication rules from the value system that they acquired from the cultural values of their parents. Rules that suggest that good parents don't argue in front of their children, that affection between spouses should be limited to the bedroom, that a husband should never cry in front of his wife, or that children should not argue with their parents usually originate from the social attitudes of parents. As children grow older, they are exposed to people and institutions with different systems of values from the family's ecosystem. When this interface occurs, some resistance to previously accepted family rules may develop. The parents may attempt to rely on punishment to enforce old rules or the rules may be renegotiated.

Finally, sometimes family members establish rules through a process of mutual exchange. Jackson (1965) refers to this process as a **quid pro quo**, which literally means "something for something." A quid pro quo is a bargain or an exchange. The idea is that one person agrees to behave in a manner desired by the other person if his or her behavior is reciprocated. This agreement can be verbally negotiated: "I'll balance the checkbook, if you will keep the income tax records." A quid pro quo can also be agreed to implicitly. Consider some of the following examples:

I'll let you watch football games on television if you will let me nag you about it.

I'll put you through college if you will show me how grateful you are.

I'll do all the housework since you are earning the money.

I'll be interested in your activities if you will be interested in mine.

I'll try to accept your friends if you will try to accept mine.

I won't bug you about your tendency to break things if you won't bug me about my tendency to forget appointments.

I won't complain about how often you visit your mother if you don't complain about how frequently I am out of town.

I'll tolerate your fits of bad temper if you will tolerate my spells of depression.

Such bargains—spoken or unspoken—are necessary to the functioning of most families, especially most marriages. Knowing that you are getting something in return for your effort makes it easier to keep up your end of the agreement. In many ways, quid pro quos allow family members to share power in the relationship.

Rules that develop out of the bargaining arrangements between people are often necessary if family members are to feel that their social system is functioning equitably. One advantage of verbally negotiating such rules is that family members can be more certain that the exchange is considered equitable by both partners.

The nature of the quid pro quo may be such, however, that family members find talking about it painful. In those circumstances a metarule frequently emerges. For instance, a rule such as, "I'll put you through college if you will show me how grateful you are," is not likely to be discussed during the period when it is in operation. Neither a parent nor a spouse is likely to admit the reward he or she receives from having an intimate feel grateful. Nor is the indebted person likely to run the risk of having his or her funds cut off by forcing the rule out into the open.

There may be, then, a conspiratorial nature to some quid pro quos. Suppose that a woman agrees not to nag her husband about his smoking if he will not nag her about being overweight. The two may conspire to keep the rule in operation and to prevent it from being discussed. She can then assume some responsibility for his smoking and he can assume responsibility for her being overweight without either of them having to assume responsibility for themselves.

ADAPTING RULES TO FAMILY SYSTEM CHANGES

Recognizing rules that create family stress is the first step in enhancing family communication. Adapting those rules to meet better the needs of the family system is the ultimate goal. Professionals who work with families seeking help often attempt to identify rules that create problems for the family. As Kidwell and her associates (1983) indicated:

> The family system of parents with adolescent children is thus one which faces realignments of or shifts in relationships through the necessary developmental changes of its members. When a family member is undergoing a developmental crisis, as in adolescence, stress is often the result because previous patterns of rule transformation (i.e., the level of rule, the rule itself, or the goals) become inadequate. . . . Family therapists should be able to achieve

some progress with a family in which the rule system is confused by helping them to decide when and how to adapt its rules of transformation to accommodate the changing situations created by a member in transition (p. 86).

Identifying Stress-Producing Rules

There are four obvious ways in which rules may contribute to family stress:

1. Some rules create stress because they are no longer appropriate, given changes in the family system.
2. Some rules produce stress because they are inflexible.
3. Metarules produce stress if they prohibit rule discussion.
4. Rules can create stress when families are unaware or pretend to be unaware that they exist.

First of all, a rule or a system of rules that cannot be renegotiated or changed without serious conflict may lead to difficulties if the circumstances under which it evolved change. It may be okay for the youngest child in the family to be labeled the "baby of the family" at age three but not at age thirty. It may be reasonable to enforce a curfew for a fifteen-year-old son or daughter but not for a nineteen-year-old young adult still living at home. A rule suggesting that a young wife is the one who is "good with people" while her husband is "good at fixing and building things" may not be appropriate when the couple has children who need to be nurtured and understood by both parents.

The most significant difficulty with such rules was perhaps best identified by Raush and his colleagues (1974): "A rigid, impermeable structure prevents learning." All families follow a natural evolutionary process. As a couple, two individuals develop rules that work for their relationship. The introduction of the first child into the family system is an event that calls for immediate change, and that change is manifested in the development of new rules. As the children grow, the rules in a smoothly functioning system are constantly renegotiated—a process of learning. The day on which a child of five or six is allowed to cross the street alone may have special significance for the family. Parents may have the sense that their child is growing up awfully fast. A rule prohibiting the child to cross the street at seven, eight, nine, or ten would probably be stress producing, however, because it fails to take into account the developmental change in the child.

Rules can also be tension producing if they are not flexible. Occasional violations of a rule probably should not result in a household uproar. If Rick forgets to make his bed or Nicholas slips and swears in front of Grandma, little permanent damage is done to the system. Nor should one person always get stuck with a disagreeable task (with family members responding to his or her cry for help with, "It's not my job"). Sally, after recovering from a long bout with the flu, may be dismayed to discover that the family took literally and applied inflexibly the rule that "Mom does the dishes." Fred and Ann may have a rule that they "always go grocery shopping on Saturday mornings," which may generally serve them well. But stress may result in the system if the rule cannot occasionally be violated to accommodate things that come up.

As Laing (1972) and Satir (1983) have both pointed out, stress in the system can result from metarules. Even though parents indicate an unwillingness to change a rule, if there is no taboo against discussing the rule, the conflict can, at least, be openly acknowledged.

APPLICATION 7.3

ADAPTING FAMILY RULES

Mark and Rita Larsen have two children. They have a rule that the children may not invite more than one other child over to play at a time. Sometimes this rule creates problems because both children are involved in group activities. Often the older child would like to invite three or four friends over to practice baseball. The elder Larsens argue that four or five children over at the same time would create too much noise and chaos. They don't enjoy having other people's children asking to use the bathroom, asking for a drink of water, and generally disrupting the tranquility of the Larsen household.

How might the Larsen family adapt this rule to meet the family's current needs?

Rules can create stress when family members are not aware (or deliberately choose to remain unaware) they exist. Many family rules are implicit; the consequence of not openly discussing a rule is the possibility that one or more family members may be unaware of its existence—until it is broken and conflict results. For example, a couple raising their first child may each implicitly develop rules about how the child should be disciplined. Those rules would be based on what each parent believes is appropriate child-rearing which, in turn, might be based on their personal experiences in their families of origin. The differences in their rules might not become apparent until one parent, who firmly believes that corporal punishment is inappropriate, becomes horror-struck after learning that the other parent has spanked the child.

Another problem arises when some family members choose to ignore the existence of a rule. Lennard and Bernstein (1969) have pointed out that "rules are not adhered to nor subscribed to with the same conviction by every member of a family." Sometimes violating a rule by pretending not to know it exists is a way to express one's power in the system and/or resentment toward someone else who has created the rule. For example, Howard may tacitly agree to a rule that suggests that the family monitor credit card use, but he can also subtly undermine the rule by saying he forgot what he had charged or by expressing surprise that a bill is as large as it is. Underlying his "mistakes" may be a resistance to the rule and to an array of rules regulating family money management, including who is to have control over the family budget.

Adapting the Rules

Having identified four stress-producing characteristics of rules, it is possible to identify family system rules that fit into those four categories. Each type of stress producer has its own implications for changing the family system.

If family rules are no longer appropriate, family members need to engage in rule negotiation, or discussion of family rules with the intent of adapting them. Returning to the opening example of Rita and Mark, consider the possibility that their rule is no longer appropriate for their dyad. The conflict at the party could provide Rita and Mark with an opportunity to discuss Rita's need to be more open and candid with their friends about some of the issues between the couple. Mark might be willing to let go of the "keep family information private" rule, at least within some specific guidelines. Rather than keep all information to herself, Rita may be able to negotiate a change in the rule with Mark that would allow her to talk with others outside the family about their shared conflicts.

If inflexible rule enforcement is the problem, family members might engage in a process of **rule evaluation**, or assessing the appropriateness of given rules. The purpose of this activity would be to identify how closely to follow family rules. If the family can identify those rules that everyone agrees should be followed inflexibly (e.g., six-year-old Martha should be supervised at all after-school activities; the kerosene heater should never be left burning when no one is in the house, etc.), it will be easier for everyone to see which rules can be violated without major impact.

Rather than becoming angry or hurt—two common ways of dealing with rule violations—family members can consider the possibility that rules are violated because they are not clearly recognized or understood by all members. Talking about the rules that are being violated is one way to create awareness. If rules are violated because certain family members are uncomfortable with them, family discussion and **rule negotiation** can bring some of these issues into the open. Some rules might be more difficult to negotiate than others. Nevertheless, listening to each other's perceptions about those rules can help all family members to understand each other better.

Increasing Awareness of Cultural Values and Rules

We would like to make a final comment about the importance of culture and ethnicity in the formulation of family rules, an issue that connects our discussion of the family ecosystem in the previous chapter to the ideas discussed in this chapter and reinforces our belief that rules are social constructions rather than descriptions of the "laws of nature." Culture and ethnicity can have a powerful influence on a family's system of rules. For example, McGoldrick, Pearce, and Giordano (1982) indicate that the dominant WASP culture "tends to value expressiveness less than many minority groups within it" (p. 11). The dominant culture tends to support rules that encourage members to manage conflict rationally, present a positive image for one another and for outsiders, appear confident, in control, and optimistic. These qualities are, perhaps, congruent with an American culture that values the entrepreneurial spirit, but as McGoldrick, Pearce, and Giordano indicate, "cheerfulness also leads to an inability to cope with tragedy or to engage in mourning. . . . Optimism becomes a vulnerability when we must contend with tragedy" (p. 11).

Other examples of cultural influences on family rules abound. Puerto Ricans have very flexible boundaries between the family and the immediate support system, while Greeks have very definite family boundaries and tend to have strong feelings about "blood lines"; African-Americans may distrust social institutions outside the family, except for the church; Chinese-Americans give the elderly more attention and respect than do other cultural groups; and so forth. While there is always the risk of making inaccurate inferences based on stereotypes, developing an awareness and understanding of a family's rules may require some real appreciation for the cultural and ethnic background of family members.

Monica McGoldrick personalizes and vividly describes her own experience with this issue:

> In 1968 I met my husband, who had emigrated from Greece at 21. (Prophetically, I had had a Greek godfather, K. P. Tsolainos, who was a close friend of my father.) I began to study Greek and to visit my husband's family in Greece. Meeting my husband and his family was a great cultural lesson, I might better say shock. He did not play by the rules my family always obeyed, like "keeping up appearances," "holding hostilities carefully in check," and never "making a scene" (McGoldrick, Pearce, & Giordano, 1982, p. 573).

Because we tend to take our cultural values and behavioral practices for granted, it may be difficult for one to recognize how culture and ethnicity influence patterns of relating in the family. Such activities as listening to stories of grandparents and seeking information about the intergenerational history of the family can be helpful in enhancing our understanding of the larger context in which family rules are embedded.

SUMMARY

Family rules form the groundwork for interaction in family systems. Rules, which may be implicit or explicit, prescribe what can, should, and should not happen in specific families. Because rules are probabilities, however, rules create predictability but not certainty in family systems. When rules are violated, other family members may sanction the rule-breaking behavior in a variety of ways. Rules exist at various levels in the system hierarchy, with rules at the interfaces incorporating the potential for conflict.

Family rules perform a variety of functions for family systems. In particular, they coordinate family interaction, establish some degree of predictability and stability, and establish and regulate the boundaries and networks in the family. Each function aids the system in maintaining equilibrium while moving toward satisfaction of its goals.

One way to distinguish among types of rules is to examine the types of behaviors which the rules govern. In this chapter we discuss six such categories: duties and responsibilities, status and authority, appropriate behaviors for specific contexts, intimate behavior, personality characteristics, and communication.

Knowing how rules originated can help families identify rules that should be negotiated, evaluated, and/or changed. Some rules simply evolve from a pattern of past behavior. Others emerge from value orientations of family members. Still others become a bargain between family members. When the functions that the rule serves no longer apply, families face the difficult task of discussing and changing those rules. Rules create stress if they are no longer appropriate, if they are inflexible, if they cannot be discussed, or if the family is unaware or pretends to be unaware that they exist. Families can adapt their rules by engaging in rule negotiation, rule evaluation, and by discussing the rules openly. Finally, we mention in this chapter the important influence of culture and ethnicity on family rules.

KEY TERMS

dyadic rules

explicit rules

extended family rules

family system rules

guilt inducements

implicit rules

personal rules

quid pro quo

rule evaluation

rule negotiation

sanctions

silencing strategies

subsystem rules

C HAPTER 8

FAMILY
STORIES

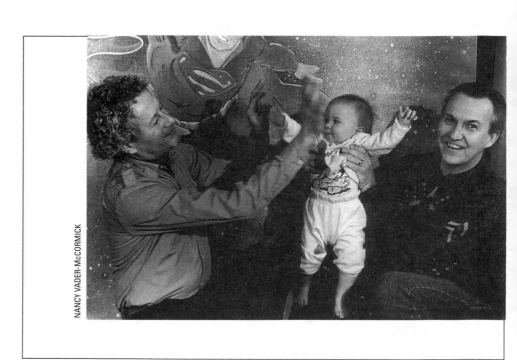

NANCY VADER-McCORMICK

L AURA'S STORY

When I was eighteen years old, a trivial argument between
my father and me turned into a nightmare. My father
repeatedly beat my face with his fists, screaming, "I wish
you were dead," while I huddled on the living room couch
trying to shield myself from the blows. He beat me until I
collapsed.

□ □ □

My dad and I had always been close. He was the one
I would go to when I needed help. He was the one I ran to
when I fell off my bike or needed my shoe tied. He was the
one who taught me to dance and bought me my first pair of
high heels. I went to him for advice when my best girlfriend betrayed my trust, when I had my first boyfriend,
and when I was having trouble in school. My friends
always referred to him as a "swell guy." They loved coming
over to my house because he made them feel welcome. He
always seemed to have the time and energy to talk with
them and participate in activities that were important to me.

Our relationship was not perfect. We had our occasional misunderstandings and arguments, but my dad
always seemed to be fair. If he thought I was wrong, he
would explain patiently why he saw things differently and
how he wanted me to change my attitude or behavior. He
was an overachiever who expected people to be dedicated
to doing their best. He pushed me to be and do the best I
could.

I viewed my father through the eyes of a child for a
very long time. He could do no wrong. I thought he was
perfect. I wanted so much to please him, to make him
proud of me so he would see how grateful I was that he was
my dad.

□ □ □

I try to open my eyes. I feel dizzy and disoriented.
My head is throbbing. I touch my face and it feels lumpy,
all swollen and abnormally hot. Where am I? What's wrong
with me? My father approaches. He tells me to relax and

gently closes my eyes as he applies a cool compress to my face. His voice is hoarse and disjointed; it cracks as he speaks. Then my mind goes blank.

□ □ □

When I was sixteen years old, some girlfriends and I had planned a night out to go bar-hopping and do some serious dancing. They were older and I was so thrilled that they had finally accepted me. I was no longer the baby of the group, even though I had skipped a year in school. They had invited me to join them for the evening. I felt like an equal for the first time.

We were to meet at 9:00 P.M. I wanted to go so badly, but I knew I would have to get my curfew time extended beyond the 11:00 deadline my father insisted upon. I approached him a few days before the big night out, rationally explained the situation, and asked him to make an exception to the rule "this one time." I told him that we were not drinkers, we just wanted to dance and that many other school friends would be there. I asked him to extend my curfew to 12:30 A.M. He said no.

I was devastated. I pleaded with him, reminding him that I had never broken curfew, never earned a grade lower than a "B" in school, did all my chores, went to religious services every week, and looked after my little brother whenever necessary. Still, he resolutely said no. We argued and raged and, finally, I gave in, or I should say, I gave up.

Our argument created new tensions in my family. I heard whispering about me behind my parents' closed bedroom door. Later, I saw in my mom's eyes a look of infinite sadness, weariness, and disappointment; and my younger brother seemed afraid that my father would take out his anger on him. The tension around the house was thick. So I gave up, feeling defeated and humiliated.

I had taken my father on and lost. Something had changed now in our relationship. Something was lost. He would not let me accept defeat peacefully. Rather he insisted on rehashing the whole event constantly, pointing out again and again why he had to say no. He mentioned mistakes I had made when I was younger, blaming me for not having had better sense. Finally, he made me apologize for being rude, demanding, and ungrateful. My mother hid in a corner of the room and cried. My father's last words on the subject, as I recall them, were to compare me to a "young sapling." When the wind blew, it would make the tree's trunk blow back and forth, but I would bounce back; the wind would not break my young trunk. On the other hand, he was an old oak tree that could not bend without being broken permanently.

□ □ □

My eyes open slowly. I see a ceiling and a wall with a flowered pattern. I recognize it. I look down and see a peach-colored comforter covering me. It is familiar. I turn my head and notice that I am in my bedroom. My father is asleep on the floor. A bowl of water and a towel are beside him. I try to lift myself out of bed, but the pain holds me back. My head throbs. My eyes burn. My throat is dry. The dim light coming in through the window tells me it is almost dusk. I reach over to the nightstand beside my bed and open the drawer, feeling for the mirror that is always there. I feel enormous pressure on my forehead. Every movement I make is excruciating. I must see what I look like, so I can know what is wrong with me. I grab the mirror out of the drawer and lift it in front of my face. When I look at myself, I begin to remember the horror of what happened. I choke at the intensity of this memory. I want to get out of here; I need to get away from this beast disguised in my father's body, lying so passively on the floor. The anger I feel grows into a hard lump in my throat and I cannot swallow. I am overpowered by a desire to run away. I grab the first clothes I see and leave.

☐ ☐ ☐

I am no longer eighteen years old. It has been six years since the beating. I left home shortly after, not able to face my father and confront him about the "event." For six years I have lived with these memories. My father and I have never talked about it. It is a taboo subject. My father and I have now established some sort of uncomfortable friendship. I visit him and he visits me. We call each other and write to each other, but we never talk about anything deep. My mother constantly tells me that he loves me "in his own way." We are two beacons of light trying to reach each other and always missing.

I am beginning to understand why my father saw himself as an old oak tree. He is so stubborn and set in his ways, so unreachable. I recall a scene I saw recently in the film version of Robert Anderson's play, *I Never Sang for My Father*. Gene Harrison, the main character in the story, says about his father, "I hate him. I hate hating him. I hate what it does to me. When I am around him I shrink." I cried uncontrollably when I heard those words. They were so close to my own unexpressed feelings; they made me feel so uncomfortable, so unresolved. Trying so hard to love someone who has provided for you and who made sure you never forgot what he did for you is a burden. There seems to be no escape for me, no way to walk away from it.

I am so sorry that my father's life has not been easier. I wish I could alleviate his worries, but I know I can't. In my own mind, I think I have forgiven him for his beastly act, but I doubt that deep down he has forgiven himself. I wish he would let me into his pain so that we could talk openly about this awful experience and reach some understanding and perhaps put it behind us. Until we do, we will remain "familiar strangers" who cannot reach the love we want to share. I am looking for an opening in his door, hoping that he can see how much I want to come through it.

UNDERSTANDING LAURA

How did you feel when you read Laura's story? Were you horrified or terrified by the violent act she describes so vividly? Could you feel the blow yourself? Did it seem like you were in the room with her when it was happening? Did you feel angry or anxious? Did it startle you to hear that these were events that happened six years before she wrote about them? Did the events described seem as if they had happened only moments earlier? Did you find yourself both thinking about and *feeling* Laura's pain and confusion and powerful desire to account for and make sense of her experience, to find a coherent explanation for her father's monstrous and "beastly" act? Do you wonder whether she really has forgiven him or whether she should? Could you sense that in telling her story Laura was actively engaged in the process of making sense of it, making it coincide with a larger set of events in her family history and in her experience with her father, drawing meaning out of confusion? Did Laura's story make you think about your own life and/or your own family? Did she give you pause to reflect on your own personal experience with your father or recall emotional events in your family that have been difficult to talk about?

Laura was a student in a course in family communication when she wrote this story. Her story brings to our attention several important aspects of personal narratives that we will emphasize in this chapter. First, *it is a true story* insofar as she has tried to be faithful to the events and feelings as she recalls them. When we call it *a* true story, we mean it is not *the* true story of what happened. If other people who were present at the time gave their accounts or versions of what took place, we would probably see or hear people expressing different aspects of and/or feelings about the event. They would be seeing the same events from a different point of view.

Second, *it is a story about concrete events.* Some writers have tried to suggest that family communication should be a largely abstract and conceptual subject, implying that theories may be more important than stories (Noller & Fitzpatrick, 1993). Laura's story suggests, however, that we don't live theories and abstractions; we live experience. The details of her experience give expression to the inner conflict she is feeling as she vacillates between loving and hating her father. Her story shows that concrete experiences and events are the "stuff" of family communication. They should not be quickly brushed aside in the haste to categorize her story as a type of family violence. It is doubtful that many of us can read books or hear lectures about family communication without relating them to our own concrete, first-hand experiences and without calling up deep-seated emotions about our family experiences. The story of how these events unfolded in Laura's "lived life" can and should be just as important and engaging to us as is the degree to which the story confirms or discounts some theory.

Third, *it is a personal, emotional, and evocative story.* Laura's description of her experience is emotionally charged. She gives us a sense of what it felt like to live through this event. It is her experience; thus, it is personal. But she evokes feelings and passions in those who read and hear her story. She is saying "look what happened to me," not "this will happen to you" (Franks, 1993). Nevertheless, many of us will call up our own memories of violence or terror in our families or we will wonder how we would have felt if placed in a similar circumstance, or we will contemplate the silences that have surrounded memorable events of a different kind in our families. Thus, Laura's story has the effect of being *both particular and universal.* It is hers but it becomes ours as we find a way to connect to it. There is a uniqueness and particularity to what happened to Laura that makes her story gripping and frightening to many, but we know that similar events have been replayed in a different form or sequence in many families by many other people.

Fourth, *Laura is the teller of her own story.* She is both the narrator and a main character in the story. Her story is told in the first person and she shifts back and forth between telling about events in the past and expressing feelings in the present. She makes us aware of the communicative dimensions of telling a story. She shows us that *it makes a difference who is telling the story and how the story is told.* By telling the story in the first person voice, she makes its meaning subjective, because the events she tells are being explicitly processed through her own consciousness. She does not hide behind the screen of the passive and objective eye of a neutral, third-person observer. Instead, she assumes responsibility for her own conclusions about these events and her attempts to persuade others who were not there that "this is the way it happened." Her telling makes us aware that *stories are told for a purpose* and require the attention of an audience. How she tells her story is important because it is "in the telling that events happen for the listener" (Reissman, 1990, p. 119). We see that she is making an effort to recreate feelings that occurred long ago and to draw us, as listeners, into her experience of what it felt like at that time. Also, we see her intense struggle to achieve a new understanding of these old but persistent feelings and events. Thus, she lays bare the confusion, ambivalence, and complexity of emotional family experience.

Laura's personal narrative is only one example of a family story. In this chapter, we describe and discuss several different forms and functions of family stories. We begin by looking at stories as an instrument for making sense of our experiences in families, a way of attaching meaning to our experiences. We identify and discuss four important qualities of family stories: sequence, time, drama, moral, and subjective truth. Then we discuss three important functions of family stories: (1) to differentiate the family from the world, (2) to integrate the family with the world, and (3) to mold character and build conscience. Next we describe three typical genres of family stories: courtship stories, birth stories, and survival stories. Stories told within families compete with or are reinforced by other narratives to which individuals are exposed outside the family. In addition to the personal narratives told within the family, we are exposed to larger "cultural narratives" through popular media such as music, television, and movies. We will discuss how these cultural forms of narrative circulate through our lives and affect our conceptions of love, romance, marriage, and divorce. We conclude the chapter by discussing the "truthfulness" and "usefulness" of family stories. Our intent is to show that meanings of stories change over time and that we can learn to "take control of our stories" instead of having them take control of us.

WHY STORIES?

Laura's narrative may be viewed as an attempt to make sense of her experience. The event she tells about was a turning point in her life. Turning points like this are referred to as **epiphanies** (Denzin, 1989). The experience of an epiphany is so emotionally absorbing for the person going through it that she may be left without a framework for interpreting the meaning of the experience. This seems to be true for Laura, who shows signs that she is still struggling to figure out why this brutal event happened, what part she played in it, and what it means for the future of her relationship with her father. Her story places these events into the wider context of her family history in an attempt also to understand them and make them meaningful.

Laura's story depicts her struggle to determine what her experience means. Although Laura's story is highly charged and deeply personal, it is not unlike much of the storytelling all of us do throughout our lives as we engage in the process of interpreting our experiences to others and to ourselves. All people accumulate stories in their lives. A person's life is a history of such stories. No one's stories are exactly like anyone else's. As our lives unfold and we share our stories with others we learn to appreciate some stories and be critical of others (Coles, 1989). *To have a self is to have a story* (Crites, 1986). People who lack a coherent story of their personal past are likely to feel rootless and uncomfortable. Without a story, they could be just anyone rather than someone in particular.

"The primary human mechanism for attaching meaning to human experiences," writes Brody, "is to tell stories about them" (1987, p. 5). When we remember events that happened to us in our families and when we tell our children, lovers, or friends about them, we tell about the events in the form of stories: who did what to whom, where, when, and why. We describe our experiences in the language of stories (Bruner, 1990). As Laurel Richardson (1990) suggests, "narrative is the best way to understand the human experience because it is the way humans understand their own lives" (p. 133). Although we often speak of "sharing our experiences" with other people, it is more accurate to say that we share *stories* of our experiences. Laura's story is not the same thing as her experience. Her story is an account of her experience, what Bruner calls an "act of meaning" (Bruner, 1990). In narrating her account, Laura selects certain details of the events to include and emphasize, whereas she ignores or omits other details of the event that she may have forgotten or considered less important.

In Chapter 2, we emphasized that family communication is largely a meaning-making activity out of which the social reality of the family and its members emerges. Family stories comprise the larger context of communicative activity by which these meanings are constructed, coordinated, and solidified. As Stone (1988, p. 244) concluded at the end of her detailed study of family stories, "our meanings are almost always inseparable from stories, in all realms of life." Family life as lived experience may thus be viewed as a process of interpretation through stories. The "stuff" of family stories—what is being transmitted and interpreted—is beliefs, values, desires, and aspirations. The content of stories is not nearly as important as the convictions that these narratives promote. Usually stories have a moral point; they encourage conviction to a way of acting, thinking, or living. Most families—at least ones that stay together—develop a corpus of stories that define their history, depict what makes them unique "as a family," establish the values and principles to which they are devoted, and characterize the identities of each family member. Many of these stories are told and retold again and again until they sink in. We hear some of them very early in our childhood "when we're as blank and unresisting as we're ever going to be" (Stone, 1988, p. 10). To a large extent, we "receive" them passively; they become "our story" though they are passed down to us by others, usually "significant others"; often, we grow into the stories until they fit as tight and are as unnoticeable as a layer of skin. In a sense, these "received stories" (Parry, 1991) have power over us. We can say aptly that they shape us or make us who we seem to be. They are our "first language" and our most private one (Stone, 1988). Later in this chapter, we consider ways in which we can take control of our stories, remaking our lives by deconstructing and reframing our received stories. First, however, we describe and discuss some of the specific features of stories.

FEATURES OF STORIES

If we examine Laura's narrative closely, we can identify certain attributes that make stories a distinctive form of expressing and organizing lived experiences. First, *stories are told sequentially*. As Bruner (1990, p. 43) states, "a narrative is composed of a unique sequence of events, mental states, happenings involving human beings as characters and actors." Clearly, in Laura's story, "one thing leads to another" (Weakland, 1981). She presents the events in her story sequentially. Even though Laura uses literary devices in her narrative, such as flashbacks and observations made in the present, we understand the story as a sequence of events that occurred in the past, that are told in the present, and that influence the future. The ordering of the story—its succession of events—provides the context through which the characters and plot are given their meaning. The predicaments that the characters face are understood, at least in part, in reference to the changes over time in the course of events. Laura tells us what happened before "the event" and what happened after. Her story has a beginning, a middle, and an end.

But Laura's story also weaves back and forth between present and past, revealing a way of layering her story which makes us aware of her struggle to make sense of it. Thus, as a storyteller, Laura shows not only that she is aware of the necessity of telling stories in an orderly, linear way but also that her experience of these events over time has not been nearly so orderly. The past intrudes on the present and the present provides a context for recreating and representing the past in a continuous way. *The present is "the pivotal point" from which Laura recollects and retrieves her experience* (Crites, 1986, p. 163). But Laura's recollections about the past are not confined to saying what happened *then*. Clearly, her interest in telling her story is primarily focused on the future. She is mainly concerned with what kind of a relationship she can have with her father *in the future*, a future that, like all futures, is ultimately unknowable. Laura does not want the future with her father to be like the past, so the meanings she attaches to her story imaginatively project a hopeful possibility that may help her adjust to the uncertainty of the future. Therefore, a second attribute is that *stories connect the past to the future from the point of view of the present* (Crites, 1986).

Third, *stories usually have a dramatic quality*. Laura's story is suspenseful and dramatic. She has faced trouble, serious trouble, and she is trying to cope with it. She has a goal, which seems to be to make her relationship with her father better and to understand why he did this "beastly" thing to her. Her story is active and alive. The scenes she sets pull you, the reader, into her life and evoke your emotions. There is some suspense as we follow the course of events, wondering what might happen next. Laura wants you to feel for her plight. She wants you to take her side. But she doesn't want her father to be seen as entirely evil. This imbalance in the natural ordering of things adds to the conflict and suspense.

Fourth, *stories have a moral*. Often, a story's plot consists of a battle contested between good and evil, right and wrong, or justice and injustice. Sometimes it is merely an attempt to show, as psychiatrist Robert Coles (1989, p. *xvii*) says, "how complex, ironic, and ambiguous this life can be." Laura's story asserts the case against her father's unexpected and unacceptable "beastliness." But Laura's story makes complex her father's actions. She wants to forgive him and wants to make it possible to see her fluctuating feelings of love and hate toward him as reasonable and appropriate. Her story reinforces certain moral norms—fathers should not act violently toward their children—but it also challenges the premise that violence should not be forgiven and cannot be explained.

Fifth, *stories show how events are interpreted by the protagonists*. There is a mental consciousness to stories as characters reveal how they felt and what their experiences meant to them. Stories make knowledge claims as well as moral claims. The truth that Laura renders, however, is a subjective truth (Bruner, 1990). By making her father's exceptional act of brutality comprehensible and coherent within her life story, Laura renders it subjectively truthful, that is, true to her experience of them.

FUNCTIONS OF FAMILY STORIES

After studying and discussing ideas about family stories in her family communication class, Debbie decided to write a letter to her mother about some of the family stories she recalls most vividly. Here are some excerpts from her letter:

Dear Mom:

I am writing this letter to you because I want to discuss some of the family stories you have told me over the years. I find that I have to stress the stories you told me, because Dad doesn't seem to tell stories. I've been thinking lately that not having anything to tell may be a story in itself. I think Dad is saying that he doesn't want to remember or that he doesn't want us to know anything that happened before he met you and his new life began. Maybe he is ashamed of his childhood or perhaps his memories of when he was a soldier in Vietnam are too painful to recount.

You may be wondering what exactly I mean by a "story." Do you remember the time I was unhappy about my job and you tried to cheer me up by telling me the story about the time when you were my age and you quit your job? Well, that was a story. I think the point was that you would have been better off sticking it out than quitting. Your story made me aware of some of the good aspects about having a job and I was glad that I listened to you. I want you to know that I admire you and respect what you have done for me. You may not realize it, but I do try to take in and use the stories you tell me. Sometimes I think you forget that times have changed and your stories don't fit my circumstances as well as they did yours, but I still try to understand what you are telling me. I guess real life is never as great as a story that is being told about it.

I've always enjoyed hearing the story about what your family was like when you were a child growing up. I remember when you and I were cleaning out the bottom drawer of the buffet where the photo albums and loose pictures were stored. I was eight years old. It was summer, a very hot and steamy day. I can still picture drinking the great iced tea you made in the glasses that would sweat. The moisture beads would slide down the sides of the glass forming a small puddle in my hand.

Remember the picture we came across of your mom and dad, the black-and-white one that had so many creases in it that it was hard to look at without moving it around to different positions. As soon as you saw that picture, you started to remember back to when they were alive and you were a child. You told me about how they spoke broken English because they had grown up in Austria. You told me what it felt like to be so poor that all the shoes and clothes were handed down from one child to another, all the way to the fifth child—you. You seemed delighted to remember that you were your father's "favorite." He would always buy you special little things and you would have to not tell your sisters or brothers about them. He did buy everyone a new outfit and new shoes for Easter every year. When you told me this story, you always emphasized how much you loved and respected your parents for all the things they managed to do for you, how much they sacrificed to make your life better. I love hearing that story. I realize now that you liked to tell it whenever one of my brothers was mean to you or didn't seem to appreciate the things you were doing for them. That story had a great impact on me. I can see that the things you do for me and the rest of the family are similar to the things your parents did for you. You always want me to have new clothes and my brothers are always telling me that I'm your favorite. You are always buying me little gifts that make me feel special. Now, as I grow older, I find that I'm doing the same things for the people I care about, my close friends and my boyfriend. I buy things for you, too. I would rather spend money on others than myself. I think someday, when I have children, I'll be telling them much the same story, but instead of your mom being in the story, it will be you.

There are also stories that you tell me that are supposed to teach me lessons or warn me against something I am about to do. One that has been very important is the story about my sister Fran's financial problems. You told me that when she turned eighteen, she received her first credit card. You were sure she would be responsible and use the card only when she needed something. But Fran went on a spending spree without realizing that she would have to pay for the merchandise sometime in the future. You also told me how often she has lost her wallet or had it stolen. The scariest part of the story is when someone stole her wallet and charged her credit card to the limit. The bank didn't believe Fran's story and you had to go to court to prove that she was in school or at work when the charges were made. What a horrible experience it was for you. And then when you found out how Paula took out loans that she didn't pay for and signed contracts for trips to health spas she couldn't afford, how angry you were. But you were always there to bail her out of those situations. Maybe she knew you would and that's why she kept buying and signing up for things. Well, now you want me to get a credit card so that I can establish good credit. I'm twenty-three years old, but I'm scared to have one. Every time I get a paycheck, I'm careful to put some of the money in a savings account. I don't like to buy myself anything unless I need it badly. I feel guilty when you take me to the mall and buy me things. I don't want to use you like Fran did. I want to pay for things myself but the irony is that I don't want to spend money. Now I wonder why you didn't tell Paula a story that would have helped her handle money and credit cards better.

Sometimes I feel that I adjust my life to fit the stories you tell. In the future I hope to tell you about how I would like to change some of the stories you tell about me to fit my life better or at least what I would like my life to be. I am grateful for the stories you have told me, which have shaped my values and taught me about life.

Love,

Debbie

How do family stories function in the development and maintenance of families and their members? Debbie's letter reveals several important ways in which family stories function in her life. When she says near the end of her letter that she sometimes feels that she adjusts her life "to fit the stories" her mother tells, she is indicating that family stories have offered her moral guidance about "how to live." The stories she recalls in this letter tell about personal sacrifice, doing nice things for people one cares about, and being responsible. These stories have become "moral companions" (Coles, 1989) for Debbie as she weighs various options about how to act and think. Thus, for Debbie, it is her conscience that is deeply influenced by family stories. The stories she received from her mother offer ideals and doctrines to live by as well as warnings and taboos against certain conduct. One of the main functions of family stories, then, is to offer concrete *moral lessons* that *promote the conscience of family members*.

Debbie's letter also shows how important the **collective memory** of the family can be. Her recollection of sorting through old family pictures with her mother when Debbie was only eight years old, an event that is vividly detailed in her letter, describes a scene that is replayed in scores of American families. Her mother's story characterizes Debbie's ancestors and recounts important experiences that took place long before Debbie was born. Telling stories for the purpose of remembering a past event that was not experienced directly by the listener(s) is one way that families function as "communities of memory" (Bellah, et al., 1985, p. 154), "remembering their past, telling the children the stories of parents' and grandparents' lives, and sustaining hope for the future . . ." Debbie promises that these stories will be passed on to her children some day, though in a different form (her mother will substitute for her grandfather). But the inspirational meanings of sacrifice and distinctiveness that she has retained, meanings that bind her to a past predating her birth, will remain. Thus, family stories function *as a cohesive*

TABLE 8.1   Functions of family stories.

Family stories teach moral lessons; they promote and build the conscience of members:

"When I feel discouraged, my father will tell me about the early days after my mother died, when I was very small. My dad and my older brothers and sisters barely made it—financially and emotionally—but we didn't give up on life; we 'hung in there' and managed 'one day at a time.' These stories are supposed to teach me that I will be fine; our family does not give up; it is important to be strong; minor setbacks mean nothing alongside losing someone you love."

Family stories connect the generations; they form and reinforce collective memories:

"My parents, who are both retired teachers, will sometimes tell the story of their political activities in the 1960s and of the demonstrations that they participated in during the civil rights movement. These stories have always made me feel proud of my parents and proud of my people, even though I sometimes get discouraged by some of the racism that I see today. I know that, in some way, I have to keep up the struggle that my parents began—and my children will have to do the same."

Family stories shape and define the identity of family members:

"I am the 'peacemaker' in the family. I am good at helping family members work out their conflicts and problems. I think that I learned this at an early age. My parents talk a lot about what an agreeable baby I was. They tell me that I would approach people, smile and laugh so much as a toddler that people enjoyed being around me. I also never fought with siblings, even though we are all close to one another in age. Sometimes this can be a burden. I really hate to see members of my family not get along."

force connecting one generation of the family to the next; passing on the family's traditions, rituals, and core values; and implying what the family should be by recalling, in stories, what they have been in the past. The corpus of stories that comprises a particular family's collective memory helps to differentiate it from other families. A family's stories help define how it is unique and special. Also, a family's stories integrate it with a community of other families, defining its connections and position in the "social order" of families according to such demographic categories as ethnicity, class, race, and religion (Stone, 1988). In the next section, we provide examples from the canon of traditional stories through which families transmit orthodox cultural norms and ideals, as well as their own particular historical meanings as a family.

The stories Debbie receives also *help to shape her personal identity*. The tales about her grandparents offer her images of sacrifice and generosity which become a standard with which she compares her actual conduct. In a subsequent letter, Debbie refers to stories her mother would tell about "how quiet and what a good kid" Debbie was as a child. Her mother still tells stories that characterize Debbie as a "sweet and quiet person who never does anything wrong." Some of these stories don't fit Debbie's present image of herself or of the person she would like to be, as she indicated when she said she wanted "to change some of the stories to fit her life better." Nevertheless, these stories loom large in her life insofar as they serve the function of *defining the family's hopes and expectations of what kind of a person she will be*. Thus, children learn who they are or who they should be largely through the stories they hear about themselves. These stories become the **stories of identity** that a family shares. As Stone (1988, pp. 167–168) writes, "We are shaped by our families' notions of our identities. . . . The primary vehicles families use to mirror us to ourselves are the family stories we hear about ourselves. These stories, especially the earliest stories about our life in the womb, our birth, and our early days of life, are a record of our family's fantasies, often unconscious, about who they hope we are or fear we are."

These three functions of family stories, (1) to build conscience, (2) to form and reinforce a collective memory that differentiates and integrates the family, and (3) to shape identity, are conservative. They constitute the received wisdom of the family, ways of thinking, acting, and feeling which protect against threats to a particular family's stability and continuity and to the general "family values" that are thought to sustain the family as a viable institution in American culture. In the next section we identify the "canonical stories" that orally transmit this "first culture," the culture of family norms and values (Stone, 1988).

CANONICAL STORIES

Laura's story shows her struggle to make her father's "beastly act" comprehensible and coherent within the larger frame of her experience of him as "a good guy." One way to read her story is to view it as an attempt to soften the image of his "beastliness" by establishing some mitigating circumstances that would allow a more sympathetic understanding of how a father could do this to his daughter. By characterizing him as a "worried" man who has led a difficult life and who, prior to this act, was "always there" for her, Laura tries to convince us (and herself) that there is sufficient reason to forgive him. The canonical form of how fathers are supposed to act physically and emotionally toward their daughters does not encompass violent beatings. Laura faces the difficult task of making his acts an

NANCY VADER-McCORMICK

Family stories help to connect the generations.

extension of the canonical form in order to find it possible to love him again or, at least, to forgive him. The difficulty of her interpretive problem is signified by her sense that it is not her father but some "beast disguised in my father's body" who physically abused her.

Canonical forms are stories that represent the generally acceptable version in a particular culture, the "right story," which eventually is taken for granted as the way things are supposed to work (Bruner, 1990). Stone suggests that families have a special interest in promoting canonical tales: "The fact is that the family, any family, has a major stake in perpetuating itself, and in order to do so it must unrelentingly push the institutions that preserve it—the institution of marriage especially, but also the institution of heterosexual romantic love, which, if all goes the way the family would have it go, culminates in marriage, children, and enhanced family stability" (p. 50). **Canonical stories** express the boundaries of acceptable cultural family practices against which alternative stories or versions are judged. When a person's actions deviate from the canonical form, the person may feel a strong need to explain, justify, excuse, or legitimize these actions. For example, Riessman (1990) notes that individuals whose marriages end in divorce must go to great lengths to explain why they are divorced; the canonical story sets the expectation that married persons will live "happily ever after." As she observes, the divorced person typically feels the need to convince other people that it was right to leave the marriage, because in our culture it is taken for granted that marriage is "a desired and honored state; one cannot walk away from it lightly" (Riessman, 1990, p. 78).

Canonical stories thus become the standard against which alternative stories are measured. Gay and lesbian relationships, interracial marriages, children born "out-of-wedlock," adopted children abandoned by "birth parents," and childless couples, to name a few notable cases, are exemplars of relational stories that are lived out against a background of "official" canonical stories, which silence, closet, or otherwise marginalize these "nontraditional" versions of lived experience.

In the following brief excerpt from her story of "a divorced kid," Lisa Biddle (1993) describes what it has been like for her to grow up with a story that falls short of the narratives of "normal kids," whose parents were still married:

My parents divorced when I was five. There was no ritual to mark the day, no day set aside for tears or stories or pasting the scrapbooks. Just a life of joint custody. On weekdays, I lived with my Mom and on weekends with my Dad. Multiple realities . . . come early for a divorced kid who lives in two houses, has two bedrooms, two backyards, two groups of neighbors, and two sets of values and rules to follow in trying to find out who she is. I had to perform one way for my mother, another for my father. I had to value my mother and devalue my father when I was with her. When I was with my father, I valued him, and devalued my mother. On holidays, for instance, I often ate four Thanksgiving meals and opened Santa's presents twice. I spent my early life on this shuttle, fashioning and refashioning one self and then another in a series of performances designed to maintain allegiances to a strangely broken, yet somehow still functioning family.

Of course, it is not necessarily easy to identify all of the canonical forms and propositions of family stories. Looking back on her own corpus of family stories, for example, Stone (1988) was amazed about the extent to which her family stories seemed weightless and invisible yet were grafted into her consciousness, almost as if she were tattooed for life. Until we begin to pay attention to the stories we have been recruited into, we don't begin to realize the impact they may have on our lives (Parry, 1991).

What family stories most typify the ways in which canonical forms are promoted and reinforced? Stone identifies several genres of stories that individuals she interviewed recalled vividly. One type of family story familiar to many people is the **courtship story**. The courtship story is a monument to love, romance, and marriage (Stone, 1988). It is a story parents tell their children, and it functions as a creation myth about the origins of the family. According to Stone, it is a love story that details the adventures and perils of romance leading to marriage, often replete with images of a fateful and irrational bond or of "love at first sight"; a strong sexual attraction; some opposition, usually familial, to the marriage; and/or some hesitancy on the woman's part to be won over by her eventual partner. The courtship story functions as a family's first collective memory. In Stone's description, it is a memory told to children who were not yet born when it happened, often embracing love's responsiveness to a calling higher than rationality and control, sometimes exaggerating a man's voracious sexual appetite, and suggesting that a woman's greater loyalty is to her family bonds rather than to her sexual impulses. Courtship stories narrate the meanings of love for men and women, how to know it when you feel it, how to react to it, what to do with it.

A second genre of typical family stories is **birth stories**. These are the family tales about each child's birth. They often include details about the child's conception, the mother's pregnancy and labor experience, and the first few weeks or months of a child's life. Long after the events take place, children are told how difficult or easy they were to conceive and to deliver, and the events surrounding the birth that made it special. Often these stories carve a place for the family's newest addition, defining how the child fits into the family's sense of itself and establishing some of the family's hopes and dreams for the child. Children become curious about their birth stories as they grow up and, without such a story, a child might wonder if there is a secret about his or her birth.

When Amy Franklin, a student in a course on communication, wrote about her "premature" birth to parents who were unmarried when she was conceived, she revealed that she did not learn about her birth story until she was sixteen years old. Her birth father, who was divorced from Amy's mother, was shocked when he learned that Amy had never been told her story. Amy recalls her father's words: "You had been in an incubator for three months because you had weighed less than two pounds at birth. No one expected you to survive. For those three months I couldn't hold you or touch you. But then my prayers came true and I picked you up for the first time. Your skin was as soft as silk and my heart did flip-flops as I held you proudly in my hands. I had never lifted anything so light, fragile, and wonderful. You were so small that I could have fit you into one of grandfather's shoe boxes." When he finished the story, Amy was convinced that her birth had been very "special" to her father and that he loved her deeply. But she also was left with the lingering feeling that her mother was ashamed of what had happened and couldn't forgive Amy for depriving her of a "chance to live a normal life."

Birth stories help to articulate a person's initial value to the rest of the family. Often, these stories convey the feeling that the child was eagerly awaited, welcomed into the world as a special gift, and deeply valued by the rest of the family. Departures from the canonical form give children cause to question how much they were wanted or loved. Adopted kids, for example, often feel robbed of a birth story and may search tirelessly to discover their origins.

A third genre of family stories is **survival stories**. One of the principal socializing functions of families is to prepare children to survive in the world by making them aware of how and where they fit. As Stone (1988, p. 145) says, "it is the first job of the family, through its stories, to explain to its members where they are positioned socially." Survival stories teach children how to cope in a world that can be dangerous, hostile, and unpredictable. To assimilate and gain some advantage in this world, individuals need to be alert and circumspect. Survival stories locate the family in a world divided into "haves" and "have-nots" or those

APPLICATION 8.1

CANONICAL STORIES

- Think about or write out the story surrounding your *birth* and first months of life. If you do not know the story or are not sure about some of the details, ask someone in the family to tell you. If you are adopted, you might prefer to explore the story of your adoption. What does this story tell you about your identity and your place in the family?

- Ask one of your parents to tell you the story of their *courtship*. What does the story tell you about your parents and their relationship? What influence do you think their courtship story has had on the family?

- Describe a *survival* story of your family's—a story that separates "them" from "us" or one that tells of the family overcoming hard times, adversity, suffering, or tragedy. What does the story say about your family and their values? What have you learned from this story?

who "dish it out" and "those who must take it" (Stone, 1988). Thus, a family's collection of survival stories often centers on distinguishing friends from enemies and preparing family members emotionally and psychologically to confront difficult and threatening circumstances. These stories also help to define the family's position in relation to other ethnic, racial, and religious groups. Regrettably, survival stories often keep racial and ethnic bigotry alive by dividing the world into "us" and "them," implicitly reinforcing racial and ethnic stereotypes that promote hatred between groups and allow prejudice to simmer beneath the veneer of friendly relations. Some of our culture's legacy of cherished clichés, such as keeping a stiff upper lip or not crying over spilt milk, are subtly advanced and reinforced in family stories that emphasize toughness, pride, and stamina. By expressing the ways in which adversity was overcome, survival stories often express the courage, guts, and self-sufficiency the family has needed to survive in the world. They also show how one can maintain dignity and self-respect in a world that is often uncontrollable and demeaning. Many families repeatedly tell their inspirational stories of how they overcame hard times, deprivation, adversity, and suffering until the values, tactics, and coping strategies these stories reflect come to be taken for granted as the natural course of the world—the way things are meant to be.

POPULAR STORIES

Family stories are personal and autobiographical narratives. Many family stories stem from specific, concrete experiences of a particular family—the Millers, the Bowers, etc.—and take on the canonical or typified story lines of courtship, birth, and survival stories. They also express a specific set of events that personalizes the plot. In this sense, they are one family's story. It is the family's way of saying, "this is what happened to us." While we have been emphasizing the ways in which personal stories promote meanings and values and connect the family to the outside world, it is important to understand that a family story is only one of the forms of narrative that circulates through our lives and the lives of others in our close relationships. In addition to our family stories, narratives drawn from popular forms of communication—music, television, and film—also play a significant role in shaping the meanings and values we attach to romance, love, intimacy, and sexuality. **Popular stories** are stories we acquire from our culture. The images and meanings that flow through cinema, television, and the mass media may unconsciously teach us ways of seeing, feeling, and thinking about the world and other people.

Some writers suggest that in our postmodern video age we are all voyeurs—observers—adrift in a sea of visual and oral symbols that shape how we experience ourselves as men and women (Denzin, 1992). These popular forms of communication may be seen as our "cultural plot" because they transmit our culture's ideals—its taken-for-granted meanings and values. What movies, television, and music have in common with family stories is the institutional role each plays in "culture-making" (Carey, 1989; Denzin, 1992). We come to know ourselves, at least partially, through the ways we see other people like us represented in the narratives of cinema, television, and popular music. Our lives become like a soundtrack of our favorite music. The film characters we most admire, and the adversities they overcome, become our own personal "field of dreams." Once we have received and integrated the meanings transmitted to us by these popular cultural forms, we begin to take them for granted. Thus, many of the meanings that we think we make and live by may actually have been chosen for us, not by us.

A good example of how the mainstream media affects us is reflected in the ways that different audiences perceived and interpreted the romance depicted in the hugely successful movie *When Harry Met Sally*. It is relatively simple for the viewer to see that this film provides an affirmative answer to the question of whether men and women can be friends *and* lovers, but it is not so simple to see how the film promotes "an ideology of love and marriage" in which it is taken for granted that women must not be single, even if they have to lie (fake orgasms) to get what they want—marriage. When audiences leave the theatre, they feel good; they are happy that Harry and Sally finally got together and lived happily ever after. What many viewers miss, however, is the sad and tragic details of what Harry and Sally had to do to achieve this marital bliss. As Denzin (1989, p. 118) suggests, *When Harry Met Sally* "is about the lies men and women tell each other." But the lies that Harry and Sally have to tell each other in order to reach their goal of achieving the traditional American marital bond go unquestioned by most viewers because they already take the need to lie for granted, though they may not realize that they do. Few people walk away from this film questioning whether it is necessary to lie to achieve a good relationship, or whether, indeed, women must be married to be happy.

Bringing the impact of cultural productions even closer to home, it is important to consider how the songs we find personally meaningful or the movies that offer us "scripts" for anticipating and enacting emotional experiences are woven into the fabric of our lived experiences in relationships. In the following personal narrative that introduces her analysis of how movies portray women's lives after divorce or breakups of close relationships, Kiesenger (1992) shows how popular music links her experience to its meanings and expressions.

> As children, my sister and I dwelled indoors on rainy summer afternoons, trying to make the best of a dreary day. Putting our imaginations to work, we transformed the barren space of our basement into a place where fantasy was born and we too were born again, transformed in play from lean, pre-pubescent forms into grown women—women we imagined we could become some day.
>
> We would transform the damp, dark basement into a schoolroom, fully equipped with a dusty chalkboard and rickety desks. Red construction paper, cut-out hearts, now faded pink, hang loosely from the cold cylinder walls. We pace the basement floor in Mother's old high heels, peering out at our students from behind over-sized glasses, whacking a click wooden rule on the desks of those who misbehave.
>
> On other days, the stage of our basement floor would be transformed into the world of "Barbie." There we would weave fantastic stories of love and loss— majestic weddings and weepy separations each time Barbie's lover betrayed her.
>
> Today, though, we huddle in the basement's musty air, dressed in oversized t-shirts and bell-bottomed jeans, our summer-tanned bare feet exposed. My little sister crouches down over the plastic, mustard-colored phonograph, carefully setting the needle down onto the record that spins. All chatter stops and the room falls silent. As the music begins to play, I lift a pink hairbrush—

my imaginary microphone—to my mouth, and begin to sing. In that moment I no longer wear the expression of a shy, shaggy-banged, giggly nine-year-old. I am now a lost and lonely woman. . . .

In the corner of the bar there stands a jukebox with selections of the best of country music old and new. You can hear your five selections for a quarter and somebody else's songs when yours are through. I've got good Kentucky whiskey on the counter and my friends around to help me ease the pain, 'til some button-pushing cowboy plays that love song—and here I am just missing you again. . . .

The song is Olivia Newton John's *Please Mr. Please.* The voice is mine, yet it is *hers* that I mimic as I sing with and over her. The narrative is a story of love and loss—a broken heart. As I sing for a small and captive audience, I enact the pain in the song. I become the woman who begs.

Please Mr. please, don't play B-17, it was *our* song. It was his song, but it's over—please Mr. please. If you know what I mean—I don't ever want to hear that song again. . . .

My voice, soft and despairing, moves my listeners as my face contorts with emotion. My eyes tear. My hands tremble. I am immersed in pain as I become a jilted woman who has lost not only love but also a sense of herself.

But I guess I better get myself together, 'cause when you left you didn't leave too much behind. Just a note that said, "I'm sorry," by your picture—and a song that's weighing heavy on my mind. . . .

When the song ended, I became nine years old again. The sound of the needle scratching as it fell off the record prompted a trickle of applause from my audience. Then, I handed the hairbrush to my sister and she took center stage to sing her song. . . .

Every once in awhile, when I hear *Please Mr. Please*, I am reminded of our play on those lazy, misty, summer afternoons. It was as if I knew what love was and how loss felt, when I transformed myself from an awkward nine-year-old kid into a vulnerable and rejected woman. I had learned the "script" of love and loss long before I had loved and lost. Later, at twenty-five, the script became my life, enacted not in imagination, but in the reality of my broken love affair. As I look back on my play as a child, I realize that many of my experiences have been informed, if not shaped, by the records I listened to, and sang with, as a little girl. When I look at the journals I've kept the past few years, I find that many of the terms I've used to express my private feelings are words I sang as a child.

DECONSTRUCTING AND REFRAMING FAMILY STORIES

Throughout this chapter we have emphasized the ways in which family stories shape and mold individuals. We have focused most of our attention on **received stories**, the stories that each of us inherits as part of our family and cultural legacy. Received stories are stories over which we seem to have little control. Initially, we are recruited into stories (White & Epston, 1990). We do not make them or give them; we *receive* them. Often, they seem to function as the taken-for-granted truth about our lives—the kind of people we are, the expectations we should have for ourselves and for others, the ideals to which we aspire. Once taken for granted, these stories can exert a power over us because, as Parry (1991, p. 52) says, "taken-for-granted means unquestioned and unexamined."

Before leaving the topic of family stories, however, it is important to emphasize the poetic and imaginative potential of narratives and to discuss ways in which received stories can be altered, revised, reframed, or deconstructed. All of us must consider whether we want to live our lives according to other people's stories or according to our own. **Deconstructing and reframing family stories** give us the opportunity to take charge of our stories.

The term *story* may be viewed as a literary metaphor. A story is a form of representation that is created, written and/or told by an author. To a certain extent, then, a story is an invention or a creation. To say that stories have authors is to say that they are told from a point of view. The problem with received stories, as Parry (1991) suggests, is that too often they are regarded as the single and only truth rather than as one point of view against which other points of view can be contrasted. When we are taught to feel or think about things in a particular way, we don't necessarily learn that there are other ways to think and feel about the same experiences.

We live in a universe of points of view. The danger is that *a* point of view may harden into *the* point of view in which case our stories become a person in which we are locked away from considering other ways of interpreting and experiencing the meaning of events. Stone (1988, p. 195) observes that "usually our family stories about ourselves are passed along to us without special regard to whether we want them or not. Often it seems . . . it is not at all what we wanted, but a burden we either live with uncomfortably or struggle later on to get rid of." As one of Stone's interviewers told her: "The stories my mother told me taught me lessons. Bad lessons. I inherited so much of that stuff. I can't wait to get rid of it" (p. 231).

Sooner or later most of us come to a decisive point in our lives when we have an opportunity to take charge of our stories, subverting the force of received and inherited stories by "drawing alternatives out of the vast realm of unremembered, neglected, minimized, and even repudiated events" in our lives (Parry, 1991, p. 53). This is the transformative point at which we can make our own meanings, find a way to be "a part of and apart from our families, a way of holding on and letting go" (Stone, 1988, p. 244).

According to Parry, in the process of deconstructing and re-forming stories one begins to see that each person's life story is connected to the stories of significant others. He points out that *"while each of us is the central character in our own stories, we are also characters in the stories of all those others with whom we are connected whether by marriage, family, friendship, or simply by being an inhabitant of the earth"* [Parry's emphasis] (1991, p. 45). This feature gives narratives a relational quality.

We expect other people in our lives to play certain roles, be certain characters, in plotting our lives. Other people also have a place for us in their stories; they assume we will play certain parts in their stories. Who we are in their stories and who they are in ours are supposed to mesh. To mess up one's lines is to introduce confusion, misunderstanding, or a sense of betrayal into the relationship. A certain degree of mutuality and agreement on the script is expected; the supportive roles we play in one another's stories help us maintain a stake in one another's lives—albeit a fragile one. In examining any particular relationship with another person, one can ask, "Who am I expected to be as a character in her story? What role do I want her to play as a character in mine?" In most cases, there is an expectation that the two stories should or will be coordinated.

In the case of marriage, however, it may be necessary to do more than coordinate the different individual stories. Usually, there is the need for a **collective story**, "our story," the couple's story (Parry, 1991). The two stories of the individuals are retained, but often there is a need to underscore the couple's togetherness by negotiating a co-authored or co-constructed story (Ellis & Bochner, 1991) that becomes a common story of their life together. At this point, they are characters in a single story of "us" rather than merely role players in each other's separate stories, which may, of course, still be retained.

Story-connecting and **co-constructing stories** (Bochner & Ellis, 1992) are active methods of creating narratives that work. They provide a way of comparing and synthesizing a partner's and/or family member's perceptions, expectations, and aspirations for the relationship. They can help each member of the family or relationship have a voice and play a part in plotting the course of the relationship, assuming the burdens of authorship and the responsibility for deciding how to live together. Parry (1991) suggests that one useful way of taking charge of one's stories is to narrate the next chapter in one's life story as one would want it to evolve, much as Laura tries to do in anticipating an opening in her father's door that will allow them to enter a new and better phase of their family life.

Stories can be enchanting or confining. If we want them to be enchanting then we must not forget, in Parry's words, "that a story always remains only a story, ours to invent, ours to tell, and ours to live" (1991, p. 53).

SUMMARY

Telling stories is one of the most fundamental communication activities of human beings. To have a self is to have a story and, usually, to want to tell your story to someone. In this chapter, we have focused mainly on family stories and to a lesser extent on the stories about relationships that are transmitted by popular forms of communication—music, television, and cinema. Most people leave their family of origin with a corpus of "received stories" that have become their taken-for-granted assumptions about themselves, their ideals, and the workings of the world. Through courtship stories, birth stories, and survival stories, we are recruited into the family values that are central to our society. If and when we begin to question some of the taken-for-granted assumptions of our stories, we enter a transformative stage of life in which we can take control of our stories and stand apart from while still being a part of our families.

Connecting your stories with the stories authored by other people in your life helps you to see how you connect to one another and how stories always are told from a particular point of view. In marriage, the couple's story—the story of "us"—often becomes the central story around which interactional life revolves. Life stories are a way of connecting the past to the future from the perspective of the present. They are dramatic, sequential, and make claims about truth and morals. Our family stories promote certain values and help the family differentiate from and integrate with the outside world. Stories are one of our most precious and magical ways of making and remaking ourselves and connecting ourselves to other people.

KEY TERMS

birth stories

canonical stories

co-constructing stories

collective memory

collective stories

courtship stories

deconstructing and reframing
 family stories

epiphanies

moral lessons

popular stories

received stories

stories of identity

survival stories

CHAPTER 9

MYTHS,
METAPHORS,
AND THEMES

NANCY VADER-McCORMICK

THE NORRIS FAMILY

As Fred Norris drives home from work he remembers how, not so long ago, he would dread going home. Almost every evening he and Ann would find themselves talking about their son, Stephen, who seemed to be drifting during his last year in high school. Recently, the situation has improved, however, and Fred is more contented than he has been in many months.

Fred owns a small printing company, and Ann sells real estate in the community where they live. Fred and Ann have worked hard all their married lives. Things were not always easy for them, and yet they have managed to reserve time for their three children. Fred is still active in the Boy Scouts, along with his younger son, Michael. When the older Norris boy was in Little League, Fred coached Stephen's team for a while. Ann Norris takes her daughter, Christie, to gymnastics lesson every Saturday morning, and both parents support the discipline required for their daughter to master the activity.

On weekday evenings Fred and Ann try to stay home with their children and monitor their homework. They take the time to know their children's teachers, reward their children's good grades at report card time, and talk as though they assume that their children will go to college. When they get together with friends they discuss problems that are related to family concerns: the cost of house remodeling and repairs, the economic climate in the community where they live, the rising expense of music lessons and sports equipment, and the stress of negotiating schedules to get children to this or that activity.

Fred's concern for his family, faith in hard work, and conviction that one needs to be prepared to meet life's difficulties come from his own family story. His father died of a heart attack when Fred was only fourteen, leaving few resources to support Fred's mother and three sisters. Mrs. Norris worked hard to get recertified as an elementary school teacher and managed to support herself and her children on her unsubstantial salary. During their teenage years, all three children had part-time jobs to help support the family and pay for extras. Fred put himself through college by continuing to work part-time for an old, established printing company.

After graduating from college with a business degree, Fred went to work full-time in the printing company and finally bought it from the original owner when the owner retired. He worked hard to adapt the business to changing consumer demands and managed to stay competitive with two national "quick-print" franchises in town. Fred acquired the belief that nothing in life is guaranteed and one can never depend on luck.

Ann's parents were raised during the Great Depression of the 1930s and she has heard stories of their hardships. When Ann was growing up, her parents emphasized the importance of hard work and of "sticking together when things get tough." In spite of the fact that there has been little love in her parents' marriage for the last twenty years, the idea of divorce is unthinkable. Ann is uncomfortable around her parents on visits home, but like them, she believes in hard work and views the family that she and Fred have built as her source of security and stability.

About two years ago, Fred and Ann spent most of their evenings talking about or arguing with Stephen, who was a senior in high school. His behavior seemed to be almost a direct affront to their values. Stephen's grades had been slipping during the last year. He made only a modest effort to study and rarely mentioned school. One evening, both parents made an attempt to talk with Stephen about their concerns; they focused on his mediocre grades, which might keep him out of the college he would like to attend. Fred and Ann also tried to make Stephen see the importance of applying himself. Stephen listened for a while and then lost his composure, telling his parents to get off his back. The relationship between Stephen and his parents remained tense for the rest of Stephen's senior year. Stephen and Fred argued regularly, often over trivial issues. Christie resented Stephen's "attitude," and she and Stephen would also fight. Stephen escaped from family tension by playing the saxophone in a small band with his friends.

Finally, Stephen announced that, instead of attending a four-year university, he was planning to register for classes at the local community college where two of his friends planned to attend. Fred and Ann were disappointed but they made an effort to accept their son's decision. They consoled themselves that at least he would be attending college.

The following year, Stephen lived at home and attended the junior college. He continued playing in the band, didn't interact much with his family, but did make respectable grades. The family declared a truce. Christie won several gymnastics awards and Michael made all-city orchestra. As much as he hated to admit it, Stephen enjoyed most of his classes at the junior college that he attended. The truce at home also made him a little less defensive, which helped to make family conflicts less intense.

This past summer, Stephen worked on a freighter on the Great Lakes. At the end of a summer away from home, Stephen seemed more confident and relaxed; he began to talk with his parents about taking out a loan to attend a four-year university in the state after finishing his two-year degree. Lately, Stephen and Christie quarrel less and display more of a sense of humor with each other. Fred and Ann do not worry as much about their son, and they feel grateful for the improved family climate.

UNDERSTANDING THE NORRISES

Think for a moment about some adjectives that you would use to describe the Norris family. The descriptions will probably come fairly easily even though the information given is limited. Some adjectives that we would use are *achievement-oriented, hard-working, supportive, enterprising, responsible, disciplined, conventional,* and *demanding.* Each of these terms describes how the family is perceived as a group and it is likely that family members would agree in general.

As you have seen from our discussion in Chapter 8 of family stories, families develop collective identities just as individuals develop self-concepts. Stephen Norris is unique: he thinks of himself as independent; he gets more satisfaction out of music than he does out of books; it is difficult for him to talk about his feelings; and he gets angry when his parents do not seem interested in how things look from his perspective. He is also "a Norris" and this means to him that he will go to college and that he will stick close to his family even though he may fight with them frequently. He also feels their pressure to "pull his own weight." The way Stephen would describe himself as "a Norris" is part of his experience as a member of a family with a collective identity and a collective memory.

In this chapter we discuss the collective identity of the family and the symbolic content of the family's communication. In addition we explore three constructs useful in describing the symbolic content of the family's communication: family myths, family metaphors, and family themes.

THE FAMILY'S COLLECTIVE IDENTITY

A family member who can say to a friend, in front of other family members and without fear of contradiction, "we work on our relationships," or "we never have any money, but we do okay anyway," or "it's never quiet around here" describes some aspect of the family's collective experience. The family's **collective identity** reflects the way that family members characterize or experience the family as a group. The family develops a set of beliefs about itself, an orientation toward the environment, and an ideology or value system that interacts with the predominant values of the culture—what Sluzki (1983) has called, "the family's world view." As Constantine (1986) suggests, a family's collective identity reflects the images a family has of itself.

> Not only does each family member carry images of what their family is and ought to be, but the family as a whole has shared images of itself as an entity, its nature, goals, and orientation (p. 212).

In addition, every family creates for its members a framework from which to view important life issues of love, death, aspiration, hope, and illusion (Henry, 1973). A family's collective identity is in part a product of its orientation toward these and other concerns, such as security, achievement, work, play, family loyalty, religion, violence, and sex. These aspects of the family's identity reflect its "world view."

The family's collective identity is often revealed by the symbolic content of the family's communication. Certainly, all communication involves symbolic activity: words, gestures, and other cues are used to represent thoughts, feelings, and experiences through the process of communication. When we discuss the concept of the **symbolic content of the family's communication** in this chapter we refer to certain acts, behaviors, narratives, and communication sequences that can come to represent concepts important to the family as a whole. Values, beliefs, perceptions, and world view are central to the family's collective identity.

Consider, for example, the fact that Stephen Norris's parents found his lack of effort in school upsetting. They worried that his attitude toward education seemed to represent a lack of concern for the future. Stephen's decision to attend a junior college and then to transfer to a four-year university had symbolic value for the family. It represented the values that Fred and Ann had brought to their family from experiences in their families of origin. Identifying acts, events, and stories from present and previous generations that symbolize important concepts in the family—such as the value of education, hard work, and achievement—helps us to understand how a family experiences itself as a group.

The symbolic content of family communication is a general description of the way that communication can have representational value—that is, the way that some events, actions, message exchanges, or stories from the past can stand for particular meanings that are important to the family's collective identity. We can understand the family's collective identity and the symbolic content of the family's communication more specifically by studying family myths, metaphors, and themes.

FAMILY MYTHS

Family myths can be defined as beliefs or attitudes about the family in which experience is selectively remembered or constructed to reflect a specific orientation of importance to the family. Myths are linked to memory and to storytelling. Suppose a grandmother is bragging to her grandchildren about their father's "gift for music" and the way he entertained a roomful of people at a church party when he was thirteen. Imagine also that the children have heard the story frequently and that occasionally the father plays a few songs for his children on his banjo in a very undistinguished way. Despite the father's somewhat ordinary abilities, there may develop in this family a myth that there are the genes of a "gift for music" among its members, perpetuated by the often-repeated story of that party where everyone had such a good time and felt such pride in one of their members. This myth, in the form of a story passed on from grandmother to grandchildren, helps the family maintain an aspect of their identity that gives them fun and pleasure.

In recent decades, scholars and writers have become interested in individual and cultural myths as representations of taken-for-granted assumptions about how life is "supposed to be," as repositories for culture and gender bias, and as potential sources for understanding ourselves and our relationships or for developing a sense of purpose in life (Campbell & Moyers, 1988; Eisler, 1988; Gergen, 1992; Goldberg, 1993; Jung, 1964; May, 1991; Richardson, 1990; Walters, Carter, Papp, & Silverstein, 1988).

Ferreira (1963) has indicated that almost all families develop myths and that myths may even facilitate the smooth operation of the family. Most researchers and family practitioners emphasize the intergenerational nature of many myths (Bagarozzi & Anderson, 1989; Pillari, 1986, 1991; Pincus & Dare, 1978). Pincus and Dare describe a myth as "a secret or unconscious belief or attitude which, through its general acceptance by succeeding generations of a family, comes to perpetuate itself in determining their responses and behavior" (p. 9). Our example of the myth of the father's "gift for music," for instance, is intergenerational and facilitates pleasure for the family.

Most often, family myths are revealed in the stories that families tell. As we indicate in Chapter 8, Robert Coles (1989) and Elizabeth Stone (1988) are among the writers who have contributed to our understanding of family myths by exploring the therapeutic value of storytelling. Family members can create and maintain family myths through their storytelling, just as the grandmother in our example sustains a family myth with the narrative of her musically gifted son. Myths are related to how individuals, social systems, and cultures have constructed their reality and satisfy important needs and longings of family members. In the following section we describe levels of family myths and the functions that myths can perform for the family.

Levels of Family Myths

We have already indicated that family myths can be identified in the stories that families tell of their lives together. The story of how father entertained a roomful of people with his "gift for music" is an example. This story reveals more than just the talents of one family member. We can think of the story as a critical event that has particular meaning for the family. It reveals fundamental lessons or assumptions of family members about themselves or even about life in general. The lessons or assumptions could be summed up in statements, axioms, or generalizations to which some or all of the family members subscribe. This story might suggest that the family believes that one's status as a person is enhanced by the attention, appreciation, and esteem of others (which a "gift for music" would provide). Or the story might represent a belief that one's esteem as a family is determined by how gifted and talented its members are or that the talents of one family member, who is adored and admired, can make up for the failures of other family members. In this way, family myths contribute to the formation of the ideal images of family members. An **ideal image** is a perception or representation of how "things should be," "how life is supposed to be," or "how things are." As we have indicated in an earlier chapter, the image of an "ideal husband" or "ideal wife" which each spouse has will influence his or her expectations for the relationship and how as a couple they will construct their social reality.

In their analysis of family myths, Bagarozzi and Anderson (1982, 1989) discuss the relationship of family myths to the ideal images that family members bring to their relationships and describe the ways in which myths function at different levels in the family. In the following section we identify four levels of family myths: (1) cultural myths, (2) personal myths, (3) couple myths, and (4) family myths.

Cultural myths include ideal images that we acquire from a particular cultural identification or from the environment at large; these images also influence our values, attitudes, and beliefs. Cultural myths are often related to cultural stereotypes. For example, one myth that our culture supports is the myth that a "normal" family is made of two heterosexual parents and one or two children, who are the natural children of their parents. A family that experiences the pain of divorce may feel that they have failed to live up to a cultural myth. They may also be confronted with the pain of loss and separation that normally accompanies divorce.

Gene and Penny are parents who have internalized this cultural ideal of the "normal family" and are having difficulty coping with the fact that their son is homosexual. The cultural myth has such a strong hold over their lives that these parents have broken off contact with their son and frequently ask themselves "how they failed" (Muller, 1987). Edith and Marshall are parents who have internalized a different ideal image of the family, one which includes gay as well as straight members. They are able to respond positively to their son's "coming out." Muller describes a similar account of a mother's reaction to the announcement that her child is gay: "She just hugged me and told me she still loved me, and it didn't matter. There was no hesitation on her part" (Muller, 1987, p. 42).

All family members internalize ideal images from the culture of what it means to be a family and these cultural myths influence their emotional responses to and interpretations of behavior and events in the family. Stephen's work (Stephen, 1992, 1994; Stephen & Harrison, 1993) has demonstrated that an understanding of the relationship of communication to cultural myths must also include an understanding of changes in family life from a *historical perspective*. For example, Stephen (1992) writes that the historical record suggests "that the present context of intimacy is unique in that relatively recent gains in the social power of women have generated forces for change that are currently only beginning to be felt within relationships" (p. 525). Unless we are aware of the influences of gender changes, changes in the expected length of life, economic changes, urbanization, and political changes on the family, our understanding of the influence of cultural myths on family communication will be limited or distorted.

Cultural myths contribute to one's personal mythology. **Personal myths** include the unique set of beliefs that each person has about herself or himself, about the ideal spouse, the ideal child and parent–child relationship, and the ideal marriage and family (Bagarozzi & Anderson, 1989). One's history of experience in the family of origin and the myths that one has internalized from the culture shape personal myths. Personal myths influence one's identity and one's expectations of intimate relationships.

Jessie Ellis grew up in an alcoholic family where life, including the family's emotional life, seemed unpredictable and out of control. As a consequence, control and predictability are very important to her. She sees herself as an organized, efficient, and somewhat reserved person, who says about herself, "I'm just not a spontaneous person." She is a loyal friend, but she is also a perfectionist who can get disillusioned with friendships easily; when this happens she tells herself, "You have to be prepared for people to let you down." She tends to keep friendships for a long time, but they tend to be of the "on again, off again" variety, and after every conflict she vows to fortify herself against the next disappointment. Bagarozzi and Anderson (1989) indicate that "individuals seek out, develop intimate relationships with, and subsequently marry persons whom they perceive to be similar to an internal ideal" (p. 17). Often spouses will "attempt to rework and correct unresolved past conflicts" (p. 20).

Jessie married Roy, someone she expected would help compensate for some of the rough times she had had as a child. Her image of the ideal spouse was someone warm, tender, predictable, cheerful, and devoted to her. She saw the ideal marriage and family as a comfortable place where there would be few surprises, where devotion would be reciprocated, and where order and calm would provide refuge from an outside world that sometimes seemed frantic and disorderly. In addition, Jessie envisioned herself as having children, to whom she would be kind and devoted, who would return her affection and confirm her image of herself as a successful parent, and who would end the alcoholic legacy of her family by being compliant, successful, happy, and energetic.

As we have indicated in an earlier chapter, each partner brings to a relationship a set of expectations and a history of experience which make up the relationship. **Couple myths** describe myths about the marital relationship which have developed from the ways the two partners have integrated their separate set of personal myths into the marriage relationship. As Bagarozzi and Anderson write, the "meshing of two distinct personal mythologies forms the basis of the couple's conjugal mythology" (p. 77).

Jessie had a clear image of her ideal spouse, described above. Because of his background, Roy was looking for a spouse with whom he could live in "peace and harmony." As he was growing up, his parents fought constantly until, after twenty-seven years of marriage, they shocked Roy and his sisters by announcing their divorce. In many ways their expectations were similar. Both Jessie and Roy had an image of the ideal marital relationship as predictable, calm, and harmonious. After they married, they constructed a couple myth suggestive of the image of themselves as a couple who "almost never fought," a couple who would work out their conflicts rationally. This myth was confirmed by retelling the story of their "biggest fight," when Roy put a deposit down on a "house in the country" without telling Jessie, who found that she hated the isolation and rustic character of the house. They both drove home from an inspection of the house in silence. Jessie did not speak to Roy for days until, finally, Roy went to get his deposit back. From time to time, Roy expresses his desire for a place in the country, but he and Jessie never talk about the issue in any detail, thus reinforcing the couple's myth that they "almost never fight."

According to the model developed by Bagarozzi and Anderson (1989), family myths include the personal mythologies of each family member, the parents' couple mythologies, as well as expectations of the children based on concepts of the ideal child that the parents brought to the family. As children are born to Jessie and Roy and as the children mature, they learn about the couple's mythology: their parents have a comfortable, harmonious marriage in which they "almost never fight." The children learn that there is a rule against expressing conflict openly in the family and they also learn how to "walk on eggs" when their parents' silence indicates that they disagree about something. When the children become young adults, they indicate that, as "ideal children," they are supposed to avoid "upsetting" their parents and avoid conflicts with each other. Everyone, in turn, gets "upset" with the youngest daughter who marries someone of another race, has a child seven months later, and gets a divorce three years later.

Occasionally the family still makes allusions to the story of the "house in the country" that Roy wanted and that Jessie hated. And recently, they told the story of the youngest daughter, who has become the "renegade in the family" with her "wild lifestyle." They also talk about how Christmas is usually "hell" because that is when the family is all together and everyone can "cut the tension with a knife." Jessie and Roy worry about their daughter and love their grandchild, but are careful not to say anything about how they feel about their daughter. The other siblings do not know why Jessie and Roy "put up with" their sister who "gets away with murder," and everyone in the family "holds their breath" and "tries to get through the day without sniping at one another." Their main goal for Christmas Day is to maintain the myth that they are a "happy and harmonious family." As you can see from this example, family myths develop and are reinforced through the family's interaction and communication.

Functions of Family Myths

A family myth can serve a number of purposes for a family (Stierlin, 1973). A distorted tale of the time when Grandmother Norris "shouted down the mayor" may reinforce the notion that the Norris women have always been strong. Telling the story may also bind the generations together and bring the family closer to one another. Jessie and Roy rationalize their avoidance of conflict by telling stories of their difficult childhoods and reinforcing their need for "peace and harmony." In particular, family myths perform four important functions in sustaining the collective identity of the family: (1) they enable the family to manage events that are painful or embarrassing; (2) they help to maintain values and beliefs important to the family; (3) they provide a rationalization for the dilemmas, role relationships, and organization created in the family; and (4) they sustain bonds between and among the generations (Ferreira, 1963; Byng-Hall, 1973; Pillari, 1986; Stierlin, 1973; Stone, 1988).

Managing Painful Events

In some families, myths may enable the family to manage events that are painful or embarrassing. Sometimes this outcome is achieved through humor. A couple may collude in restructuring disastrous, uncomfortable, and awkward events during their honeymoon by emphasizing and exaggerating the humor of the events as they retell the story together.

Sometimes the management of painful events through a myth is achieved with more seriousness. A son's failure to do well in several critical swimming meets may be overlooked as family members talk about what a swimming champion he was in high school. Through the family myth, the family chooses to remember and to perceive that which is congruent with the image of their son as a champion. Family myths enable members to collaborate in their perceptions of themselves and to avoid ownership of images that they find untenable, uncomfortable, or painful. In talking about their son, the swimming champion, the painful memory of his losses, as well as his failure to gratify the family's need to feel important, fades. The myth may even help the family avoid acknowledging and talking about the sense of failure that the whole family experiences as a consequence of the father's depression. Through their talk, events are restructured; painful memories are suppressed, and the myth that the son was a champion makes the family feel better about itself.

Family myths are also related to how the family copes with painful events when a particular event is interpreted as a kind of crisis or epiphany for the family. An *epiphany*, as we mentioned in Chapter 8, is a crisis situation or story that becomes a turning point in the family's experience and has a profound effect on the family (Denzin, 1989; Ellis & Bochner, 1992). The Won-Lee family tells the story of how they rebuilt their urban business after their store was destroyed in a fire on their block. For the Won-Lee family, the fire was a crisis event that tested the strength of all the family members who had previously been drifting apart because of the cultural differences between the generations. Refusing to succumb to their despair after the fire, the Won-Lees rebuilt their store over a period of years. During this period the children's father became very ill and died, which added to the family's sense of tragedy and loss. The eldest daughter took over the management of the family business and was instrumental in pressuring relatives and neighbors to take a more active role in community relations.

The fire did more than test the family's strength; the crisis made the family aware of how connected their fate was to the fate of their somewhat fragile neighborhood. The crisis that the Won-Lee family experienced produced the family myth that they could be strong in the face of disaster and heartbreak. It also helped to create a related myth that their fate was linked to the fate of their community. We can see how the myth altered and fortified their values, beliefs, and moral vision and helped the family cope with pain and loss. For the Won-Lees, the fire and the events following the fire constituted a turning point in their lives.

Maintaining Family Values and Beliefs

Family myths can be used to reinforce central attitudes, beliefs, and choices of the family. Pillari (1986) describes three generations of Crosby women who choose men who discredit themselves and treat the women in their lives badly.

Each time a woman in the family marries, she and her husband maintain the family myth that men are "bad people interested only in exploiting women for sexual purposes" (p. 64). Three generations of Crosby women have married alcoholics whom they view as weak and undependable. Each generation of Crosby women has learned from her mother to dislike sex and to use it as a reward and punishment strategy. Coalitions are formed between mothers and daughters against an alcoholic father (and later a daughter's alcoholic husband) who is perceived as no good. Because they are sexually manipulated, negatively labeled, and treated like outsiders, the Crosby men receive reinforcement for their feelings of failure. As their rage and alcoholism become worse, they turn to violence, and the family myth that men are no good is confirmed.

Not all myths that are related to the maintenance of family values and beliefs are as negative, of course, as the Crosby example. Gary and Frieda Sloan, for instance, both tell the story that two acres of land they bought for $350.00 "made them rich." In the early years of their marriage, they bought some land from an acquaintance just outside the city limits "in the middle of nowhere." A few years later, they sold the land for a modest profit and invested it in a small appliance store. Because of their inexperience, the store went broke after two years. Three years later Gary's father helped them to open a new store. For years they worked hard to keep the new store going. In time, their hard work and long nights paid off. They made enough money to open a second store and, eventually, a third store. After several decades, their business had made them relatively wealthy.

The Sloans did not attribute their good fortune to hard work and help from Gary's father, however. They never mention the first store that went broke. Instead, they repeatedly tell the story that their $350.00 investment "made them rich." They believe that life is an adventure and that one must take risks. They encourage their children to experiment, to get involved in Junior Achievement projects, and to set their economic goals high. They emphasize these values as they retell the story that reinforces the family myth. In both the Crosby and Sloan families, a family myth helps to sustain values and beliefs that are central to the collective identity of the family.

Rationalizing Tools

Family myths can provide rationalizations for the dilemmas, role relationships, and organization created in the family. Rationalizations provide plausible explanations for situations when actual feelings and circumstances are too difficult or painful for the family to face. Ann Norris' parents have been partners in an unhappy marriage since Ann was in her teens. Ann's father "dealt with the situation" by investing himself in his work. At one point in their marriage, Ann's mother became severely depressed, primarily because of the couple's inability to improve a lifeless marriage. During this period, she relied heavily on tranquilizers and slept more than usual. The myth that emerged in the family suggested that menopause, rather than the lack of intimacy in the marriage, was the source of the problem. Through the family's communication the myth developed in conversations that Ann's mother was not very strong emotionally, got depressed easily, and had a hard time coping with middle age. Emotional difficulties in the marital relationship were rationalized as consequences of "the change of life." The couple was caught in a dilemma: they were fearful of talking about and facing their marital difficulties and yet believed that they should "stick together, no matter what." The "change of life" myth helped them to explain the stress in their marriage without forcing them to confront the deeper issues of their relationship.

In their discussion of family myths, Pincus and Dare (1978) discuss the ways in which families use family myths to rationalize failures in paternal performance. A myth that emerges represents an exaggerated altering of reality.

> Mr. Shields was one year old when his father returned home from the Boer War as an invalid. Whether any specific illness had been diagnosed was not clear to the son, but he knew that his father never worked again and spent the rest of his life drinking on his wife's meager earnings and treating her violently when she complained. Mr. Shields joined his mother and sisters in fearing and despising the drunken father, but with the help of photographs of father in army uniform and a medal from the Boer War, the family cherished an image of him as a war hero. They had been brought up to cherish the memory of their grandfather, the father's father, who they believed had been a great soldier, and died young as a result of service injuries. Much later, this turned out to be a complete invention (p. 14).

The Shields family maintained an image of the father as a war hero in place of the actual fear and hate that they felt toward him. They distorted the real events surrounding the father's life, just as they had done for the grandfather. Through the myth they were able to reconstruct the family's organization, however unrealistically and painfully, to include the guiding presence of a strong masculine figure.

Sustaining Bonds Between the Generations

Family myths can help to build bridges between the generations, reinforce the importance of the family's history, or maintain continuity from one generation to the next. Eleanor is mother to three married daughters, each of whom has children. She has worked hard all her life, but she has never known how to relate to her daughters to their satisfaction. Early childhood experiences of abuse, a young life preoccupied with hard work, and several husbands contributed to the difficulties that she had in developing any closeness between herself and her daughters. She is

APPLICATION 9.1

FAMILY MYTHS

Think about your own family of origin or, if you are married, your family of procreation. Identify three myths that you have heard or (better yet) that you tell. Identify the benefits that your family receives from perpetuating these myths.

not very close to her grandchildren, either; somehow they make her nervous. The oldest daughter, Katherine, has a good relationship with her own daughter, Amy. Katherine finds the distance between herself and her mother and between grandchild and grandmother painful. To give the grandchild a more positive image of grandmother, she tells the story over and over again of how grandmother raised three daughters during the Great Depression. Eleanor was raised in Mexico and spoke Spanish fluently. She was able to get secretarial and bookkeeping work, which was hard to find during the depression, because she lived in a large Texas border town and was bilingual. Katherine painted a picture for her daughter of Eleanor as a woman of courage, caring, and good humor. The primary bond between her and her grandmother came from the myth that Amy acquired from her mother's exaggerated story.

Other kinds of myths sustain claims, values, or beliefs from one generation to the next. Christie Norris hears of her grandmother's exploits from her parents. In her own achievements, Christie reinforces the family myth that the Norris women have always been strong, worked hard, and gone after what they wanted. The family myth links the values and beliefs of generations.

In our discussion of family myths we have tried to convey the powerful influence that myths can often have over the lives of family members and how family myths can influence communication in the family. We have described how cultural myths, personal myths, couple myths, and family myths are interrelated. Finally, we have discussed four functions of family myths. In the next section we will discuss family metaphors as another tool for understanding the symbolic content of family communication.

FAMILY METAPHORS

A **family metaphor** is a specific event, object, image, or behavior that represents for family members some aspect of their collective identity (Yerby, 1989). A couple married for only a short time may describe their marriage as comfortable—like an old shoe—or they might describe their marriage as a tropical storm or a refuge. In conversations that include these kinds of images, the couple describes how the marriage feels and what it means to them.

Sean and Tamara describe their relationship as a "marvelous two-headed beast." The image represents the symbiotic interdependence of two strong-willed, sensual, and charismatic personalities. They talk about their relationship in terms that remind one of creatures from Greek, Roman, and Eastern mythology. They speak of their attachment and affection as intensely emotional and therefore not without pain or conflict. Their image is a romantic one, to be sure, but it illustrates how a metaphor can be used to characterize the marital unit.

Metaphors provide information about how the family is experienced by its members as a collective unit. Frank Norris has a set of beliefs about himself that makes up his identity. In the same way that Stephen does, he will also think of himself as "a Norris." What does it mean to be *a Norris?* How would he characterize his family? Suppose he thinks of the family as hard working and close? If he has an image of the family as close, is that closeness experienced as controlling and suffocating or supportive and encouraging? Could the family be imagined as a hard-working and dependable Maytag? Or would an overloaded washing machine, foaming with too much detergent and too little room for the clothes, be a more representative image of the family? If Frank Norris were remembering the family of his childhood, would he recall family picnics on the Fourth of July or conversations at the dinner table in which each child was to demonstrate what he or she learned at school that day? The images with which he recalls these events are metaphors for his early experience in his family of origin.

Several of the metaphors that we have discussed are figures of speech in which a word or descriptive phrase is used to represent some aspect of the family's experience (Jorgenson, 1988; Krueger & Ashe, 1986; Owen, 1985; Rawlins, 1989; Stephen & Enholm, 1987). The statement, "Our house was like a three-ring circus when our children were little," is a metaphor, a figure of speech, representing the chaotic life of a family with young children.

Metaphors can be more than figures of speech, however. As Haley (1976) has pointed out, behaviors, acts, and episodes can have representational value for the family. A family that routinely argues over dirty dishes left in the sink may not only be talking about whose job it is to do the dishes; the dirty dishes may be a metaphor for a struggle over whose standards of neatness and cleanliness will apply in the family.

Haley (1976) writes of the importance of understanding the metaphoric content of family interaction in helping families to change. Haley is specifically concerned with the use of metaphors to make statements about the relationship problems in the family. For family members certain behaviors may represent such things as regard, status, or value differences. As Haley indicates, "The fight a married couple may have over who is to pick up whose socks does not necessarily have socks as a referent but rather what the socks have tended to mean in the context of the relationship" (p. 84). Perhaps the socks "stand for" a struggle over the kinds of demands that each partner may make on the other. What the couple *seems* to be talking about may not be what they *are* talking about.

Imagine a family issue revolving around the amount of time that a husband and father spends in his workshop. The workshop is meticulously organized, stocked with a wide variety of tools, and furnished with a complex array of shelves and cupboards. The children, two boys, are not allowed to explore the workshop. The justification is that expensive and dangerous tools might get broken or someone might get hurt (good "reasons," of course). Whenever the household gets noisy or a conflict ensues, the father drifts down to his workshop. Though she has never said so directly, his wife hates the workshop. She protests when her husband spends money on tools, says that it is damp in winter and asks,

"How can you stand it down there?" She is restrained in admiring the objects that her husband builds for the family. The taboo against entering the workshop mystifies the space for the children. In addition, the mother supports their prejudice against the workshop. As part of their turning away from the workshop, the children become awed and intimidated by machines and tools and take up the music skills of their mother.

The workshop becomes a family metaphor for the emotional, psychological, and physical distances among family members. The wife complains about the workshop, which represents the withdrawal that she experiences from her husband. The more hostility that she directs toward her husband's workshop activities, of course, the more he feels the need to retreat to the solace and quiet of the basement. Family tensions focus on the workshop. The central, unspoken problem is that the workshop symbolizes *distance* among members of the family. New alternatives for handling tension, maintaining privacy, or regulating interpersonal distance—issues that the workshop represents—are not explored. They are not explored because the family cannot share its stories of what the workshop represents to them or how they feel about each other. The symbolic content of the workshop, its value as a metaphor, makes it especially significant to the family.

In recent years, family therapists have started exploring ways to help families who want to change to develop new metaphors for their relationships. Sharing and developing new metaphors, as well as new myths, stories, and narratives, will provide the family with alternative ways of constructing their reality and framing or interpreting their experience (Combs & Freedman, 1990; Gilligan & Price, 1993; Hoffman, 1990; McNamee & Gergen, 1992; Parry, 1991; Anderson & Goolishian, 1988; Sluzki, 1992; Gustafson, 1992). As Combs and Freedman suggest:

> Any single metaphor is a particular vision of a particular part of the world. When people have only one metaphor for a situation, their creativity is limited. The more metaphors they have to choose from for a given situation, the more choice and flexibility they have in how to handle it. Finding metaphors expands the realm of creativity (p. 32).

Expanding your awareness of family metaphors and of the possibility for developing new family metaphors can create a sense of movement, optimism, and energy in the family as options for reconstructing family stories are widened (see also Rawlins, 1989).

Functions of Family Metaphors

We have suggested that one method of understanding how meanings are generated in the family is to identify the metaphoric function of the family's communication (Yerby, 1989). In the following section we identify three types of metaphors that are related to family communication: metaphors as representational acts, metaphors as collective images for the family, and metaphors as connecting links between events and meaning.

Representational Acts

Metaphors can be **representational acts**—behaviors or messages that function as symbols for other messages, values, or concerns in the family. The act of stopping

The experiences and values of a parent can be a source of family themes.

by the candy store on the way home from work to pick up a box of chocolate-covered cherries for her husband, who has been harassed by a colleague at work, can represent an expression of affection and concern from wife to husband. Pearce and Cronen (1980) and their colleagues (Cronen, Pearce, & Harris, 1979; McNamee & Cronen, 1981) have argued that people in social systems develop particular rules, which Pearce and Cronen identify as **constitutive rules,** in that one type of message or action represents a behavior or attitude at another level of abstraction. Harris (1980) gives the example of a relationship in which the message "wipe your feet" counts as "nagging." Lakoff and Johnson (1980) describe this process as "understanding and experiencing one kind of thing in terms of another" (p. 5).

Imagine Ann Norris getting upset with her son Stephen for leaving wet towels on the bathroom floor. Stephen says that he cannot understand why his mother has to get irritated over something so trivial. Yet both Stephen and Ann know that the issue is not trivial because "wet towels on the bathroom floor" stands for "sloppy housekeeping" and abuse of Ann's role as primary housekeeper for the family. Ann reacts intensely because the towels are a metaphor for a struggle between Stephen and her.

Families develop a vast array of acts and messages that represent other and often more fundamental issues in the family. In the Norris family does arguing with a parent indicate rebellion and disrespect? Does being late for dinner stand for resistance to adapting to family norms? Sometimes family members may not be aware of what a particular issue, act, or behavior represents. Feelings can emerge quickly and with a sense of urgency, often leaving family members confused about why their reactions were so intense. As Napier (1988) indicates:

> Even if the couple says, "We fight about money" (or sex, or their in-laws), these issues are more like summary metaphors. Because the deeper issues are more painful and threatening, the real sources of their distress remain hidden behind a veil of repression and denial. Sometimes only the agony is visible (p. 44).

Families develop a series of metaphors in which particular behaviors not only stand for broader meanings but seem to require or warrant specific reciprocal responses. When Fred Norris fixes his daughter's bicycle, does that count as an expression of affection and warrant an appreciative hug? The appreciative hug that Christie Norris gives her dad is a reciprocal response. When Christie takes too long to get ready for school and is about to be late (as she chronically does), the reciprocal response from her father is a short lecture on punctuality as an indication of responsible behavior. Being late is a metaphor for irresponsible behavior and warrants a brief lecture from her father. A conversation between mother and daughter late at night, a frown from a parent to a child, a particular facial expression from a child to a parent, wet towels on the floor, being late, and a gift of candy are all behaviors that can have metaphoric content in the family.

Collective Paradigms and Images for the Family

Metaphors that represent collective paradigms or images for the family are symbols, adjectives, or events that are descriptive of the family as a unit. In his discussion of what he calls "relational metaphors," Owen (1985) makes the point that couples, especially in their early years of marriage, often develop metaphors that represent their marriage and in conversations about their relationship use language that reflect this metaphor. Owen illustrates his point with the example of a couple who see their relationship as a machine—a typical metaphor in our culture. The couple use such phrases as, "we're clicking," "we shifted into high gear," "the friction was burning us out," "timing is important to a smooth-running relationship," and other similarly related phrases that reveal this central image they have of themselves.

Families, as well as couples, may also develop central metaphors for their collective experience. Consider the example of a family who see themselves as "a ship at sea." They might think of the marital relationship as occasionally "rocky" and worry that older children are "drifting" without enough purpose in life. Therapists sometimes help families identify such central metaphors for themselves as a way of helping the family to look at issues that might be difficult or painful for them to examine (Combs & Freedman, 1990; Duhl, 1983).

Labels or adjectives that reflect or reinforce the family's view of the world can also be metaphors for the family. For example, the Norris family might label themselves as "well disciplined" and "somewhat tense," while their neighbors might describe themselves as "disorganized" and "spontaneous." Such adjectives become labels that reflect the family's image of themselves. They also reflect the family's value system and world view. In this way, adjectives can become metaphors for family paradigms.

Paradigms may be statements or aphorisms that suggest an orientation to the world or supply a piece of wisdom that serves as a guide for the family. Reiss (1981) argues that paradigms influence how the family relates to the environment (or to the family's ecosystem), as well as how family members relate to each other. Constantine (1986) describes a paradigm as a governing framework for the family, an image or a model that structures the family's behavior: "A paradigm is a model, a model of both the actual and the ideal. But a paradigm is more than just a model or representation; it is a way of seeing and knowing as well. A paradigm is really a model of the world, a world view" (pp. 4–5). Perhaps the Clark family lives by the assumption that "the world is a cruel and a harsh place." This piece of "wisdom" represents their collective family experience and represents a family paradigm.

Metaphors help to reflect and reinforce paradigms that present the family's collective experience. Suppose one of the Clark children is involved in a minor bicycle accident; the accident may become a metaphor that reinforces the family paradigm: "The world is a cruel and a harsh place." Sometimes families live by paradigms that may create problems. The family can fail to acknowledge aspects of family life that are not consistent with their collective family image. A family that sees itself as always "cheerful" or "in control" may not be able to deal with a severe trauma such as the illness or death of a child. This is part of the tragedy of the family in the film *Ordinary People*. Napkins neatly inserted in napkin rings, a perfectly set dinner table, and conversation that avoids emotion are metaphors for the order and control that fail the family when confronted with the tragic death of one of its children. When the oldest son in the family dies in a boating accident, the family falls apart. Metaphors that represent collective paradigms or images for the family are often central to the family's identity and can be difficult to change or reconcile with contradictory events that happen to the family.

Connecting Links Between Events and Meaning

The term *connecting links* as a description of some family metaphors is borrowed from the work of Duhl (1983). Metaphors that function as **connecting links** involve a process of translating or framing a specific experience or event into meaning for the family. (In Chapter 3 we discuss what we mean by "frame.") What is the meaning of unemployment for the family, for instance? When William Brown temporarily loses his job because of layoffs, does he feel like a failure? Does the family as a group experience the loss of employment with shame and a sense of failure? After a while, are they able to adapt and pull together? Might they be able to say later, after Bill finds another job, that this period was rough but that the family "stuck together"? Ultimately they may see their period of hardship as a test of their courage and caring for each other—a metaphor for their cohesiveness. When the Browns find themselves moving to another city to take advantage of an employment opportunity that emerged, do they see the move as "uprooting" or do they frame the experience as a "fresh start" for the family?

As families go through various stages of their lives together, they are confronted with diverse life passages: children are born into the family and later start school; parents' careers evolve; family members mature emotionally and change physically as they age. The metaphors that families use to connect events to meaning and their stories to each other are interpretations of such life passages. Imagine a mother and father helping their six-year-old daughter learn how to ride a two-wheel bicycle. For the family, the first time she rides around the block by herself represents the child's passage from babyhood to a more independent stage of childhood.

Parents can experience their children going off to college with sadness and loneliness—the *metaphor* of the "empty nest." Or they can interpret the event as a stage of "liberation" from parental responsibility and a chance to spend more time together, in spite of the fact that they miss the companionship of their children. How a family *frames* events such as unemployment, moving to a new city, children going off to college, or divorce and remarriage can be understood by the metaphors that the family uses to translate the event into meaning for themselves.

While the content of a family's talk may be about dirty dishes, socks on the floor, workshops, or children going off to college, the family frequently is talking

APPLICATION 9.2

FAMILY METAPHORS

Identify three metaphors that you believe describe your family. Explain why each is appropriate. Indicate whether or not other family members would agree with your description. Why or why not?

about other, more primary, relationship issues as well. Usually these issues deal with questions of distance, affection, fear of abandonment, trust, control, avoidance, and so on. Examining the metaphoric content of a family's communication can help you to identify the nature of the tensions, divisions, and bonds of the family.

FAMILY THEMES

As its members accumulate a common experience, a family begins to acquire an array of interpersonal metaphors and myths that constitute the family's ideology and view of the world. A family's myths and metaphors will reveal and reinforce particular themes in the family. **Family themes** represent important preoccupations and relationship definitions in the family as well as provide the focus for the family's energy. Hess and Handel have defined a theme as "the centering of the family's interaction" and have suggested that "the identification of family themes may be a useful procedure for understanding some of the binding forces in families" (Hess & Handel, 1959, p. 31). An analysis of family themes can provide a description of the major issues, goals, concerns, or values of the family. The final section of this chapter (1) discusses two potential sources of family themes, (2) identifies three types of family themes, and (3) describes how family themes are integrated in the conversation of family members.

Sources of Family Themes

The Beliefs of Parents as a Source of Themes

One source of family themes can be found in the stories and history of experience of the parents (Hess & Handel, 1959). For instance, a theme in the Norris family emerged from the parents' belief, which is related to cultural values, that education and hard work are fundamental to economic security and family stability. Most of the family's energy goes into working hard to maintain careers and support the children's education. Interaction in the family often centers on the theme of the need for economic security and stability. Thus, the possibility that Stephen might not go to college becomes a real source of stress in the family. Stephen and his parents argue frequently when Stephen suggests that he wants to experiment with being independent and might postpone his education to pursue his interest in music. Stephen becomes defensive about his need for independence and his lack of interest in school. Fred and Ann discuss how they feel about Stephen and what strategies they will take in dealing with him. They worry that if Stephen pursues his interest in music, he will not gain economic security and he will abandon his education. They want to protect him from failure and help him avoid making mistakes. They would like to see him sacrifice some of his spontaneity and impulsiveness for a more secure future. The parents alternately become frustrated in their attempt to influence Stephen and avoid talking about the issue to prevent the tension from escalating. Christie supports the family theme in her complaints about Stephen's attitude. When Stephen makes a decision to go to college the climate in the family improves.

Answers to basic questions about a family can help to identify a family's themes: What are some important concerns of family members? What do family members talk about and avoid talking about in their conversations with one another? Which rule violations seem to produce the strongest sanctions? How does the family use its energies and resources? What behaviors evoke positive responses from one another? What truisms do family members seem to regard as fact? What behaviors are regarded as important and which ones are viewed as insignificant? The Norris family theme of the need for economic security and stability, which emerged from the experiences of the parents in their families of origin, provided the focus for much of their energy and interaction.

Dialectical Processes as a Source of Themes

Competing demands in the family can provide the focus for the family's energy and interaction. For instance, in the Norris family there was a struggle between Stephen's efforts to differentiate himself from the family and his parents' obligations to provide guidance that would be integrated with the family's value system. A significant amount of interaction in the Norris family centered on the tension between Stephen's need to develop his own autonomy as he maintained some degree of interdependence with other family members.

FIGURE   9.1   Types of symbolic family experience.

Myths	Beliefs and stories about family members that allow families to gain some measure of pleasure, stability, or continuity in their sharing.
	Examples: Grandpa was a war hero. The Clearys have always been lucky. Men have to be tough.
Metaphors	Images, objects, events, and behavioral acts that have specific representational value for family members.
	Examples: Our family is like a clock that is wound up too tight. The move to Wilmington represented a fresh start for the Shannons. John's burning the grilled cheese sandwiches represented his lack of enthusiasm for sharing household responsibilities once Becky had returned to work.
Themes	Preoccupations, central concerns, ways of experiencing contradictions, and relationship definitions in the family which provide the focus for the family's energy and help to center their interaction.
	Examples: We have to work hard, avoid risks, and look out for each other because no one will be looking out for us. As parents in a stepfamily we have to make it clear that the marriage is here to stay. My dad and I just don't connect.

Hess and Handel have discussed the tendency of family themes to emerge in the tensions that many families experience between autonomy and interdependence (Handel, 1965; Hess & Handel, 1959). **Autonomy** represents family members' assertions of their unique identities and self-sufficiencies. **Interdependence** is related to the extent to which family members find support, get their needs met, and establish interests, attitudes, and goals that are congruent with those of other family members. The tension between autonomy and interdependence is related to the ways that families manage differentiation and integration in the family. Hess and Handel (1959) have used the term "separateness and connectedness" to describe the family's need to maintain balance in their relationships between autonomy and interdependence. Nearly every family is confronted with conflicts over autonomy and interdependence at certain stages of its development. Tension and energy expenditure in the Norris family is related to Stephen's efforts at asserting his own independence and his right to decide whether or not he will go to college.

In interviews with stepfamily couples regarding their experiences in building a stepfamily, Cissna, Cox, and Bochner (1989) have illustrated how family themes can emerge from the competing demands of family relationships. Stepfamilies are faced with particular problems in differentiating and integrating their relationships. The newly married couple is confronted with the task of establishing and nurturing their new relationship. At the same time, multiple relationships in the stepfamily must be managed that have not yet developed. A stepparent is confronted with the obligation of helping to raise another individual's children, with whom bonds may not be firmly established. Differences in parenting styles and ambiguities in the role of the stepparent may make that obligation especially difficult or conflictual. In addition, the stepchildren in the family may resent the presence of the stepparent or of other stepchildren. The newly married couple is confronted with having simultaneously to nurture the marriage, coordinate definitions of their parenting roles, establish stable relationships with the children, and facilitate functional relationships among the siblings. The adults may experience competition between the need to nurture the marriage and manage the stepparenting relationships in the family. Cissna, Cox, and Bochner (1989) found the theme of the perceived tension between marital and parental relationships to be universal among those stepfamily couples interviewed. As they indicate:

> Within the stepfamily, a natural tension, or "relationship dialectic," seems to exist for the adults between maintaining a spousal relationship—their own marriage—and simultaneously developing a relationship with one or more children. This is difficult because the children are not the biological offspring of both parents. The children represent a previous marital relationship that no longer exists, and they sometimes resent and work to undermine the new marital relationship. The more time and energy invested in the marital relationship, the less is available to work with the children—and vice versa. Yet both relationships are vital to the success of the reorganizing stepfamily. These relationships must be balanced against one another, and every successful family finds a continuing though constantly changing point of balance. Thus, an inherent conflict exists between the two kinds of relationships (marital and parental), which are simultaneously interdependent with one another. The process of change or reorganization within the stepfamily depends on the successful management of this relationship dialectic (p. 8).

The theme of managing the tension between marital and parental relationships is not unique to the stepfamily, of course. All families have the tendency to focus energy and interaction on those struggles that are of significance to them at a particular stage in their life cycle (Carter & McGoldrick, 1980; Constantine, 1986; Kantor & Lehr, 1975). However, the struggles of a stepfamily as it reorganizes itself helps to demonstrate the ways in which a family theme can provide the focus for the family's energy and interaction.

Types of Family Conversational Themes

We have indicated that the function of family themes is to provide a focus for the family's energy. That is, family themes represent a centering of the family's interaction and reveal important preoccupations in the family. We have also described some of the sources of family themes in the experiences and values of parents and in the family's struggle with dialectical processes. In this section we will describe a hierarchical model for identifying and discussing family themes and examine how family themes are related to conversation in the family.

In their explorations of how relationship definitions can be revealed in the conversational themes of married couples, Sillars and his colleagues (Sillars, Burggraf, Yost, & Zietlow, 1992; Sillars, Weisberg, Burggraf, & Wilson, 1987; Sillars & Wilmot, 1989; Sillars & Zietlow, 1993) have contributed to our understanding of the importance of communication in the development and recognition of family themes. The following description of types of family themes and how themes are integrated in the conversation of family members is based on the work of Sillars and his colleagues.

Given a particular topic of discussion, such as money, agendas, affection, conflict, or decision making, each couple will approach the topic differently (Sillars, et al., 1987, 1992). For example, in discussing the topic of money, one couple might recall their joint efforts to save for a new house; another might launch into a criticism of each other's spending habits; or a third couple might discuss how changes in the economy have restricted their budget. A **topic** is a specific issue that leads to an initial conversation among family members. The way family members approach a particular topic provides information about how they have constructed their relationships. For example, regarding the topic of money, the couple who chooses to discuss its cooperative effort to save for a new house is describing something that each of them shares. The couple who discusses the topic of money by disclosing potentially embarrassing or critical stories of each other is

---

APPLICATION 9.3

FAMILY THEMES

Identify two themes that guide your family's behavior. Identify events in your family's experience and history that both fit in with these themes and help to support them.

revealing something about the competitive and individualistic nature of the relationship. Finally, the two spouses who see themselves as victims of external forces beyond their control are defining their relationship in terms of outside factors that impact on their relationship. Each of these examples illustrates a different type of conversational theme, which provides a different view of how each couple has constructed the relationship. In their study of couple communication, Sillars and his colleagues describe three types of conversational themes: communal themes, individual themes, and impersonal themes (Sillars, et al., 1987, 1991).

Communal themes are represented in conversation that conveys a joint description of the relationship. Conversation that suggests a sense of togetherness, alludes to efforts at cooperation, or reveals aspects of interdependence in the relationship focuses on communal themes and presents *a definition of the relationship as one that is unified and connected*. Imagine the following dialogue between Fred and Ann Norris:

Fred: I think that one of the things that has helped us out is that Ann and I share the same goals.

Ann: We haven't always been easy on Stephen, but we always had his best interests at heart. It has been hard for us not to push him. We've always believed that hard work and a good education would pay off for him in the long run.

Fred: Yes, overall, but we've been together on the fundamentals.

As they talk about their relationship, Fred and Ann tend to speak in "we" terms. They indicate what they have in common rather than differentiate between their points of view. They describe common goals and indicate that they have tried to influence their son in ways that are congruent with their jointly constructed values.

Individual themes in family conversation suggest separateness between family members, differences in or criticisms of one another's personality, and issues related to individual role performance. Individual themes can *reveal the competitive or conflictual nature of the relationship*. A conversation between Fred and his son, Stephen, illustrates individual themes:

Stephen: Sometimes I resent the way you try to make decisions for me.

Fred: That's difficult to understand. I've only been concerned about your welfare. And, frankly, sometimes I worry about your judgment. You haven't always made decisions that reflected the necessary degree of maturity. It's my job to give you advice.

Stephen: Even now, you sound kind of high and mighty, so sure that you're right. Sometimes when you talk like that it makes me want to do the opposite of what you want.

Fred: That seems self-destructive to me.

As Fred and Stephen talk, we have the sense that each is criticizing the other's personality and arguing, at the same time, for some understanding of his own individual experience and point of view. Father and son each make competing attributions of their relationship. Fred attributes their interaction to Stephen's immaturity, while Stephen attributes interaction in their relationship to his father's rigidity and lack of empathy. Fred alludes to how he sees his role as father and Stephen criticizes how his father performs his role. Rather than presenting a communal image of their relationship, father and son present an image of two separate individuals with distinctly different perceptions.

Impersonal themes are themes that suggest that a *particular relationship is governed by factors largely or partly beyond the control of family members.* Impersonal themes tend to attribute major aspects of the relationship to factors outside the relationship, such as organic properties, nature, or environmental influences, and they often reveal an attitude of stoicism and acceptance of forces that are beyond the power of family members to change. For example, Fred might make the following comment about his interactions over money with Ann. "There is no point in arguing about things that can't be changed. People have to work hard for a living if they want to get ahead, so it's important for us to live within our means." Ann might describe their interactions with Stephen in terms that reflect impersonal themes. "Of course we want him to finish college. These days no young person can get anywhere without an education—that's just a fact of life."

Communal themes can be identified in the conversation between individual family members that reveal a unified description of the relationship and a cooperative, shared view of a situation. In contrast, *individual themes* can be identified by language that is more argumentative, critical, conflictual, and suggestive of alternative viewpoints and experiences. *Impersonal themes* are suggested by language that describes certain factors outside the family that have to be accepted by family members.

Integration of Family Themes

Sillars and his colleagues use the terms *hierarchy* and *continuity* to describe how family themes are related to each other and how they are integrated in the family's communication. Each of the three previously described types of family themes found in the conversations of specific family members may also be included in an overarching, higher-order theme that governs the family (Hess & Handel, 1959; Sillars, et al., 1987, 1992). The dialectical processes of differentiation and integration (which are sometimes referred to as separateness vs. connectedness, autonomy vs. independence, or the self vs. the system) and the process of balancing stability and change may be thought of as higher-order themes as well as sources of family themes. The concept of **hierarchy of family themes** is used to describe this idea that some family themes may be subsumed by broader, more overarching themes.

Distinguishing among the three types of family themes may be useful in understanding how family members have defined their relationship. **Conversational continuity** in family themes is a term used to describe how the themes of specific family members are integrated in their conversations or narratives. That is, how is the structure of conversation related to the themes expressed by individual family members?

Sillars and his colleagues suggest that continuity is achieved in family themes as comments by one family member invite comments from another family member and "a chain reaction of feelings, memories, stories, and personal philosophies" is produced (Sillars, et al., 1992, p. 136). **Thematic chaining** refers to the ways that family members organize their conversation, that is, how they

FIGURE 9.2   Types of family themes.*

Communal themes: Relationship themes that reveal a sense of togetherness, allude to efforts at cooperation, and/or present an image of the relationship as unified and connected.

- "We share the same things."
- "My mom and I are almost like sisters."
- "If one of us is depressed, that will affect the rest of us."
- "We have the same values."
- "Dad and I are alike in a lot of ways."

Individual themes: Relationship themes that emphasize a sense of separateness between family members, focus on individual differences between family members, and/or reveal criticism of the other's personality and role performance.

- "Sheila likes to argue too much."
- "You always walk over things rather than pick them up."
- "I need more time alone than you do."
- "I can't stand being at home all day Sunday. It's boring."
- "Stephen can be really stubborn."

Impersonal themes: Relationship themes that suggest that a particular relationship is governed by circumstances largely beyond the control of family members and that attribute influence in the relationship to natural forces, social factors, or environmental conditions.

- "Men don't show their feelings. It is not in their nature."
- "There is no point in talking when nothing will change."
- "In this culture, we have no time for each other. We are too busy and our agendas are too full."
- "All families have problems. You don't sit around and cry about it."
- "We discipline according to the Bible."

*Adapted from Sillars, A. L., Weisberg, J., Burggraf, C. S., & Wilson, E. A. (1987). *Human Communication Research, 13,* pp. 506-507.

structure their individual contributions to the conversation in ways that create some degree of integration and continuity around one or more family themes.

Thus, there is a hierarchical relationship among (1) the topics which provide the initial impetus for conversation and the creation of family themes, (2) the three types of *conversational themes* that we can identify in the conversation of specific family members, (3) the *conversational structure* of those who interact (i.e., interaction chains), and 4) *higher-order themes* (such as the tension between separateness and connectedness), which tend to be broader and more encompassing. In the following paragraphs we discuss three thematic chains in conversational structure that Sillars and his colleagues have identified in their analysis of the structure of conversational themes: blending chains, differentiating chains, and balancing chains.

Blending chains are made up of conversational segments in which there is mutually confirming, reinforcing, and overlapping talk. Conversational partners express agreement about both negative and positive aspects of their relationship and openly acknowledge shared rules, interpretations, and common experiences with a significant amount of redundancy and similarity in points of view. Ann might say, "We have both agreed that we need to spend more leisure time with each other." Fred supports her comment by adding, "It is true; we both want to make more time to be together—just to relax together."

Blending chains most often include communal themes. Impersonal themes may also be identified in blending chains when partners feel influenced by forces larger than their relationship. For example, a partner might make a comment, which the other partner reinforces, that "hard economic times made us realize how much we need to stick together," or another couple might support each other in asserting that "our marriage is based on a unity that includes our religious faith."

In contrast, **differentiating chains** in the conversational structure of a couple or two other family members tend to reveal unintegrated perceptions of the relationship, irreconcilable personality differences, and the tendency to make self-assertions rather than to confirm, reinforce, or build on the comments of the other person. Differentiation in conversational patterns includes talk that reiterates the identities of each person as distinct, different, and immutable. Such conversation usually does not include much continuity from one speaker to another or much direct disagreement. Instead, *differentiating chains include shifts in the topic, evasive replies, or competing narratives.*

Sillars and his colleagues found that a substantial number of differentiating conversational chains in couples focused on wives' discontent with the perceived inexpressiveness of husbands, which confirms much of the research on gender conflicts in communication. For example, Marie complains to her husband, "You just do not communicate." Floyd counters by commenting, "There's no point to it.

FIGURE 9.3   Hierarchy of family themes.

Higher-Order Themes

Overarching themes that influence a wide variety of family concerns and often suggest how the family has managed the dialectical processes of differentiation/integration and stability/change in the family.

Example : Ann and Fred Norris tend to emphasize integration at the expense of differentiation. They are united in their feelings about Stephen's future and feel that his going off to college is consistent with the family's values. They often feel uncomfortable with Stephen's effort to express his individuality, which they tend to interpret as immaturity.

Thematic Chains in Conversational Structure

Integration of individual family themes in the conversational structure of family members as they interact with one another.

Types of thematic chains: blending, differentiating, and/or balancing chains

Example: Ann and Fred tend to exhibit blending chains in their conversation as they talk about their desire for Stephen to go to college. They tend to reinforce each other in their conversation, agree with each other's assessments of the situation, and respond directly to each other without arguing or providing different perspectives of Stephen's situation.

Conversational Themes

Themes that can be identified in the conversation of specific family members.

Types of conversational themes: communal, individual, impersonal

Example : In the Norris family, Ann's conversation suggests a communal theme because she refers to the fact that she and Fred "both want the same things for Stephen; we want him to have a comfortable, financially secure future."

Topics

Specific issues that may be responsible for initiating conversation in the family.

Example: Ann and Fred Norris' relationship with their son Stephen.

Everyday life isn't a social event. I do my job and try to enjoy myself a little without too much fuss." Furthermore, both partners account for their lack of connection by identifying intractable personality differences: Floyd might say that he is "not a talker," while Rita might say that she is "outgoing." It is not surprising that Sillars and his colleagues found that differentiating chains can be related to feelings of incompatibility and dissatisfaction in a relationship.

Blending chains provide a unified image of those who are interacting and tend to reveal communal or impersonal themes; differentiating chains convey a fragmented, separated picture of two people interacting and reveal more individual themes in their conversation. **Balancing chains** provide a compromise between the alternatives of blending and differentiating chains and include individual themes interspersed with communal themes. For example, Ann might say, "I don't like the way that you get angry so quickly. It really got us into trouble with Stephen a while back; he was able to provoke you so easily. But we are really doing much better now." Fred responds by saying, "Well, I sometimes had the feeling that you were on his side, but we can usually talk it through once I have cooled off. I think that has helped us a lot." Notice how *Ann and Fred present different points of view, but there is also a sense of engagement between them;* and both of their comments include communal themes that suggest the notion that "we can work it out together."

The work of Sillars and his colleagues helps us to understand more about the relationship between family themes and communication or discourse in the family as family members blend, differentiate, or balance themes in their conversations with one another. We can also identify a relationship among communal, individual, and impersonal themes that are revealed in the family's conversation and themes that emerge from dialectical processes in the family.

For example, communal and impersonal themes may be identified in the Norris family, for whom integration is especially important and differentiation is seen as a threat to family unity. The conversational structure of Ann and Fred Norris is characterized by a significant number of blending chains. As we have indicated, the tension between differentiation and integration could be thought of as a kind of higher-order theme that could include communal and impersonal themes. Blending chains describe the way that communal and impersonal themes are integrated in the conversation of two people. In another family there might be more energy focused on differentiation than on connectedness. For this family, individual themes emerge in their conversations, which are characterized by more differentiating conversational chains than in the Norris family. A third family, for whom the tension between differentiation and integration is less emotional and is managed with more of a sense of balance may exhibit both individual and communal themes and more balancing conversational chains than do the other two families.

Sillars and his colleagues (Sillars & Wilmot, 1989; Sillars & Zietlow, 1993) also make the important point that the types of themes and how family members integrate themes in their conversation is related to the family's stage of development. For example, a young couple's conversation might include their attempts to negotiate individual identities and priorities and to coordinate competing work schedules, whereas an older couple's conversation may reveal more individual themes. Individual themes might also be more apparent in an adolescent family, for whom issues of individuation and the development of a separate sense of self are important. A middle-aged couple may have worked through many of their

APPLICATION 9.4

THEMATIC CHAINS

The next time that you have time to observe and listen to two or more members of your family interact with one another, try to identify blending chains, differentiating chains, and/or balancing chains in their conversation.

Blending chains: Do conversational participants in a family use "we" language in talking with each other or about their relationship? Do they reinforce what the others say and convey a sense of unity in their perceptions?

Differentiating chains: Do some members' conversations seem to be going in different directions, without much sense of connection? Do particular conversational partners explain a situation in terms of personality differences, criticize each other's behavior, personality, or role performance, make shifts in the topic, or offer a different account of the situation?

Balancing chains: Does the conversation of family members seem to acknowledge personality differences while, at the same time, identifying potential commonalities? Do they express disagreements directly and also suggest the potential for acceptance and/or negotiation of conflicts? Can you identify communal themes as well as individual themes in their conversation?

conflicts, launched children into adulthood, and come to rely on each other for companionship more than they may have in earlier years. Their conversation may reveal more communal themes. The themes that emerge in a family's conversation may also depend upon its unique characteristics or problems. Emotional, social, or economic stress, and particular cultural values may influence the types of themes that can be identified in the family.

It is important to remember that the conversational themes of families have the potential for change and can be influenced by a variety of factors, including the passage of time and the circumstances of the context. Overall, a family's conversational themes can be an indication of the family's view of the world, how family members have defined their relationships, and the central issues that prevail in their interactions.

SUMMARY

In this chapter we define the collective identity of the family as a description of how family members characterize or experience the family as a group. In the context of the family's collective identity, we discuss the symbolic content of the family's communication as acts, behaviors, and communication sequences that represent concepts important to the family as a whole. We argue that understanding more about the family's collective identity and the symbolic content of the family can help to locate potential conflicts and identify goals in the family system. The myths, metaphors, and thematic concerns that make up a family's meaning system characterize its collective experience.

Family myths are beliefs or attitudes about the family in which actual experience is selectively remembered to reflect a specific orientation of importance to a family. Family myths enable the family to manage events that are painful or embarrassing; maintain values and beliefs important to them; provide a rationalization for the dilemmas, role relationships, and organization created in the family; and sustain bonds across the generations.

A family metaphor is a specific event, object, image, or behavior that represents some aspect of the family's collective identity. We have discussed three types of metaphors in this chapter: metaphors as representational acts, as collective paradigms and images for the family, and as connecting links between events and meaning.

Family themes identify a family's orientation toward major issues, goals, relationship definitions, concerns, or values. Family themes represent important preoccupations in families and provide the focus for family energy. Family themes can evolve from the parents' unique background of experiences and values. They can also emerge from attempts by the family to balance dialectical tensions. The tensions that families experience between autonomy and interdependence and from competing demands in family role relationships often provide a focus for the family's energy and interaction. In our discussion of family themes, we explore two sources of family themes, identify three types of family themes, and describe how themes are integrated into the conversation of family members. We hope that this discussion of family myths, metaphors, and themes has given you the opportunity to explore—and perhaps reconstruct—your own family's collective identity.

KEY TERMS

autonomy	family themes
balancing chains	hierarchy of family themes
blending chains	ideal image
collective identity	impersonal themes
communal themes	individual themes
connecting links	interdependence
constitutive rules	paradigms
conversational continuity	personal myths
couple myths	representational acts
cultural myths	symbolic content of
differentiating chains	communication
family metaphors	thematic chaining
family myths	topic

C H A P T E R   10

ROLES
AND
FAMILY TYPES

NANCY VADER-McCORMICK

BARBARA GARLAND'S FAMILY

The moment that Cliff returned from Vietnam in 1966, I knew that there would be an "us." We felt like a couple and had the same dreams and plans. We wanted to build our future together—to have our own home and to raise our own children with the same values that we had. We were in love and our love has grown deeper and stronger with time, but we have also changed over the years. When we were married, I thought of Cliff as my "hero." I think that he thought of himself that way, too. He has often said that he fell in love with me in part because I made him feel good about himself. He also liked my self-confidence, my sense of humor, and my ease with people.

Cliff filled my need for stability and security. My father died when I was young, and I used to hear stories about my grandfather. He and my grandmother emigrated from Europe in the late 1800s to build a better life for themselves. My grandfather worked very hard as a carpenter to provide a living for his wife and four sons. However, my grandfather was an alcoholic and he physically abused his sons, especially after he had been drinking. These facts were secret for many years. Apparently my grandmother died an embittered, old woman because of the turmoil and abuse that my grandfather periodically inflicted on his family. Even today there is a source of shame about this. After my father died, my uncles looked after me, my mother, and my brothers and sisters. They rarely mentioned my grandfather's name with any feelings of warmth. My mother and uncles always said that when I married I should find someone who was hard working but also dependable and kind—like my father. Cliff seemed to be that person; he was dependable and kind, and he came from a stable farm family.

Our union was made official on April 8, 1967. Nine months and ten days later we were blessed with our daughter, Colleen; 19 months later our son, Mitch, was born, and

23 months later our son, Duffy, was born. During their childhood, my children kept us so busy that we had very little time for each other. Time was "eaten up" with responsibilities, children's games and crises, and day-to-day chores. Most of the time Cliff has worked two jobs. He took over the management of the beef cattle farm that had been in his family for years and he has also worked for a large seed company. Cliff has really enjoyed working for the seed company, but he has often had to travel for two or three weeks at a time in that job. When Cliff is gone, it has been up to me to manage farm and the "homefront." I have kept the books for the cattle farm on a regular basis, kept the house clean, done all the shopping, looked after Cliff's parents (who were in ill health), and raised the children as well as I could. I enjoyed the responsibility and independence that I had when Cliff was away.

The children learned to do things around the farm from the time that they were very small. They would help me and Cliff (when he was home) in a variety of ways; we would all work together "picking stones" from the fields in the spring, putting up hay in the summer, and harvesting our corn in the fall. The children learned responsibility early, but having fun was something that tended to occur only on vacations or on rare weekend trips.

We have had some wonderful vacations and whenever the five of us are together for a holiday or birthday, we inevitably tell stories about some adventure or mishap that occurred on one of our vacations. These stories give us a chance to laugh together, something we never really had time to do in the course of daily living. Our vacations have included trips to Mammoth Cave, Disneyworld, Mount Rushmore, the Henry Ford Museum, Greenfield Village, Buffalo Bill Museum, a trip to the Colorado Rocky Mountains, and numerous camping trips to the Smoky Mountains and to Jackson Hole, Wyoming. Not only did these trips give us lasting memories but they also helped us to develop bonds with one another. Despite some of our problems, my children still comment to me about how great they thought our trips were.

Cliff and I never had much time to enjoy being with each other apart from our children. As the children have begun to leave home, we are focusing a little more on our relationship. This has been no easy task, however. Because of the nature of Cliff's work, he is out of town much of the time, and the amount of time that he spends away has gradually increased over the years. When he returns, it takes us two days to mesh again into a couple.

As I said earlier, when Cliff is out of town, I take care of everything at home. When Cliff returns, he tends to "check over" what I have done. He asks a lot of questions and is sometimes critical of my decisions; if one of the children (usually the boys) has done something he does not like, he will confront them. He also does maintenance chores around the house and checks out the cars, which I find helpful. When Cliff is home he then becomes the family auditor, looking over the budget, checking on the children, and monitoring the household. I know that this is his way of participating in the family's life and I appreciate much of what he does, but sometimes it can be difficult for me.

After a day or two, he usually relaxes and then we can connect a little. We pack three weeks of events, problem solving, and joy into that one week when he is home. We argue intensely; we love with sweet abandon. By the time that he is ready to leave again, we are usually feeling like a couple once more. This process has repeated itself for years. The routine can also leave us with issues that are never quite resolved.

We have managed to make this relationship work. However, Cliff's work has always been a source of tension and emotional complexity for us. I know this arrangement could not work for everyone. In the past, we have even discussed the possibility of Cliff's leaving his job so that we could live together like a "normal" married couple. This situation has not been all negative, and as I look ahead I see my "job" changing. During these past years I have become more assertive and independent. Not only have I balanced the books and run the farm, but I've gone alone to the children's basketball games and school functions and listened to my children's problems, wondering if I was giving them the right advice. Now, as they are growing up I have returned to college to become a counselor. My old friends have supported me and I have made wonderful new friends at school. The independence that I have gained over the years has given me the will and confidence that I can do this.

However, it is difficult for some of the family to understand that, after all the years of caring for them, I need to do something for myself. My daughter understands my need to have my own career, but my husband and sons are having a difficult time accepting the change. Cliff does not fully appreciate why my return to college is so important to me. He worries about what will happen to the farm—I have told him that we can hire someone to help out, and he can take over when he cuts back on his job in three or four years, which he has planned to do. I try to suggest that if he does more at home, he will probably not worry as much. He might also have more time to spend with the boys before they move too far away or both get married.

I think that the changes ahead of us are disturbing for Cliff. I suppose that I am a little scared also, afraid of what these changes in our roles will mean for our relationship. Another difficulty is that education is not as important to Cliff as it is to me. I have always had a dream of going back to school. During these years that Cliff has been away, I have occupied myself with reading and thinking about what I might do with my life someday. I wish that I could say that Cliff supports me in my decision to return to school. I'm deeply grieved that he fails to understand this basic part of who I am. However, with encouragement and help from two dear friends, I plan to continue my education.

Despite this unresolved part of our relationship, I know that I can always count on Cliff in numerous other ways that are very important to me. He is a responsible husband and father. He makes repairs around the house, provides financial support for the family, maintains our cars, is faithful to me and proud of our children. This is how he lets me know how important his family is to him. Most of all, by being affectionate and holding me when I am afraid or sad or just need to feel his arms around me, he makes me feel loved.

Our children are independent, responsible adults—just like their parents. Colleen has been married for only a few months and is a registered dietician in Cincinnati, Ohio. She and I have always been close, and she has been a great source of emotional support, help, and companionship for me. Our relationship was strained for a while after she got married and moved to Ohio. I felt a real loss when she left and I think that I withdrew a little. I recently went to visit her and her husband and since then we have been doing much better; she even calls me more often. Colleen and her father do not talk with each other very much, but he is proud of her and I think that she knows that.

Mitch will be married in July to a wonderful woman he has dated for four years. She is a nursing student who will be finished at the end of this school year.

Mitch has been thinking about going to veterinary school. In a sense, Mitch is a mediator between his father and me. He talks to his father about my returning to school and tries to help me understand why my career goals are difficult for Cliff. Mitch tells me that after working so hard all these years, I should begin to slow down and enjoy life with his father. Although I sometimes resent Cliff's and Mitch's unwillingness to understand my point of view, I do appreciate Mitch's concern for his father. Perhaps Mitch is closest to his father because, during the time before Cliff began traveling so much, they spent more time together than Cliff and Duffy did.

In a sense, Duffy is the "rebel" in the family—he does not want to work on the farm, but he is not sure what he wants to do yet. Sometimes he can be moody and unpredictable, and he does not talk very much to either me or Cliff, although he and Mitch are pretty close. When Cliff is home, he and Duffy will inevitably get into a fight. Cliff will ask Duffy questions about "what his plans are" and Duffy will get defensive and evasive; this will irritate Cliff, and then Duffy will stomp out of the house. On several occasions, Duffy has managed to do something stupid after he leaves the house—get into an accident or forget a family engagement—and then he and Cliff will get into an argument when he gets home. Cliff will tell him that he is irresponsible and Duffy will tell his dad to quit harassing him. Sometimes Cliff will try to repair things between them before Duffy leaves again, but they are typically silent around each other toward the end of Cliff's time at home. I worry about Duffy a little, but I know that he has to find his own way.

In spite of some of the tensions and changes we are going through, our family is generally secure, and I am somewhat optimistic that Cliff and I can work out our problems. I believe that going back to school has helped to give me a new zest for living. Once Cliff's work situation changes, perhaps he will better accept my goals and be willing to take on more responsibilities at home. Meanwhile, I will continue my education and do what I can to manage my obligations at home, and Cliff will continue to juggle his work and family schedule.

UNDERSTANDING THE GARLANDS

Each member of a family develops a repertoire of communication behaviors associated with his or her position in the family. As part of her role as mother, Barbara Garland has taught her children how to work on the farm, maintained a household, attended her children's basketball games and school functions, listened to their problems, and given them advice. Her energy, self-confidence, adaptability, and capacity to dream and set goals for herself also make her a positive role model for her children. She exchanges emotional support and companionship with Colleen, expresses pride in Mitch's choice of a spouse, and avoids putting pressure on Duffy. In his role as father, Cliff has worked at two jobs to support his family, has functioned as the "family auditor," communicates his approval of Colleen and Mitch, confides in Mitch, and makes an effort to get Duffy to be "more responsible." Cliff and Barbara also make choices about how to behave in their relationship. They support each other's independence, have developed a pattern for coping with Cliff's traveling, and are affectionate with each other. Colleen's primary role as daughter is to provide support for her mother. Mitch provides support for his father and functions as a mediator between his parents, while Duffy contributes a degree of unpredictability, impulsiveness, and spontaneity to the family climate. For the Garlands, as for other families, a description of their family roles is a way of answering such questions as: What am I entitled to expect and to demand from other members of the family? What am I held responsible for? What should I say and do as a mother, as a daughter, as a father, as a husband in this family? What are my functions in the family system?

In this chapter we explore family roles and role relationships from a communication perspective. We begin our discussion with a definition of family roles and describe two characteristics of family roles that are relevant to a communication perspective for understanding the family. We discuss role conflict and its inevitable consequences for communication in the family. We also describe types of marriages and families on the basis of how relationships are organized. Finally, we discuss the relationship of gender to the family's role functions and role structure.

CHARACTERISTICS OF FAMILY ROLES

A **role** is a term used to describe a set of prescribed behaviors that a family member performs in relation to other family members. In all families "each individual seeks and negotiates for himself a place in the social system" (Kantor & Lehr, 1975, p. 179). In our discussion of family roles we are interested in the behavior of family members as "players in the family system" (p. 180).

A particular role describes behaviors expected of an individual in the family, but it is the family as a system that helps to sustain the role. Roles do not reside in individuals, but are rather the outcome of how the family system is organized; they emerge from and are sustained by cultural values and habits of interaction. The meaning of one family member's behavior is found in the responses of other family members. Duffy's occasional acts of rebellion may keep the family from becoming too rigid; Cliff's resistance to Duffy keeps a rein on his rebellion; and Barbara's lack of involvement in the conflict keeps it from becoming too threatening for the family. The point is that family roles are not so much behaviors associated with the personalities of family members—though individual predispositions can influence role performance. Rather, roles grow out of the organized patterns of interaction in the family and larger social system.

Most individuals have some idealized images about their family roles. Most of us also adapt our role behavior to fit unique and/or new situations and experiences. In a family that claims its values are traditional, a father may view housekeeping as a task he is not suited for because that is his wife's domain, and he may, therefore, resist doing housekeeping chores. He may, however, do much of the family cooking because he enjoys it. Family roles are products of historical evolution, cultural stereotypes, and the unique adjustments that family members make to each other and to their system.

There are two characteristics of family roles that are associated with a communication perspective in understanding the family: (1) family roles reflect the functions that family members perform in the system, and (2) family roles and role relationships change and evolve as the family grows and changes.

Roles as Functions

In her role as wife and mother, it is Barbara's job to help manage the family's cattle farm as well as to maintain the household. As part of his role as son in the family, it may be Mitch's job to mediate conflicts between his parents, while it is Colleen's role to support her mother. Perhaps it is Duffy's responsibility to test the limits of the family system now and then so that the family does not get too bored with its orderliness.

In every family there are specific kinds of activities that certain family members perform. Most families have to formulate and manage a budget, maintain a household, and take care of children (Nye & Bernardo, 1973). The Garland family has developed particular patterns for these tasks, which Barbara generally performs on a day-to-day basis and Cliff monitors or "audits" when he is home.

Family roles also relate to other functions that help maintain the structure and stability of the family. The mediator role that Mitch plays in the conflict between his parents can maintain the stability of the system. The role that Colleen has played in supporting her mother may have helped Barbara avoid becoming overwhelmed by her responsibilities and kept her from becoming consumed by the family's needs. The mediator role that Mitch plays in the conflict between his parents can help to maintain the stability of the system. Mitch provides support for his father, which can help reduce Cliff's anxieties about changes in the family, as Barbara makes the transition from focusing on the family to focusing on furthering her education. Duffy is less predictable and more intense than the other family members. His role may be to keep the legacy of responsibility from becoming too oppressive in the family, and it also functions to gain his father's interest and attention.

In other families someone may perform the role of "family achiever." The son or daughter who always makes good grades, gets admitted into a good university, and is successful at his or her career may help to reinforce positive images of the family. From time to time, families may need one or more of their members to enact the role of family clown, listener, hero, adventurer, eccentric, confronter, mediator, achiever, or scapegoat in the family. These roles often perform important functions in maintaining the family system.

In some families, family members may perform roles for the family that have painful effects. As Boszormenyi-Nagy and Spark (1984) have indicated, troubled families often assign one or both adults and the children inappropriate generational and sexual roles in the family. Family members who take on such roles assume a one-dimensional character, suppressing other aspects of themselves in order to perform some important function for the family. Boszormenyi-Nagy and Spark describe the role of "the family pet" in compensating a family for its feelings of failure:

> The pet is described by the families as the carefree or nonsymptomatic child. They cause no overt troubles. They may act clown-like, do silly, annoying things, or tease, but it never is with serious intent to hurt or make anyone angry. They are rarely taken seriously. It is as if these children exist to bring the family lightness and laughter. They may also be depicted as good students. This child's goodness and nondemandingness is frequently used as a model against the siblings who express their hostile feelings. But close to the surface the child's affect is one of sadness and depression (pp. 260–261).

Family role functions are related to the responsibilities and privileges of family members. **Responsibilities** are the obligations and duties that family members are assigned by or assume in the family system. The responsibility of "the family pet" may be to bring lightness and laughter to the family. It has been

Barbara's responsibility to manage the cattle farm when Cliff is away, and Cliff's responsibility to make repairs on the house and maintain the cars when he is home. Mitch has the responsibility of supporting his father in resisting Barbara's new career aspirations. Duffy has the responsibility of playing the family rebel. Colleen's responsibility is to support her mother.

Privileges are the rights that particular family members assume in the family. Sometimes privileges involve the legitimacy of the demands that family members can make on other members. Cliff has the privilege of expecting that his family adjust to his schedule as he periodically exits and enters the family. In their roles as parents, Barbara and Cliff have a legitimate right to ask their children to help with the work of the farm.

The Changing and Evolving Nature of Roles

Family role relationships are constantly changing and new role behaviors are learned as members of a family go through various stages of life together. As Barbara finishes her education and pursues her goal of becoming a counselor, this will mean changes in her role and in the roles that Cliff has performed in the family. Barbara may attempt to get Cliff to take on more responsibility for supervising the cattle farm and maintaining the household as his traveling begins to slow down. Cliff may find himself having to adjust to Barbara's schedule rather than Barbara adjusting to his schedule.

Changes that individual family members experience affect the whole family. The toddler who is learning to assert herself demands specific adaptations from her parents. Her parents' responses, in turn, influence the child's behavior. Certainly the role expectations of children are different at six than at sixteen. The role of a parent who has taken time off to be with an infant child will be a little different when he or she starts back to work. A family with teenaged children may have a different set of role relationships than the same family did when the children were younger. When she was younger, Colleen was a major source of support and companionship for her mother. Now that Colleen is married and has a job in another state, Barbara is trying to let go of the particular kind of closeness that she previously had with her daughter. Role changes can also be observed in relationships between middle-aged adults and their parents. Barbara used to argue with her mother-in-law's advice when she was first married; now she finds herself *giving* her mother-in-law advice.

The concept that role relationships in the family are usually not static but changing and evolving reflects a developmental perspective of family roles that is

FIGURE 10.1   *Characteristics of family roles.*

Family roles identify the functions that individuals assume in the family system.

Cliff Garland is responsible for earning a significant portion of the family's income in a job that requires him to travel; Barbara Garland maintains the house, cares for the children, and manages the family's cattle farm.

Family roles change as the family grows and develops.

Now that their children are almost grown, Barbara wants to shift some of her responsibilities to Cliff so that she can return to school and pursue a career outside the home. Colleen's function as a companion for her mother has changed now that she is married and has a job in another state.

similar to our discussion of change in Chapter 11. Not only do family members assume different "jobs" or functions in the family as they grow and develop but they also change how they converse with one another about their relationships in the family. The developmental perspective reflects how the family's communication changes as the family progresses through stages in the life cycle. Fran and Dave are a couple with children in their late teens. When their children were small, conversations between Fran and Dave tended to focus on schedules, agendas, and tasks that needed to be done. Now that the children are more independent, Fran and Dave have routinized more of their tasks and spend more time conversing about their jobs, exploring their needs as a couple, and trying to provide support for each other. They *talk* with each other differently at this stage in their lives than they did a few years ago. In Chapter 11, we discuss stages in the life cycle in more detail.

ROLE CONFLICT

Family roles are related to differentiation and integration in the family system. Individuals and subsystems in the family are differentiated from one another and integrated into the family system by the roles that they enact. As we have indicated previously, a family is a system that carries out its functions through subsystems (Minuchin, 1974). Roles in the spousal subsystem focus responsibility on maintaining attraction and closeness between partners. Roles related to the parental subsystem involve executive and supportive functions necessary for guiding and nurturing children. The sibling subsystem can also be differentiated from the spousal and parental units. Children require guidance and nurturance, but they also need areas of autonomy appropriate to their age and development so that they can gain confidence in their ability to manage their lives apart from their parents. Each of these subsystems has a set of role functions to perform.

How do family members handle the multiple expectations of belonging to several role relationships simultaneously? This process does not always run smoothly and is not without conflict. By **role conflict** we mean the potential for incompatibility or contradiction in the demands of particular roles that specific members are expected to perform in the family (Minuchin, 1974). Role conflicts are related to the complexity of family structure.

Cliff Garland's job requires him to be away from his family for two or three weeks at a time. When he is away, Barbara Garland and her daughter take care of the family's domestic life; Colleen and the other children provide Barbara with companionship and often help in the decision making around the house. When Cliff enters the family, he is initially an "outsider." This puts Barbara in a delicate position. She needs to maintain the support system that she has with the children when Cliff is not home and, at the same time, support the parental authority that she and Cliff share when he is home. Barbara has become used to managing everything on her own when Cliff is not home; when he enters the family again, she must somehow share the roles that she has previously performed alone and refocus her attention on the marital relationship. Barbara's predicament might be described as one involving role conflict—she has to manage simultaneously her role as primary caretaker of her family and her role as a member of a spousal dyad. As the children get older, they find themselves wanting to differentiate themselves from the family system and find their own identities; this is hard to do, as Duffy's behavior illustrates, without challenging the parental subsystem that has nurtured and guided them.

Minuchin (1974) has discussed role conflict from a structural perspective by describing some of the dilemmas that family subsystems have to manage. Cliff and Barbara are spouses *and* parents. Duffy is evolving toward freedom from adult authority *and* lives in a house under the care and control of his parents. There is an inevitable tension between the demands of these double roles. Most every family experiences these two types of role conflict: (1) the parents in the family can experience conflict between their marital and parental obligations, and (2) parents and children can experience role conflict as they negotiate the parent–child relationship.

Conflict Between Parental and Spousal Roles

In a nuclear family, the husband and wife are partners in two subsystems whose competing demands can create role conflict. As husband and wife, they need affection and validation. For the health of the relationship and the stability of the family, the spousal dyad needs to develop a strong boundary around itself that protects its integrity. A husband and wife require what Minuchin (1974) calls a "psychosocial territory of their own—a haven in which they can give each other emotional support" (p. 57). If the boundary between husband and wife is extremely rigid, children in the family may be isolated and left to function without adequate support. If the boundary between husband and wife is not clearly defined, however, then children, relatives, and in-laws may interfere with the functioning of this primary relationship. When Cliff is home, he and Barbara always take an evening to do something romantic with each other, even if it is no more than going out to dinner together. This is one way that they have established a boundary around their marriage relationship—by spending time exclusively together.

A husband and wife are parenting partners as well as spousal partners. Sometimes the demands of the parenting relationship can interfere with the needs of the marital relationship. The most typical example of this kind of problem is the couple who find that they have very little time for each other after the arrival of their first baby (Rubin & Rubin, 1989; Stamp, 1992). The parental role can also conflict with the spousal role in other ways. Suppose a couple finds it difficult to identify, acknowledge, or negotiate important issues in their relationship. Children may be drawn into the unresolved conflict between husband and wife. One spouse may try to make an ally of one of the children in order to gain power in a struggle with the other spouse. In another family, differences in parenting philosophy between husband and wife can trigger a conflict over values between spouses that may be difficult to resolve. If the disagreement between spouses becomes serious, one or both spouses may try to use parenting roles to manipulate or punish the other.

Sometimes unresolved problems in the spousal system influence the parenting style of the couple, or the problems of parenting may interfere with maintaining closeness in the marriage. In families where these patterns develop, the spousal and parental roles can become too undifferentiated (Haley, 1963, 1976; Napier & Whitaker, 1978; Minuchin, 1974). It is important to remember that most families struggle with these role conflicts to some degree at different stages in their lives. Adults in a nuclear family are members of two primary subsystems

APPLICATION 10.1

RECOGNIZING ROLE CONFLICT

How would you answer the following questions?

1. To what extent did your parents have conflicts over their parenting roles?

2. How do you think parents can effectively maintain the separation between their parental roles and their spousal roles?

3. To what extent did your parents encourage or discourage your "gradual aspirations for independence"? Did you ever experience a conflict between wanting protection and longing for independence?

4. How might the problem of role conflict be different in stepfamilies or in single-parent families?

How would you describe each of the issues presented in the questions above as communication problems?

simultaneously—the spousal subsystem and the parental subsystem. Managing the demands of one relationship can seem difficult; managing the demands of two, sometimes competing, subsystems can seem impossible.

Conflict Between the Child's Needs for Protection and Self-Realization

In families with children, the kids are children *and* siblings. As children, they are dependent on their parents; as siblings they are learning to relate to their peers as equals (even a child without brothers and sisters is a peer to her friends and class-mates). Parents are obligated by their children's dependence; at the same time, they must support their children's gradual aspirations for independence. Parents are also assigned the role of socializing their children according to the tenets of the parental value system. Socialization requires discipline, authority, and disapproval of behaviors not consistent with the family's value system. However, a parent must provide guidance while facilitating enough self-confidence so that the child can gradually assume control of his or her own life.

Parents have a responsibility to provide protection for their children and, at the same time, to allow their children to take risks that help them grow and mature. For their part, children are asked to conform to the demands of their parents with enough acquiescence to ensure that their parents will continue to care for them as long as they need care. At the same time they normally want to experiment with enough resistance to test parental authority and develop a sense of individuation that will allow them to form independent lives eventually (Rubin & Rubin, 1989). Duffy longs for attention from his father, but when his father expresses interest and concern about his future, Duffy seems to push him away. Barbara has learned that she must wait for Duffy to approach her and take care not to sound judgmental or critical or ask many questions if she is going to try to get Duffy to open up to her.

Children contribute energy and vitality to the family system; they also absorb energy and make excruciating emotional and financial demands on the system. Minuchin (1974) makes the point that parenting is so difficult that most mothers and fathers end up with scars from the experience. About the time parents want to be closer to their children, the children want a life of their own and strive to put distance in the relationship.

Single-parent families have particular difficulties in managing role conflict. Single parents often experience unique emotional and economic problems (Hogan, Buehler, & Robinson, 1983; Norton & Glick, 1986; Weiss, 1979a, 1979b). Excessive demands can lead them to rely on their children in ways that two-parent families do not. Children may be asked to provide emotional support for the parent and assume greater responsibility for the household than is customary for children their age. Greater reliance on children leads to a blurring of generational boundaries in which a peer relationship between parent and children develops (Glenwick & Mowerey, 1986). The roles in the family can become unclear. Single-parent families may demand greater self-reliance from children and at the same time draw them into a mutually dependent role (Nock, 1988). Providing support for their children's eventual independence, while simultaneously nurturing and guiding children is an especially difficult challenge for single-parent families, who often must struggle with reduced economic resources and added stresses.

CONSTRUCTING THE PARENTAL ROLE

Our preceding discussion of the potential for role conflict in the parent/child relationship because of the contradictory needs of children for protection and for self-realization makes it clear that negotiating this often rewarding but difficult relationship is no easy task. Parenting has become a difficult process in a changing and complex world. Although we do identify some of the characteristics that are related to optimal family functioning in Chapter 11 and believe that successful parenting is related to the well-being of the whole family, we are hesitant to suggest specific ways to be a parent. Certainly a case can be made for the positive effects of empathy, patience, letting children speak for themselves, establishing clear boundaries, tolerating individual differences, and allowing the expression of a full range of feelings (Hauser, 1991; Beavers & Hampson, 1990). We discuss some of the behaviors of optimally functioning families in Chapter 11. However, as we indicate there, interpersonal warmth and caring are about the only behaviors that empirical research has conclusively associated with effective parenting (Stafford & Bayer, 1990). It is important to think about how you construct the parental role and to identify some significant contemporary parenting issues. We identify four issues that are related to the parents' construction of their parental roles: (1) coping with the dialectic of authoritarianism versus nurturance in the parental role, (2) the need for parents to develop a more egalitarian relationship with their children as the children grow older, (3) the struggle to integrate the parenting styles of the parents, and (4) the difficulties of integrating the obligations and satisfactions of parenthood with the demands of work and the need for personal growth and development.

The Dialectical Tension Between Authority and Nurturance

This issue is related to the issue of role conflict, which we mention in the above section. Much of the literature about the family suggests that it is crucial for the parents to establish themselves as role models or authority figures, especially when their children are young (Haley, 1963, 1976; Minuchin, 1974). However, as we have indicated in our discussion of role conflict, parents also have an obligation to nurture their children by reinforcing their children's self-esteem, helping to provide opportunities for children to express their feelings, helping their children to develop their gifts, encouraging them to take responsibility for their own lives, and supporting them as they differentiate themselves from other family members.

Because nurturing behaviors facilitate the development of a child as a unique person, nurturing behaviors have the tendency to undermine the role of the parent as an authority figure. Nurturing another person's uniqueness and self-confidence tends to reinforce egalitarian relationships rather than authoritarian relationships between people. Further, if one constructs parental authority as the parent's right to control his/her child, the child's sense of self can be inhibited or even damaged. If one constructs parental authority as a status issue related to the parents' right to gain respect for their needs, values, and beliefs, then children may legitimately demand that "respect" be mutual or reciprocated. In contemporary American culture, the obligation to nurture children's individuality and talents can conflict with the construction of the parental role as grounded in status and authority. One major dialectic in the construction of one's role as a parent is the cultural demand for parents to be role models and authority figures for their children and to provide adequate socialization and moral development for their children while simultaneously supporting their children's freedom to become their own persons.

The Need to Adapt the Parental Role over Time

We have suggested that when children are young, they can thrive with parents who are authority figures and role models, parents who protect and are responsible for them; but as they move through adolescence, adulthood, and maturity, they gradually need parents who are more egalitarian and accepting of their uniqueness (Williamson, 1991). However, as we indicate in Chapter 11 when we discuss transitions in the family life cycle, making the transition from one stage of parenting to another is no easy task. What makes the transition from one life cycle stage to the next so difficult is that fundamental changes in how parents and children construct their relationship are required as children move toward adulthood and grow older. Williamson argues that, for many adults, reconstructing their relationship with their parents as they get older requires no less than a revolution in the way that parents and children relate to one another:

> The essence of this revolution is the renegotiation and termination of the hierarchical power boundary between the parent and the child. . . . Grown sons and daughters give up the parent as one who protects and provides for, guides

and nurtures, and carries ultimate responsibility for their general well-being. . . . The threat for many parents is emotional abandonment, with the resulting loss of role and an important part of the self, namely, self-as-parent, as well as the loss of a potential return on a major life investment. Second, there is the fear of a failing grade in the performance as parent. The most difficult problem for a son or daughter is *intergenerational intimidation* [Williamson's emphasis] (pp. 7–8).

As Williamson suggests, intergenerational intimidation can inhibit necessary change in parent/child relationships. Parents who have difficulty relinquishing earlier constructions of their parenting role may use intimidation strategies to resist change. For example, Jason's mother continues to make subtly disapproving comments about Jason's wife, Miriam, even though Jason and Miriam have been happily married for twenty years. Every time she does so, Jason feels embarrassed, angry, and frustrated, just as he did when he was a little boy and his mother would make judgments about his friends.

In making observations about intergenerational intimidation and other parental orientations, we wish to emphasize that *the construction of the parental role through the life course is a communication process*. For example, the parent of an older child may talk about the "consequences" of engaging in activity that seems risky or unwise ("If you stay overnight at Libby's you won't get your homework done"); when the child was younger the parent was more inclined to tell the child that she was "not allowed" to do something that the parent thought was risky or unwise. Parents may also rely more on guilt inducements rather than on direct orders (Socha, 1991) as their children get older ("I would expect you to be more considerate of your mother's feelings"). In launching their child into adulthood, the parents of an adolescent may indicate their "preferences" for how they would like their adolescent to behave rather than "tell them what to do"; they may also reduce the amount of advice they give their child and express more curiosity about their child's needs and goals ("I'd rather you didn't work after school"; "What is it about this boy that attracts you?"). In order to facilitate a stronger peer relationship with parents, Williamson even suggests that adult children who are working on reconstructing their relationship with their parents call their parents by their first names. As parents and children reconstruct their relationship over time they change the way that they talk with one another.

Integrating Different Parenting Styles

In Chapter 1 we described the difficulties that Ted and Joan Nelson have in integrating their parenting styles. Ted's parenting style is more reactive, prescriptive, and authoritarian than is Joan's. When Jamie cries and screams in public, Joan's tendency is to weather out the behavior, respond firmly but calmly, and take her son to the car or go home. Ted thinks that Jamie's behavior is self-centered, manipulative, and tyrannical; he believes that it is important to try to control Jamie and feels justified in punishing him with a severe spanking if Jamie does not comply with Ted's demands. Ted sees himself as "disciplining" Jamie. Joan sees Ted's parenting style as excessively harsh, unempathic, inappropriate, and even potentially damaging to Jamie. Ted sees Joan's parenting style as overprotective and likely to lead to Jamie's becoming a "spoiled" child. Parenting differences such as these can create intense conflicts between parents, whether the parents are members of a heterosexual, intact family, two gay or lesbian parents with different values and beliefs about parenting, a stepparent couple, or a grandparent and daughter who share responsibility for taking care of and raising a child.

These issues are so *intense* because how we construct our parenting role is related to our values and beliefs about appropriate social conduct, our view of morality and integrity, our sense of fairness and equality, our comfort or discomfort with status and authority relationships, and our view of ourselves. Ted feels resentful, angry, and defensive at the suggestion that he might be "damaging" Jamie. Joan feels insulted and anxious at Ted's suggestion that she "spoils" Jamie.

It is inevitable that parents will have some differences over how to parent their children simply because they are different persons. Even minor differences, however, can seem insurmountable and threatening to parents who have constructed a parenting role for themselves which they experience as congruent with their values, beliefs, view of the world, history of experience, and self-image. Counseling and the passage of time helped Ted and Joan weather the storm. For other parents, compromising, reacting with less emotional intensity to their parenting differences, or talking with each other about their differences without being judgmental might be helpful. In any case, differences in how each parent constructs his or her parenting role can be an important issue in the family.

Integrating the Parental Role with the Demands of Work and Needs for a Separate Sense of Self

Because most women work outside of the home today and because the popular culture has created an opportunity for dialogue about the roles of men and women, we have become sensitive to the issue of how parents negotiate their work lives, their needs to develop themselves as persons, and their parental needs and obligations. Later in this chapter, we discuss the relationship of gender to family roles. Certainly, gender is important in how parents construct conflicts among their work, family, and personal lives. Deciding how to share child-care responsibilities when both parents work, deciding whether to have one parent stay home with the children during a particular stage in the family's life, and deciding to what extent one or both parents will pursue interests and goals apart from their involvement with the family all have implications for how men and women construct their roles in the family. Regardless of the implications for gender roles in the family, the sense for some parents that one is constantly "torn" between work and family can be physically and emotionally exhausting.

As our culture begins to recognize some of the stresses placed on parents, more resources may become available for affordable child-care, counseling, flexible work arrangements, and other kinds of support. In the meantime most parents must cope with complicated choices about where to invest their energy, time, and attention. Too much investment in the family can lead to the loss of one's sense of self; too little investment in the family can lead to inadequate nurturance of children and of all relationships in the family. But how is one to know and who is to decide what is too much and what is too little? Are the long hours that Martin works an indication of his efforts to provide a good income for his family or an indication of the distance that he puts between himself and his children and of his reliance on his wife as the nurturer in the family? Does Emily's decision to put long hours into her work in order to get a promotion mean that she is a good role model for her children or that her children will grow up missing the attention that a less ambitious mother could give her children? Does Pat's decision to put her family before advancement at work mean that she has overinvested in her family as a way to avoid realizing her own potential? None of these questions is easily answered and the answers will be influenced by cultural attitudes and historical circumstances as well as by individual predispositions. As we suggested in our description of the family systems concept of equifinality, different orientations toward work and family life can be successful for different families. How parents construct their relationships to work, family, and their personal selves, however, can be a source of difficulty for the family if there is conflict about this issue or if parents cannot find ways to cope adequately with the stresses that they experience.

Earlier in this chapter we discussed the significance of role conflict for the family and identified some important issues in the parents' construction of their parental roles. In the following sections, we explore how different types of families have organized their role relationships in ways that will influence how they manage these issues.

MARITAL AND FAMILY RELATIONSHIP TYPES

Role relationships is a term that describes the ways that two or more family roles have been organized in relationship to other roles in the family. Family roles are labels for individual roles in the family: Duffy is the rebellious one in the family; Barbara is the family caretaker; Cliff is the family auditor; Mitch is the mediator. Role relationships are labels for relationships rather than labels for individual behavior. If the tension between Cliff and Barbara escalates to the point where all they seem to do is quarrel, we might be tempted to label their relationship "conflictual." Family role relationships describe reciprocal roles at various levels in the family system. A husband/wife relationship may be egalitarian rather than traditional. A nuclear family may be more democratic than authoritarian. These are labels that we can attach to relationships at various levels in the system. Such labels indicate how the family is organized and describe the structure of responsibilities, privileges, and authority in the family.

Definition of Relationship Typologies

How would you characterize your parents' marital role relationship? In what ways do the role relationships in your family differ from other families that you know? Family roles and role relationships are related to the functions that family members perform. How a family structures its roles and role relationships, however, depends upon its orientation to the goals and work it must accomplish as a family. As Constantine (1986) has argued, "There is more than one basic way for families to accomplish what they need to do as families" (p. 6). Marital and family typologies help to describe and explain some of these differences.

Relationship typologies identify dimensions along which couples and families may be differentiated and reflect how couples and families have organized their relationships (Yerby & Stephen, 1986). In this section we discuss several examples of relationship typologies that have advanced our understanding of communication in families. These typologies provide a means for understanding the different patterns of organization that families develop.

A family with a young child will have different life tasks than a family at a different stage in the life cycle.

Marital Types: Fitzpatrick's Model

Fitzpatrick (1977, 1988) has developed a model of couple types that is based on her survey of available literature identifying dimensions of relational life. Fitzpatrick collected information about how couples perceive their relationships. Her analysis of the data produced three primary dimensions of marital relationships: the extent to which couples subscribe to a *conventional ideology* toward marriage; the degree of *autonomy* desired by the partners; and the extent to which they value *avoidance of conflict* in the marriage. Using couples' scores on her Relational Dimensions Instrument, Fitzpatrick identified three basic types of relationships: **Independents**, **Separates**, and **Traditionals**.

Pure couple types are defined by the extent to which husband and wife agree on descriptions of the relationship. A *Pure Traditional type,* then, would be a couple in which both husband and wife had similar perceptions of their marriage as consistent with the Traditional description of the relationship. **Mixed couple types** include those couples in which the husband's definition of the relationship is different from the wife's. Approximately 60 percent of the couples in Fitzpatrick's research were identified as Pure types. Of the Mixed types—the remaining 40 percent of the couples—there is some evidence to suggest that the Separate/Traditional couples (in which the husband identifies the relationship as Separate and the wife identifies the relationship as Traditional) occur most frequently. Profiles of the three Pure types are given below.

Traditionals

Traditional couples have conventional values about marriage and tend to emphasize stability over spontaneity. There is a significant amount of interdependence in the marriage with a high degree of sharing and companionship and a tendency not to avoid conflict about issues they believe are important. The Traditional couple relies on cultural stereotypes in its management of male and female roles in the marriage; the male is expected to be task-oriented, concerned with problem solving, and dominant, while the wife is expected to be nurturant and concerned with the emotional aspects of the relationship. Husbands and wives in Traditional relationships tend to share their feelings with one another to a moderate degree while using restraint in expressing negative feelings. High marital adjustment is attributed to the couple's lack of a need to continually renegotiate expectations and because of their ability to use accepted cultural standards to evaluate their relationship. Fitzpatrick (1988) provides the following example of a Traditional couple:

> Tom and Jennifer have the same philosophy of life; they believe that their marriage is very important and that both should sacrifice some personal independence for the good of the marriage. They believe in stability; they stress the importance of being able to predict each other and their life together. Marriage provides them with a stable, committed relationship that helps to tie them into their community. Tom and Jennifer spend a lot of time together, working on their home and in leisure pursuits. They make time for each other during the day by keeping a regular daily schedule and eating their meals together. They avoid conflict in general and say that when they do disagree, they try to argue only over very important issues. Part of their philosophical agreement about life involves the nature of male/female roles; Tom sees himself as analytical, assertive, and dominant in the marriage, and Jennifer sees herself as warm, expressive, and nurturing. They are good at predicting one another's moods and feelings (p. 20).

Independents

Independent couples are less conventional in their orientations toward marriage than Traditionals. While there is a high level of companionship and sharing in the marriage, Independents tend to value individual freedom and to subscribe less to traditional male/female roles than do Traditionals. Just as the Traditionals, they tend not to avoid conflict. Independents also seem to work harder at their relationship. They continually renegotiate their expectations, emphasizing personal growth and individual autonomy as important aspects of their marriage. Both husbands and wives adopt masculine and feminine personality traits and roles, and they express a wide range of positive and negative feelings, including feelings of vulnerability and anger. Rather than follow culturally prescribed roles, the couple tends to negotiate roles unique to the needs of their relationship. It may be the constant process of negotiation and change that tends to lead Independents to describe their relationship as less adjusted than Traditionals. Open communication and the honest expression of feelings and conflict are signs of the vitality of the relationship for these couples. Scott and Missy have an Independent relationship (Fitzpatrick, 1988):

> Scott and Missy have the same philosophy of life; they believe that love and marriage primarily exist for the psychological gratification that the relationship gives to spouses. They believe that a marriage should be based on the satisfaction that each partner derives from the relationship. . . . For this couple, the most freedom in marriage stems from allowing each partner some privacy and independence. Scott and Missy try to spend a lot of time

together, but they do not keep regular daily schedules and they both have out-side friends and interests.

Scott and Missy thrive on conflict; neither is afraid of openly expressing their views. Part of their philosophical agreement about life involves the nature of male/female roles; they both believe in egalitarianism. . . . Scott and Missy both believe that they can disclose their innermost thoughts, feelings, and anxieties to one another. They disclose both positive and negative feelings about each other (p. 22).

Separates

Separates tend to have conventional attitudes toward marriage, but they also value individual freedom over relationship maintenance. These couples place less emphasis on companionship and sharing than the other two types. There is less interdependence, more psychological distance between spouses, more of a ten-dency to avoid conflict, greater withdrawal from conversational opportunities, and less intimacy than couples in the other two types of relationships. They rarely experience strong emotion in the relationship and do not engage in much self-dis-closure of their feelings. The moderate marital satisfaction attained by the Sepa-rates seems to be based on freedom to pursue individual interests, support for conventional role relationships, and a communication strategy that keeps them relatively uninvolved with and unaroused by one another. Frank and Eleanor have a Separate relationship (Fitzpatrick, 1988):

Frank and Eleanor's marriage provides them with a stable relationship that ties them into the community yet includes little personal closeness. They try not to spend very much time together, either working around the house or pursuing leisure activities. Their major points of contact occur at mealtimes or other regularly scheduled daily events. Frank and Eleanor will go to great lengths to avoid conflict. A strong bond between them is their commitment to conventional male and female roles. . . . Frank and Eleanor feel that they can-not express their innermost thoughts to one another, and they do not. . . . When Frank and Eleanor talk about their marriage, they talk about having separate time, activities, and interests, and about each of them having distinct personalities. They see their marriage as the product of factors that are out-side of their control, factors that are part of normal stages of life (pp. 22–23).

Based on Fitzpatrick's work, an important generalization can be made about marital role relationships that is consistent with our earlier discussion of roles and role relationships: The type of communication "appropriate" for a couple may depend upon the type of spousal relationship. For the Traditionals, marriage may be a way of performing important tasks learned through socialization; for Indepen-dents, marriage may be more of a route to individual growth and personal achieve-ment. Intimacy, emotional expressiveness, and closeness are not always outcomes of the marital relationship. Separates seem to value the interpersonal distance that they have achieved in their relationship. Complete honesty in the marriage, open acknowledgment of disagreement, as well as negotiation of needs and roles, for example, are behaviors that may be important priorities for Independent relation-ships but not for Traditional relationships, where more moderate levels of expres-siveness are likely to produce greater adjustment. Marital typologies help us to understand the complexity of marital role relationships and the impact that relationship goals have on perceptions of what is satisfying, effective, or functional.

Representative Models of Family Types

Family typologies provide a description of the ways that families can differ in defining their reality and structuring their relationships. Bernstein's typology of families differentiates families on the basis of the family's orientation toward generalized cultural values. Kantor and Lehr's model is based on the family's management of resources in the achievement of systems goals. Reiss's family types reflect differences in the problem-solving orientation of families. Finally, the Olson model distinguishes between families on the basis of the family's degree of adaptability and interrelatedness.

Bernstein's Model

A major task of any family is to integrate personal orientations and family roles with cultural expectations. Bernstein (1971) describes families as either Person-oriented or Positional, depending upon whether role differentiation among family members is based on the individual and psychological characteristics of family members or on the formal, culturally defined status of family members.

Positional families differentiate among their members on the basis of what each family believes is appropriate to the person's position or status in the family. In Positional families, roles are based on generalizations about a class of people. Children, women, mothers, fathers, and grandparents are expected to behave in specific ways because such conduct is "right," "good," or "correct" for someone occupying that position. Hence, positional families tend to rely on such admonitions as, "daughters don't act that way," "you know how you are supposed to behave," or "don't be disrespectful to your mother." Positional families apply standards for behavior which they perceive to exist outside their small unit and to be "greater than themselves."

According to Bernstein's model, the role structure of Positional families functions within a **restricted code of communication**. A restricted code depends upon generalizations. Requests are frequently assumed, unspoken, or stated indirectly. Feelings are not usually discussed; a child might be required to control the expression of anger rather than be encouraged to discuss its source and direction.

Roles in **Person-oriented families** depend more on the family's adaptations to the needs and personalities of the individuals in the family. Roles such as breadwinner, cook, listener, budget manager, and problem solver tend to be more specific to the situation and to be performed by or shared by family members who are suited to the task.

Members of Positional families can make themselves understood by communicating axiom-like messages (e.g., "mind your manners, now!"), which are accompanied by message-laden vocal cues and gestures. A family organized in terms of personal roles develops a more elaborated communication code. An **elaborated communication code** includes descriptions and explanations of the personal feelings and unique experiences of family members. Family members tend to exchange their reactions to specific behaviors ("I get nervous when you make so much noise") rather than speak in language that has more generalized meanings.

Person-oriented families depend less on social prescriptions and widely accepted meanings which originate outside the family than do Positional families. For the Person-oriented family, behavior is evaluated as good or bad on the basis of its effect on other family members and on the need of individual family members for self-growth. Does it hurt someone's feelings, ignore his needs, inconvenience her, or make the other feel good? A mother in conflict with her daughter is more inclined to indicate that her daughter has "hurt her feelings" rather than to say that "good daughters don't behave that way toward their mothers."

As Bernstein (1971) suggests, a Person-oriented system requires a more sophisticated awareness and use of communication in order to maintain stability than does a Positional system. In the family where role relationships are organized on the basis of the rights, privileges, and duties assigned to positions by the culture, it may be enough to suggest to a family member that he or she should behave in a specific way: "It is the children's duty to be obedient and respectful to their parents." Such prescriptions become inadequate once the family begins to place greater value on the personal fulfillment and mutual understanding of its members. Family members are then required to develop skills in disclosing and sharing feelings, in negotiating needs, and accepting responsibility for personal behavior. The rewards of such relationships can be fragile since they do not depend on cultural prescriptions ("I will obey you because you are my mother") to keep them together.

Kantor and Lehr's Model

Kantor and Lehr (1975) argue that the main activity of the family is the regulation of distance within itself and between itself and the environment. Families are defined as information-processing systems and information about distance regulation is carried by the family's communication. Through communication, a family maintains its territory; it also regulates both the degree and kind of physical and emotional closeness of its members.

The *spatial metaphor* can be explained by a variety of examples. Physical territory is a type of distance regulation. Fences, high shrubbery, unlocked doors, tricycles on the sidewalk, closed drapes, objects on the porch or in the entrance hall all communicate information about how the family regulates its territory. An open bathroom door while someone showers, a chair belonging to a father, a study area for a daughter, shared secrets, a pat on the back, a hug at bedtime also carry information about distance regulation.

Of central concern to Kantor and Lehr are the strategies families employ to reach certain "targets." **Target dimensions** represent desirable goal states of affect, power, and meaning. The strategies that family members employ to achieve particular goal states relate to the ways that the family utilizes particular resources. **Access dimensions** are the resources of space, time, and energy that the family manipulates to achieve desirable target states.

Affect is a target dimension that includes the manifestation of preferred levels of intimacy, nurturance, and caring in the family. The *power* dimension refers to the desired degree of freedom family members have to decide what they want and the ability that they have to get it. The *meaning* dimension describes the family's philosophical framework, which provides it with an explanation of reality and which defines the identity of its members. Values, attitudes, and beliefs about the self, others, and the world are included in this dimension, as well as the extent to which such meanings are shared by all the family members.

The family's manipulation of *space* includes such things as traffic control—how family members come together to share the same space for common or overlapping activities. It also includes how the family manages its territory; screens information and people coming into the family; distances members from one another (without deserting each other); and maintains privacy. How a family manipulates *time* also influences the affect, power, or meaning in the family. How do families spend their time, set up routines, manage schedules, become available to one another, orient themselves to the past, present, and future? The family's manipulation of *energy* includes such things as the intensity of involvement in encounters, the choices the family makes in expending and recharging its energy. Are family energies squandered? Do members have satisfying outlets for their energies? Do family members try to expend more energy than they can possibly supply? Using this basic model, Kantor and Lehr (1975) have developed a typology that identifies a family as closed, open, or random.

In a **closed family**, space is fixed and traffic is regulated by those in authority. Information is censored, strangers are screened, and operations to bring the family together are also controlled by authority. Parents set up rules about when, where, and with whom the children can go out. They might, for example, establish obligatory attendance at a family reunion, pronounce the father's study off limits, and prohibit eating in the living room. Time is regulated; routines and schedules are maintained and deviation from them is considered a legitimate cause for conflict. The family tends to be past- or future-oriented and views a present orientation as self-indulgent and hedonistic. Energy is steady energy. Expressions of emotion are restrained. Family members are closely regulated as to how and when they may spend their leisure time. Family loyalties are more important than friendships and affection is manifested primarily as a feeling of belonging. Power is expressed through authority, discipline, and regulation. Meaning in the family comes from traditional ideological values. Change is resisted. Verbal communication is formal, limited, and reflects a judgmental orientation toward others as well as a high degree of certainty that the family's belief and value system reflects universal truth.

In the **open family**, space is moveable and flexible. Boundaries tend to be regulated by group consensus rather than by those in authority. Family territory extends easily into the larger community; there is less censorship of information, screening of people entering the family, and control over excursions of family members into the environment than in the closed family. Intimacy is encouraged, but temporary distance, privacy, and personal secrets are permitted. Time is more variable and flexible; clocks and schedules are not as important as in the closed family. The past and future are important only insofar as they are related to the present. Energy expenditures are more flexible than in the closed family. The open family also demands more variety in their energy investments. The open family is more comfortable with minor crises and conflicts in daily living than with constrained, regulated, or controlled energy expenditures. As a consequence, the open family is willing to risk the values of stability, order, and dependability in favor of exploration and change.

Open expressions of affection are more acceptable in the open family. Children can reveal their anger at their parents without the fear of being called disrespectful. Joy and even ecstasy are viewed as authentic experiences. Power is dispersed through the family rather than being the exclusive possession of the parents. Members are given the freedom to choose their own activities and are encouraged to develop their talents. There is more interest in group decision making. Persuasion is utilized more than authority; negotiation tends to be more prevalent than coercion. In establishing family meanings, the open system is dominated by a concern that different points of view can be heard. Beliefs are subject to doubt. The family tolerates and accepts different identities. A conservative businessman is likely to be comfortable with his college-age son's lifestyle and belief system being different from his own.

The **random family type** maintains an optimum degree of divergence in a pluralistic-like culture. Space is characteristically dispersed space without much concern for order or integration. There may be as many territorial guidelines as there are persons in the family. Territory may extend into the yard, where arguments and embracing may both take place in view of the neighbors. Guests and strangers wander in and out freely. There may be a circus-like atmosphere in the household, with individuals drifting in and out and crises constantly occurring. Each member is free to design his or her own space without any concern as to how the design fits in with the rest of the household. Time is irregular; there are no schedules for such things as eating or family meetings. The family, in fact, tends to avoid routines and seldom make plans for future events. Things just happen and are reacted to when they occur. Random families tend to make fluctuating energy investments rather than controlled or steady energy expenditures. There is a sense of constant chaotic activity and coping with crises is viewed as a way of retaining the vitality of life. Affections also fluctuate; they can be intense during an episode and then disappear quickly. Emotions tend to be characterized by excitement and

FIGURE 10.2   Kantor and Lehr's family typology model.

The ways that the family manipulates its resources to achieve desired goals determines the type of family.

Access Dimensions: Family Resources

Space: territory, privacy, emotional distance, closeness, psychological and physical distance

Time: scheduling, use of time, availability, past/present/future orientations to time

Energy: amount of energy required for activity, investment and commitment, choices of where to put energy

Target Dimensions: Desirable Goals

Affect: preferred levels of affection, intimacy, and nurturance

Power: desired orientation toward freedom to decide, ability to get what one wants, and authority and status orientations

Meaning: identity confirmation, reinforcement of world view, beliefs, and values

Family Types:

Closed: fixed space, regular schedules, rigid rules for time and energy, change governed by authority, space controlled by parents, meanings established by parents, events regular, repetitive, and consistent, traditions and rituals carefully observed

Open: moveable space, no individual's rights including children's may be violated, goals are subject to change by consensus, time and energy are flexible, family traditions are present but flexible

Random: personal and family space is individualized, people come and go as they please, no set territory, time is irregular, events are spontaneous, tasks may be left uncompleted, energies fluctuate, few family rituals or traditions

passion. Originality and imagination are highly valued in the random family. The exercise of power also tends to be anarchistic, guided primarily by emotional inspiration rather than reference to authority or persuasive reasoning. Individual identity and independence are strongly guarded. Creativity, uniqueness, individuality, and even eccentricity are valued traits among family members. In contrasting these family types, Kantor and Lehr maintain that different types of families use different standards for evaluating their success and happiness. They seek different goals and focus on different concerns.

Reiss's Model

Reiss (1981) has developed a family typology based on the family's belief and value system and their problem-solving orientation. He describes what he calls differences in the family's "consensual experience." The concept of consensual experience refers to the idea that each family develops its own shared set of constructs or principles about how the world operates and about the relationship of the family to its social environment. This concept is similar to our description of the family's collective identity discussed in an earlier chapter. The Townsend family, for instance, may view the world as a basically hostile environment where survival depends upon the extent to which family members can "stick together." Reiss's model provides a description of how different family types approach problems, coordinate their behaviors, and create varying degrees of continuity between past and present experience. Reiss differentiates among families on the basis of their adoption of one of three distinct orientations to consensual experience: the Consensus-sensitive family, the Interpersonal distance-sensitive family, and the Environment-sensitive family.

Consensus-sensitive families share an experience of the environment as threatening, chaotic, and basically unknowable. Given this view of the world, the family's role is to protect each other. Problem solving is experienced as an opportunity to maintain a close and uninterrupted agreement among family members. Answers to problems are perceived as embedded in family consensus rather than requiring integration between the family and the environment. Decisions are often reached prematurely in an effort to gain consensus; relevant outside information in the environment is either distorted and oversimplified or not sought and acknowledged at all.

Interpersonal distance–sensitive families perceive their interactions with the environment and the problems presented by the environment as opportunities for family members to demonstrate their independence and mastery apart from the family. Accepting the suggestions, observations, or ideas of others is experienced as a personal sign of weakness. Each member of the family views problems as manifestations of his or her own personal universe with its unique set of laws and values. Family members make an effort to exchange minimal information with one another and tend to view themselves as relating to the environment independently from the family.

Environment-sensitive families do not perceive the world as hostile but as responsive to knowledge and mastery. Solutions to problems are perceived as possible with adequate information and the application of reason and logic. Exchange of information within the family that family members have collected from outside the family is thought to be important. New ideas and observations that family members share with one another are valued. These families work toward solutions that are the result of sharing ideas as well as individual efforts to analyze problems.

Consider, for example, how a family might cope with a move to a new neighborhood. The Yeagers, who tend to be environmental sensitive, assign family members tasks to help them get integrated into the new neighborhood. As soon as all the furniture and boxes are unloaded from the truck, Eric Yeager sets out to find the local hardware store in order to replace the utility knife that he lost, locates a grocery store with the most reasonable prices, and identifies where the closest discount drug store is located. While in the front yard, shaking out sheets and blankets that she found wrapped around some table lamps, Bonnie Yeager introduces herself to a neighbor whom she sees watering flowers. In the course of the conversation, she identifies the name of a reliable teenaged babysitter. Seven-year-old Rick heads off down the street on his small bicycle the minute it is lifted off the moving truck. On his ride down the street he pauses to watch some boys about his age kicking around a soccer ball; although he only watches from a distance because he is a little shy, he decides that maybe "this place won't be so bad after all."

That evening the three Yeagers eat pizza on the floor of their new house. Each of them has a story to tell. Dad shares information about the local shopping resources that he discovered. Mom talks about her conversation with the neighbors and Rick shares what he discovered on his bicycle ride. The family's communication behaviors are the "repository" of this family's governing paradigm. Not

F I G U R E 1 0 . 3   Reiss's model of family types.

Consensus-Sensitive Families

The family's role is to protect each other.

It is important to maintain close ties among family members and to achieve agreement; disagreement produces anxiety.

Solutions to problems are found in the family; outside information and ideas divergent from family viewpoints are viewed as threatening.

Information outside the family may be distorted, oversimplified, or not sought out or acknowledged.

The environment is viewed as threatening.

Interpersonal Distance–Sensitive Families

Problems are viewed as opportunities to express individual differences and to rebel against the authority or control of other family members. Any agreement among members seems to provoke resistance.

Family members express little value of one another's opinions and make little effort to exchange information. Solutions are thought to reside in the individual rather than in the family or in the environment.

Environment-Sensitive Families

Family members exchange information within the family; they are encouraged to share information from the outside environment.

New ideas of family members are viewed as useful and open to testing.

Knowledge is found within the environment.

Reason and logic are valued.

only does the family assign different roles to members in foraging out into the neighborhood, but they exchange with one another the information each member has gathered while they share their pizza. They have begun working on the problems of moving to a strange neighborhood, of coordinating information and perceptions, and of establishing some continuity in their lives by relying on roles familiar to each family member and by communicating with one another what they have learned about the environment beyond the four walls of their new house.

Olson's Model

We have already indicated that a framework for examining family types provides some method for analyzing the structure of relationships in the family. Olson and his colleagues (Olson, et al., 1983; Olson, Sprenkle, & Russell, 1979) developed a typology of families based on their efforts to integrate dimensions of family relationships identified by other family researchers. The Olson typology is a theoretically based typology in which families are assessed along two dimensions of family functioning: cohesiveness and adaptability. Sixteen family types are identified along a grid made up of four dimensions of cohesion (disengaged, separated, connected, and enmeshed) and four dimensions of adaptability (chaotic, flexible, structured, and rigid). Families are clustered in terms of their tendency to be balanced, mid-range, or extreme on the grid.

The concept of **cohesiveness** deals with the sense of separateness or connectedness in the family, a dimension originally identified by Hess and Handel (1959) in their study of the whole family and later elaborated on by Minuchin (1974) and Hoffman (1975). Cohesiveness identifies the extent to which family members are involved in one another's lives, maintain rules that reinforce agreement among family members, and establish identities and routines that promote family togetherness. The **adaptability** dimension describes the tendency and/or ability of families to change their relationship and rule structures in order to adjust to various stages in the life cycle. Some families can be described as being rigid, having difficulty adapting their rules and role relationships to developmental and environmental changes confronting the family. Other families are able to generate so little stability and predictability in their relationships that their system appears chaotic. Families that tend to be neither rigid nor chaotic are balanced. Olson's dimensions of cohesiveness and adaptability have parallels in the dialectical processes of integration/differentiation and stability/change discussed throughout this book.

We might, for example, describe the Yeager family as "flexibly connected," exhibiting balanced amounts of adaptability and connectedness. Roles in the family are clearly delineated—it's Dad's job to locate resources in the community and Mom's job to initiate social attachments—but the family's assignment of roles is flexible enough to enable them to adapt to a new neighborhood with relative ease and even some sense of adventure. There is also a sense of connectedness in the family which facilitates both the independent exploration of the neighborhood and the sharing of the information that they have collected. Olson and his colleagues reinforce the idea that the ways families manage the dimensions of cohesiveness and adaptability depend upon the communication in the family.

APPLICATION 10.2

IDENTIFYING FAMILY TYPES

Select one of the four family typology models described by Bernstein, Kantor and Lehr, Reiss, or Olson and his colleagues.

- Describe your family in terms of one of the types identified in the model.
- In what ways does this model seem to fit your family?
- What family patterns can you identify that would classify your family as one of the types described in the model?
- Are there some ways in which your family does not fit the model?
- What can you say about the utility of family typologies?
- What are their limitations and how are they useful?

GENDER AND FAMILY ROLES

Previous sections of this chapter have discussed role functions and models for structuring family roles and organizing family relationships. Thus far, our discussion has not focused on the relationship of family roles to gender and the politics or power relationships in the family. However, the functions that family members perform for the family and the idealized models upon which they base their orientation toward intimacy and authority are inseparable from how men and women construct their identities, their relationships with each other and with their children, and their relationships to institutions outside the family. In the following section we explore some of these issues.

There is some evidence that gender roles in the larger culture are changing. Women are entering the workforce in record numbers. Many women, similar to Barbara Garland, are taking on new careers as their children get older. Sociological change in the workforce and change in the control that women have over their reproductive lives have intersected with women's traditional responsibilities for child-care, maintenance of the marriage, and of the emotional well-being of the family. In recent years, attention has been given to how these changes have affected roles in the family.

To a significant degree, changes in family roles can be understood only in relationship to the larger social context. Attitudes about men and women, which are reinforced in the larger culture, influence the structure of marital and parental roles in the family. At the same time, individuals also learn what it means to be a man or a woman, a husband or a wife, a mother or a father, a daughter or a son in the family environment in which they grow up.

Walters, Carter, Papp, and Silverstein (1988) identify two orientations toward models of family organization that have significance for our understanding of gender roles in the family. The first of these represents a more traditional, patriarchal model of family organization or role structure based on role complementarity. The second model of family organization is based on more egalitarian relationships in the family which are characterized by role symmetry. In the following section we define and explore the implications of these two different structures for organizing family roles.

Role complementarity suggests that men and women have different contributions to make to the family which emerge from their inherently different natures. In this model, men are seen as primarily engaging in instrumental tasks such as supporting the family financially; bridging the relationship between the family and institutions outside the family; taking responsibility for significant decision making; and maintaining the quality and safety of the tools, vehicles, and physical artifacts of family life. Women are seen as having primary responsibility for nurturing and rearing the children; for maintaining the marital relationship; for monitoring the emotional climate of the family; for creating and overseeing the aesthetic environment at home; and for sustaining the social relationships between the family and the extended family, friends, and others with whom the family comes into contact. A student of one of the authors has described her parents in a way that is consistent with these differences in gender roles:

> I love my dad, but we really don't talk very much. He is usually too busy working. If I need help with my car or something like that, he is always there to help me out. And he gives me a lot of advice about how to manage my finances and find a job after I graduate. But if I am hurting or have a problem with a boyfriend or a roommate, my mom is the one I can talk to. She listens and tries to figure out what's going on with me.

Role complementarity is supported by cultural attitudes that specify important personality differences between men and women (see, for example, Heilbrun, 1976). In studies that asked participants to identify some adjectives they would use to describe men and women, women were characterized as nurturing, emotional, sensitive, sentimental, submissive, dependent, warm, empathic, intuitive, supportive, expressive, and affiliative. Men have been characterized as aggressive, confident, dominant, forceful, industrious, strong, instrumental, logical, rational, goal-oriented, and competitive.

The role complementarity view suggests that both of these sets of traits are necessary for family life and that women function as the primary providers of the emotional and nurturing needs of the family, while men are needed to ensure the financial stability and protection of the family. However, as Walters and her colleagues (1988) argue, there are problems with the role complementarity model of organizing the family. This model significantly disadvantages women and may, in the long run, also disadvantage men in their intimate relationships.

The model grants women less power over their lives than it does men. As the "primary breadwinners" for the family, men are assigned more autonomy and independence than are women, a circumstance that often leads to men emotionally disconnecting from the family. They are freer to move in and out of the family than are women and they are given more support than are women for developing their individual identities. Conversely, women are assigned the role of maintaining the connectedness of the family but often at the expense of their self-sufficiency, which leaves them dependent upon and vulnerable to their husbands for economic survival. As Walters and her colleagues (1988) indicate:

> A major conceptual error is to assume that traits such as "autonomy" or "dependency" are intrinsic to the person of men or women rather than

assigned to them by a patriarchal society on the basis of gender. Thus men are assigned "autonomy" with both the power and emotional disconnectedness that goes with it, while women are assigned "dependency" with both the emotional connectedness and the powerlessness that goes with it. Although being disconnected and being dependent both have drawbacks, it is clearly a far more serious threat to survival to be dependent (p. 19).

In addition, since men are thought to be best suited to relating to the outside world, their ways of relating tend to govern most social, economic, and educational institutions. Work organizations, corporations, and social institutions often do little to take into account the needs of their workers' families. Because men have more social and institutional power than women—through the positions they hold, the money they earn and control, the legislative power they have, and because of their numbers in the professions—masculine values, ways of knowing and relating to the world, also tend to have more status and prestige than do feminine ways of knowing (Gilligan, 1982; Brown & Gilligan, 1992). As a consequence, when women work for remuneration outside the home, they often find themselves taking on two jobs—caring for the family and working at their job outside the home. Even though husbands may help with the instrumental *activities* of family life—shopping, cooking, babysitting, and housekeeping—wives may still be primarily responsible for maintaining the social-emotional climate of the family. The female-attributed aspects of family life are typically considered less essential to the family's economic survival and, hence, have less value.

As we have indicated, the role complementarity model associates male identity with emotional unexpressiveness, detachment, and psychological distance. This leaves women with the additional obligation of maintaining the family's cohesiveness. Furthermore, there is increasing evidence suggesting that changes in women's roles have not led to significant changes in men's roles. Walters and her colleagues (1988) argue that changes in roles have usually meant that women simply add working outside the home to their responsibilities:

> Most of these changes [*in women's roles*], however, are behavioral and have been in the direction of women entering the work force and shouldering permanently a portion of the economic burden of the family. There has been no significant shift in men's focus toward family life, nor any real change in the basic attitudes of most men and women about the organization of family life—although there are more isolated cases of shared roles than there used to be. . . . In spite of unequal opportunity and unequal pay, and the lack of social supports, women are working more outside the home, some out of necessity, others for the freedom of choice and fulfillment it gives them. Whatever the reasons, now women have gained for themselves the freedom to work full-time at two jobs—career and family—and have lost the legal and social expectation that they, and their children, would be financially supported by men (p. 19).

In their work on the parental role of fathers, Fink and his colleagues (Fink, 1993; Fink, Buerkel-Rothfuss, & Buerkel, 1993) have found evidence suggesting that a transformation in the father role as women have entered the workforce cannot be supported by current research. Fathers, in general, remain emotionally distant and detached from their families. For example, in reporting the results of an empirical study of the father/daughter relationship, Fink, Buerkel-Rothfuss, and

Buerkel (1993) indicate that, while daughters seemed to be generally satisfied in their relationship with their fathers, daughters also "wished that they could have been at least somewhat more involved in their fathers' personal lives" (p. 26). Fink and his colleagues poignantly quote Osherson (1986), who concludes from his interviews with men in their thirties and forties that "the psychological and physical absence of fathers from their families is one of the great underestimated tragedies of our times" (p. 4).

Belenky and her colleagues (1986) conducted interviews with women that also supported this profile of the emotionally distant father. They concluded:

> If our interviews are an index of current trends, it appears that fathers are having great difficulty fulfilling their parental roles at this point in history. To a degree that surprised and disturbed us, we found women describing their fathers as unable to see others in their own terms, as dictatorial and sometimes violent, and as fleeing from family life and their children (p. 167).

In sum, proponents of the role complementarity model suggest that the role functions that wives and husbands each contribute to the family, while distinctly different, are equally important. Yet, so-called feminine traits tend to be viewed as symptoms of weakness in the larger culture, while our social institutions tend to reinforce the dominance of "masculine" traits and values. Women's economic dependence on men makes it difficult for them to speak with the same voice of authority that men use or to support themselves if they separate from their husbands or if their husbands abuse or leave them. And if women do work, they often find themselves having to be both economic earners and social-emotional providers for the family.

Walters and her colleagues (1988) describe an alternative to the role complementarity model of family life, which they refer to as **role symmetry**. In families characterized by role symmetry both the man and the woman perform instrumental and expressive functions for the family: "This model reflects an egalitarian approach to power between male and female, and a more democratic and consensual approach to parental management of children" (p. 18). In families that have greater role equity, both partners function as providers for their family's economic security and for their emotional well-being. Role symmetry suggests that husbands and wives share the housekeeping and child-rearing tasks in the family. The model also suggests that husbands participate in the maintenance of the marital relationship and connect with their wives and children emotionally.

Family structures that support role symmetry are characterized by (1) greater balance in their orientations toward idealized images of masculine and feminine role functions, (2) more interchange between men and women in the affective and instrumental activities of the family, and (3) an equal distribution of power in the family. A woman's identity can be redefined to include "self-reliance" along with "connectedness to others" and a man "can be a good husband and father without having to be overresponsible toward his wife and overprotective toward his daughter" (Walters, et al., 1988, p. 126). Men are able to listen receptively, empathize without passing judgment, provide support as well as give advice to family members, initiate in the maintenance of the marriage, and sometimes follow their partner's lead without becoming passive. Women feel comfortable sharing child-care responsibilities with their husbands, can be assertive in describing their needs as well as attending to the needs of other family members, and feel confident in their ability to contribute to the financial security of the family and to share in making major decisions for the family.

Both partners *value*, as well as acquire, behaviors and traits that are typically associated with feminine ways of relating to the world: nurturing, emotional expressiveness, collaboration, and sensitivity. And both partners are able to utilize typically masculine traits to take control over their lives and pursue their own goals: rationality, assertiveness, inner-directedness, and self-confidence.

The work of family therapists such as Walters, Carter, Papp, and Silverstein (1988) suggest that integrated persons who balance their tasks and their ways of relating within the family may provide the healthiest models for relationships. For men to expand their affective relations in their family and for women to become more assertive in the world, however, changes may have to occur simultaneously in our social institutions and in our families.

Cultural values, problems of discrimination, and lack of accessibility to education and employment opportunities can make the issue of gender and family roles even more complex. In a social environment that makes it difficult for either parent to provide adequately for the economic stability of children and family, the issue of gender roles may be complicated by the wives' desires to emotionally support their husbands. While they are careful to point out the "diversity that exists among Black families and communities," Hines and Boyd-Franklin (1982) describe the dilemmas of Black husbands and wives:

> The role of the Black male as father and mate varies. But Black fathers, regardless of income, are likely to demand and receive recognition as head of the household from their wives and children. Their identity is tied to their ability to provide for their families. Yet their chances for success in fulfilling this function are often limited because of discriminatory practices (see Pinderhughes, Chap. 5). Black males have had the highest job loss rates in the labor force. When employed, the number engaged in managerial and professional jobs is relatively small. The essence of these realities is that Black males may have to expend great time and energy trying to provide the basic survival necessities for their families. . . . [A] woman may feel empathy for her husband's frustrations with a racist society and have difficulty holding him responsible for his behavior or the situation. Furthermore, most Black females are keenly aware of the extent to which they outnumber Black males. The ratio is skewed as high as 44 to 1 in some geographic and socioeconomic areas of the country. Black males have a much lower life expectancy than Black females (or Whites of either sex). Their availability is reduced also because of lower educational levels, incarceration, mental or physical disabilities, and deaths frequently associated with their greater participation in active military service and other dangerous job situations (pp. 88–89).

In Black families, as well as in other ethnic and minority groups (many of whom are becoming the majority in some urban areas), issues of culture and gender are interrelated. It is apparent that for men and women to share roles in the family or to establish patterns of role symmetry in their relationships, educational and economic opportunities need to be available to both partners.

We can make some of the issues related to gender and roles in the family more immediate if we apply them to our example of the Garland family. It is apparent that Cliff Garland cares about and loves his wife and his children. However, because the organization (or social institution) for whom he works requires

APPLICATION 10.3

GENDER AND FAMILY ROLES

- How would you describe the influence of gender on the ways that your parents (or another couple with whom you have experience) have organized their relationship?
- Would you describe their relationship as one based on role complementarity or one that includes aspects of role symmetry?
- Suppose that you are a close friend of Cliff Garland, but you also feel supportive of Barbara Garland's desire to finish her education and pursue a career as a counselor. What would you say to Cliff that might help him understand Barbara's point of view?

that Cliff spend a significant amount of time traveling, Barbara is left at home as the primary provider for her family. In addition, she also has responsibility for running the household, overseeing the cattle farm, and looking after Cliff's parents. When Cliff does come home, he feels the necessity as the "family breadwinner" to assume leadership of the family, audit Barbara's bookkeeping, and monitor the household, which limits further the amount of time and energy that he might spend connecting with his children. While Cliff begins to look forward to a period when he can spend more time at home, Barbara looks forward to accomplishing her goal of furthering her education, developing her career, and turning the general maintenance of the farm over to Cliff. And, finally, we see Colleen aligned with her mother and Mitch aligned with his father, as Cliff and Barbara confront the changes that lie ahead of them.

The family typologies we described earlier in this chapter are relevant to our discussion of gender roles in the family. Role complementarity can be thought of as similar to the Positional role structure described in Bernstein's model and similar to the Traditional type of marriage described in Fitzpatrick's model. Family role structures that are more flexible than rigid, more open than closed, and more connected in ways that support the personal growth and development of all members of the family generally allow for healthier family relationships. In Chapter 11 we discuss some of the behaviors and metaphors that can be used to characterize healthy families.

SUMMARY

In this chapter we define a family role as a set of prescribed behaviors that a family member performs in relation to other family members. We indicate that the concept of roles is used to describe behaviors associated with one's responsibilities and privileges in the family system. Family role relationships describe the ways that two or more family roles have been organized in relationship to other roles in the family. We discuss two characteristics of roles that are related to the communication approach to understanding families: family roles serve functions for the family system and they change and evolve as the family grows and changes.

We also discuss role conflict as the potential for incompatibility or contradiction in the demands of particular roles that specific members are expected to perform in the family. Role conflicts emerge from the problem of differentiating spousal roles from parenting roles and from the inherently conflictual nature of the parent–child relationship.

We identify several marital and family typologies that are useful in explaining alternative ways that couples and families may organize their relationships and relate to their environment. Fitzpatrick's typology of marital couples identifies three basic types of relationships: Independents, Separates, and Traditionals. Bernstein makes the distinction between Person-oriented and Positional families based on the family's use of either an elaborated or restricted code of communication. Kantor and Lehr's model describes families as open, closed, or random based on how the family members regulate distance among themselves and between themselves and the environment. Reiss's typology of families identifies families as either consensus-sensitive, interpersonal distance-sensitive, or environment-sensitive, based on the family's view of its relationship to the environment and its need for family members to maintain agreement with one another. The typology developed by Olson and his colleagues attempts to differentiate families on the basis of their orientation toward cohesion and adaptability.

We discuss issues related to gender and role functions in the family based on the distinction made by Walters and her colleagues between role complementarity and role symmetry. Role complementarity reflects a more patriarchal model of family organization which separates the role functions of men and women. This model, however, tends to reduce the power that women have over their lives and may facilitate men's emotional disconnectedness from the family. Role symmetry represents a family structure in which both sexes share instrumental and expressive functions and are involved in the economic and emotional well-being of the family. We also discuss how this model is related to the other models of family functioning described in this chapter.

Overall, we address some important issues in the relationship of communication to family organization. Family organization is related to particular functions members assume in relationship to other family members as the family moves toward the accomplishment of its goals. Family organization is also related to the fact that while each family is unique it is also part of the larger cultural environment. In addition, family members are participants in various, sometimes competing, subsystems in the family. The type of family system that family members create for themselves depends upon and reveals the goals, values, and ideology of the family system. Increasing your awareness of alternative ways that families can organize their roles and role relationships can help to increase your understanding of the importance of communication in maintaining the structure of relationships that each family develops for itself.

KEY TERMS

access dimensions

adaptability

closed family

cohesiveness

consensus-sensitive family

elaborated communication code

environment-sensitive family

Independents

interpersonal distance–sensitive
  family

mixed couple type

open family

Person-oriented family

Positional family

privileges

pure couple type

random family type

relationship typologies

responsibilities

restricted code of communication

role

role complementarity

role conflict

role relationships

role symmetry

Separates

target dimensions

Traditionals

CHAPTER 11

CHANGE
AND
GROWTH

JANET YERBY

DIANE'S FAMILY

Diane speaks:

My parents, Gil and Sheila, are in their mid-forties and are self-employed insurance agents. I also have a brother, Mack, who is 19 and also sells insurance. My family unit is small, which has tended to make us closely knit. My father and mother seem to have a solid and successful marriage. They have never fought excessively or indicated to my brother and me that they are anything but happy with each other. They both work hard and share most of the responsibility for earning the money and caring for the family. My brother and father are also very close, and I would even go so far as to say that they are best friends. They hunt and fish together, and my father is teaching my brother the business. My brother and I have always been extremely close, too. In fact, I cannot recall ever arguing as children the way other siblings do. My brother gets along well with my mother. I feel close to both of my parents; however, there is considerable tension between my mother and me. Sometimes I have the feeling that our family unit is too close. We tend to get overinvolved with one another's lives and become frustrated and panicky when things do not go the way we want them to. This may be why the tension between my mother and me is difficult for the two of us and for the whole family to handle.

Since I left for college almost four years ago, a central theme has developed in conversations and interactions with my parents about separating from them and establishing my own identity. I will be graduating soon and I feel very concerned about my future. During my freshman year of college I was overwhelmed. I was exposed to different cultural experiences and points of view that were different from anything I had ever known. Sometimes this made me feel insecure and sometimes I questioned my parents' ideas and values. Growing up, I thought that my parents' beliefs about the world were the only way to view certain issues and cultures. I think that the process of developing one's own ideas and beliefs is interesting because as young adults, once we are away from our parents' protection, we tend to become more open and liberal. During the last two years, I have challenged my parents' beliefs and openly clashed with them. Sometimes they will make a comment about politics or some stereotyped perception they have, and I will disagree with them—even lash out at them—with an intensity that seems to catch all of us off guard. My impatience, frustration, and anger at something my parents will say surprises even me.

What I am realizing is that I am learning that I have a right to think and believe differently than they do. As children, my brother and I were raised to respect our parents and to believe that everything that they told us was the truth. Now, I tend to question almost everything they say. I am not speaking of disillusionment, but I am speaking of the identity stage of development when I am trying to become my own person and to separate from my parents' assumptions about me, about how I should think, and about what is good for me. It's not that what my parents taught me to believe is wrong, but as children my brother and I were like puppets who obeyed our parents and accepted their value system without question. They loved us; they took good care of us; they taught us their values; we trusted and believed in them. Specific political, religious, and social beliefs were ingrained in us—beliefs which, only until a couple of years ago, reflected what I considered to be the only way to view certain issues.

I do not blame my parents for any of this "brainwashing" and I do know that some of my behavior has been difficult for them to reconcile. However, as children, my brother and I respected and loved our parents and longed for their approval so much that we took on their ideas to avoid offending them. Over the last several years it has been difficult for me to define my own identity. I believe that it is important to let children know that there are ways of looking at the world other than through their parents' eyes. This is a concept that seems very difficult for my parents to accept.

At this point in our lives, the struggle between my parents and me seems to be the central theme in our family. I am beginning to view the struggle as an issue related to normal development and growth, but my parents cannot view it this way and object to my developing beliefs and goals that are different than their own. I find myself feeling upset every time I go home because, since I have moved out of their house, they seem to constantly disapprove of decisions I have made. Even my brother has difficulty understanding my feelings; he still lives at home and doesn't understand why I do not do more to try to keep the peace. Because I love my parents, I am confident that this period of conflict will eventually work itself out, but until then I know that the decisions I make will be under careful scrutiny. I wonder when my parents will realize that they cannot control me or my opinions anymore.

What makes the process of separating from my parents' protection and guidance especially hard is the fact that I must continue to rely on them for financial help. This gives my parents leverage to use against me, which makes me resentful. Some examples of these two central themes in my family involve recent incidents when I freely voiced my opinion and shared decisions that I had made about my living situation and my college career. I have recently decided to move in with my boyfriend. We have been thinking about getting married sometime in the future and since we spend so much time together anyway, we decided to find an apartment together. I have also decided to change my major from management to sociology. I feel uninspired by the business courses I've taken and have really enjoyed a couple of sociology courses that I took as electives. My parents let me know, in a not-so-subtle way, that they did not agree with either of these decisions and hinted that I might have to pay for my own tuition next year if I did not reconsider. They were shocked that I might consider living with my boyfriend before getting married and worried that I will not be able to find a job after college if I major in sociology. They seem to be genuinely concerned about my welfare, but it is almost impossible for them to understand how I feel about these two issues. I also have the feeling that they are asking themselves, "Where did we go wrong?" At first, their response made me doubt my own judgment and then it made me very angry.

I know there are risks in both of these decisions, but I did not make either of these decisions hastily and I feel betrayed and let down that they cannot support me. We have argued intensely—yelling and calling each other names—but have not been able to settle anything. I'm still not certain what I am going to do. The fights we have often leave me feeling guilty and bitter. Occasionally, I consider not telling my parents anything of importance about my life—or lying to them. Thoughts of withholding feelings from them, however, make me feel isolated, lonely, and depressed. I yearn for my parents' respect and approval—that may never change—but these confrontations wear me down. I also feel that I have to stand up for myself and begin to make some decisions on my own sometime. I hope that we can work out this separation/identity process eventually and that our struggle can be resolved.

I hang on to the hope that my family can continue to grow and become even closer and that my separation from the family will get easier. When I am calm, I realize that we are slowly improving our ability to confront each other, to listen to each other, and to work on our conflicts in a more functional way. I try to be optimistic about the future and accept the fact that even the healthiest family cannot avoid the kind of turmoil we are experiencing. Sometimes it is difficult, however—painfully difficult.

Sheila speaks:

Diane makes her father and me sound so unreasonable, but it is also difficult for her to see our point of view. My husband and I have worked very hard for what we have: we have a terrific family and are, generally, financially secure, and we live in a state that has suffered a 15-year depression with numerous economic ups and downs. We have raised our children to be thoughtful and caring, with strong moral values, in the best way that we could. Our family and our religion are important to us, and we believe in the work ethic. I don't feel like I should have to apologize for that. To some extent, we have shielded the children from the hardships of life: the bedroom fights that Gil and I have had about money, Gil's high blood pressure, or our worries about my elderly mother. We worry also about what the kids will do with their lives: will the business be able to support Mack? Will Diane find a career for herself?

Diane has always been independent, and sometimes she doesn't take our advice or listen to what we have to say. Lately, she "flies off the handle" when we least expect it and she seems to make impulsive decisions that worry her father and me. Even if she is at college and on her own, we are still her parents and we still want her to be okay. We do not want her to make decisions to suit us, but we would like her to be more open to our opinions—especially since we have an investment in her education also. I know of several young people who have had to move back in with their parents after college; that put a strain on the whole family.

We want her to prepare herself for the future—they say that her generation is likely to have a tough time of it—and we don't see how changing her major because she "enjoys" some courses more than others is going to help her in the years ahead.

As far as moving in with her boyfriend—that just doesn't make sense to me. He is a nice boy, but he is no more certain about his future than Diane is about hers. His parents recently got a divorce—after twenty-seven years of marriage—and he was so upset that he dropped out of school for a semester. I think he is using Diane right now for emotional support. I know that he has been engaged before. What if it doesn't work out between them? What if she gets hurt? Diane needs to focus on her education for now. If they are meant for each other, Diane and her boyfriend can move in together after they get married. Living together to see if you like each other does not fit my idea of a strong, loving relationship. I know I sound like a moralist, but that is what I believe—and I thought that is the way we raised Diane. Diane wants to make her own decisions and run her own life, but she doesn't always indicate to her father and me that she can exercise good judgment. Would we be responsible parents if we just supported everything she did, in spite of what we know is right? I would like some acknowledgment from her that independence brings with it responsibility as well as freedom.

The fights we have with Diane are no easier on us than on her. She accuses us of not listening to her or taking her feelings into account, but she does not seem very willing to listen to us and take *our* feelings into account. She didn't ask how we felt about these two decisions she has made—without warning, she just announced what she was going to do. We would have liked to have been consulted; we would have liked her to talk things over with us, to listen, at the very least, to our input rather than just declare her plans after the fact. In general, I find it very difficult to talk with Diane about almost anything these days—she argues with every opinion I express and sometimes I think that she says things just to shock me. She told me the other day that she doesn't know if she believes in God anymore. I wondered later if she said that just to hurt me or get a rise out of me. When she comes home for a visit, she spends half her time on the phone and the other half sleeping. I feel grateful if all four of us are able to squeeze in a nice dinner together without feeling tense and uncomfortable.

I have talked to other parents who have children in college, and they have expressed some of the same concerns that Gil and I have. I know that what we are going through is fairly normal, but when you have a twenty-two-year-old daughter screaming at you in the kitchen, it does not feel normal. It is easy to lose your perspective and sense of humor. We all love and care about one another in this family, but sometimes that's just not enough.

UNDERSTANDING DIANE'S FAMILY

Diane and Sheila each have very different stories to tell about how they are currently experiencing each other and the family. However, we can identify common themes in their stories. Both of their narratives reveal feelings of frustration, ambivalence, and uncertainty in the family's attempts to launch children into adulthood. Diane needs the approval and support of her parents, but she also wants to make decisions on her own—decisions that she knows might not always be

consistent with her parents' values and views of the world. Sheila wants an independent, secure, and happy future for her daughter. Sheila also wants to be
included in Diane's decision making and has difficulty supporting Diane when she
believes that Diane's actions are not wise or consistent with the family's values.
Diane and Sheila also share the belief that their conflicts are normal and have
some faith that their love and caring for each other will see them through this trying period of change.

This chapter focuses on the processes of change and growth in families. One
of the most common sources of stress in family life is the tension between stability
and change. In previous chapters, we examined the ways in which families
develop stable and relatively predictable patterns of relating. Although each family
may develop a somewhat unique pattern of interaction, all families share the tendency to repeat certain routines and sequences of behavior over and over again.
The sequences may be different in different families, but every family will have
some recurrent and stable sequences of interaction. On the other hand, families
also are systems in flux. Every family must confront the forces of change brought
on by the forward movement of time.

At about the time a couple has become secure in their patterns of relating to
each other as husband and wife, their first child is born. The new demands of
parenting the child can challenge or interfere with their pattern of relating to each
other as spouses. They must now learn how to function both as spouses and as
parents. Another example is the case of parents of adolescents. As the children
become teenagers, the parents discover that they are being asked to allow their
children more independence and to relate to them more as peers than as parents.
This adaptation requires a change in the interactional rules of the family. Moreover, the children seem to want more distance from their parents at about the same
point in time that the parents want more closeness to their children. These apparent cross-pressures can make matters difficult, indeed. As children enter adulthood, they need to feel confident in making their own decisions, and yet, like
Diane, they need the approval and support of their parents. Another common
example of the requirement for change occurs when "the nest is emptied." After
years of focusing on parenting and togetherness as a whole family under a single
roof, parents must come to grips with being alone again.

In family life, the demand for change is matched against the demand for
stability. Sometimes change is welcomed; often it is resisted. Haley (1963) refers
to resistance to change as "the first law of human relationships." According to
Haley, whenever change in the definition of relationship is attempted, it is
resisted. If Haley is correct, then all of us must sooner or later face a troubling
dilemma. The forces of biological, social, and cultural change mandate that we
must change—one cannot not change; yet when change is attempted, it will probably be resisted. Change is also related to issues of differentiation and integration
in the family. Periods of change provide opportunities for family members to
differentiate themselves from the family, to redefine themselves, and to assert
their identities. Differentiation can also lead to anxiety and fears of rejection and
isolation. This dilemma may explain why change so often is experienced as disruptive, difficult, and/or disturbing. Change is inevitable and so is resistance to
change!

The purpose of this chapter is to enlarge your understanding of how and
why families change. Many of the changes that occur in families are predictable
and can be anticipated; but some changes come with no forewarning and these

unexpected developments can shock and disrupt even the most secure and stable families. How many of us are ever sufficiently prepared for the death of a parent, the loss of a job or stable income, the breakup of a marriage, or some similarly intense family crisis? In our opinion, the most truthful answer is that few of us are prepared to cope effectively with these blows of fate. Yet each of us is likely to be forced to face some kind of family crisis at some point in our lives.

Considering what is known about family dissolution, teenage childbirth, and violence in the home, it is probably a good idea to question any utopian images you may have about the "normal" or "average" American family. More than fifty percent of persons under seventy who have been married also have been divorced. Today, nearly twenty percent of all births in the United States are to unmarried women; many of these are children born to children. Another twenty percent are children of divorced parents who are raised by a single parent or in blended families where one of the parents is a stepparent. One of the most significant and distressing social problems of our time is family violence. Gelles (1979, p. 11) bluntly stated that "people are more likely to be hit, beat up, or even killed in their own homes by another family member than anywhere else, or by anyone else, in our society." Tragically, more than six million men, women, and children are subjected to some form of severe physical abuse at the hands of parents, spouses, or adult children each year (Gelles, 1979). These data suggest that, instead of being a place of love, warmth, and security, the family context too often becomes a source of pain, fear, and disappointment.

The developmental perspective discussed in this chapter encompasses the predictable historical changes that most families experience as they grow older together and the unpredictable and/or unexpected blows of fate. This developmental perspective presents a focus on the family ecosystem. The chapter is divided into four sections. The first section describes the family life cycle and discusses transitions between stages that may require changes in rules and roles. The second section distinguishes between the family life cycle and processes of family development. This distinction has been advanced by Wynne (1984), who emphasizes the relational processes associated with functional adaptability to new stages in the family life cycle. What we like most about Wynne's developmental approach is his emphasis on the interpersonal skills associated with successful adaptation to changes in the family's stage of life. In the third section, we discuss the irony and tragedy of family violence. The topic of family violence draws attention to the crucial importance of understanding how stable patterns of communication can turn into vicious cycles of self-reinforcing, destructive communication. The final section of the chapter reviews the contradictions of family life that form the foundations of personal growth and summarizes what we have learned about optimal family functioning.

SOURCES OF CHANGE IN THE FAMILY LIFE CYCLE

Many social scientists have described families as social systems that change over time (Carter & McGoldrick, 1980; Haley, 1973; Hill & Rodgers, 1964; Hill, 1970; Duvall, 1977; Olson, et al., 1983). The term **family life cycle** is used to describe a sequence of developmental stages associated with the passage of time during which members of the nuclear family enter, exit, and mature, and the performance of important life tasks that accompany each stage of development. One of the main advantages of a life cycle perspective is that it helps us to understand the demands placed upon families and the problems they can expect to face at particular points in time.

Individuals normally become members of a family through birth, adoption, marriage, or blending (as in stepfamilies). The family is unique insofar as it is the only organization into which some of its members are born (McGoldrick & Carter, 1982). You do not choose to be a member of the family into which you are born.

Exit from a family occurs when children grow and establish lives apart from their family of origin or when a family member dies. Family members mature as they age and pass through various biological, physical, cognitive, and moral stages of development. As each member of the family changes, the family as a whole changes too. Sometimes these changes are too small or subtle to notice; at other times, they are too obvious to miss. As a family adjusts to the birth of a new child, adapts to the departure of a young adult, or tries to cope with parents in "midlife crisis," changes in family rules and role relationships occur.

Family life tasks provide the primary focus for goals, energy, and activity in the family at various stages in the family's life cycle. In a family with young children, for example, life tasks normally revolve around the socialization and nurturance of the children, the advancement of careers for the adults, and the management of the economic and emotional stability of the family. Life tasks for a family in which the parents are much older and the children about to finish college would be different than for a family with young children. Life tasks for two divorced households, whose parents are entering new spousal relationships and whose children and stepchildren are defining their relationships to one another, present still a different challenge to the family.

All families do not experience stages in the life cycle in the same way or at the same point in biological time. For example, dual-career couples often have their first children in their late thirties or early forties, after their careers have been established. Married couples who blend children from previous marriages sometimes decide to wait until these children are almost grown to have children of their own. Men and women frequently launch new careers in midlife; grandparents may take on the responsibility of helping to raise grandchildren; and some children return to live at home after finishing college or experiencing a marital separation. These variations in the sequences of family experience make it very difficult to generalize about "normal" or "natural" patterns of family development.

A focus on stages in the life cycle helps to highlight the ways in which communication functions and changes as a family evolves over time. For example, when Diane was younger she says that she accepted, without question, her parents' values and beliefs about the world. She felt protected and cared for by her parents and seldom disagreed or fought with family members. Once she entered college, she became exposed to new ideas and cultural views that challenged her parents' ideas. As she began to develop opinions and ideas of her own, she found herself arguing with her parents more frequently and displaying feelings of impatience, anger, and irritation during some of their conversations. Sheila expresses her frustration and discomfort with Diane's style of communicating and with the changes in Diane's behavior. The transition to adulthood in this family is characterized by interaction that tends to be tense, unpredictable, and modestly confrontational.

The communicative problems experienced by Diane and Sheila may be seen as one of the natural outcomes of intergenerational influences in the family (Carter

& McGoldrick, 1980; Kramer, 1985; Pillari, 1986). **Intergenerational influences** can be defined as communication between the generations, the influences of one generation on the next, or the transmission of patterns of relating from one generation to the next. To a significant degree, Diane is going through a process of constructing her own beliefs and value system by contrasting the new ideas to which she has become exposed with those of her parents.

Intergenerational influences also include relationships between the family of origin and the extended family, as we discussed in Chapter 6. Many important questions come to mind. How do the parents' experiences in their families of origin influence the way that they respond to a noncompliant young adult child? How does the family of origin communicate with the nuclear family when a grandchild is born? How do in-laws influence the marital relationship at various stages in the family's life cycle? How do midlife parents relate to or care for older parents while, simultaneously, launching children into independent lives of their own? Clearly, relationships inside the family can be strongly influenced by transactions across these generational boundaries.

Our discussion of family tasks centers on five stages in the family life cycle: the newly married couple; the family with young children; the family with adolescents; the launching family; and the empty-nest and retirement family.

STAGES IN THE FAMILY LIFE CYCLE

The Newly Married Couple

In Chapter 5 we discussed some of the relationship tasks that a newly married couple must face as they co-define two realities into one relationship. They must work through many new rules about who can say and do what to whom under what conditions (Haley, 1973) and they must develop a satisfactory connection to both spouses' families of origin. The life cycle perspective focuses particular attention on the relationship of the couple's family of origin in the process of the

APPLICATION 11.1

INTERGENERATIONAL ISSUES

Interview your family or a family that you know and ask them the following questions:

- How is communication between parents and children different than it was five years ago (or when the children were younger)?
- What is the relationship between the parents and grandparents of the family? How have these relationships influenced the nuclear family system?
- How have the parents' patterns of communication influenced the children's patterns of communication?

transition to marriage. The "baggage from the family of origin," which individuals bring into marriage, is so important that McGoldrick and Carter (1982) have referred to tying the marital knot as "the joining of families through marriage." According to these writers, the crucial issue may boil down to how effectively each spouse has managed the separation from his or her family of origin. This issue was discussed as an important aspect of courtship and commitment in Chapter 4.

The Family with Young Children

As you learned in Chapter 5, communication for the newly married couple focuses primarily on the processes involved in co-defining reality and building the marriage relationship. For families with young children, however, the focus shifts to how effectively the spouses can balance the pressures of parenting against the pressures of maintaining an intimate relationship with each other. Nurturing and caring for children, managing authority relations between parents and children, and sustaining affection for each other and a satisfactory sexual relationship are crucial life tasks during this cycle of family history. Patterns of relating established at the previous stage of the family life cycle—before the couple had children—will influence what occurs, just as unresolved issues from the family of origin continue to influence the marriage relationship. This shift becomes most intense, perhaps, during the transition to parenthood, when parents need to adjust their role expectations and support each other in the performance of parental roles (Stamp, 1994). The patterns established at one stage change but, even as they change, they influence communication at a later stage.

The Family with Adolescents

Families with adolescents are confronted with the task of preparing their children for roles of adulthood. This involves adapting old rules and forming new ones that reflect the need for more responsibility and independence normally associated with adolescent development. Children begin to reach out for independence while still needing clear messages about authority in the family. As McGoldrick and Carter (1982) indicate, the goal is for families to "make the appropriate transformation of their view of themselves to allow for the increasing independence of the new generation, while maintaining appropriate boundaries and structure to foster continued family development" (p. 183).

Max and Tim Wiley are a case in point. These two sixteen-year-old twin brothers have developed a small lawn-mowing business. Though they argue frequently, they do work well together. Their mother, Annette, who is a single parent, used to intervene; now she tries not to unless the twins begin to "drive everyone crazy." She also does not exert control over how the boys manage the money that they make. Annette does, however, make it clear that certain chores are their responsibility—for instance, the twins usually do the grocery shopping for her every other Saturday morning so that Annette can visit with her married daughter and see her grandson. Annette also tries to keep a sense of humor about the mood swings of her sons and what she calls their "back talk." None of this is easy, for as Minuchin (1974) suggests, and we concur, few parents are able to escape the perils of parenting unscathed.

The Launching Family

The primary life task of launching families is to help young adults to establish independent lives for themselves and to help parents redefine their personal goals after children leave. The difficulties that this stage may bring often depend upon the family's experience in the previous stage. For some families, it is the adolescent stage that is most challenging. For Diane's family, the conflicts and assertions of independence that are often the hallmarks of adolescence have become pronounced in the launching stage, as Diane enters adulthood. New experiences outside the family have caused her to differentiate her own beliefs from those of her family. Rather than seeing these challenges to their belief system as appropriate, Diane's parents respond with resistance, which makes the process of Diane's separating from her parents tense and strained. If Sheila were able and willing to communicate her confidence that Diane could make decisions on her own and that any mistakes that Diane makes would not likely be fatal (and are necessary to Diane's learning and growth), perhaps Diane could feel less defensive. Then she could experience the support she needs to forge a life on her own and become more accepting of her parents.

The Empty-Nest and Retirement Families

The primary issue for empty-nest and retirement families is to attend to marriage issues and develop goals that no longer focus centrally on children. A couple who has directed most of their attention toward the needs of their children or their own careers may need to reestablish their importance to each other and redefine their relationship. Once the children are launched, the couple may find themselves struggling with significant relationship issues that were never addressed when their attention was primarily directed to working and parenting. There is now more pressure to relate one-to-one, and face-to-face. Conversations that previously involved the children may seem awkward and unnatural. On the other hand, there may be more time and opportunity for sharing recreational activities or for getting to know each other in new ways. This stage simultaneously presents communication difficulties and opportunities. As the couple ages, financial problems and deteriorating health may have to be confronted or one member may be left alone after the other dies. As they experience the deaths of friends and relatives, separation from children and careers, and/or disassociation from old landmarks such as their place of residence and neighborhood, elderly spouses face new and sometimes terrifying changes and challenges. Often they want or require involvement with their children; sometimes children must become parents to their parents. This change in family patterns often can be full of growth and also stressful for family members of both generations.

FAMILY CHANGE: POINTS OF IMPASSE

Transitions in Family Development

We have already made the point that families develop predictable patterns of relating at particular points in time. As a family moves from one stage of the family life cycle to another, changes in rules and roles may be necessary. The period

FIGURE 11.1   Stages in the family life cycle.

The Newly Married Couple
- co-define reality
- establish relationship rules
- join two family histories

The Family with Young Children
- nurture and care for children
- manage authority relations with young children
- sustain affection
- maintain a satisfactory sexual relationship in the marriage

The Family with Adolescents
- balance responsibility, authority, and independence in parent–child relations

The Launching Family
- help young adults establish independent lives
- help parents redefine their personal goals when children leave

The Empty-Nest and Retirement Families
- attend to marriage issues
- develop goals that no longer focus on children

marked by changes from one stage in the family life cycle to another is called a **transition**. Diane's family is having a difficult time launching children into adulthood. The parents' concern about the consequences of their children's decisions and the children's need for approval from their parents make the transition to adulthood conflictual for the family. Transitions can be relatively natural and the shift from one stage to another may occur without any direct awareness of change on the part of family members. More often than not, however, transitions bring difficulties. Family members may begin to sense that their stability as a family is threatened or that the family is somehow regressing. For instance, LaRossa (1986), in his work on the transition to parenthood, found that egalitarian marriages tend to regress toward a more traditional division of roles after the birth of the first child. Families with children in the early stages of adolescence may find it difficult to redefine parental authority to provide increased freedom and control for the teenaged children. Ironically, about the time a family reaches some degree of security and stability within a particular stage in its life cycle development, the security and stability is threatened by new demands for changes in rules and roles.

For example, since her children were babies, Charlene and her two children have lived with her mother in the house where Charlene grew up. In more recent years, their neighborhood has become threatened by the invasion of drugs, gangs, and random acts of violence. When the children were small, in order to combat some of the negative influences of the neighborhood, Charlene and her mother developed a set of strict rules about where the children could go and with whom they could play. The children went everywhere with the two adults or were looked after by one of them. These rules worked well—they gave the family a sense of security and cohesion—primarily because Charlene and her mother had forged a formidable alliance. As the children have gotten older, however, it has become more difficult to keep them at home. Charlene knows that she must "loosen the leash" a little, but she spends sleepless nights worrying about her children and quizzes them incessantly about their friends, what they are doing, and the need to "stay out of trouble."

Adapting communication and relationship structures that are appropriate at one stage of development to the current stage of development is the primary challenge of family life cycle transitions. Even simple patterns can present difficulties. Penny and Jeff were the parents of a six-year-old daughter, Anna, to whom they gave a new bicycle as a birthday present. It was the first two-wheel bicycle Anna had received and, with her father's help, she worked hard to learn how to ride it. Once she learned how to ride her bicycle, Anna's view of the world changed. She wanted to go exploring beyond the front yard and her immediate street. One evening after supper, Penny and Jeff told Anna that she could ride around the block alone on her bicycle. Both parents sat on the lawn as they watched their daughter heading down the street. They waited until Anna appeared around the corner as she completed her short journey. As Anna reached the driveway, Penny and Jeff realized that all three of them had entered a new stage and that Anna would continue to push the boundaries of their neighborhood (and their parental authority). It was wonderful, exciting, and a little frightening too. The old rule was that Anna stayed within one or two houses of their yard. How would the new boundary be defined? How would they decide? How would they talk about it?

Family Crisis

A significant number of family therapists view family problems as outcomes of life-cycle adjustments. Strategic and structural family therapists (Minuchin, 1974; Haley, 1973, 1976; Madanes, 1983; Palazzoli, et al., 1978) perceive families seeking help as caught in communication patterns and role relationships potentially relevant to one stage of development but inappropriate for the family's current stage in the life cycle. Unable to make the transition to the next stage of development, the family experiences itself as "being stuck" in dysfunctional patterns, often resorting to scapegoating or blaming particular family members. A family may not be able to launch their late-adolescent child into adulthood because the parents, who have an unhappy marriage, will be left alone to confront their marital relationship. Struggling with a rebellious adolescent helps the family to avoid "saying good-bye" to a particular kind of companionship provided by the adolescent and to avoid confronting serious issues and grievances that were never adequately communicated in the marriage (see, for example, Napier & Whitaker, 1978). In Diane's family, Diane's need to question her parents' values and views of the world threatens the family's identity and creates conflict.

Families may become stuck in patterns appropriate for a previous stage of development in several different ways. Penny and Jeff, who became parents in their early forties, always wished for more children. They went through a difficult period when they argued about their parenting styles, worried excessively about their daughter, Anna, and found that letting Anna become more independent was painful. A family therapist helped them to mourn the fact that they would not have any more children. They acknowledged their decision to have only one child, felt sad for a brief time, and began to realize that they needed to enjoy Anna's development instead of try to hang on to her as if she were still a baby and needed protection. Once they were able to finish and leave behind the babyhood stage of family development, everyone seemed to relax somewhat. They began to develop patterns that would accommodate Anna's slow but inevitable maturing and to discover how to have fun with each new stage in Anna's growth rather than panic at how fast she seemed to be reaching out to the world and away from them.

When families are unable to let go of previous stages in their lives together, the family can reach a point of impasse that inhibits its ability to change. Families that are confronted with unpredictable change must also overcome points of impasse in their development. A point of **impasse** is represented by the experience of being stuck in a cycle of destructive conflict, pain, or anxiety because the family is not ready to leave behind previous patterns of functioning and relating to one another that may no longer be appropriate. Family members may argue with one another without resolving issues or changing patterns. Patterns that provide stability for the family at one stage in their lives may be very difficult to change even though circumstances and individuals in the family have changed. Family systems are continually seeking stability and, at the same time, continually changing. Understanding the family from a developmental perspective helps to give us additional insight into the evolving and reflexive nature of family communication and experience.

RELATIONAL PROCESSES AND FAMILY DEVELOPMENT

Wynne (1984) makes a distinction between family life cycles and family development that has important implications for understanding family communication. Stages in the life cycle do not wait for us to prepare for them. Children are sometimes born into the family before parents are ready for them; a child may leave home before she or her parents have been readied for the separation; and few people ever adequately anticipate how they will react to the death of a parent, grandparent, or sibling. Life cycle events move inexorably forward through time without regard for the preparedness or skills of family members.

Wynne argues that family development, in contrast to family life cycles, does not progress with the same forward inevitability. Family development is qualitative movement in the family. *Developmental stages* are identified by qualitative changes in the interaction of family members rather than by life cycle events. A couple, for example, who spent their early married years negotiating work schedules and making time for social life with each other finds that their world is turned upside down when they have a child. Their relationship seems to be terribly strained for a time by the demands of parenthood. And then, as if giving in to their exhaustion, they find themselves sharing more of their feelings with one another, making more concessions to one another, and quietly talking about things that they never before discussed. Their relationship, from Wynne's perspective, takes a developmental leap.

Developmental leaps can be thought of as qualitative shifts in family communication patterns. Changes in the family life cycle often are associated with specific events: a baby is born; a child enters school or acquires a driver's license; children leave home, marry, and begin their own careers; a grandmother moves to the same town where her middle-aged children are living. Qualitative movement in the family's communication patterns, however, does not always move forward logically through time; it often has its own inner logic. It is possible that Diane will graduate, marry, and continue to experience tension when she is around her parents. Gil and Sheila may be unable to accept Diane's views on religion, politics, and relationships. Diane may continue to be frustrated with her parents' inability to support her unique beliefs and values, and yet she may also feel a need for their closeness and support.

Wynne's definition of family development as qualitative movement calls attention to some of the emotional or irrational aspects of communication in families. Sometimes relational processes associated with change can be identified even when specific events leading to change cannot be identified. The couple for whom qualitative changes in their relationship have occurred may be able to describe how their relationship is different than it used to be, though they may not be able to describe any sequence of events that brought them to where they are. Understanding and recognizing the importance of these relational processes provides additional insights into the functions of communication in the family.

Four Features of Wynne's Model

We will emphasize four features of Wynne's (1984) model of family development:

1. the distinction between the family life cycle and family development stages
2. the idea that stages of family development are sequential, with each one building on a previous stage
3. the qualitative progression of relational processes at each stage of family development
4. the identification of dysfunctional, as well as functional, aspects of relational processes at each stage of development

Family development is seen as a sequence of different stages of relating among family members. Family life cycle events, on the other hand, sometimes bring changes in the way members relate to one another; sometimes they do not. The term **epigenesis** is used by Wynne to describe the sequential movement of developmental stages in which each stage builds on the skills acquired or on ways of relating achieved at the previous stage. Developmental stages have a hierarchical quality in that each stage is more complex than the previous stage; each stage incorporates behaviors and ways of relating achieved at the previous level. Wynne uses the term "epigenesis" in the same way that we have used the concept of levels in a system. Each level in a system incorporates the characteristics of components at previous levels but the system as a whole is more than the sum of its parts. A family system has particular characteristics such as rules and role structures that integrate the needs, expectations, and histories of individuals. The system functions, however, are more than the sum of these individual attributes.

Epigenesis describes communication patterns as evolving qualitatively, with each level incorporating more complex and sophisticated behaviors and ways of relating than the previous level. Wynne emphasizes changes in the nature or quality of the relational processes at each stage of development. He also indicates that there are dysfunctional or negative aspects of behavior at each developmental stage. An example is communication that maintains an exaggerated overinvolvement, detachment, or rejection between or among family members.

Five Stages of Family Development

Wynne identifies five stages of family development, each of which is defined by a particular relational process: (1) attachment/caregiving, (2) communicating, (3) joint problem solving, (4) mutuality, and (5) intimacy. The label for each of the five stages is descriptive of a "positive side of a domain of relatedness." Negative forms of relatedness for each of the developmental stages are also identified. The chart in Table 11.1 summarizes negative and positive aspects of relating for each of the five stages.

Attachment/caregiving. Wynne describes **attachment and caregiving** as complementary functions. The growth of parental love for an infant, the reciprocal tie of infant to parent, and the care that a parent administers to an infant are examples of attachment and caregiving. Attachment refers to the bond that develops between family members. Bonding is a fundamental and essential process in the development of strong parent–child relationships and in establishing a child's sense of self-worth and ability to care for others. In a parent–infant relationship, attachment/caregiving is established primarily through nonverbal communication—through embrace, touch, tone of voice, and facial expression.

In his review of the research literature on attachment, Wynne identifies three characteristics of attachment: the need to be close to the attached person in times of distress, the sense of heightened comfort and reduced anxiety in the presence of an attachment figure, and the increase in discomfort and anxiety when accessibility or availability of the attached person is threatened. "Falling in love" is an experience that is associated with attachment. Caregiving is related to the ability to attend to the survival and comfort needs of the attached person.

Attachment/caregiving is the most basic relational process. Without the ability to attach and give care appropriately, it is doubtful that one could even begin to establish a personal relationship with another human being. When a relationship terminates, participants in the relationship may suffer from loss of attachment, in spite of the fact that more complex levels of relational development were never achieved. Negative aspects of attachment/caregiving are emotional overinvolvement (in which family members experience extreme anxiety in the absence of the other person or experience an inability to function as separate individuals), detachment, excessive criticism, and withdrawal.

Communicating. According to Wynne, **communicating** involves the ability to develop shared meaning among family members. The capacity to communicate builds upon the attachment/caregiving capacity of family members. Without some degree of attachment/caregiving, concern for the other would not be possible. At this stage of development, family members have the ability to understand how other members of the family feel and think. They develop shared codes of communicating and of interpreting behaviors. Negative aspects of the communicating stage of relational development involve communication pathologies (such as double-bind communication), guarded communication (in which family members must be "overcareful" about their communication with one another so as not to provoke each other), and fragmented communication (where communication between family members is indirect and unclear).

Joint problem solving. Wynne makes the point that "when attachment/caregiving has not taken place, a shared cognitive and affective perspective cannot be well

TABLE 11.1   Wynne's five stages of relational development.

STAGES CHARACTERISTICS	EXAMPLES	DYSFUNCTIONAL ALTERNATIVES
Attachment/Caregiving • development of bonds between family members; the need to be close in times of distress; sense of comfort and reduced anxiety in the presence of the attachment figure; discomfort or anxiety when faced with lack of availability of the attached person; ability to attend to the survival and comfort needs of the attached person	• falling in love; parental care of a child; basic caring of one spouse for another	• emotional over-involvement; extreme anxiety in the absence of the other; inability to be involved with family members
Communicating • ability to develop shared meanings; ability to decenter and take the point of view of the other person; developing coordinated communication code	• attending to what others say with interest in understanding them; direct and clear requests and inquiries that are not emotionally laden; empathic understanding	• guarded communication so as not to be provocative; fragmented communication where messages are indirect and unclear
Joint Problem Solving • flexible role structures; comfortable coordination of tasks; managing differences and conflicts; successful movement from one life cycle stage to another	• negotiation; shared decision making; testing solutions; provisionalism; behavioral flexibility	• cyclical repetitions of conflicts; avoidance of problem solving; disruptive and emotional disagreements; blaming and scapegoating
Mutuality • ability to develop and try new forms of relating that will lead to relational renewal or termination (if appropriate); requires members to stand back from the relationship temporarily to observe the relationship; often motivated by a sense of dissatisfaction with the current relationship	• a couple assessing their relationship and making changes; deciding to terminate a marriage; planning a new lifestyle; children and parents relating as adults when children are grown	• pseudomutuality or preserving a fixed and stable but painful pattern at the expense of individual needs; repeating old conflicts with no commitment to take relational risks in order to change
Intimacy • intense emotional sharing; reciprocal self-disclosure that could make the speaker vulnerable and that assumes total trust of the listener; high relational risk taking; knowing the other person as one knows oneself	• a couple deeply in love and who share aspects of themselves in an intensely revealing way	• fixation on the relationship; inability to balance the intimate relationship with other relationships and responsibilities; over-reliance on intimacy in order to give meaning to one's life

established. However, when communication processes build upon attachment/ caregiving, the participants draw upon abundant information that can be taken for granted" (p. 307). In a similar way, the **joint problem-solving** stage of family development builds upon the previous stages of relating and on skills established in the attachment/caregiving and communicating stages. Through joint problem solving family members are able to develop informal role structures, coordinate task activities, and manage differences and conflicts in the family.

Wynne sees the joint problem-solving stage as essential to facilitating the successful progression of families from one important life cycle stage to another. For instance, imagine a family that has not been able to resolve attachment/ caregiving issues and achieve some degree of shared meaning and understanding (or empathy) in their communication with one another. They will have difficulty managing the transition from being a family with young children to being a family with adolescent children who require new, and less formal or socially prescribed, family role functions. Negative patterns associated with the joint problem-solving stage of development include such behaviors as cyclical repetitions of solutions that do not work, avoidance of problem solving about important issues, and disruptive disagreement (which, in the case of violent families, may become dangerous). Wynne makes the point that joint problem solving requires sufficient emotional attachment and the ability to communicate: "Without a background of attachment/caregiving and communication skills, joint problem solving is doomed to be muddled and dysfunctional" (p. 307).

Mutuality. The **mutuality stage** involves negotiations associated with long-term relational renewal, reengagement, and, in some cases, termination. At this stage of development, there is the recognition that previous forms of relating are no longer adequate and new patterns must be developed. Diane and Sheila, in our opening story, express the difficulties they are having in negotiating and redefining their relationship. In another family, successful launching of their children may mean that parents need to make changes in the spousal relationship. A couple that has launched four children into adulthood may, for instance, find themselves rattling around the house and bumping into each other until they begin to redefine their relationship in terms of their new childlessness. Mutuality can also mean that two partners in a relationship no longer wish to stay married. Whether mutuality involves redefining and revitalizing a relationship or terminating a relationship, the processes involved at this stage build on joint problem-solving skills.

Mutuality differs from joint problem solving. Not every family attains a high level of mutuality; nor is a high level of mutuality necessary to the experience of a rewarding and satisfying family life for everyone. It requires partners or family members to stand back from the relationship temporarily and observe the functioning of the relationship. This is often the function of marital counselors who are asked to help couples achieve more rewarding ways of relating to one another. The therapist can describe what he or she observes about the marriage and, thereby, provide the opportunity for the participants to step outside their adversarial roles and take on participant–observer roles in order to make their own evaluation, assessment, and commitment to new patterns of relating. Renegotiation of old patterns may involve global reevaluations of the relationship or smaller, more specific concerns. One couple may be planning a new lifestyle for themselves in New Mexico after retirement; another may be negotiating the reorganization of household management tasks when one of them begins a photography business after the children are grown.

The process of mutuality is related to the family's ability to separate their identities from a relationship problem and to externalize or objectify the problem as outside of themselves and between or among family members (Friedman, 1993; Gilligan & Price, 1993; White & Epston, 1990). In becoming observers of their interactions rather than defenders of their identities, family members can gain the detachment necessary to develop a new perspective of their situation and explore alternative versions of the story that they tell about the situation. Diane and Sheila might talk about how difficult the process of moving from adolescence to adulthood can be for families (which they have already begun to do). They could verbalize their awareness that each of them has different and sometimes contradictory needs at this stage in their lives: Diane would like to feel free to take some risks and make decisions on her own; Sheila would like to be included in Diane's decision making and would like to have the family's values validated. In conversing about the problem in this way, Diane and Sheila free themselves "from being defined by the problem" and open the door for change and mutual resolution of the problem (Freeman & Lobovits, 1993, p. 190).

Intimacy. Of all the relational processes that we have described, intimacy is the most difficult to define. Intimacy involves intense emotional sharing distinct from sexual passion. Wynne describes the **intimacy stage** as requiring more significant degrees of personal disclosure and trust than sexual passion. Intimacy can give one a sense of connectedness and transcendence that is exhilarating—in a sense, a way of escaping the boundaries of our private, mortal existence. But intimacy is not only difficult to attain, it also is risky. As Wynne (1984) writes:

> I believe that intimacy is best characterized as the inconstant, subjective side of relatedness, the sharing of personal feelings, fantasies, and effectively meaningful experience associated with each of the stages that have been described. These processes are relational, between persons, but are not necessarily symmetrical. They include emotionally charged verbal or nonverbal self-disclosures of a kind that connote an acceptance of the listener, who could betray or exploit the speaker but is trusted not to do so. This definition suggests that intimacy can be a deeply powerful, meaningful, humanizing experience, subtly and emotionally complicated, seductive but frightening. . . Erotic elements, joint inspiration, and reciprocal self-disclosure are some of the more obvious elements that surely contribute to intimacy beyond the elemental starting point of attachment/caregiving. . . . Paradoxically, preoccupation with intimacy as a goal, as with simultaneous orgasm, interferes with its attainment and also distracts, at the very least, from attention to other forms of relatedness (p. 310).

Wynne's model describes family communication as a hierarchy of relational skills. At the most elementary level is the sense of attachment and caregiving that family members give and communicate to one another. By building on a foundation of mutual attachment and caring for one another, individuals are able to understand how other family members perceive experiences, and they can then create the shared meanings and sense of mutual understanding that makes joint problem solving possible. Joint problem solving enables family members to coordinate agendas, negotiate tasks, resolve differences, and adapt roles to meet

Attachment and caregiving are fundamental to the qualitative development of family relationships.

life-cycle changes. Mutuality in family relationships requires skills in joint problem solving as well as the ability to step outside of the relationship in order to assess the potential of the relationship. Intimacy is characterized by intense personal sharing and requires the use of relational skills achieved at each of the previous stages of development. It is, perhaps, the most emotionally rewarding and infrequently achieved stage of relational growth and the stage most fraught with risks to the participants.

Wynne's developmental model describes a hierarchy of relational skills which provides a repertoire of responses to the changing goals of the family and the changing demands of the life cycle.

FAMILY DEVELOPMENT AND FAMILY VIOLENCE

In this section, we apply Wynne's stages of relational development to a specific form of family crisis—family violence. There are many important forms of family problems that could be discussed here, including families characterized by drug or alcohol abuse (Stanton, 1981a), families having members with eating disorders (Minuchin & Fishman, 1981), and families manifesting a variety of other problem behaviors (Palazzoli, Cirillo, Selvini, & Sorrentino, 1989). We have chosen family violence as our case in point for two reasons. The first reason is the extremely high incidence of family violence. The fact that each year millions of people are victims of some form of physical abuse by other family members indicates that family violence is not rare, occasional, and confined only to "sick families" (Gelles, 1979, 1980; Straus, Gelles, & Steinmetz, 1980; Steinmetz, 1977; Lystad, 1986; Pagelow, 1984). None of us can hide from the stark reality that, instead of being an individual aberration, violence "is a pattern of family relations in millions of American families" (Gelles, 1979, p. 11). The second reason for focusing on family violence is its emergent and developmental quality. Families do not normally start out with a pattern of violence and abuse. More likely, a pattern of violence develops, is perpetuated, and escalates over time. Moreover, violence and abuse can interfere with healthy developmental progress and growth in the family, creating a crisis environment and an impasse in the family so severe that the lives and self-worth of family members are threatened, a circumstance especially painful and tragic for its most vulnerable members.

Our discussion of family violence will be limited and focused. By **family violence** we mean the spirals of family conflict that escalate into physical attacks upon family members. This broad definition of family violence does not distinguish among the various specific forms of family violence such as wife-battering and spouse abuse, child abuse and neglect, sexual abuse of children and marital rape, sibling abuse, abuse of elderly relatives, psychological abuse of family members, and violence by children. Family violence can include any member of the family and a wide range of behaviors. The severity of violence in the family can also vary, as can the vulnerability of the victims of family violence. Considerations of the specific types, forms, and patterns of family violence is beyond the scope of this chapter's narrower focus on change.

Violence in families is the most profound and devastating irony of human relationships. "Love and violence," writes R. D. Laing (1967, p. 58), "properly speaking, are supposed to be polar opposites. Love lets the other be, but with affection and concern. Violence attempts to constrain the other's freedom, to force him to act in the way we desire, but with ultimate lack of concern, with indifference to the other's existence or humanity." The profound irony of family violence is that in the one social unit where members have the highest potential for supreme joy, they often inflict tremendous pain. As anthropologist Jules Henry (1973) stated so poetically, "life lures us with small favors to commit great crimes."

Following Giles-Sims's (1983) application of systems theory to the problem of wife-battering, we distinguish between the question of *why* family violence occurs and *how* it occurs. Discussions of why family violence occurs requires that we identify the causes of family violence. There is evidence to suggest, for instance, that unemployment, rigid sex-role orientations, social isolation, cultural approval of violence, use of corporal punishment in disciplining children, and the use of violence in one or both of the spouses' families of origin may contribute to family violence (Gelles, 1979). It is important to acknowledge that family violence is most often a consequence of **power inequities** in the family which are embedded in cultural attitudes. Those with the least power, women and children, are most likely to be the victims of family abuse and violence (Gelles & Straus, 1988). A concern for why family violence occurs calls for a systematic analysis of the family ecosystem.

Focus on the interaction processes associated with family violence will help to determine whether episodes of repetitive patterns that erupt into violence can be identified, understood, and changed. Consistent with the developmental and systematic orientation of this book, we center our attention on how family violence occurs rather than why it occurs, specifically sequences in the cycle of violent episodes in families, characteristic dysfunctions in the structure of rules, and role relationships in families prone to violence. We then apply Wynne's developmental model for understanding family violence.

Stages in the Cycle of Violent Episodes

Families that respond violently to each other or to their more vulnerable members often progress through interaction stages that culminate in violence. Giles-Sims (1983) has identified the following interactional sequence characteristic of episodic violence in families:

1. an equilibrium or precompetition stage
2. a stage of competition and increasing tension

3. a crisis event in which emotions escalate and violence erupts
4. contrition or withdrawal leading toward a renewal of equilibrium

The **equilibrium or precompetition** stage is characterized by moderate levels of temporary stability in which family members maintain enough detachment from one another to avoid provoking each other. The **competition and increasing tension** stage is marked by an accumulation of unexpressed grievances among family members. The **crisis event** stage involves an escalation of emotions that erupt into violence. The **contrition and/or withdrawal** stage is characterized by conciliation after a period of emotional and physical distance.

Tom Gilchrist feels angry, frustrated, suspicious, and depressed by the circumstances of his recent job loss. He and his wife have recently spent time apart, allowing the couple to create some distance in what has become a tense relationship. Tom spends the day doing what he can to find work and completing mechanical repairs on a car so that the couple will have two functioning automobiles available to them. Their two children are at school most of the day. Janine, Tom's wife, is employed on a part-time basis. On this particular day, Janine brings home fried chicken; everyone eats dinner, watches a little television, and then goes to bed tired. For today, at least, some degree of quiet association has been maintained. The family is in the equilibrium or precompetition stage.

The next afternoon and evening are different. During the stage of competition and increasing tension, family members begin to experience their relationships as an accumulation of grievances. Janine has the day off and becomes increasingly frustrated by Tom's lack of interest and concern about the condition of the house. Tom does not express his feelings. He says little in response to Janine's requests and complaints, which he perceives as nagging. The less responsive Tom is, the more frustrated Janine feels and the more intensely she expresses her frustrations. Tension between the couple builds. Janine begins complaining about Tom to the oldest child in the family, who is torn between his alliances to both parents.

During the third stage of the cycle, the tension increases until a crisis event produces an escalation of emotions that erupts into a violent episode. Sometimes the triggering behavior can be a trivial issue. The previous night Tom Gilcrist had told Janine that he was going out to have a few beers with some friends. Tom felt that he had to get away from Janine's nagging. Janine felt resentful about spending the night alone.

Tom came home late—long after Janine had gone to bed—and collapsed on the couch. The next day, he got up late and spent most of the afternoon working on the car he was repairing. During the early evening hours, he fell asleep on the couch while he was watching television. Janine, who was still irritated about being left at home the previous night, told the children not to wake him for dinner. That evening when he woke up, the children had eaten and were upstairs and Janine was reading in the bedroom. Tom was furious that no one had tried to wake him for dinner. When he found the youngest child in the kitchen, he grabbed her arm in a painful grip and yelled, "Why the hell didn't you get me up for dinner?" Terrified, the child ran to her mother in the bedroom. Tom followed. Holding the child in her arms, Janine told Tom to control his temper; she indicated that she thought Tom had wanted to sleep and that he would only be "ugly" if she or one of the children tried to get him up. Tom's fury increased. He yelled at Janine, "You want to see ugly? I'll show you ugly!" Janine got up off the bed and Tom grabbed her

FIGURE 11.2   Stages in the cycle of violent episodes.

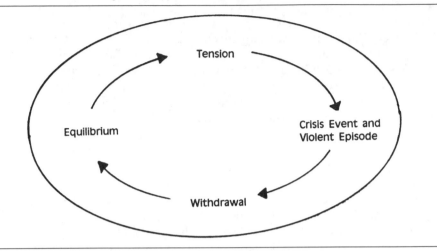

by the shoulders and shoved her against the wall. Janine called him "a son of a bitch" and Tom punched her in the face. Janine worked herself free and ran to the kitchen, threatening him with a butcher knife. Both children ran to the kitchen crying and screaming at their parents to stop. Tom stormed out of the house and did not return that evening. Janine cried all night. The next day she went to work.

Tom returned two days later with a gift. They sat on the couch in the living room. Tom cried and promised not to hit Janine again. Janine did not say much, but she was touched by Tom's efforts at conciliation. In this fourth stage in the cycle of violence, family members may experience some degree of contrition or, at least, establish a safer emotional distance. A degree of stability is temporarily achieved until competition and tension in the system is triggered by some new incident and escalates again.

In describing the stages of family violence, we do not mean to sanction Tom Gilcrist's behavior or to define his behavior as "provoked." In discussing family violence, there is always the chance that identifying one member's behavior as "provoking" another's may be misleading or suggest that the violent behavior of a stronger family member against a weaker one can be rationalized or justified. This certainly is not our view. Indeed, we cannot think of any nonviolent behavior that can be considered as legitimate provocation for the violent physical assault of one family member against another. The cycle of violence depicted in this example is intended to illustrate how violent families can find themselves caught up in family patterns that tend to repeat and escalate.

Application of Wynne's Developmental Model

Wynne's model can be used to examine violence in families as a developmental crisis in relational processes. At the attachment/caregiving level, violent families may vacillate between severe criticism of each other's behaviors and withdrawal from accepting responsibility for influencing other family members. Rather than sustaining basic complementary bonds of affection, attachments among family members prone to violence are more likely to be characterized by emotional over-involvement in which minor behaviors evoke intense emotional responses; small signals provoke large responses.

Because of their inability to develop functional levels of attachment and caregiving, the violent family may have difficulty communicating adequately (Chandler, 1986; Whitchurch, 1987). Members of violent families rely less on argumentative skills in resolving conflicts and more on verbal aggressiveness or verbal abuse (Sabourin, Infante, & Rudd, 1990). Moreover, in violent families, there is an unwillingness or an inability to understand the other's perspective and subsequently to develop shared meanings. Understanding the other's perspective requires more individuation than members of these families are able to achieve. Developing shared meanings requires an ability to exchange information about needs, feelings, and perceptions and to understand "where the other is coming from." Without a sense of what it means to share another's perspective, family members are unable to exchange messages that take into account the point of view and probable response of the other person.

We see this communicative difficulty in the Gilcrist family. Tom does not share his feelings of inadequacy and helplessness over his unemployment situation with Janine. In an attempt to get Tom involved in the family, Janine complains about his thoughtlessness around the house. Tom is unable to understand how Janine might experience his silence as isolating himself from her and how she might be using her "nagging" as a way to get him to connect with the family. As a consequence, each person experiences the other's behavior as a source of provocation.

In Chapter 7, we discussed "communication as metaphor." The influence of actions and behaviors is a function of the meanings they are assigned as messages. People respond according to what they think others are trying to do to them; that is, what others "mean" by what they say or how they act. Family members who behave violently often see their behavior as a fitting response to being "provoked." Messages do not necessarily have unambiguous and unequivocal meanings. A problem in violent families is that family members are prepared to respond to each other's actions as threatening and provocative. Consider what stands for provocation for the Gilcrists. Tom's lack of concern for things around the house "provokes" Janine into nagging him. The failure of Janine and the kids to wake up Tom for dinner is sufficient to provoke his rage because he views it as a purposeful attempt to agitate him. The inability to view the situation from the other's perspective may distort the other's intentions and provide all the justification one requires to fly into uncontrollable rage.

Without a foundation of adequate caregiving and shared understanding about each other's experience, joint problem solving is impossible. Violent families often seem unable to coordinate basic tasks and negotiate agendas. Even more importantly, there may be an "evasion of problem solving," to use Wynne's phrase (1984). Important issues are not addressed; instead, accusations are exchanged. And, of course, without adequate ability to attach, communicate, and jointly solve problems, mutuality cannot be sustained. Connections and interaction patterns among family members become rigid (Gelles & Maynard, 1987). There is little acknowledgment and tolerance for divergent self-interests of other members of the family. Family members, especially parents, also have little ability to step back from the system in order to analyze the needs of relationships in the family. Lacking this ability, members of violence-prone families too often view differences among them as a threat to the survival of the family or themselves. They fight when they ought to resist (Henry, 1973).

Moreover, families inclined toward violence find it extremely difficult to break their destructive cycle of anger and pain, a circumstance that is influenced by social constraints and opportunities (Goodrich, Rampage, Ellman, & Halstead, 1988; Gouldner, 1985). Women find it difficult, sometimes next to impossible, to overcome their economic and emotional dependency upon their husbands and, given the wage discrepancies between men and women, to support themselves and their children on their own should they choose to leave an abusive situation. Children seldom get help from persons outside the family who are willing or legally authorized to intrude on parental rights and the family's privacy in order to intervene on the children's behalf. Male socialization makes it relatively easy for men to avoid taking responsibility for their lack of empathy for the pain they inflict and for their use of family members as *objects* of their frustration and rage. Reconciliation, which often completes a cycle of family violence, offers false hope and reinforcement for staying in the relationship (Walker, 1979; Giles-Sims, 1983). This reinforcement makes it more difficult to contemplate or discuss separating or terminating the marriage. Members of violent families have not developed skills to distance themselves from their cycle of destructive interaction and to talk about their family relationships in objective ways that could lead to radical change or termination. Consequently, they are inclined to repeat their cycle of projected blame, provocation, violence, and reconciliation.

In the previous sections of this chapter we have discussed various ideas that explore how life stages, developmental phases, and repetitive cycles can facilitate or inhibit change and growth in the family. Families develop ways of relating as members are born into, enter, mature, develop new loyalties, exit, and die. How families cope with the changes that accompany natural life processes depends to a significant degree on the quality of their communication. In spite of the difficulties confronting them, some families are able to achieve a degree of joint problem solving, mutuality, and detachment which supports every member's integrity. Other families seem to repeat painful episodes that leave all or most of its members diminished and depleted. Diane feels crowded by her parents' expectations and simultaneously feels dependent upon them for love and nurturance. Sheila feels pushed away by her daughter and anxious about her daughter's future. And yet, in both of their stories, Diane and Sheila can find spaces to breathe, to grow, and to accept each other's different perspectives, even if they do not converge conveniently. They can talk about their feelings, acknowledge positive aspects of their relationship, discuss their problems with some degree of objectivity, and express their caring for each other and their hope for the future. In the following section we discuss more specifically our views of the characteristics of optimally functioning families.

OPTIMAL FAMILY FUNCTIONING

In this book we have purposely avoided such value-laden terms as "healthy," "normal," and "adjusted" families. It would be so comforting to be able to conclude our book by presenting a set of techniques or behaviors that would guarantee everyone a healthy and fulfilling family life. But we realize that it can be dangerous and presumptuous to give advice about how to be a family, primarily because there are so many different ways to be a family and so many different beliefs and values about what constitutes a "healthy family." All of us have to struggle with the paradoxes and contradictions of relational life discussed in this book. If there is a secret, it is that there is no secret. We can only cope with the confusion and uncertainty; we cannot resolve it.

Nevertheless, the topic of change provides an inspiration for considering what is better and what is worse for families. Many of us want to do better, and think we can, than our parents did with us; families that pay to get help from therapists usually expect to change for the better rather than for the worse. But what is better and what is worse and how big is the difference? The main difference between "them" and "us," according to Jules Henry (1973), is that they (extremely disturbed families) "seem to go to extremes and do too many things that are upsetting." Yet even in these "very disturbed" families, there is usually some alleviating health that makes family life seem tolerable and "normal." Our awareness of cultural diversity and history has also heightened our sensitivity to being judgmental about what is normal family functioning (Ho, 1987; Sue & Sue, 1990; McGoldrick, Pearce, & Giordano, 1982; Stephen, 1994; Stephen & Harrison, 1993).

This paradox—that is, the need to be cautious in making prescriptions about effective family functioning and the need also to identify the processes that "make things better" rather than "make things worse"—raises the question of precisely what is meant by the term *normal family*. Too often, normality merely represents the absence of some clinical definition of abnormality. What is "normal" then becomes confused with what is conventionally acceptable, which is not necessarily the same as what is "good" or "right." Indeed, the famous psychiatrist Don Jackson (1977) suggested many years ago that the concept of a normal family is a myth:

> As a student of the family for many years, I think it is *safer* to say there is no such thing as a normal family any more than there is a normal individual. There are parents who appear to live in extreme harmony together but who have nervous children, and parents who get along miserably but whose children appear to be functioning well. When one hears the expression, "Gee, they're a normal family," the speaker is usually referring to some facet of family living and not to the total family interaction, which is unknown to the casual observer. Such statements are usually made by persons who value conformity and see this family as one that lives up to all the ideals of the ladies' magazines, including the cardinal principle of "togetherness." Truly, such behavior has little to do with mental health. There are cultures and families within our own culture in which the family structure is very different from what is commonly considered normal. Yet the individuals therein are creative and productive (p. 161).

In more recent years, researchers, clinicians, feminists, and writers have demonstrated that particular conceptions of the "normal family" can in fact be viewed as "dysfunctional," depending upon one's perspective. Family roles that assign women to expressive, social-emotional roles and men to instrumental, task roles in the family have the tendency to reduce women's economic and decision-making power in the family and in society and to diminish men's capacity for intimacy. The tendency to view women as too often "overinvolved" in the family can be viewed as a tendency for men to be "underinvolved" and emotionally distant.

The Western cultural emphasis on individual autonomy, achievement, and expressiveness in the family can be viewed as "dysfunctional" in a culture that values family cohesion, connectedness to nature, intergenerational ties, and a sense of community above individual identity. It is our view that any description of the "normal family" can benefit from understanding that defining normality involves a selection process among competing perspectives of the family and should be presented tentatively, primarily as a way to begin a dialogue. Given these cautionary observations, can we make some generalizations as a starting point for a conversation about potential goals for optimal family functioning? In recent years, researchers and clinicians have identified several characteristics of optimal family functioning. Our discussion draws heavily from Beavers and Hampson's (1990) synthesis of the literature and their study of "successful families," the work of Hauser and his associates with adolescents and their families (1991), and from other articles by Bochner and Eisenberg (1987) and Walsh (1982, 1993). In the following section, we identify ten characteristics of optimally functioning families:

1. *Optimally functioning families tend to be more egalitarian than chaotic or authoritarian.* Egalitarianism is related to issues of power and leadership in the family (Beavers & Hampson, 1990). In chaotic families, no one seems to be in charge, attempts at directing family members may be covert or manipulative, and there is a lack of clarity about the responsibilities of each generation. For instance, the oldest child in an alcoholic family may take on child-care responsibilities usually assigned to a parent. In authoritarian families, leadership is characterized by dominance, rigidity, and the efforts of certain family members to control other family members. Beavers and Hampson state that less-than-successful families often vacillate between authoritarian and chaotic leadership. A rigidly authoritarian family may not be able to sustain the efforts of some members to dominate others; rigidity may mask an underlying insecurity and attachment to stereotyped family roles, provoking resistance and rebellion. In contrast, families characterized by **egalitarian leadership** provide opportunities for all family members to influence family decisions and to legitimately get their needs met in ways that promote everyone's self-worth. Children's opinions are not discounted because they come from children, and there is enough provisionalism about what is considered "right" and "wrong" to give the family the flexibility to handle different situations as they arise. Egalitarianism does not prescribe equality in every area of family functioning, but there is enough freedom for all family members to feel that their point of view is respected and valued.

2. *Optimally functioning families exhibit a congruence between the family's mythology and its actions.* In optimally functioning families there is a general agreement between the images that family members have of themselves and how they act. For example, a family does not maintain the myth that "we are a happy family" when it is apparent to everyone in the family that several members are angry and depressed. Alcoholic families that are "in denial" often maintain the myth that "everything is fine," even when the drinking of one or more members of the family causes considerable pain and despair for other family members. To some extent, we can see a lack of congruence between the family myth and the actions of family members in our opening story. Diane refers to the family myth that "we are a close family." At the same time, she describes how difficult it is for her parents to understand her needs and to support her efforts to launch herself into adulthood. Sheila also complains that Diane does not understand her parents'

point of view. Would a "close" family be more understanding of the needs of a young adult? If the family were "close," would Sheila be better able to share her feelings with her daughter without making Diane feel that she is judging or controlling her?

3. *Optimally functioning families develop strong dyadic relationships without excluding members or forming coalitions against one another.* In healthy families parents do not consistently exclude children by being preoccupied with each other, nor does a parent and a child form a coalition against another parent. Beavers and Hampson (1990) observe that "Parents may undermine each other's authority at times, and even solicit some support from the children, but the consistent parent–child coalition is not evident, nor is there evidence of unresolved love relationships between parents and children" (p. 17). The family, instead, provides the opportunity for dyadic relationships to develop among family members that do not provoke consistent anxiety and distress among other family members. A mother helps to facilitate a positive relationship between her daughter and her husband. Mother and father are able to parent in ways that do not strangle their marital relationship. Father and son are able to bond without forming a coalition against mother.

4. *Optimally functioning families develop emotional closeness and bonds of attachment while also maintaining personal boundaries and individuation.* In optimally functioning families, closeness is a consequence of the appreciation of the uniqueness of each member's needs, preferences, personality, and identity. Family members respect one another's differences (Hauser, 1991; Wynne, Ryckoff, Day, & Hirsch, 1958). They do not assume that they can speak for one another's feelings ("You're not angry; you're just tired"), pressure each other to conform to a unified world view represented by the family's ideology ("We can't trust anyone outside the family"), or relate to each other almost entirely as role performers ("Husbands are supposed to control their feelings"). Family members can engage in activities that may not interest other family members, maintain strong friendships outside the family, and have political views that differ from the rest of the family without endangering their acceptance and participation in the family's group life. A family that is functioning optimally somehow finds a way for its members to achieve satisfactory separateness without damaging the family's sense of wholeness. This issue is related to our earlier discussion of negotiating the dialectic of differentiation and integration, and it is part of Diane's struggle in our opening story. Diane wants to maintain a sense of closeness with her family without feeling that she has to sacrifice her own feelings, opinions, and decision-making power in order to do so. In fact, she experiences the inability of her parents to let her become her own person as a threat to the closeness that she wants and needs in the family.

5. *Optimally functioning families encourage every family member to participate in the problem-solving process and can stay focused on the task.* In optimally functioning families there is a tendency for everyone to be involved in identifying problems, negotiating solutions, and making decisions. Once a decision is made everyone is able to commit to following through and assessing the outcomes. This process requires a willingness of family members to discuss their own issues and concerns or those of other family members, to make known their reservations about proposed solutions, and to carry out a contract with other family members. Beavers and Hampson (1990) write, "The husband who accedes to his wife about

a marital issue but then passively grumbles or sabotages, the sullen adolescent who refuses to discuss disciplinary problems with parents, and the dictator-like spokesperson who assumes all responsibility for family negotiation—all produce or contribute to ineffective negotiation processes" (p. 21). Families that function well tend not to have members who remain consistently disengaged, distant, and aloof from the problem-solving processes of the whole family.

6. *Optimally functioning families tend to be more empathic, affiliative, and warm than oppositional.* They do not use their communication intentionally and regularly to hurt, intimidate, or control one another. Family members do not make "enemies" of other family members; they do not feel that they have to "defend themselves" against one another or believe that they have the "right to punish" and "destroy" one another (Henry, 1973, p. 448). They are not looking to blame the others or to find a scapegoat for their problems. They do not behave "coldly" among themselves. In optimally functioning families there is an effort to understand everyone's point of view, an awareness that one's perspective is related to his or her developmental stage, and a tendency to be receptive rather than resistant to appreciating the struggles of all family members. As Stafford and Bayer (1993) indicate in their review of parent–child interaction, "In all the variables studies, from all frames and theories, the expression of interpersonal warmth and responsiveness appears beneficial to the child and to the family" (p. 168).

Diane and Sheila are each seeking, longing for, some empathic understanding of their respective perceptions and struggles as a young adult and as a parent. We sense in each of their accounts some hope for common ground in achieving mutual acceptance and warm feelings of regard that have not been crowded out by their feelings of disappointment and frustration. They each express a desire for reconciliation rather than a desire to retaliate against or punish the other.

7. *Optimally functioning families give all family members the opportunity to find and express their own feelings and stories.* These families actively solicit the feelings of individual family members and are "respectfully responsive" when members do express themselves (Beavers & Hampson, p. 22). For the most part they can listen to one another, acknowledge their individual experiences, and do not attempt to block one another. Optimally functioning families recognize that each member has ambivalent feelings, experiences divided loyalties, and must struggle and come to terms with the contradictions and dialectical processes of life. These families experience and can tolerate a wide *range* of emotions. For example, they do more than go through repetitive cycles of calm, anger, depression, and remorse; they can sometimes laugh at their problems, feel compassion for one another, acknowledge their frustrations, experience resignation, mourn, celebrate their successes, share their neediness as well as withdraw from one another, and so forth. Hauser and his colleagues (1991) have described with sensitivity the importance of tolerating ambiguity and enduring uncomfortable emotions in the families of adolescents who have been able to nurture rather than interfere with the growth and positive ego development of their children:

> Enduring and even making authentic attempts to engage with an abusive or rejecting son or daughter may be one of the most meaningful acts a parent can perform during these adolescent years. . . . Being willing and able to weather storms of disruptive and at times deeply offensive feelings, such as intense anger and rejection, is an important general family strength, one especially called upon during the adolescence of one of its members (p. 242).

In the successful families of Hauser's study, parents endure intense and complex emotions and accept the expression of a wide range of emotions as a way of helping their children find their own voices and come to terms with the problems and possibilities of life.

8. *Optimally functioning families encourage family members to take personal responsibility for their actions and do not punish them for acknowledging their mistakes.* Family members acknowledge the effects of their behaviors rather than avoid, minimize, or scapegoat one another for their errors, weaknesses, or inadequacies. Mistakes can include minor problems, such as getting a speeding ticket or hurting a relative's feelings. Mistakes can also inflict major damage and pain on others in the family, such as having an affair, or verbally abusing or physically harming someone. Accepting responsibility for one's mistakes requires honesty and trust in the family. In optimally functioning families, family members do not blame others for their actions ("Your brother deserved it"; "You have not been very exciting lately"; "She provoked me"), lie about their actions ("I didn't have anything to drink this afternoon"), or dismiss the problem as unimportant ("Why are you making such a big deal out of this?"). In some families, withdrawal of love and affection, overdramatization ("I can't believe that you would do such a thing—this will destroy me!"), or fear of retaliation may make family members fearful of accepting responsibility for their actions. In other families, ownership of one's actions tends to make the situation "better" rather than "worse" because members are not punished for their forthrightness. In optimally functioning families, family members are encouraged to accept the consequences of their actions ("Your father and I want you to help pay for your speeding ticket"), but they are not belittled for having been honest ("How could any responsible person daydream while driving a car?"). Being able to take responsibility for one's mistakes without fear of family reprisals is related to role modeling and to habits of relating in the parents' families of origin. If a parent was made to feel guilty and ashamed as a child whenever she or he made a mistake, the tendency will be to discount or blame others for mistakes as an adult. That parent, in turn, will not be an effective role model for the children. Supporting family members in acknowledging their mistakes is strongly related to intergenerational patterns and rules in the family.

9. *Optimally functioning families are more spontaneous, playful, and optimistic than introspective.* These families are more energized and emotionally connected. They have fun together; they are humorous and witty. They can laugh at their problems and be playful. They do not take life too seriously, nor do they "have a compulsion to murder pleasure" (Henry, 1973, p. 452). They notice their successes and can acknowledge the times that they overcame problems. The climate of less healthy families feels heavier; interactions are often tense, abbreviated, and confused; family members may experience feelings of depression, discouragement, and hopelessness about their ability to function as a family. In contrast, optimally functioning families are able to keep things in perspective, rejuvenate and nourish themselves even in "the worst of times," and tend not to be obsessive about their problems. The pleasure and comfort that they take in one another's company has more significance for them than do the difficulties that they experience. We are aware of the difficulties in Diane and Sheila's family in part because there are no references in their story to any fun times or to the times they manage to shift the focus away from their struggles and take a break from the

"tug-of-war" in the family. Moments of fun, play, and spontaneity provide spaces for family members to experience aspects of their life together in positive ways and to distance themselves from day-to-day negotiations.

10. *Optimally functioning families are able to negotiate conflicts and move forward rather than repeat the same conflicts without resolving issues*. These families are flexible and adaptable enough to change when they are confronted with problems. Successful families are able to make the transitions from one developmental stage to the next without developing coping strategies that damage its members or become problematic. Unlike the violent families we have described, optimally functioning families tend not to get caught in typical cycles of avoidance and confrontation which produce only "more of the same" (Dailey, 1992; Yelsma, 1984). They tend to be confident that differences that cannot be endured can be discussed and alternatives can be explored. Conflicts between family members do not become "life and death" struggles without room for some degree of a mutually satisfying outcome.

It is important to keep several thoughts in mind when you consider our description of the characteristics of optimally functioning families. The presence of a struggle or "inadequacy" in one or even several areas does not mean that your family or any family is "dysfunctional." It is also apparent that the presence of intense emotions is not a sign that a family is "falling apart" or has failed in some way. Notice the significance that enduring engagement, the coming to terms with the uniqueness of each person's experience, and the willingness to navigate opposing forces in the family (stability and change; differentiation and integration) has for the family. It is, perhaps, most useful to view these ten characteristics of optimally functioning families not as end states, which your family has either achieved or not achieved, but as processes that are constantly changing or *goals* that can be periodically renewed.

In our example of Diane and Sheila, it is possible to identify the ways that their different perspectives represent both problems and strengths in the family.

TABLE 11.2   Characteristics of optimally functioning families.

OPTIMALLY FUNCTIONING FAMILIES

1. tend to be more egalitarian than chaotic or authoritarian
2. exhibit a congruence between the family's mythology and its actions
3. develop strong dyadic relationships without excluding members or forming coalitions against one another
4. develop emotional closeness and bonds of attachment while also maintaining personal boundaries and individuation
5. encourage every family member to participate in the problem-solving process and to stay focused on the task
6. tend to be more empathic and affiliative than oppositional
7. give each family member the opportunity to find and express his or her own feelings and story
8. encourage members to take personal responsibility for their actions and do not punish them for acknowledging their mistakes
9. are more spontaneous, playful, and optimistic than introspective
10. are able to negotiate conflicts and move forward rather than repeat the same conflicts without resolving issues

APPLICATION 11.2

OPTIMALLY FUNCTIONING FAMILIES

- Select several characteristics of optimally functioning families which seem to be difficult for your family. For each characteristic think of a particular episode that seems to illustrate a problem related to the characteristic you have identified.
- Then, think about situations when each of these same issues was not a problem. For example, if you are concerned that leadership in your family tends to be more authoritarian or chaotic than egalitarian, can you think of a time when that was not the case? What helped the family function in a more egalitarian way? How did you feel and how did everyone react when that happened?
- Finally, identify at least one characteristic of optimally functioning families that your family does relatively well. Think of a situation that illustrates your assessment. Are there other areas where your family seems to function in ways that make family life "better" rather than "worse"? Can you relate these to any of the characteristics of optimally functioning families?

Diane describes her family as "perhaps too close" and her assessment may be accurate; the family seems to be having trouble allowing Diane to have her own opinions and make her own decisions. But it is also "true" that the closeness of which she speaks has the potential to motivate the family to work on their problems and to accept one another's different perceptions and points of view more comfortably. Both Diane and Sheila indicate their frustrations about not feeling understood, and yet it is to their credit that neither is ready to scapegoat or punish the other person.

SUMMARY

This chapter discusses family change from a developmental perspective. We briefly describe family life tasks and potential intergenerational interfaces that may influence communication in newly married couples, families with young children, families with adolescents, launching families, and empty-nest and retirement families. Sometimes families have difficulties making transitions from one stage in the life cycle to the next. We describe the family crisis that may emerge if the family reaches a point of impasse at some stage in the life cycle.

Qualitative changes in the family do not always progress chronologically. This is one of the points that Wynne makes in his model of family development. Wynne discusses family development as qualitative changes in the interaction of family members. Using the term *epigenesis* to describe the sequential nature of developmental changes, Wynne identifies five epigenetic stages of family development: (1) attachment/caregiving, (2) communicating, (3) joint problem solving, (4) mutuality, and (5) intimacy. As a case in point we have applied Wynne's model of family development to the problems of violent families. First we discuss stages in the cycle of violent episodes and then examine violence in families as developmental dysfunction in relational processes. In the final section of the chapter we explore family change as it relates to optimal family functioning and identify several generalizations that can be made about optimal family functioning.

Optimally functioning families tend to foster a sense of equity among members; their beliefs about themselves as a family typically fit how they behave; they can be connected while being respectful of the integrity of individual family members; they are able to share responsibility for problems; they try to understand rather than blame each other; they encourage family members to express their feelings and take responsibility for themselves; they are not punitive when family members own up to their mistakes; they can enjoy one another and are able to live with or resolve their differences.

We believe that the future is not unalterably constrained by the past, and the possibility for achieving a satisfying (if not happy) "ending" to a family story may depend upon the extent to which a family can grieve over its failures, laugh at its mistakes, and acknowledge its resources. Perhaps in the years ahead, Diane and Sheila will have a different story to tell about the comforts, complexities, and frustrations of their relationship.

As you conclude this text we suggest that you reflect upon some of the ideas you have explored and discussions you have had while reading this book that have affected how you think and feel about families in general and about your family in particular. Some of your reflections could also be formulated into assertions about optimally functioning families or goals for the future. Has thinking about some of the issues presented in this book changed how you communicate with your family or influenced the kind of family relationships that you might help to create? As the future unfolds, what new narratives might you be able to tell about your family life? We hope that this book can influence your own family stories—just as the experience of writing and living has influenced ours.

KEY TERMS

attachment/caregiving stage

communicating stage

competition and increasing tensions
   stage

contrition and/or withdrawal stage

crisis event stage

developmental leaps

epigenesis

egalitarian leadership

equilibrium or precompetition stage

family life cycle

family life tasks

family violence

impasse

intergenerational influences

intimacy stage

joint problem-solving stage

mutuality stage

power inequities

transition

REFERENCES

Ainsworth, M. D. S. (1982, March). *Attachment: Retrospect and prospect.* Presidential address to the biennial meetings of the Society for Research in Child Development, San Francisco.

Allen, C. V. (1980). *Daddy's girl.* New York: Simon & Schuster.

Altman, I., & Taylor, D. (1973). *Social penetration: The development of interpersonal relationships.* New York: Holt, Rinehart, & Winston.

Anderson, H., & Goolishian, H. A. (1988). Human systems as linguistic systems: Preliminary and evolving ideas about the implications for clinical theory. *Family Process, 27,* 371–394.

Aponte, H., & Van Deusen, J. (1981). Structural family therapy. In A. Gurman & D. Kniskern (Eds.), *The handbook of family therapy* (pp. 310–360). New York: Brunner/Mazel.

Ariel, S., Carel, C., & Tyrano, S. (1984). A formal explication of the concept of family homcostasis. *Journal of Marital and Family Therapy, 10,* 337–349.

Askham, J. (1976). Identity and stability within the marriage relationship. *Journal of Marriage and the Family, 38,* 535–547.

Askham, J. (1984). *Identity and stability in marriage.* New York: Cambridge University Press.

Auerswald, E. H. (1971). Families, change and the ecological perspective. *Family Process, 10,* 263–280.

Ault-Riche, M. (1986). A feminist critique of five schools of family therapy. In M. Ault-Riche (Ed.), *Women and family therapy* (pp. 1–15). Rockville, MD: Aspen Systems Corp.

Bagarozzi, D. A., & Anderson, S. (1982). The evolution of family mythological systems: Considerations for meaning, clinical assessment, and treatment. *The Journal of Psychoanalytic Anthropology, 5,* 71–90.

Bagarozzi, D. A., & Anderson, S. (1989). *Personal, marital, and family myths.* New York: Norton.

Barber, B. K., Chadwick, B. A., & Oerter, R. (1992). Parental behaviors and adolescent self-esteem in the United States and Germany. *Journal of Marriage and the Family, 54,* 128–141.

Barnett, R. C., Kibria, N., Baruch, G. K., & Pleck, J. H. (1991). Adult daughter-parent relationships and their associations with daughters' subjective well-being and psychological distress. *Journal of Marriage and the Family, 53,* 29–42.

Bateson, G. (1970). A systems approach. *International Journal of Psychiatry, 9,* 242–244.

Bateson, G., Jackson, D. D., Haley, J., & Weakland, J. H. (1956). Toward a theory of schizophrenia. *Behavioral Science, 1,* 251–264.

Baxter, L. A. (1982, May). *Towards a dialectical understanding of interpersonal relationships: Research and theory in the 1980s.* Keynote address presented to the California State University, Fresno, 9th Annual Communication Conference.

Baxter, L. A. (1988). A dialectical perspective on communication strategies in relationship development. In S. W. Duck (Ed.), *A handbook of personal relationships* (pp. 257–273). New York: Wiley.

Baxter, L. A., & Bullis, C. (1986). Turning points in developing romantic relationships. *Human Communication Research, 12,* 469–493.

Baxter, L. A., & Wilmot, W. (1985). Taboo topics in close relationships. *Journal of Social and Personal Relationships, 2,* 253–269.

Beavers, W. R. (1977). *Psychotherapy and growth: A family systems perspective.* New York: Brunner/Mazel.

Beavers, W. R., & Hampson, R. B. (1990). *Successful families: Assessment and intervention.* New York: Norton.

Beck, D. F. (1969). Marital conflict: Its course and treatment as seen by caseworkers. In R. S. Cavan (Ed.), *Marriage and family in the modern world* (pp. 581–598). New York: Thomas Y. Crowell.

Belenky, M. F., Clinchy, B. M., Goldberger, N. R., & Tarule, J. M. (1986). *Women's ways of knowing: The development of self, voice, and mind.* New York: Basic Books.

Bellah, R. N., Madsen, R., Sullivan, W. M., Swidler, A., & Tipton, S. M. (1985). *Habits of the heart.* New York: Harper & Row.

Berger, P. L., & Kellner, H. (1974). Marriage and the construction of reality: An exercise in the microsociology of knowledge. In D. Brissett & C. Edgley (Eds.), *Life as theatre: A dramaturgical sourcebook* (pp. 219–233). Chicago: Aldine Publishing Company.

Berger, P. L., & Luckman, T. (1966). *The social construction of reality.* Garden City, NY: Doubleday & Company, Inc.

Bergman, I. (1974). *Scenes from a marriage.* New York: Pantheon Books.

Berlo, D. K. (1960). *The process of communication: An introduction to theory and practice.* New York: Holt, Rinehart, & Winston.

Bernstein, B. A. (1971). A sociolinguistic approach to socialization, with some reference to educability. In J. J. Gumpers & D. Hymes (Eds.), *Directions in sociolinguistics: The ethnography of communication* (pp. 465–497). New York: Holt, Rinehart, & Winston.

Bertalanffy, L. von. (1968). *General systems theory: Essays in its foundation and development* (Rev. ed.). New York: Brazilier.

Biddle, L. (1993). *Modernity and divorce: A performance by a divorced kid.* Paper presented at the annual meeting of the Southern Communication Association, Louisville, KY.

Bochner, A. P. (1976). Conceptual frontiers in the study of communication in families: An introduction to the literature. *Human Communication Research, 2,* 381–397.

Bochner, A. P. (1984). The functions of human communication in interpersonal bonding. In C. C. Arnold & J. W. Bowers (Eds.), *Handbook of rhetorical and communication theory* (pp. 544–621). Boston: Allyn & Bacon.

Bochner, A. P. (1994, in press). Perspectives on inquiry II: Theories and stories. In M. Knapp & G. R. Miller (Eds.), *Handbook of interpersonal communication* (2nd ed.). Newbury Park, CA: Sage.

Bochner, A. P., & Eisenberg, E. M. (1987). Family process: Systems perspectives. In C. R. Berger & S. H. Chaffee (Eds.), *Handbook of communication science* (pp. 540–563). Beverly Hills, CA: Sage.

Bochner, A. P., & Ellis, C. (1992). Personal narrative as a social approach to interpersonal communication. *Communication Theory, 2,* 65–72.

Bolton, C. D. (1961). Mate selection as the development of a relationship. *Marriage and Family Living, 23,* 234–240.

Bopp, M. J., & Weeks, G. R. (1984). Dialectical metatheory in family therapy. *Family Process, 23,* 49–61.

Boss, P. G. (1983). The marital relationship: Boundaries and ambiguities. In H. I. McCubbin & C. R. Figley (Eds.), *Stress and the family: Coping with normative transitions* (Vol. 1, pp. 26–40). New York: Brunner/Mazel.

Boszormenyi-Nagy, I., & Spark, G. M. (1984). *Invisible loyalties.* New York: Brunner/Mazel.

Braiker, H. B., & Kelley, H. H. (1979). Conflict in the development of close relationships. In R. L. Burgess & T. L. Huston (Eds.), *Social exchange in developing relationships* (pp. 135–169). New York: Academic Press.

Broderick, C., & Pulliam-Krager, H., (1978). Family process and child outcomes. In W. R. Burr, R. Hill, R. I. Nye, & I. L. Reiss (Eds.), *Contemporary theory about the family* (Vol. 1, pp. 604–614). New York: The Free Press.

Broderick, C., & Smith, J. (1979). General systems approach to the family. In W. R. Burr, R. Hill, F. I. Nye, & I. L. Reiss (Eds.), *Contemporary theories about the family* (Vol. 2, pp. 112–139). New York: The Free Press.

Brody, H. (1987). *Stories of sickness.* New Haven: Yale University Press.

Brown, L. M., & Gilligan, C. (1992).

Meeting at the crossroads: Women's psychology and girls' development. Cambridge, MA: Harvard University Press.

Bruner, J. (1990). *Acts of meaning.* Cambridge, MA: Harvard University Press.

Bryson, J., & Bryson, R. (Eds.). (1978). *Dual-career couples.* New York: Human Sciences.

Buckley, W. (1967). *Sociology and modern systems theory.* Englewood Cliffs, NJ: Prentice-Hall.

Buerkel-Rothfuss, N. (1981). Coordination: A rules-based approach to human communication. *Michigan Speech Association Journal, 16,* 20–36.

Buerkel-Rothfuss, N., Greenberg, B. S., Atkin, C. K., & Neuendorf, K. (1982, Spring). Learning about the family from television. *Journal of Communication, 32 (3),* 191–201.

Burgoon, J. K. (1985). Nonverbal signals. In M. L. Knapp & G. R. Miller (Eds.), *Handbook of interpersonal communication* (pp. 344–390), Beverly Hills, CA: Sage.

Burr, W. R., Herrin, D. A., Day, R. D., Beutler, I. V., & Leigh, G. K. (1987, November). *An epistemological basis for primary explanations in family science.* Paper presented at the annual meeting of the National Council on Family Relations, Atlanta, GA.

Burr, W. R., Leigh, G. K., Day, R. D., & Constantine, J. (1979). Symbolic interaction and the family. In W. R. Burr, R. Hill, F. I. Nye, & I. L. Reiss (Eds.), *Contemporary theories about the family* (Vol. 2, pp. 42–111). New York: The Free Press.

Byng-Hall, J. (1973). Family myths used as defense in conjoint family therapy. *British Journal of Medical Psychology, 46,* 239–250.

Byrne, D. (1969). Attitudes and attraction. In L. Berkowitz (Ed.), *Advances in experimental social psychology* (Vol. 4). New York: Academic Press.

Byrne, D. (1971). *The attraction paradigm.* New York: Academic Press.

Campbell, J., with Moyers, B. (1988). *The power of myth.* New York: Doubleday.

Capra, F. (1982). *The turning point.* New York: Bantam Books.

Carey, J. (1989). *Communication as culture: Essays on media and society.* Boston: Unwin and Hyman.

Carter, E. A., & McGoldrick, M. (Eds.). (1980). *The family life cycle: A framework for family therapy.* New York: Gardner Press.

Chandler, T. A. (1986). *A profile of interaction in acute battering incidents.* Unpublished doctoral dissertation, Purdue University.

Chang, J., & Phillips, M. (1993). Michael White and Steve deShazer: New directions in family therapy. In S. Gilligan & R. Price (Eds.), *Therapeutic conversations* (pp. 95–111). New York: Norton.

Charny, I. W. (1986). An existential/dialectical model for analyzing marital functioning and interaction. *Family Process, 25,* 571–589.

Charny, I. W. (1992). *Existential/dialectical marital therapy.* New York: Brunner/Mazel.

Chilman, C. S., Nunnally, E. W., & Cox, F. M. (Eds.). (1988). *Variant family forms.* Newbury Park, CA: Sage.

Cissna, K. N., Cox, D. E., & Bochner, A. P. (1989). The dialectic of marital and parental relationships within the stepfamily. *Communication Monographs, 57,* 44–61.

Cohler, B., & Grunebaum, H. (1981). *Mothers, grandmothers, and daughters: Personality and child care in three-generation families.* New York: Wiley.

Coles, R. (1989). *The call of stories: Teaching and the moral imagination.* Boston: Houghton Mifflin.

Combs, G., & Freedman, J. (1990). *Symbol, story, and ceremony.* New York: Norton.

Compton, N., & Hall, O. (1972). *Foundations of home economics research: A human ecological approach.* Minneapolis, MN: Burgess Publishing.

Constantine, L. L. (1983). Dysfunction and failure in open family systems, I: Application of a unified theory. *Journal of Marriage and the Family, 45,* 725–738.

Constantine, L. L. (1986). *Family paradigms: The practice of theory in family therapy*. New York: Guilford Press.

Cooper, P. J. (1988). *Speech communication for the classroom teacher* (3rd ed.). Scottsdale, AZ: Gorsuch Scarisbrick, Publishers.

Craddock, A. E. (1984). Correlations between marital role expectations and relationship satisfaction among engaged couples. In D. H. Olson & B. C. Miller (Eds.), *Family studies review yearbook* (Vol. 2, pp. 361–374). Beverly Hills, CA: Sage.

Crane, D. R., et al. (1987). Diagnosing relationships with spatial distance: An empirical test of a clinical principle. *Journal of Marital and Family Therapy, 13,* 307–310.

Cronen, V. E., Pearce, W. B., & Harris, L. M. (1979). The logic of the coordinated management of meaning: A rules-based approach to the first course in interpersonal communication. *Communication Education, 28,* 22–38.

Crites, S. (1986). Storytime: Recollecting the past and projecting the future. In T. Sarbin (Ed.), *Narrative psychology: The storied nature of human conduct* (pp. 152–173). New York: Praeger.

Cuber, J. F., & Harroff, P. (1965). *The significant Americans: A study of sexual behavior among the affluent.* New York: Appleton-Century-Crofts.

Cushman, D. P., & Craig, R. T. (1976). Communication systems: Interpersonal implications. In G. R. Miller (Ed.), *Explorations in interpersonal communication* (pp. 37–57). Beverly Hills, CA: Sage.

Cushman, D. P., & Whiting, G. (1972). An approach to communication theory: Toward consensus in rules. *Journal of Communication, 22,* 217–238.

Dailey, W. O. (1992, May). *Explaining a family conflict dialectic.* Paper presented at the annual meeting of the International Communication Association, Miami, FL.

Dell, P. (1982). Beyond homeostasis: Toward a concept of coherence. *Family Process, 21,* 21–41.

Demo, D. H. (1987). Family relations and the self-esteem of adolescents and their parents. *Journal of Marriage and the Family, 49,* 705–715.

Denzin, N. (1989). *Interpretive interactionism.* Newbury Park, CA: Sage.

Dodson, J. (1988). Conceptualization of black families. In H. P. McAdoo (Ed.), *Black families* (pp. 63–81). Newbury Park, CA: Sage.

Doherty, W. J. (1986). Quanta, quarks, and families: Implications of quantum physics for family research. *Family Process, 25,* 249–264.

Duhl, B. S. (1983). *From the inside out and other metaphors: Creative and integrative approaches to training in systems thinking.* New York: Brunner/Mazel.

Duvall, E. (1977). *Marriage and family development.* Philadelphia, PA: J. B. Lippincott.

Eisler, R. (1988). *The chalice and the blade.* New York: Harper & Row.

Ellis, C., & Bochner, A. P. (1992). Telling and performing personal stories: The constraints of choice in abortion. In C. Ellis & M. G. Flaherty (Eds.), *Investigating subjectivity: Research on lived experience* (pp. 79–101). Newbury Park, CA: Sage.

Ferreira, A. J. (1963). Family myths and homeostasis. *Archives of General Psychiatry, 9,* 457–463.

Ferreira, A. J., & Winter, W. D. (1968). Information exchange and silence in normal and abnormal families. *Family Process, 7,* 251–276.

Fink, D. S. (1993). *Father-son relationships: Relational closeness and fathers' parenting style as predictors of sons' expected parenting style and communicator style similarity.* Unpublished master's thesis, Central Michigan University.

Fink, D. S., Buerkel-Rothfuss, N., & Buerkel, R. (1993, November). *Father-daughter relational closeness and similarity of communicator style.* Paper presented at the annual meeting of the Speech Communication Association, Miami, FL.

Fishbein, M., & Ajzen, I. (1975). *Belief, attitude, intention, and behavior: An introduction to theory and research.* Reading, MA: Addison-Wesley.

Fitzpatrick, M. A. (1977). A typological approach to enduring relationships. In

B. Rubin (Ed.), *Communication Yearbook 1* (pp. 263–275). Rutgers: Transaction.

Fitzpatrick, M. A. (1988). *Between husbands and wives.* Beverly Hills, CA: Sage.

Fitzpatrick, M. A., & Badzinski, D. M. (1985). All in the family: Interpersonal communication in kin relationships. In M. L. Knapp & G. R. Miller (Eds.), *Handbook of interpersonal communication* (pp. 687–736). Beverly Hills, CA: Sage.

Ford, F. (1983). Rules: The invisible family. *Family Process, 22,* 135–145.

Framo, J. (1992). *Family-of-origin therapy.* New York: Brunner/Mazel.

Franks, A. (1993). The rhetoric of self-change: Illness experience as narrative. *The Sociological Quarterly, 34,* 39–52.

Freedle, R. (1975). Dialogue and inquiring systems: The development of a social logic. *Human Development, 19,* 97–118.

Freeman, J. C., & Lobovits, D. (1993). The turtle with wings. In S. Friedman (Ed.), *The new language of change: Constructive collaboration in psychotherapy* (pp. 188–225). New York: Guilford.

Friedman, S. (Ed.). (1993). *The new language of change.* New York: Guilford.

Gelles, R. J. (1979). *Family violence.* Beverly Hills, CA: Sage.

Gelles, R. J. (1980). Violence in the family: A review of research in the seventies. *Journal of Marriage and the Family, 42,* 873–885.

Gelles, R. J., & Maynard, P. E. (1987). A structural family systems approach to intervention in cases of family violence. *Family Relations, 36,* 270–275.

Gelles, R. J., & Straus, M. A. (1988). *Intimate violence.* New York: Simon & Schuster.

Gergen, K. J. (1985). The social constructionist movement in modern psychology. *American Psychologist, 40,* 266–275.

Gergen, K. J. (1992). Toward a postmodern psychology. In S. Kvale (Ed.), *Psychology and postmodernism* (pp. 17–30). Newbury Park, CA: Sage.

Giles-Sims, J. (1983). *Wife-battering: A systems theory approach.* New York: Guilford Press.

Gilligan, C. (1982). *In a different voice.* Cambridge, MA: Harvard University Press.

Gilligan, S., & Price, R. (Eds.) (1993). *Therapeutic conversations.* New York: Norton.

Glenwick, D. S., & Mowerey, J. D. (1986). When parent becomes peer: Loss of intergenerational boundaries in single parent families. *Family Relations, 35,* 57–62.

Goldberg, J. G. (1993). *The dark side of love.* New York: Putnam.

Goodrich, T. J., Rampage, C., Ellman, B., & Halstead, K. (1988). *Feminist family therapy: A casebook.* New York: Norton.

Gottlieb, G. (1968). *The logic of choice.* New York: Macmillan.

Gottman, J. (1982). Emotional responsiveness in marital conversations. *Journal of Communication, 32,* 108–120.

Gouldner, V. (1985). Feminism and family therapy. *Family Process, 24,* 31–47.

Guerin, P. J. (1976). Family therapy: The first twenty-five years. In P. J. Guerin (Ed.), *Family therapy: theory and practice* (pp. 2–22). New York: Gardner Press.

Gustafson, J. P. (1992). *Self-delight in a harsh world: The main stories of individual, marital, and family psychology.* New York: Norton.

Haley, J. (1963). *Strategies of psychotherapy.* New York: Grune & Stratton.

Haley, J. (1973). *Uncommon therapy: The psychiatric techniques of Milton H. Erikson, M.D.* New York: Norton.

Haley, J. (1976). *Problem-solving therapy.* New York: Grune & Stratton.

Hall, F. S., & Hall, D. T. (1979). *The two-career couple.* Reading, MA: Addison-Wesley.

Handel, G. (1965). Psychological study of whole families. *Psychological Bulletin, 63,* 19–41.

Hanson, S. L., & Ooms, T. (1991). The economic costs and rewards of two-earner, two-parent families. *Journal of Marriage and the Family, 53,* 622–634.

Hare-Mustin, R. T. (1978). A feminist approach to family therapy. *Family Process, 17,* 181–194.

Harre, R., & Secord, P. F. (1973). *The explanation of social behavior.* Totowa, NJ: Littlefield, Adams.

Harris, L. (1980). Analysis of paradoxical logic: A case study. *Family Process, 19,* 19–44.

Hauser, S. T., with Powers, S. I., & Noam, G. G. (1991). *Adolescents and their families.* New York: The Free Press.

Heilbrun, A. B. (1976). Measurement of masculine and femine sex role identities as independent dimensions. *Journal of Consulting and Clinical Psychology, 44,* 183–190.

Henry, J. (1973). *Pathways to madness.* New York: Vintage Books.

Hess, R., & Handel, G. (1959). *Family worlds.* Chicago: University of Chicago Press.

Hill, R. (1970). *Family development in three generations.* Cambridge, MA: Schenkman.

Hill, R., & Rodgers, R. H. (1964). The developmental approach. In H. T. Christensen (Ed.), *Handbook of marriage and the family* (pp. 171–211). Chicago: Rand McNally.

Hines, P. M., & Boyd-Franklin, N. (1982). Black families. In M. McGoldrick, J. K. Pearce, & J. Giordano (Eds.), *Ethnicity and family therapy* (pp. 84–107). New York: Guilford Press.

Ho, M. K. (1987). *Family therapy with ethnic minorities.* Newbury Park, CA: Sage.

Hoffman, L. (1975). "Enmeshment" and the too richly cross-joined system. *Family Process, 14,* 457–468.

Hoffman, L. (1981). *Foundations in family therapy.* New York: Basic Books.

Hoffman, L. (1990). Constructing realities: An art of lenses. *Family Process, 29,* 1–12.

Hogan, M. J., Buehler, C., & Robinson, B. (1983). In H. I. McCubbin & C. Figley (Eds.), *Stress and the family: Coping with normative transitions* (Vol. 1, pp. 116–132). New York: Brunner/Mazel.

Hook, N., & Paolucci, B. (1970). The family as an ecosystem. *Journal of Home Economics, 62 (5),* 315–318.

Hopper, R., & Naremore, R. (1978). *Children's speech: A practical introduction to communication development* (2nd ed.). New York: Harper & Row.

Huston, T. L., Surra, C. A., Fitzgerald, N. M., & Cate, R. M. (1981). From courtship to marriage: Mate selection as an interpersonal process. In S. Duck & R. Gilmore (Eds.), *Personal relationships 2: Developing personal relationships* (pp. 53–90). New York: Academic Press.

Jackson, D. D. (1965). The study of the family. *Family Process, 4,* 1–20.

Jackson, D. D. (1970). The question of family homeostasis. In D. D. Jackson (Ed.), *Communication, family and marriage* (pp. 1–11). Palo Alto, CA: Science & Behavior Books.

Jackson, D. D. (1977) The myth of normality. In P. Watzlawick & J. H. Weakland (Eds.), *The interactional view* (pp. 157–163). New York: Norton.

Jorgenson, J. (1988, November). *Metaphoric patterns in definitions of "family."* Paper presented at the Speech Communication Association Convention, New Orleans.

Jorgenson, J. (1989, Spring/Fall). Where is the "family" in family communication?: Exploring families' self-definitions. *Journal of Applied Communication Research, 17,* 27–41.

Jorgenson, J. (1993). Mothers who work out of the home. Unpublished personal correspondence with the author.

Jung, C. G. (Ed.). (1964). *Man and his symbols.* New York: Doubleday.

Kantor, D., & Lehr, W. (1975). *Inside the family.* San Francisco, CA: Jossey-Bass.

Kempler, W. (1974). *Principles of gestalt family therapy.* Salt Lake City, UT: Deseret Press.

Kempler, W. (1981). *Experiential psychotherapy within families.* New York: Brunner/Mazel.

Kerckhoff, A. C., & Davis, K. E. (1962). Value consensus and need complementarity in mate selection. *American Sociological Review, 27,* 295–303.

Kerr, M. E., & Bowen, M. (1988). *Family evaluation.* New York: Norton.

Kidwell, J., Fisher, J. L., & Dunham, R.

M. (1983). Parents and adolescents: Push and pull of change. In H. I. McCubbin & C. R. Figley (Eds.), *Stress and the family* (Vol. 1, pp. 74–89). New York: Brunner/Mazel.

Kiesenger, C. (1992). *Discovering me apart from him: An investigation of female scripts of self-development as portrayed in film.* Unpublished paper, University of South Florida.

Kissman, K., & Allen, J. A. (1993). *Single-parent families.* Newbury Park: Sage.

Kline, M., Johnston, J. R., & Tschann, J. M. (1991). The long shadow of marital conflict: A model of children's postdivorce adjustment. *Journal of Marriage and the Family, 53,* 297–309.

Knapp, M. L. (1978). *Social intercourse: From greeting to goodbye.* Boston: Allyn & Bacon.

Kramer, J. R. (1985). *Family interfaces: Transgenerational patterns.* New York: Brunner/Mazel.

Krueger, D. L. (1985). Communication patterns and equalitarian decision making in dual-career couples. *Western Journal of Speech Communication, 49,* 126–145.

Krueger, D. L., & Ashe, N. (1986, November). *Metaphor as an index of marital culture.* Paper presented to the Speech Communication Association Convention, Chicago.

Laing, R. D. (1967). *The politics of experience.* New York: Ballantine Books.

Laing, R. D. (1972). *The politics of the family.* New York: Vintage Books.

Lakoff, G., & Johnson, M. (1980). *Metaphors we live by.* Chicago: University of Chicago Press.

Laosa, L., & Sigel, I. (1982). *Families as learning environments for children.* New York: Plenum.

LaRossa, R. (1986). *Becoming a parent.* Beverly Hills, CA: Sage.

Laszlo, E. (1972). *Introduction to systems philosophy: Toward a new paradigm of contemporary thought.* New York: Gordon & Breach.

Lederer, W. J., & Jackson, D. D. (1968). *The mirages of marriage.* New York: Norton.

Lennard, H., & Bernstein, A. (1969). *Patterns in human interaction.* San Francisco, CA: Jossey-Bass.

Lerner, G. (1986). *The creation of patriarchy.* New York: Oxford.

Leslie, L. A., & Glossick, M. L. (1992). Changing set: Teaching family therapy from a feminist perspective. *Family Relations, 41,* 256–263.

Levinger, G. (1974). A three-level approach to attraction: Toward an understanding of pair relatedness. In T. L. Huston (Ed.), *Foundations of interpersonal attraction.* New York: Academic Press.

Lewis, D. K. (1969). *Convention: A philosophical study.* Cambridge, MA: Harvard University Press.

Libow, J. A., Raskin, P. A., & Caust, B. L. (1982). Feminist and family systems therapy: Are they irreconcilable? *American Journal of Family Therapy, 10,* 3–12.

Littlejohn, S. W. (1992). *Theories of human communication* (4th ed.). Belmont, CA: Wadsworth.

Luepnitz, D. A. (1988). *The family interpreted: Psychoanalysis, feminism, and family therapy.* New York: Basic Books.

Lystad, M. (1986). *Violence in the home: Interdisciplinary perspectives.* New York: Brunner/Mazel.

MacEwen, K. E., & Barling, J. (1991). Effects of maternal employment experiences on children's behavior via mood, cognitive difficulties, and parenting behavior. *Journal of Marriage and the Family, 53,* 635–644.

MacKinnon, L. K., & Miller, D. (1987). The new epistemology and the Milan approach: Feminist sociopolitical considerations. *Journal of Marital and Family Therapy, 13,* 139–155.

Macklin, E. D. (1983). Nonmarital heterosexual cohabitation: An overview. In E. D. Macklin & R. H. Rubin (Eds.), *Contemporary families and alternative lifestyles: Handbook on research and theory.* Beverly Hills, CA: Sage.

Madanes, C. (1983). *Strategic family theory.* San Francisco, CA: Jossey-Bass.

Massey, R. (1986). What/who is the family system? *American Journal of Family Therapy, 14*(1), 23–39.

May, R. (1991). *The cry for myth.* New York: Norton.

McAdoo, H. P. (Ed.). (1988). *Black families* (2nd ed.). Newbury Park, CA: Sage.

McGoldrick, M., & Carter, E. (1982). The family life cycle. In F. Walsh (Ed.), *Normal family processes* (pp. 167–195). New York: Guilford Press.

McGoldrick, M., Pearce, J. K., & Giordano, J. (Eds.). (1982). *Ethnicity and family therapy.* New York: Guilford Press.

McLain, R., & Weigert, A. (1979). Toward a phenomenological sociology of family: A programmatic essay. In W. R. Burr, R. Hill, F. I. Nye, & I. L. Reiss (Eds.), *Contemporary theories about the family* (Vol. 2, pp. 160–205). New York: The Free Press.

McNamee, S. (1989). Creating new narratives in family therapy: An application of social constructionism. *Journal of Applied Communication Research, 17,* 92–112.

McNamee, S., & Cronen, V. E. (1981, November). *The ability of untrained subjects to understand the dynamics of convoluted interpersonal logic.* Paper presented at the annual meeting of the National Council on Family Relations, Milwaukee, WI.

McNamee, S., & Gergen, K. J. (1992). *Therapy as social construction.* London: Sage.

Mesarovic, M. D. (1970). *Theory of hierarchical multi-level systems.* New York: Academic Press.

Micklin, M. (1973). *Population, environment, and social organization: Current issues in human ecology.* Hinsdale, IL: The Dryden Press.

Millar, F. E., & Rogers, L. E. (1976). A relational approach to interpersonal communication. In G. Miller (Ed.), *Explorations in interpersonal communication* (pp. 87–203). Beverly Hills, CA: Sage.

Miller, G. R., & Knapp, M. L. (1985). Background and current trends in the study of interpersonal communication. In G. R. Miller & M. L. Knapp (Eds.), *Handbook of interpersonal communication* (pp. 7–23). Beverly Hills, CA: Sage.

Miller, J. G. (1978). *Living systems.* New York: McGraw-Hill.

Miller, S., Wackman, D., Nunnally, E., & Miller, P. (1988). *Connecting with self and others.* Littleton, CO: Interpersonal Communication Programs, Inc.

Minuchin, S. (1974). *Families and family therapy.* Cambridge, MA: Harvard University Press.

Minuchin, S., & Fishman, C. H. (1981). *Family therapy techniques.* Cambridge, MA: Harvard University Press.

Moen, P. (1991). Transitions in mid-life: Women's work and family roles. *Journal of Marriage and the Family, 53,* 135–150.

Montague, A. (1971). *Touching: The human significance of the skin.* New York: Harper & Row.

Montgomery, B. (1992). Communication as the interface between couples and culture. In S. Deetz (Ed.), *Communication yearbook 15* (pp. 475–507). Newbury Park, CA: Sage.

Morgaine, C. A. (1992). Alternative paradigms for helping families change themselves. *Family Relations, 41,* 12–17.

Muller, A. (1987). *Parents matter: Parents' relationships with lesbian daughters and gay sons.* Tallahassee, FL: Naiad Press.

Napier, A. Y. (1988). *The fragile bond.* New York: Harper & Row.

Napier, A. Y., & Whitaker, C. A. (1978). *The family crucible.* New York: Harper & Row.

Nichols, M. P. (1987). *The self in the system.* New York: Brunner/Mazel.

Nock, S. L. (1988). The family and hierarchy. *Journal of Marriage and the Family, 50,* 957–966.

Noller, P., & Fitzpatrick, M. A. (1993). *Communication in family relationships.* Englewood Cliffs, NJ: Prentice-Hall.

Norton, A. J., & Glick, P. G. (1986). One parent families: A social and economic profile. *Family Relations, 35,* 9–17.

Nye, F. I., & Bernardo, F. M. (1973). *The family.* New York: Macmillan.

Odum, E. (1971). *Fundamentals of ecology* (3rd ed.). Philadelphia, PA: W. B.

Saunders.

Olson, D. H., McCubbin, H. I., Barnes, H. L., Larsen, A. S., Muxen, M. J., & Wilson, M. A. (1983). *Families: What makes them work.* Beverly Hills, CA: Sage.

Olson, D. H., Sprenkle, D., & Russell, C. (1979). Circumplex model of marital and family systems I: Cohesion and adaptability dimension, family types, and clinical applications. *Family Process, 18,* 3–28.

Osherson, S. (1986). *Finding our fathers: The unfinished business of manhood.* New York: The Free Press.

Owen, W. F. (1985). Thematic metaphors in relational communication: A conceptual framework. *Western Journal of Speech Communication, 49,* 1–13.

Pagelow, M. D. (1984). *Family violence.* New York: Praeger.

Palazzoli, M. S., Boscolo, L., & Cecchin, G. (1978). *Paradox and counterparadox.* New York: Jason Aronson.

Palazzoli, M. S., Cirillo, S., Selvini, M., & Sorrentino, A. M. (1989). *Family games: General models of psychotic processes in the family.* New York: Norton.

Paolucci, B., Hall, O. A., & Axinn, N. (1977). *Family decision making: An ecosystem approach.* New York: Wiley.

Parry, A. (1991). A universe of stories. *Family Process, 30,* 37–54.

Pearce, W. B. (1976). The coordinated management of meaning: A rules based theory of interpersonal communication. In G. R. Miller (Ed.), *Explorations in interpersonal communication* (pp. 17–36). Beverly Hills, CA: Sage.

Pearce, W. B., & Cronen, V. (1980). *Communication, action, and meaning.* New York: Praeger.

Pepitone-Rockwell, F. (1980). *Dual-career couples.* Beverly Hills, CA: Sage.

Pepper, S. (1972). Discussion: Systems philosophy as a world hypothesis. *Philosophy and Phenomenological Research, 32,* 548–553.

Pillari, V. (1986). *Pathways to family myths.* New York: Brunner/Mazel.

Pillari, V. (1991). *Scapegoating in families.* New York: Brunner/Mazel.

Pincus, L., & Dare, C. (1978). *Secrets in the family.* New York: Pantheon Books.

Pinsof, W. M. (1984). Integrative problem-centered therapy: Toward the synthesis of family and individual psychotherapies. In D. H. Olson & B. C. Miller (Eds.), *Family studies review yearbook: Vol. 1* (pp. 587–603). Beverly Hills, CA: Sage.

Rabkin, R. (1967). Uncoordinated communication between marriage partners. *Family Process, 6,* 10–15.

Raush, H. L., Barry, W. A., Hertel, R. K., & Swain, M. (1974). *Communication, conflict, and marriage.* San Francisco, CA: Jossey-Bass.

Raush, H. L., Grief, A. C., & Nugent, J. (1979). Communication in couples and families. In W. Burr, R. Hill, F. I. Nye, & I. L. Reiss (Eds.), *Contemporary theories about the family* (Vol. 1, pp. 468–492). New York: Free Press.

Rawlins, W. (1983). Negotiating close friendship: The dialectic of conjunctive freedoms. *Human Communication Research, 9,* 255–266.

Rawlins, W. (1989, Spring/Fall). Metaphorical views of interaction in families of origin and future families. *Journal of Applied Communication Research, 17,* 124–154.

Reiss, D. (1981). *The family's construction of reality.* Cambridge, MA: Harvard University Press.

Richardson, L. (1990). Narrative and sociology. *Journal of Contemporary Ethnography, 19,* 116–135.

Riessman, C. (1990). *Divorce talk: Men and women make sense of personal relationships.* New Brunswick, NJ: Rutgers University Press.

Rogers, L. E. (1972). *Dyadic systems and transactional communication in a family context.* Unpublished doctoral dissertation, Michigan State University.

Rogers, L. E. (1983, November). *Analyzing relational communication: Implications of a pragmatic approach.* Paper presented at the annual meeting of the Speech Communication Association, Washington, D. C.

Rogers, L. E. (1984). Research potentials in family communication. In J. Yerby (Ed.), *Research directions in family* communication: *Proceedings of the Northwestern Conference on Family Communication Research.* Annandale, VA: Speech Communication Association.

Rogers, L. E., & Bagarozzi, D. A. (1983). An overview of relational communication and implications for therapy. In D. Bagarozzi, A. P. Jurich, & R. Jackson (Eds.), *Marital and family therapy: New perspectives in theory, research and practice.* New York: Human Sciences Press.

Rogers, L. E., Courtwright, J. A., & Millar, F. E. (1980). Message control intensity: Rationale and preliminary findings. *Communication Monographs, 47,* 201–219.

Rogers, L. E., & Farace, R. V. (1975). Analysis of relational communication in dyads: New measurement procedures. *Human Communication Research, 1,* 222–239.

Ronai, C. R. (1994). Multiple reflections of child sex abuse: An argument for a layered account. *Journal of Contemporary Ethnography,* in press.

Rosenblatt, P. C. (1994). *Metaphors of family systems theory: Toward new constructions.* New York: Guilford.

Rubin, J., & Rubin, C. (1989). *When families fight.* New York: William Morrow.

Rubin, L. (1976). *Worlds of pain: Life in a working class family.* New York: Basic Books.

Sabourin, T. C., Infante, D., & Rudd, J. (1990, November). *Argumentativeness and verbal aggression in interspousal violence: A test of the argumentative skill of deficiency model using couple data.* Paper presented at the annual meeting of the Speech Communication Association, Chicago, IL.

Sager, C. J. (1976). *Marriage contracts and couple therapy.* New York: Brunner/Mazel.

Sager, C. J. (1981). Couples therapy and marriage contracts. In A. S. Gurman & D. P. Kniskern (Eds.), *Handbook of family therapy* (pp. 85–130). New York: Brunner/Mazel.

Satir, V. (1972). *Peoplemaking.* Palo Alto, CA: Science & Behavior Books.

Satir, V. (1983). *Conjoint family therapy* (3rd ed.). Palo Alto, CA: Science & Behavior Books.

Sears, H. A., & Galambos, N. L. (1992). Women's work conditions and marital adjustment in two-earner couples: A structural model. *Journal of Marriage and the Family, 54,* 789–797.

Shimanoff, S. B. (1980). *Communication rules: Theory and research.* Beverly Hills, CA: Sage.

Shon, S. P., & Ja, D. Y. (1982). Asian families. In M. McGoldrick, J. K. Pearce, & J. Giordano (Eds.), *Ethnicity and the family* (pp. 208–228). New York: Guilford Press.

Sieburg, E. (1985). *Family communication: An integrated systems approach.* New York: Gardner Press.

Sillars, A. L., & Scott, M. D. (1983). Interpersonal perception between intimates: An integrative review. *Human Communication Research, 10,* 153–176.

Sillars, A. L., & Weisberg, J. (1987). Conflict as a social skill. In M. E. Roloff & G. R. Miller (Eds.), *Interpersonal processes: New directions in communication research.* Newbury Park, CA: Sage.

Sillars, A. L., & Wilmot, W. W. (1989). Marital communication across the lifespan. In J. F. Nussbaum (Ed.), *Lifespan communication: Normative processes* (pp. 225–253). Hillsdale, NJ: Lawrence Erlbaum.

Sillars, A. L., & Zietlow, P. H. (1993). Investigations of marital communication and lifespan development. In N. Coupland & J. Nussbaum (Eds.), *Discourse and lifespan development.* Newbury Park, CA: Sage.

Sillars, A. L., Burggraf, C. S., Yost, S., & Zietlow, P. H. (1992). Conversational themes and marital relationship definitions: Quantitative and qualitative investigations. *Human Communication Research, 19,* 124–154.

Sillars, A. L., Weisberg, J., Burggraf, C. S., & Wilson, E. A. (1987). Content themes in marital conversations. *Human Communication Research, 13,* 495–528.

Simmel, G. (1950). *Soziologie* (4th ed.). (K. H. Wolff, Ed. & Trans.). Glencoe,

IL: Free Press. (Original work published 1908.)

Sluzki, C. (1983). Process, structure, and world views: Toward an integrated view of systemic models in family therapy. *Family Process, 22,* 469–476.

Sluzki, C. E. (1992). Transformations: A blueprint for narrative changes in therapy. *Family Process, 31,* 217–230.

Smith, J. M., & Smith, D. E. P. (1976). *Child management.* Champaign, IL: Research Press.

Socha, T. J. (1991, November). *The parental guilt episode: Exploring parents' messages.* Paper presented at the annual meeting of the Speech Communication Association, Atlanta, GA.

Speer, D. (1970). Family stress: Morphostasis and morphogenesis, or is homeostasis enough? *Family Process, 9,* 259–278.

Stafford, L., & Bayer, C. L. (1993). *Interaction between parents and children.* Newbury Park, CA: Sage.

Stamp, G. H. (1994). The appropriation of the parental role through communication during the transition to parenthood. *Communication Monographs, 61,* 89–112.

Stanton, M. D. (1980). Family therapy: Systems approaches. In G. Scholevar, R. Benson, & F. Blinda (Eds.), *Treatment of emotional disorders in children and adolescents.* New York: Spectrum.

Stanton, M. D. (1981a). Family treatment approaches to drug abuse problems: A review. *Family Process, 18,* 251–280.

Stanton, M. D. (1981b). Strategic approaches to family therapy. In A. Gurman & D. Kniskern (Eds.), *The handbook of family therapy* (pp. 361–402). New York: Brunner/Mazel.

Steier, F. M. (1989, Spring/Fall). Toward a radical and ecological constructivist approach to family communication. *Journal of Applied Communication, 17,* 1–26.

Steier, F. M., Stanton, D., & Todd, T. C. (1982). Patterns of turn-taking and alliance formation in family communication. *Journal of Communication, 32 (3),* 148–160.

Steinglass, P. (1978). The conceptualization of marriage from a systems theory perspective. In T. J. Paolino & B. S. McCrady, *Marriage and marital therapy: Psychoanalytic, behavioral, and systems theory perspectives* (pp. 298–365). New York: Brunner/Mazel.

Steinmetz, S. K. (1977). *The cycle of violence: assertive, aggressive, and abusive family interaction.* New York: Praeger.

Stephen, T. (1984). A symbolic exchange framework for the development of intimate relationships. *Human Relations, 37,* 393–408.

Stephen, T. (1992). Communication, intimacy, and the course of time: Commentary on Montgomery. In S. A. Deetz (Ed.), *Communication yearbook 15* (pp. 522–534). Newbury Park, CA: Sage.

Stephen, T. (1994). Communication and the shifting context of intimacy: Marriage, meaning, and modernity. *Communication Theory,* i press.

Stephen, T., & Enholm, D. K. (1987). On linguistic and social forms: Correspondences between metaphoric and intimate relationships. *Western Journal of Speech Communication, 51,* 329–344.

Stephen, T., & Harrison, T. (1993). Interpersonal communication, theory, and history. *Communication Theory, 3,* 163–172.

Stewart, L., Cooper, P., & Friedley, S. (1986). *Communication between the sexes.* Scottsdale, AZ: Gorsuch Scarisbrick, Publishers.

Stierlin, H. (1973). Group fantasies and family myths: Some theoretical and practical aspects. *Family Process, 12,* 111–125.

Stone, E. (1988). *Black sheep and kissing cousins: How our family stories shape us.* New York: Random House, Times Books.

Straus, M. A., Gelles, R. J., & Steinmetz, S. K. (1980). *Behind closed doors: Violence in the American family.* Garden City, NY: Doubleday/Anchor Press.

Stryker, S. (1972, Spring). Symbolic interaction theory: A review and some suggestions for comparative family research. *Journal of Comparative Family Studies, 3,* 17–32.

Sue, D. W., & Sue, D. (1990). *Counseling the culturally different* (2nd ed). New York: Norton.

Sunnafrank, M. (1984). A communication-based perspective on attitude similarity and interpersonal attraction in early acquaintance. *Communication Monographs, 372–380.*

Taggert, M. (1985). The feminist critique in epistemological perspective: Questions of context in family therapy. *Journal of Marriage and the Family, 11,* 113–126.

Tannen, D. (1986). *That's not what I meant! How conversational style makes or breaks your relations with others.* New York: William Morrow.

Tannen, D. (1990). *You just don't understand: Women and men in conversation.* New York: William Morrow.

Terkelsen, K. G. (1980). Toward a theory of the family life cycle. In E. A. Carter & M. McGoldrick (Eds.), *The family life cycle: A framework for family therapy* (pp. 21–52). New York: Gardner Press.

Turner, R. H. (1970). *Family interaction.* New York: Wiley.

Von Foerster, H. (1984). On constructing a reality. In P. Watzlawick (Ed.), *The invented reality* (pp. 41–61). New York: Norton.

Walker, L. E. (1979). *The battered woman.* New York: Harper & Row.

Walsh, F. (Ed.). (1982). *Normal family processes.* New York: Guilford Press.

Walsh, F. (Ed.). (1993). *Normal family processes* (2nd ed.). New York: Guilford.

Walters, M., Carter, B., Papp, P., & Silverstein, O. (1988). *The invisible web: Gender patterns in family relationships.* New York: Guilford Press.

Watzlawick, P. (1976). *How real is real?* New York: Random House, Vintage Books.

Watzlawick, P., Beavin, J. H., & Jackson, D. D. (1967). *Pragmatics of human communication.* New York: Norton.

Weakland, J. H. (1981). One thing leads to another. In C. Wilder-Mott & J. H. Weakland (Eds.), *Rigor and imagination: Essays from the legacy of Gregory Bateson* (pp. 43–64). New York:

Praeger.

Weeks, G. R. (1986). Individual-system dialectic. *The American Journal of Family Therapy, 14,* 5–12.

Weiss, R. S. (1979a). *Going it alone: The family life and social situation of the single parent.* New York: Basic Books.

Weiss, R. S. (1979b). Growing up a little faster: The experience of growing up in a single-parent household. *Journal of Social Issues, 35,* 97–111.

Weiss, R. S. (1982). Attachment in adult life. In C. M. Parkes & J. Stevenson-Hinde (Eds.), *The place of attachment in human behavior.* New York: Basic Books.

Whitchurch, G. G. (1987, July). *Linkages in conjugal violence and communication: A review and critical appraisal.* Paper presented at the third national Family Violence Conference for Researchers, Durham, NH.

White, M. (1993). Deconstruction and therapy. In S. Gilligan & R. Price (Eds.), *Therapeutic conversations* (pp. 22–61). New York: Norton.

White, M., & Epston, D. (1990). *Narrative means to therapeutic ends.* New York: Norton.

Williamson, D. S. (1991). *The intimacy paradox: Personal authority in the family system.* New York: Guilford Press.

Wilmot, W. W. (1987). *Dyadic communication* (3rd ed.). New York: Random House.

Winch, R. (1977). *Familial organization.* New York: The Free Press.

Wynne, L. C. (1984). The epigenesis of relational systems: A model for understanding family development. *Family Process, 23,* 297–318.

Wynne, L. C., Ryckoff, I., Day, J., & Hirsch, S. (1958). Pseudo-mutuality in the family relations of schizophrenics. *Psychiatry, 21,* 205–220.

Yelsma, P. (1984). Functional conflict management in effective marital adjustment. *Communication Quarterly, 36,* 94–107.

Yerby, J. (1989, Spring/Fall). A conceptual framework for analyzing family metaphors. *Journal of Applied Communication Research, 17,* 42–51.

Yerby, J. (1992, November). *Family systems theory reconsidered: Integrating social construction theory and dialectical process into a systems perspective of family communication*. Paper presented at the annual meeting of the Speech Communication Association, Chicago, IL.

Yerby, J., & Buerkel-Rothfuss, N. (1982, November). *Communication patterns, contradictions, and family functions*. Paper presented at the annual meeting of the Speech Communication Association, Louisville, KY.

Yerby, J., & Stephen, T. (1986, November). *The development and application of an instrument to measure the family's communication environment*. Paper presented at the annual meeting of the Speech Communication Association, Chicago, IL.

Zinker, J. (1977). *Creative process in gestalt therapy*. New York: Brunner/Mazel.

Zuk, G. H. (1965). On the pathology of silencing strategies. *Family Process, 4,* 32–49.

GLOSSARY

access dimensions in the Kantor and Lehr model of family types, those resources of space, time, and energy that the family manipulates to attain specific family system goals.

adaptability dimension in the Olson model of family types that deals with how families manage their resources and relationships at various stages of family development.

addiction form of escalator in premarital relationships in which love is like a potent drug that can produce a constitutional dependency.

alliances subsystems that join together for some generally positive purpose.

alternate the strategy in coping with the identity-relationship dialectic in which a couple goes through different phases of stressing either the stability of the relationship or the personal identities of the partners.

architects of the family the relationship of the husband and wife which provides the foundation of the family.

attachment refers to the social bonds that develop between family members.

attachment/caregiving stage stage at which family members show their affection for and connectedness to one another.

autonomy behavior that represents family members' assertions of their unique identities and self-sufficiencies.

balancing chains provide a compromise between the alternatives of blending (i.e., mutually confirming, reinforcing, overlapping) and differentiating conversational segments.

birth stories stories about each child's conception and birth that often explain how the family feels about the child and how the child fits into the family and establish the family's hopes and dreams for the child.

blending chains conversational segments in which the talk between partners is mutually confirming, reinforcing, and overlapping.

boundary an arbitrary dividing line that defines what is to be considered inside and outside of a given system.

canonical stories stories that express the boundaries of acceptable family practices against which alternative stories or versions are judged.

causality one family member's behavior cannot be said to cause another family member's behavior, but rather is the product of the interdependence of all family members.

change the tendency of family systems to reorganize themselves and adapt new patterns as the family grows, matures, and copes with unexpected events.

closed family family type in the Kantor and Lehr model characterized by closely regulated use of space, time, and energy with rigid boundaries and rigorous screening of inputs and outputs.

coalitions alliances formed as a way to exert power or influence over other family members.

co-constructing stories partners and/or family members share their individual experiences of an event and develop a shared story about their experience.

co-defining reality how marriage partners reconstruct their perceptions, identities, and beliefs through the management of everyday activities.

cohesiveness dimension in the Olson model that deals with the sense of separateness or connectedness in the family.

collective identity a description of how family members characterize or experience the family as a group.

collective memory the repository of the family's history revealed in stories told to a listener(s) for the purpose of remembering a past that was not experienced directly by the listener(s); stories about the past become part of the community's knowledge about itself.

collective stories stories of relationships which are the stories of the couple's life together; e.g., the couple's story, the family story.

commitment form of escalator in premarital relationships referring to private and/or public expressions of the special meaning of the relationship.

communal themes conversational themes that convey a joint or mutually shared description of the relationship; communal themes suggest a sense of togetherness, cooperation, and interdependence.

communicating stage stage in Wynne's model of family development that involves ability to develop shared meaning among family members.

communication approach examines processes, patterns, and sequences of verbal and nonverbal messages in the family.

communication code a set of unspoken principles used to translate words and behavior into meaning.

communication pattern an organized sequence of communication exchanges that tends to be repeated.

community system a system that includes positive and negative influences from the norms, values, and expectations of the community in which the family resides.

competition and increasing tension stage family violence stage marked by an accumulation of unexpressed grievances among family members.

competitive relationships the partners in a marriage continually struggle or compete for control of the relationship.

complementary relationships one partner consistently gives in or relinquishes control of the relationship in certain significant areas.

components the parts that work together to create the system as a whole.

compromise some degree of relationship integrity is achieved, while at the same time, each partner has some degree of independence in managing the identity-relationship dialectic.

congruence the extent to which a couple's expectations are similar or compatible.

connecting links metaphors that translate or frame a specific experience or event into meaning for the family (e.g., a move can be "uprooting" or a "fresh start").

consensus-sensitive family family type in Reiss's typology in which family members share an experience of the environment and of individual differences in the family as threatening.

constitutive rules a form of communication in which one type of message or action counts as or stands for a behavior or attitude at another level of abstraction.

constructionist view a systems and social construction perspective that focuses on meaning-making processes in the family.

content level of a message information about the literal meanings of messages.

context of communication the background and frame of reference that makes up the situation in which the interaction occurs.

contrition and/or withdrawal stage stage in family violence characterized by conciliation after a period of emotional and physical distance.

control patterns a reciprocal process reflected in the behavioral transactions of a couple which describes how the couple has managed control in the relationship; how each partner functions as an equal, subordinate, or superior in various dimensions of their life together.

conversational continuity how family themes or the central recurring concerns and orientations of family members are integrated into their conversations or narratives.

conversational liquidation changing how a friendship is viewed through conversations between marriage partners about a friend.

coordinating a communication code acquiring mutually understood interpretations of the meaning of messages.

couple myths describe myths about the marital relationship which have evolved from the ways in which two partners have integrated their separate set of personal myths into the marriage relationship.

courtship as decision making the decision to marry is a prediction about how one person's life with another will evolve in the future based largely on how it has evolved in the past.

courtship stories stories told by parents to their children which function as a creation myth about the origins of the family, a love story that details the adventures and perils of romance ending in marriage.

creating meaning interpretations, significance, and order are attached to actions and words within the marriage relationship.

crisis event stage stage in family violence involving an escalation of emotions that leads to physical violence.

cultural myths ideal representations of reality and of relationships which we acquire from a particular cultural identification or from the larger environment which influence our values, attitudes, and beliefs about "the way things are."

deconstructing and reframing stories including parts of one's experience that have been neglected or minimized in order to add new elements to or create an alternative to the story that has been told.

developmental leaps in Wynne's model of family, development qualitative shifts in family communication patterns.

dialectical process the process of coping with opposing forces that typically relate to integration versus differentiation and stability versus change including the sometimes contradictory demands made on individuals, role relationships, and the family as a whole.

differential contact the tendency for the field of eligibles to be confined to one's social network.

differentiating chains self-assertive statements and other contributions of family members to conversation which tend to reveal unintegrated perceptions of relationships and irreconcilable points of view, in contrast to conversation which tends to confirm or build on others' comments.

differentiation provides for the unique needs and contributions of various subsystems in the family (i.e., individuals, dyads, and subgroups) and may also compete with the forces of integration in the family.

diffuse boundaries boundaries that fluctuate freely and are easily permeated.

dyadic rules rules that govern behavior in a dyadic relationship.

ecosystem refers to a depiction of all conceivable interrelated systems, from the smallest subsystem to the largest macrosystem, and to the study of the nuclear family system in relationship to its various subsystems and its surrounding environment.

egalitarian leadership an orientation to leadership in the family that provides opportunities for each family member to influence decisions in the family and to legitimately get his/her needs met in a way that promotes the self-worth of all family members.

elaborated communication code includes descriptions and explanations of the personal feelings and unique experiences of family members.

environed unit the system of interest, such as the nuclear family.

environment refers to the larger systems surrounding the system of interest, such as the neighborhood, the city or town, the state, and the various systems operating within those boundaries.

environment-sensitive family family type in Reiss's typology that does not perceive the world as hostile but as responsive to knowledge and mastery.

epigenesis in Wynne's model of family development, the sequential movement of developmental stages in which each stage builds on the skills acquired or on ways of relating achieved at the previous stage.

epiphanies emotionally absorbing and transforming experiences which often become turning points in the lives of family members.

episode a communication event that includes a sequence of actions or messages in which some internal structure or routines can be determined.

equifinality refers to the fact that systems may achieve the same goal through a variety of means.

equilibrium or precompetition stage stage of family violence characterized by moderate levels of temporary stability in which family members maintain enough detachment from one another to avoid provoking each other.

escalators sequences of action that have a built-in momentum pushing a couple toward marriage.

expectations a collection of images, unspoken assumptions, and attitudes about what a partner expects to give in return for what he or she expects to receive in a marriage relationship.

explicit rules rules that are openly discussed and verbally agreed to.

extended family network a system composed of the husband's and the wife's families of origin and the family and environmental factors that influenced them.

extended family rules rules that govern the interactions at the interfaces between the nuclear family and families of origin.

family communication the symbolic, transactional process of generating meaning in the family.

family life cycle describes the sequence of stages of development associated with the passage of time as members of the nuclear family enter, exit, and mature, and the performance of important life tasks that accompany each stage of the cycle.

family life tasks tasks that provide the primary focus for goals, energy, and activity in the family at various stages in the life cycle.

family metaphor a specific event, object, image, or behavior that represents for the family some aspect of their collective identity.

family myths beliefs or attitudes about the family in which experience is selectively remembered or constructed to reflect a specific orientation of importance to the family.

family stories the narratives that family members construct about their lives together.

family system rules rules that govern the behavior of the family as a whole.

family themes describe how the family has oriented itself toward major core issues, ideals, goals, relationships, or values.

family violence spirals of family conflict that escalate into physical attacks upon family members.

fantasy form of escalator in premarital relationships in which the relationship becomes a symbol for a privately held fantasy to which the individual attaches substantial importance.

feedback any response to an operation or behavior that provides information about that operation or behavior.

feedback mechanism sensor that detects signs that the family is moving toward or away from accomplishment of its goals.

filtering process the tendency for individuals to apply different tests of compatibility as they progress toward increased commitment.

focus energy the strategy for coping with the identity–relationship dialectic in which the couple attends to one end of the polarity at the expense of the other.

focusing movement in the relationship the way in which a couple's interactions and activities become more predictable and goal-oriented once they are married.

frame the process of attaching meaning to events and behavior in such a way as to label or categorize the experience; for example, a mother can frame her daughter's behavior as "rebelliousness" or "healthy self-assertion."

functional nature of communication the tendency of communication to achieve goals and produce consequences for the individuals, the relationship, or the family as a whole.

generation of meaning the process by which family members interpret events and each other's behavior on the basis of what the behavior represents in their social world.

goal that which a system attempts to accomplish or achieve at any given point in time.

guilt inducements attempts to control the other person's behavior by making him or her responsible for the discomfort or unfair treatment of other family members.

heterogamy theory of mate selection based on the complementarity of differences between partners.

hierarchy defines the relationships between two or more system boundaries, especially defining differences in responsibility for authority, guidance, and nurturance between parents and children.

hierarchy in family themes refers to the idea that some family themes may be subsumed by or included under broader, more overarching themes.

hierarchy of subsystems a series of ever-smaller subsystems embedded in each other and in the same system.

hierarchy of suprasystems a series of ever-larger suprasystems, each encompassing the others.

historical frame of reference influence of previous interactions in the current interaction.

homogamy theory of mate selection based on similarity of the partners.

ideal image a perception or representation of "how things should be" or "how life is supposed to be," often acquired from experiences in one's family of origin or from cultural myths.

idealization form of escalator in which each person tends to inflate the image of the other.

identity–relationship dialectic situation in which the needs for individual identity and relationship integrity each depend upon the other for their satisfaction, and at the same time, fulfillment of one has the potential to undermine the other.

impasse the family becomes stuck in a cycle of destructive conflict, pain, or anxiety and often resorts to patterns of scapegoating or blaming because it is not able to leave behind previous patterns of functioning and relating that are no longer appropriate for its stage of development.

impersonal themes conversational themes which suggest that a particular relationship is governed by factors that are largely or partly beyond the control of family members.

implicit rules rules that remain unspoken and perhaps not even part of individual family members' conscious awareness until they are violated.

Independents couple type in Fitzpatrick's model that has a high level of companionship and sharing in the marriage but also values individual freedom and subscribes less to traditional male/female roles than do the other types.

individual perceptions, feelings, and cognitions involves the process by which family members take in information from the senses, make interpretations of the data from their unique characteristics and background of experience, react emotionally to those interpretations, and identify behavioral options based on the interpretations.

individual themes conversational themes suggestive of differentiation and separation of family members that may reveal criticisms of personality, role performance, or other issues of a competitive or conflictual nature.

inputs resources and information received and used by the system to perform its designated function or achieve its goals.

integration allows family members to function as a whole or to work together with a significant degree of connectedness; often competes with the forces of differentiation in the family.

interactional view a systems perspective that focuses on the the transaction of messages in the family system.

interdependence each family member's behavior influences and is influenced by every other family member's behavior; also the extent to which family members find support, get their needs met, and establish interests, attitudes, and goals that are congruent with those of other family members.

interfaces the points at which influence occurs between two subsystems or systems.

intergenerational influences communication between the generations, the influences of one generation on the next, or the transmission of patterns of relating from one generation to the next.

interpersonal distance–sensitive family family type in Reiss's typology in which family members perceive their interactions with the environment and the problems presented by the environment as opportunities for family members to demonstrate their individual autonomy and independence.

intimacy sharing secrets, revealing vulnerabilities, and intense emotional involvement with one another that makes the family unique as a communication context.

intimacy stage stage in Wynne's model of family development that involves intense emotional sharing and high levels of self-disclosure.

involvement form of escalator in premarital relationships in which interpersonal sequences have the effect of coordinating one individual's activities and plans with others'.

joint problem-solving stage stage in Wynne's model of family development in which family members are able to develop informal role structures, coordinate task activities, and manage differences and conflicts in the family.

linear causality a person, an object, a series of events, or a set of variables is perceived as being responsible for a particular outcome: A causes B.

longevity of family influence the influence that the family has on family members over the course of their lives.

marriage contract identifies what each partner expects to get in return for what he or she is expected to give or do for the partner.

meaning-making the way that meanings are coordinated in the family through the family's communication.

meanings values, beliefs, interpretations of events, and constructions of reality that family members attach to people, events, and behaviors.

metacommunication family members' communication about their communication.

metarules rules about rules (who can make them, who can break them, etc.), often unconscious agreements that identify who has the right to establish certain rules.

mixed couple couple in which the husband's definition of the relationship is different from the wife's.

momentum the tendency for a couple to be propelled toward marriage by events that seem "bigger than both of them."

moral lessons a function of family stories that is related to promoting the conscience of family members.

morphogenesis a family system's tendency to change as it evolves over time.

morphostasis a family system's tendency to seek stability.

multigenerational emphasizes the hierarchical nature of relationships between parents and children and the influence of the family of origin.

mutual influence each person in an interaction situation influences the behavior of the other person at the same time that he or she is influenced by that person.

mutuality stage stage in Wynne's model of family development in which there is recognition by family members that previous forms of relating are no longer adequate and new patterns must be developed.

narrowing alternatives the ways in which commitment to the marital relationship typically limits options for the partners.

nonsummativity because the whole is greater than the sum of the parts, a family system cannot be understood by summing up the characteristics of individual members.

nonverbal communication nonlinguistic forms of communication including facial expressions, vocal cues, eye contact, gestures, posture, touch, odor, physical appearance, dress, silence, and the use of space, time, and objects.

nonvolition the fact that family members do not choose to be born into a specific family makes the family unique.

norm of exclusivity a relationship rule in which each partner agrees to seek sexual and emotional intimacy within their relationship only.

objectification a premarital relationship begins to be perceived as something that is as objectively "real" as the individuals who constitute it.

open family family type in the Kantor and Lehr model in which many inputs are sought and there is much interaction with the outside environment; characterized by flexible use of space, time, and energy.

organization a description of the structure that exists among interdependent parts and patterns that reinforce and reflect how family members function as equals, subordinates, or superiors in various relationships.

outputs outcomes or by-products of the system's activity that are returned to the environment.

paradigm statements or aphorisms that suggest an orientation to the world or supply a piece of wisdom that serves as a guide for the family; in Reiss's model of family types, the particular set of shared assumptions about reality and the world in which the family lives.

parallel relationships one partner controls certain areas of the relationship and the other partner controls other, equally important, areas of the relationship.

perception of marriageability the self-perceptions, perceptions about the other, and perceptions of the relationship associated with increased closeness and greater interdependence of premarital couples.

personal myths the unique set of beliefs that each person has about herself or himself, about the ideal spouse, the ideal child and parent–child relationship, and the ideal marriage and family.

personal rule a rule developed by one person that governs only that person's behavior.

Person-oriented family family type in Bernstein's model that has role structures based upon the family's adaptations to the needs and personalities of the individuals in the family.

place as context influence of the physical location, setting, or environment on the communication.

popular stories stories that we acquire from our culture, primarily from cinema, television, and the mass media.

Positional family family type in Bernstein's model that has role structures based on what the family believes is appropriate to the person's position or status in the family.

power inequities an unequal distribution of the physical, financial, or psychological resources in the family which makes it possible for some members of the family to inflict their will on other family members.

privileges the rights that particular family members assume in the family.

process orientation views communication as complex, ever-changing, and influenced by past actions while simultaneously influencing future interactions.

psychological approach examines the effect of the family on the development of the individual.

punctuation the process of attributing causality on the basis of one's point of view, as though one were only reacting to the behavior of the other person rather than influencing it.

pure couple types couple in which the husband and wife define their relationship similarly.

qualitative purposes the prominence of emotionality, connectedness, altruism, and nurturing in family life and their significance.

quid pro quo a bargain or negotiated set of rules in which one family member agrees to do something if another family member will do something in exchange.

random family type family type in the Kantor and Lehr model characterized by regard for individual differences and minimum regulation of space, time, and energy.

received stories stories that family members inherit as part of their family and cultural legacy; persons are often recruited into received stories that are damaging or destructive or that they have not owned.

reflexive and evolving communication emerges from, is influenced by, and is dependent upon the previous messages or interaction experiences of the participants and simultaneously influences or directs the course of future communication.

relationship level of messages information about how the other person should interpret and respond to a message.

relationship typologies identify dimensions along which couples and families may be differentiated and reflect how couples and families have organized their relationships.

representational acts metaphors that are behaviors or messages that function as symbols for other messages, values, or concerns in the family (e.g., being late represents inconsiderate behavior).

responsibilities the obligations and duties that family members are assigned by or assume in the family system.

restricted code of communication depends upon generalizations, clichés, or folk sayings that do not require specific elaboration by family members.

rigid boundaries boundaries that are clearly defined and difficult to penetrate.

role   describes a set of behaviors that a family member is expected to perform in relation to other family members, based on the rules established for specific relationships.

role complementarity   gender role structures which suggest that men and women have different contributions to make based on their different natures; men are seen as primarily engaging in instrumental tasks while women have primary responsibility for the nurturance and emotional life of the family.

role conflict   the potential for incompatibility or contradiction in the demands of particular roles that specific members are expected to perform in the family.

role relationships   describes how two or more family roles have been organized in relationship to other roles in the family.

role symmetry   gender role structures in which both sexes engage in instrumental tasks and help provide for the nurturance and emotional life of the family.

rule evaluation   assessing the appropriateness of given rules.

rule negotiation   discussion of family rules with the intent of adapting them.

rules   relationship agreements, established through interaction episodes, that prescribe and limit the behavior of family members, specifying which behaviors are allowed, which are recommended, which are expected, and which are forbidden in the system or subsystem of interest.

salience   the importance of the congruence or incongruence of a couple's expectations.

sanctions   behaviors intended to enforce rules or to punish offenders who violate them.

scapegoat   the person who temporarily assumes a set of negative symptoms in a family system.

self-concept   the composite of positive and negative feelings that a family member has about his or her self-perceptions.

Separates   couple type in the Fitzpatrick model that tends to have conventional attitudes toward marriage but also values individual freedom over relationship maintenance.

shared history   the shared experiences, images, meanings, and values associated with a family unit as it functions and evolves through time.

shared memory   how family members recall their previous interactions; memories are related to the stories that family members create about their experience together.

silencing strategies   maneuvers designed to avoid dealing with an issue or to punish an individual for some transgression by isolating that person in silence.

simultaneous orientation   the tendency for family members to engage in several activities and pursue several goals at the same time.

social construction theory   maintains that reality is not an objective fact but rather something that family members create as they interact with each other.

social reality   meanings that are created from our experience of ourselves, other people, and our relationships.

social support system   the arenas outside of the family system in which family members receive emotional support, financial recognition, intellectual stimulation, cultural and aesthetic exposure, and reinforcement of their values and beliefs.

sociological approach studies the relationship between characteristics of the family and social forces in society.

space access dimension in the Kantor and Lehr model that refers to the physical and psychological distances that family members share and maintain between each other, including how the family manages its territory, screens information and persons coming into the family, distances members from one another without deserting each other, and maintains privacy.

stability the tendency of the family to develop predictable patterns of relating that will ensure maintenance of the system.

stories of identity stories that define the family's hopes and expectations for what kind of a person a family member will be.

structural view a systems perspective that focuses on the social organization of the family.

subsystem rules rules governing dyadic, three-person, and larger subsystems within the nuclear family.

subsystems components of a larger system.

suprasystem system that is composed of other identifiable systems.

survival stories stories that teach children how to cope in a world that can be dangerous, hostile, and unpredictable.

symbolic content of communication certain acts, behaviors, narratives, and communication sequences that come to represent concepts important to the family's collective identity.

symbolic interaction assumes that people live in a symbolic world created and sustained through symbolic behavior and that the meaning and interpretations people attach to behavior are central to social relationships.

system an integrated whole in which parts or members are interconnected with one another in a complex web of relationships.

system elements the physical features of the family system.

system processes the characteristics of human systems that work to keep the system functioning.

systems theory maintains that, although a family comprises individuals, the behavior of family members can be understood only in relation to each other and to the functioning of the family as a whole.

target dimensions in the Kantor and Lehr model, desirable goal states of affect, power, and meaning.

thematic chaining refers to the tendency for family members to organize their conversation in ways that create some degree of integration and continuity around particular family themes.

themes of a relationship the core issues or ideals that form the basis for prolonged commitment in a couple's relationship.

topic a specific issue or subject which is responsible for initial conversation between or among family members.

Traditionals couple type in the Fitzpatrick model that has conventional values about marriage and tends to emphasize stability over spontaneity.

transactions activity between systems, generally in the form of communication.

transition period marked by changes from one stage in the family life cycle to another.

triangulation refers to situations in which a third person serves as a go-between for two other family members (sparing them from interacting directly), two members form a coalition against a third member, or one family member competes with another for the attention of a third.

turning points decisive episodes in which a premarital relationship can either soar to higher levels of commitment or fall apart.

unintentionality communication can take place in spite of family members' intent not to communicate or lack of awareness that certain of their actions have communication value for other family members.

verbal symbols use of language symbols to create meaning.

AUTHOR INDEX

SUBJECT INDEX